D1593012

BALDWIN THWARTS THE OPPOSITION

BALDWIN
THWARTS THE OPPOSITION

THE BRITISH GENERAL ELECTION OF 1935

TOM STANNAGE

CROOM HELM LONDON

© 1980 Tom Stannage
Croom Helm Ltd, 2-10 St John's Road, London SW11

British Library Cataloguing in Publication Data

Stannage, Tom
    Baldwin thwarts the opposition
    1.   Great Britain. Parliament — Elections, 1935
    I.   Title
    329'.023'41083   JN955

    ISBN 0-7099-0341-3

Printed in Great Britain by
Biddles Ltd, Guildford, Surrey

TO MY MOTHER AND FATHER

CONTENTS

ACKNOWLEDGEMENTS

I wish to thank Dr Henry Pelling for his kindly and helpful guidance throughout the writing of this manuscript, which was originally submitted for the degree of PhD at the University of Cambridge.

I am grateful to the following people and institutions for granting me access to material in their care: Mr A.J.P. Taylor, Hon. Director of the then Beaverbrook Library, and the Trustees of the First Beaverbrook Foundation; the Executors of the late Lord Samuel, and the Clerk of Records, House of Lords; Viscount Simon and the Librarian of the Institute of Historical Research; the Librarian of the University of Cambridge; the Librarian of Churchill College, Cambridge; the Curator of Historic Records, Scottish Record Office; the General Secretary and Librarian of the Labour Party; the Secretary of the National Union of Conservative and Unionist Associations; Mr G.D.M. Block and the Librarian of the Conservative Research Department; Mr Percy Cohen CBE; the Secretary of the Scottish Conservative and Unionist Association; the General Secretary of the Scottish Liberal Party and the Librarian of the University of Edinburgh. Transcripts of Crown-copyright records in the Public Record Office appear by permission of the Controller of HM Stationery Office. I am also grateful to the Librarian of the University of Birmingham for permission to cite the papers of Neville Chamberlain. I wish also to thank the Master, Senior Tutor and Fellows of St John's College, Cambridge, for granting me a Laski Foundation Award. The study was made possible by the award of a Hackett Overseas Scholarship from the University of Western Australia and by a travel grant from the Research School of Social Sciences of the Australian National University. Mrs Phyllis Langley typed the manuscript.

The book is dedicated to my mother and the memory of my beloved father.

INTRODUCTION

There is a flatness about the 1935 general election which has as depressing an effect on the historian as it had on the voters at that time. Perhaps this explains why at least three historians have taken up the subject, only to turn from it to other areas of study. It is so orderly an affair, so lacking all sense of excitement; and this was due principally because it was agreed, even among Labour leaders, that the National Government was in no danger of defeat. And events justified such a feeling, for the National Government was returned with an overall majority of almost 250 seats. But although it lacks the glamour of a close contest or an unexpected result, the 1935 general election is not without interest or importance. It was after all the last election of the interwar years, and it determined the composition and character of the House of Commons for the next decade. It left in office a sort of national administration, rather than a clearly identifiable party one, with a majority large enough to ignore backbench and opposition pressure for major changes in policy. It was *the* election of the 'Age of Wireless', while the use of film was an important and fascinating ingredient in the electoral mix. Furthermore, the 1935 general election provides the historian with an opportunity to explore the political climate of the 1930s, and the role of the most interesting and extraordinary politician in twentieth-century British political history — Stanley Baldwin.

There is also a more mundane but probably important consideration. The 1960s saw an upsurge of interest in elections, both contemporary and historical. For the twentieth century the general elections of 1906, 1910 (two elections), 1922, 1923 and 1929, have been the subjects of either doctoral or B.Litt. theses, while most of the others have been discussed in articles or in books on related topics. And of course the Nuffield series of election studies had begun as long ago as 1947, developing in sophistication of technique if not in elegance of presentation with each volume. In this situation there is something to be said for filling any gaps remaining after this flurry of activity; and the 1935 general election is one such gap. The 1931 election has also come through relatively unscathed; but to the present writer it seemed that in his book *Nineteen Thirty-One: Political Crisis* (1958) Reginald Bassett had put and answered the more interesting questions concerning that election, even though he had left his work uncluttered with reams of statistical tables which we have come to associate with serious election studies. Hence this study of the 1935 general election.

But the historian of the 1935 general election works within a decade rather bare of soundly researched party histories. Lord Blake, Roy Douglas, and G.D.H. Cole have produced twentieth-century histories of the Conservative, Liberal and Labour Parties respectively; but each of them treats the 1930s rather cursorily, and none is particularly interested in electoral politics. John Ramsden's recent *A History of the Conservative Party: The Age of Balfour and Baldwin 1902-1940* (1978), while admirable on the period 1911 to 1930, is thin on the 1930s, especially for party organisation. Other books, such as Naylor's solid *Labour's International Policy: the Labour Party in the 1930s* (1969), have more limited objectives; and anyway there are regrettably few of them. There is still no 'life and times' study of Sir John Simon, while David Marquand's *Ramsay MacDonald* (1977) appeared too late to affect the judgements made in this book. I have felt bound, in any case, to include much descriptive matter on parties and electoral politics in order to provide the necessary background to the 1935 general election.

Unlike the writers of the Nuffield series of election studies, historians of interwar elections do not have to provide a chronological account of the parliamentary history of the inter-election years. Indeed the student of interwar elections is singularly fortunate in being able to draw on a number of stimulating, and in some cases well-researched, general histories, pre-eminent among them the late C.L. Mowat's *Britain Between the Wars 1918-1940* (1955). Most recently Margot Heinemann and Noreen Branson have published a work directly on *Britain in the Nineteen Thirties* (1971), while Chris Cook and J. Stevenson have produced *The Slump*, a popular account of the depression years. Hence the student of interwar elections is spared the necessity of drawing in detail the contours of political, economic and social development, though he is of course bound to make the connections between those lines and his own generalisations.

From the moment of its creation the National Government was the central fact in British political life, and this study underlines its centrality. One cannot, as several historians have done,[1] write off the National Government as yet another Conservative administration. To do this is to deny the politics of the 1930s its quintessential flavour. The policies of the National Government were the product of a greater

degree of compromise than was usual for a purely Conservative administration. Even a cursory glance at the Cabinet minutes shows that deci-
sions were a very long time in the making, and, when reached, too often
bore little resemblance to the proposals as originally conceived; and,
as often, the resulting policy proved either to be administratively unworkable or was simply inadequate to cope with the problem. These
were the reasons why it appeared that the Cabinet lacked the will to
deal quickly with the overriding problems of the day. Put another way,
the machinery created to deal with the immediate problem of the financial crisis proved to be too cumbersome to solve the vital long-term
problems of unemployment and war and peace. Chamberlain's actions
after 1937 perhaps should be seen as a belated recognition of this.

   Furthermore, it should not have escaped the notice of historians that
the Baldwin of the 1930s is rather different from the Baldwin of the
1920s, and that this is of some importance to the political history of
the 1930s. Throughout the 1920s Baldwin had been fearful of the possible emergence of a Centre Alliance composed of Lloyd George and
some prominent Conservatives. In 1930 and 1931 he faced and
defeated challenges to his leadership from Winston Churchill and the
press lords; but it had been a 'damned near thing'. By bringing into the
House of Commons nearly 150 Conservative MPs whose political survival was dependent on the continuation of 'national' government and
Baldwin as leader of the party, the 1931 election had placed Baldwin in
an unassailable position. This in part explains why Baldwin's attitude
to Lloyd George changed from being one of fear and apprehension to
one of condescension and affected affability. It also explains why he
seems to have considered the row over unemployment regulations in
the winter of 1934-5 to be fraught with greater danger than the rebellion
of the diehards over India: on the latter issue he could rely on the bloc
support of the Conservative MPs whose political survival rested with
former Labour and Liberal voters; on the former, perhaps not.

   To write of the National Government as a Conservative Government
is also to to deny Ramsay MacDonald a leading role in the politics of
the 1930s. From about 1933, as is shown in Chapter 1, MacDonald
seems to have seen himself as a captive in the camp of the Conservatives, but for a captive he enjoyed and exercised considerable freedom
of movement and expression, both at Cabinet meetings and in speeches
at large. If his performances in the House of Commons seem deserving
of the epithet 'Rambling Ramsay', this is not so of his performances at
Cabinet meetings, where he was not exposed to the unrelenting
hostility of his former colleagues which sometimes rendered him inartic-

ulate in the House.

To deny the National Government its national character is to give the India issue a centrality in the history of the party in the 1930s which it does not deserve. The India issue was only one, though a most serious one, of a range of issues arising out of the interests and policies of the National Government which produced a furore in the rank and file of the Conservative Party, leading on the one hand to a call for the formation of a National Party, and on the other to a demand for withdrawal from the National Government. Larger than the India issue was the question of the nature of Conservatism, and it was this that was the true centre of debate within the party. It was the proximity of a general election and the ability of Baldwin and his Ministers to convince the rank and file that participation in the National Government was as Conservative as Disraeli that made it possible for the party to present a united front to the electorate; but the consensus was a long time coming.

Analysis of the 1935 election is complicated by the difficulty of comparison with earlier and later elections. The 1945 election was fought on straight party lines; and, for example, to compare the National Government vote at the 1935 election with the Conservative vote at the 1945 election would be to distort the nature of both elections. Similarly with a comparison of the 1929 and 1935 elections. Even comparison between the 1931 election and the 1935 election is less rewarding than, say, comparison of the 1951 and 1955 elections: in 1931 the Liberals fought as partners in the National Government, but in 1935 they were opposed to the National Government. Furthermore, the lack of uniformity in contest-type exacerbates the problem of valid statistical comparison between the 1935 and earlier elections. Nevertheless, while paying due deference to these limitations an attempt is made to look backwards to the 1920s and forward to the 1940s.

This is a study of electoral politics in Britain between 1931 and 1935, with particular reference to the 1935 general election. It seeks to elucidate the varying long-term responses to the 1931 crisis and election, and to the by-elections, as well as the development of party strategies. It examines the timing of the 1935 election, the role of the mass media in electoral politics, and the campaign and its outcome. It concludes with a brief comment on the meaning of the 1935 general election result for the last years of the peace.

Note

1. See for example, C.L. Mowat, *Britain Between the Wars 1918-1940* (1955), p. 412; N. Branson and M. Heinemann, *Britain in the Nineteen Thirties* (1971), p. 2; A. Marwick, *Britain in the Century of Total War: War, Peace and Social Change 1900-1967* (1970), p. 210. The 'National Government' does not appear in the index to K. Middlemas and J. Barnes, *Baldwin: a biography* (1969).

1 THE CONSERVATIVE PARTY AND ITS ALLIES, 1931-35

From August 1931 to the eve of the 1935 general election the Conservative Party sought to define its relations with National Labour, and the Samuelite and Simonite wings of the Liberal Party. To many Conservatives co-operation with former opponents was anathema — a betrayal of the essence of Conservatism. To others it seemed to offer an opportunity for the party to maintain, indeed extend, its credibility with the new mass electorate. To still others it was a matter of personal political survival in the short term. This chapter explores the attitudes and actions of Conservative MPs, Central Office officials, and constituency organisers, to their party's commitment to the continued existence of the National Government. It also discusses the efforts at self-preservation made by the National Labour Group and the Liberal Nationals.[1] The politics of these years take their shape from the events of August-October 1931, and it is on these events that attention must first be focused.

The chain of circumstance leading to the formation of the National Government is well known and need not be discussed in this chapter.[2] However, the role of one link in the chain needs to be explored in some detail: namely, that the general expectation that once the financial crisis had been met, the National Government would cease to exist and the ensuring general election would be fought on traditional party lines,[3] was not fulfilled. Less than two months later an election took place at which the protagonists were the National Government and the Labour Party, and the campaign's principal issue was whether or not the government should be given a free hand to deal with the emergency.[4]

Most of the leaders of the Conservative Party had hoped that the Liberals who followed Sir Herbert Samuel would refuse to participate in such an election, but to their surprise and chagrin Samuel had agreed to the proposal.[5] Thus the Conservative Party found itself fighting a general election alongside a party which it had hoped to discredit, and the Liberals alongside the party which, in Lloyd George's words, 'they had always been pleased to call the Stupid Party'. This unnatural alliance, coupled with that of the Conservative Party and the National Labour Group, created a set of problems for national and constituency

16

oganisations the resolution for which had to be found in the space of three weeks. It will be shown that the efforts made to secure electoral co-operation were fitful rather than wholehearted and that they met with only limited success; and that a conditioning factor in the future relations of the parties composing the National Government was the sense of grievance inspired by the need for electoral co-operation.

On the day following his announcement of the date of the general election, MacDonald wrote to Baldwin, the leader of the Conservative Party, to complain about the unwillingness of Conservative Central Office to co-operate with MacDonald's twenty or so followers, by which he meant the fact that Conservative candidates, apparently with Central Office's blessing, were being put up against National Labour candidates. In particular, he was annoyed by Central Office's claim that it could not find a Conservative Association which was willing to support the candidature of W. Jowitt, a follower of MacDonald and Attorney General in the National Government, who had been forced to forsake the constituency he had represented in the 1929 Parliament. MacDonald was inclined to think that Central Office was annoyed that the election was not going to be fought on the principle of free trade versus protection and wished to opt out of electoral co-operation:

> The feeling, therefore, steadily grows that the Conservative Head Office is not at all recognizing the national emergency and is declining to show the spirit which I understood was common to all of us at this moment.[6]

This, in fact, was less than just, for Lord Stonehaven, the effervescent chairman of the Conservative Party Organization, had taken steps to ensure that the Prime Minister's followers were not opposed by Conservative Party candidates: in no less than thirteen constituencies he arranged for the withdrawal of Conservatives, and in at least eight of these, Conservatives would have won the seats on a normal swing of the pendulum.[7]

But this sacrifice was no more than MacDonald expected of Central Office; and indeed was something less than he expected and demanded. And in several constituencies there were clashes between National Labour candidates and local Conservative Associations which Stonehaven was unable to resolve or in which he was unwilling to interfere. MacDonald appeared to be under the impression that there was an agreed rule governing National Government candidatures; namely, 'that the Party in possession ought to claim the national candidature, so that no partisan advantage may be gained from the national crisis'.[8] But Baldwin and Stonehaven, and several constituency Conservative Associations do not appear to have shared his view. Stonehaven was unable to prevent a Conservative from standing at Everton, where in 1929 Labour had only narrowly won the seat from the Conservative Party, and for Combined English Universities, to which Jowitt had moved when he failed to get the support of the Conservatives at Preston. At Chatham, Preston and Central Wandsworth, National Labour candidates were compelled by Conservative Associations to withdraw before nomination day; while at Colne Valley, a National Labour candidate withdrew after nomination day. Just prior to nomination day, MacDonald demanded of Stonehaven that he withdraw Conservative candidates from South-East Essex and Central Newcastle. Stonehaven refused to countenance this and when nominations closed the National Government was still represented by both Conservative and National Labour candidates, though in the latter constituency the National Labour candidate subsequently withdrew. But their late decision to contest the seats had prompted Stonehaven to write angrily to MacDonald that

> In both cases by the intervention of your candidate at the very last moment, there is a grave risk of two seats being handed over to the opposition. But what is still more serious is that your insistence on the withdrawal of members of our Party, who have promised and, if elected, will give you unqualified support, in favour of unknown candidates introduced at the very last moment by yourself, cannot fail to convey the impression that you have doubts as to the support which the Conservative Party is prepared to give the National Government.

He added that in the light of the sacrifices which the Conservative Party was making in the national interest, the Prime Minister's actions were grossly unfair and not in accord with his own 'very proper denunciation of attempts to gain Party advantage out of the National crisis'. Now thoroughly aroused, MacDonald gave Stonehaven's letter to Baldwin;[9] but the latter appears to have refused to intervene in a dispute which persisted throughout and, indeed, after the election campaign.[10] It was MacDonald's sense of grievance and Stonehaven's feeling that he and his party were being imposed upon that hampered good relations between the Conservative Party and the National Labour Group throughout the years 1931 to 1935.

If relations between the National Labour Group and the Conserva-

tive Party were not altogether harmonious, those between the Conservative Party and the Liberal Party, or rather between the Conservative
Party and the Samuelite wing of the Liberal Party, were marked from
the start by an overt hostility which intensified as the campaign
proceeded. Prior to 9 October, the Conservative Party in general, and
Central Office in particular, had been given the impression by Baldwin
that although Ministers of the National Government had agreed to
refrain from attacking each other over questions relating to ideology
and policy, the rank and file of all the National Government parties
were not so bound — that Liberal freetrade candidates would be
attacked as strongly as Labour candidates.[11] (It was understood that as
the Simonites were prepared to support a general tariff they were in a
different category from the Samuelites.) Central Office was therefore
very surprised when in the course of a speech at Birmingham on 9
October, Baldwin expressed his annoyance that Samuel was being
opposed by A.C. Graham, a Conservative.[12]

Central Office did not wholeheartedly accept this apparent modification in their leader's position and Sir Patrick Gower, the Chief Publicity
Officer, was authorised to prepare a memorandum on the subject which
was to be brought to Baldwin's attention. In the memorandum —
which reached him on 15 October — Baldwin was informed that his
Birmingham speech had offended and upset many Conservatives who
felt that he had been unduly severe with Graham, especially in view of
the fact that Samuel's election literature was focused on a denunciation of tariffs rather than on the need for a free hand to deal with the
national emergency. Reviving memories of 1930, Gower warned
Baldwin that his appeasement of the Samuelites was tending to react
against his leadership; he also emphasised that:

> The unity between the Free Trade Liberals and ourselves is merely
> artificial, whereas the unity of the Conservative Party is a substantial
> reality.[13]

It would appear that Baldwin took heed of Central Office's opinion
and thereafter took a firmer line against the Samuelites, as the
following incident suggests. Within two days of receiving the Central
Office memorandum, Baldwin also received a note from Samuel, who
wanted to know what arrangements were to be made in regard to
messages of support to National Government candidates.[14] Samuel
himself suggested several possible courses: first, that no messages should
be sent; secondly, if messages were sent they should be sent only to

constituencies where there was one government candidate; thirdly, where there were two government candidates, the leaders should agree on which of the two candidates should receive the message of support; fourthly, and for the same situation, a free hand should operate and messages should be sent to both candidates. In short, Samuel sought to rationalise a state of affairs which was in danger of getting out of hand. He himself regarded the third possibility as impracticable, there being too little time in which to reach an acceptable agreement and the whole thing smacking too much of a 'coupon', which he regarded as undesirable; but he invited Baldwin to comment on all the courses he had suggested.

Baldwin's letter in reply is not in the Samuel Papers, nor is there a copy in his own papers, but there can be no doubt that he did in fact reply, for on 22 October Samuel wrote to say that he approved of the course which Baldwin intended to adopt.[15] It is difficult to determine precisely what this course was. In his letter of 22 October, Samuel wrote that he intended to send messages of support to Liberal Ministers, especially to those being opposed by Conservatives. The following day he again contacted Baldwin to ask him whether it was true that he had sent a message of support to a Conservative opponent of a Liberal Minister.[16] From these two statements, together with the knowledge that he did not send messages to a Liberal Minister at Mid-Beds.,[17] it can be deduced that in his reply to Samuel's initial approach Baldwin had said that he was sending messages of support only to Conservative Ministers. If this was the case, Samuel's surprise on being told that Baldwin had sent a message of support to a rank-and-file Conservative who was opposing a Liberal Minister is easily understood. And concerning Samuel's query about a message of support allegedly sent to E.D. Simon's Conservative opponent at Penryn and Falmouth, Baldwin merely recorded that no arrangements had been made which prevented a Conservative from getting a message of support from his leader. He added that:

> If Simon had stuck to his old constituency the situation would have been different.[18]

In summary, it appears that Baldwin's attitude late in the campaign was that a Conservative could oppose a Liberal in any constituency except where the Liberal was a Minister and was defending his seat. But the question of messages was not yet fully resolved.

As the campaign entered its final week, relations between the Conservative Party and the Samuelite Liberals became even more strained. On the one hand Samuel was aggrieved that whereas all thirty Conservative Ministers were unopposed by Liberals, no less than five Liberal Ministers were being opposed by Conservatives, as were many rank-and-file Liberal MPs and candidates. On the other hand Central Office was intensely annoyed by what it regarded as blatant free trade propaganda issued, apparently with Samuel's consent, by the Liberal Publication Department. On 20 and 21 October the pages of *The Times* were enlivened by an acrimonious correspondence between Stonehaven and the chairman of the Liberal Election Committee, Lord Stanmore, over a questionnaire on free trade which had been issued by the Liberals to all candidates. Stonehaven sought to show that the questionnaire contravened the agreed formula of a free hand, but Stanmore insisted that his party's questionnaire was concerned with the 'ultimate goal' rather than 'immediate measures', and therefore did not contravene the agreed formula.

The debate had not been resolved to the satisfaction of either man when on 23 October the Liberals issued the last of their *Notes for Speakers*, which contained a scathing denunciation of tariffs and a reaffirmation of the virtues of free trade. Its publication caused Stonehaven to protest to Baldwin that the Liberals 'really are over the limit and I do hope that you will see your way to take the matter up at once and most energetically with Samuel'. And he added:

> You will see from attached letters that Donald McLean and
> E.D. Simon and others want you to do something for them. Quite
> apart from all that you have done for them already I think the
> Liberal Notes for Speakers makes it impossible for you to do any
> more for any Liberal.[19]

Once again Baldwin heeded the advice of Central Office, and within the next three days he rejected the appeal from Sir Donald McLean to send him a message of support,[20] and he issued messages of support to every Conservative candidate except Graham at Darwen and one or two others.[21] One is justified therefore in asking how real was the co operation between the parties composing the National Government?

There can be no doubt that there were many instances where a Conservative Party candidate withdrew from a contest, apparently in the interests of national unity; but their number and importance have been exaggerated. In his study of the 1931 crisis, Reginald Bassett estimated that the Conservative Party withdrew candidates from no less than 44

constituencies in order to give Liberals a free run against the Labour
Party, and from thirteen in order that National Labour candidates
should have a free run against the Labour Party.[22] It has already been
shown that the figure for withdrawals in favour of National Labour
candidates, though accurate, disguises the fact that several of the constituencies had never been and could not be won by the Conservative
Party. Similarly with the seats 'sacrificed' by the Conservatives in
favour of the Liberal Party. Following Bassett, Middlemas and Barnes
claim that 44 seats were 'sacrificed' this way, and they add that in all of
these seats the Conservative Party would have stood an excellent chance
of success.[23] But this was hardly the case. In putting the number of
Conservative 'sacrifices' at 44, Bassett appears to have followed the list
issued by Lord Stonehaven to the press on 15 October, and published
the next day. After the publication of this list, however, there were
several more withdrawals, and about one of the 44 Stonehaven had
been misinformed and a Conservative was in fact contesting the seat.
The actual number of Conservative withdrawals in favour of Liberals
was 54.[24]

This figure would appear to strengthen the claim by Middlemas
and Barnes that the Conservative Party made considerable sacrifices in
the national interest; but in fact this is not so. Even a cursory glance at
the list of seats involved reveals that well over half the 'sacrifices' were
made in Scotland, Wales and East Anglia, areas of traditional Liberal
strength. Of the total number, moreover, three had not been contested
by the Conservative Party in 1929 and in a further 28 the Conservative
Party had finished at the foot of the poll in three-way contests. In
another 15 the Conservative Party had finished in second place behind
the Liberal Party, in many cases well behind, though in perhaps five a
Conservative candidate might have defeated a Liberal in the exceptional circumstances of 1931. Apart from these, however, there were
only about ten seats where *vis-à-vis* the Liberal Party the Conservatives
made real sacrifices in the interest of national unity.

Most of the sacrifices were made to the estranged and less representative section of the Liberal Party, namely the Simonites.[25] On the
whole, seats held by Simonite Liberals tended to be more safely Liberal
than were seats held by the Samuelite Liberals. For this and the even
more important reason that the Simonite Liberals were prepared to
support the introduction of a general tariff, the Conservative Party
made greater concessions to Simon's followers than to Samuel's. Of the
54 constituencies where Conservative candidates were withdrawn, no
less than 35 supported Liberal Nationals; that is, there were only 19

Conservative withdrawals in the Samuelite Liberal interest. Put another way, whereas there were 26 straight fights between the Conservative Party and the Samuelite Liberals (and a further three between the Conservative Party and independent Liberals, all of whom followed Lloyd George), there was only one straight fight between the Conservative Party and the Liberal Nationals; and of the 89 clashes between the Conservative and Liberal candidates, 81 were between the Conservatives and the Samuelite Liberals, and only four were between the Conservative Party and the Simonites.[26] At the election, ten Liberal MPs from the 1929 Parliament were defeated by Conservatives: of these no less than eight were Samuelites.[27] Thus while it can be shown that the Conservative Party did make some sacrifices in the national interest, the Samuelite Liberal Party had reason to be unimpressed.

At first sight it is the Liberal Party which made the greater sacrifices. At the 1929 general election the Liberal Party had contested 513 seats, but at the 1931 general election it contested only 159.[28] Samuel frequently pointed out that the Liberal Party was not putting up candidates against Conservative and National Labour Ministers and had refrained from doing so against many backbench Conservative MPs as well. He admitted that the financial difficulties of the Liberal Party would have prevented it fielding more than 300 candidates at a normal general election; but he asserted that at least 150 Liberals had withdrawn from contests to avoid splitting the National Government vote.[29] This, if true, was a sacrifice of considerable proportions.

After the election, however, the *Liberal Magazine*, which represented the opinion of Liberal Party Headquarters, published a different set of calculations:

> In many constituencies the Liberal candidate was withdrawn in order to ensure the election of a supporter of the National Government, but in something like three hundred constituencies there was no Liberal candidate chiefly because the Liberal Party unexpectedly found itself without the necessary funds at the very last moment, when it was too late adequately to repair the defect.[30]

If the *Liberal Magazine*'s assessment of the situation was correct, then the Liberal Party sacrificed about 60 seats in the national interest; if Samuel's assessment is correct, about 150 seats were sacrificed. There seems no way of finding out which seats were left uncontested for financial reasons and which in the national interest, but it can be safely argued that in the great majority of both groups, the sacrifice would have been more apparent than real, that most would undoubtedly have not returned a Liberal, and that in many a split in the National Government vote would still probably have resulted in a victory for the Conservative Party, so weak would have been the Liberal vote. However, perhaps about 100 Conservative MPs owed their victory to the fact that fo one reason or another the Liberal Party left seats uncontested.[31]

When Stonehaven referred to Conservative Party sacrifices he meant in effect that had he been able to exploit the situation fully he might have been able to see about 520 Conservative candidates elected, instead of the 469 who were. When Samuel mentioned sacrifices, he meant in effect that while his party could not have gained more seats than it did, it had generously given about 100 Conservative candidates an easy passage to the House of Commons.

There was, however, every appearance of unanimity. Shortly after nominations had closed, *The Times* noted that whereas in 1929 there had been only 102 divisions in which there were straight fights, in 1931 there would be 409; this, it claimed, testified to the efforts which had been made to avoid splitting the National Government vote.[32] But in reality this state of affairs owed far more to Lloyd George's decision to withhold funds from the Liberal Party than to any other factor,[33] for there can be no doubt that had money been available the Liberal Party would have contested many more seats; and if it had done so it is possible, on the evidence of the ill feeling between the leaders and between the Liberal and Conservative constituency parties in the 81 instances where there was a clash, that the National Government might have broken up during or sometime immediately after the general election.

The main features of the Conservative position were described in the previous section. As a result of the 1931 general election there were about 100 Conservative MPs who owed their seats to Liberal withdrawals and to whom continued good relations with the Liberals were of the utmost importance; and at the same time there were nearly 60 Conservative Associations which had refrained from putting up candidates only at the behest of Stonehaven and Baldwin. There were a further 90 associations which had had their candidates opposed by Liberals or National Labour men and consequently regarded the National Coalition as a farce. Both of these — particularly the latter — were anxious to see a return to party politics on traditional lines. If the party was not to split apart at the seams, the desires of these groups had somehow to be reconciled.

Within a month of the general election taking place, Conservative
Central Office was forced to deal with the problem. On 27 November
the party's leading officials, among them Lord Stonehaven, the chairman
of Party Organization, Sir Patrick Gower, the Chief Publicity Officer,
Sir Robert Topping, the principal agent, and Sir George Bowyer, the
officer responsible for examining the credentials of potential parliamentary candidates, held a meeting

> to consider requests for advice which have been received from
> organizations throughout the country as to whether they are at
> liberty to use the word 'National' in the titles of constituency asso-
> ciations.[34]

Central Office was not unsympathetic to the idea, for it recognised that
the desire appeared to be 'general and growing', and was particularly felt
in constituencies where the return of the Conservative or Liberal
member had been secured through the combined effort of Conservatives, Liberals and Labour people, 'and where it was realized that only
by the maintenance of a similar combination could the seat be held'.
It was also aware, however, that in other constituencies 'where the
Liberal candidates, although supporting the National Government, had
not cooperated with the Conservative Party in one way or another,
the position was not without its difficulties'.
    In considering the possible courses open to it, Central Office had to
take into account the Prime Minister's intentions. If MacDonald himself
invited 'in the near future' all those who supported the National
Government to form a National Party, it seemed wise for the present to
retain the separate identities of the parties composing the National
Government. Although this was a contingency which could not be
ignored, it was not the ideal solution. Central Office hoped that a
different situation would arise — in the words of the conference report:

> The Simon Liberal wing would probably join with the Conservative
> wing before long, thus forming a very strong combination. The other
> wings would then have to decide either to join that combination or
> go into opposition, and in this way the old two party system would
> be restored.

The report went on:

> The Conference were unanimously of the opinion that it was desir-

able that the position should develop on the lines indicated, and that, subject of course to the approval of the Leader, the Central Office should use its influence in that direction while the National spirit was still strong in the country.

The conference agreed also, however, that it was desirable that the proposal for the formation of a National Party should be brought to the notice of the Prime Minister, but only after Baldwin and Captain Margesson, the Conservative Chief Whip, had been consulted as to the wisdom of such a course. Central Office resolved that until this was done

> every encouragement should be given to the cooperation of all parties in support of the National Government, and, where local conditions would permit, to the establishment of any organization likely to keep together those supporters who worked to secure the return of the National candidate at the last election.

There is no evidence to suggest that MacDonald intended to form a National Party, though with his keen desire to keep the Samuelite Liberals in the National Government he may have considered forming a 'left alliance' of progressives from within the government and in the constituencies.[35] It is more likely, however, that under pressure from Lord De La Warr and H. Usher, his private secretary, he intended to keep things as they were, and even institutionalise the existing state of affairs by forming a separate National Labour Party.[36] Baldwin probably shared MacDonald's attitude. If Central Office did approach him about the possibility of the Conservative Party changing its name, his reply would almost certainly have been along the lines which the conference itself had wished to adopt, namely that he wished to keep things as they were and to encourage the Simonites to join the Conservative Party. This certainly was the course taken by Central Office, presumably with Baldwin's authority, from late in 1931, and it formed the substance of the New Year messages to the party agents.[37]

In his message Stonehaven first congratulated the party on the victory it had recently achieved:

> The triumph of 470 Conservative candidates, and the public-spirited withdrawal of 40 others in favour of National Labour and Liberal National candidates entitles the Party to be proud of its share in the victory of the National Government.

He then stated:

> So far as the future is concerned, our object must be to do our
> utmost to retain the support of many former Liberal and Labour
> electors whose votes contributed to the overwhelming majorities
> polled by our candidates at the Election. The longer that collabora-
> tion can be maintained both in Parliament and in the country the
> better, and we ought to do our utmost to cultivate a National rather
> than a Party spirit in politics with that object in view.

It remained to be seen whether Conservative organisations would
respond to Stonehaven's appeal, and whether they could cultivate a
'national' spirit without sacrificing traditional Conservative ideology,
policies and organisation. Stonehaven had addressed himself to those
constituencies which had returned Conservative MPs with the assistance
of Liberal and Labour votes, but Topping, in his New Year message to
the party agents, addressed himself to those constituencies which had
withdrawn Conservative candidates and promoted the candidature of
representatives of other parties and groups:

> Once more we have been called upon in the national interest to make
> party sacrifices and, in some instances, personal sacrifices. In the
> circumstances this was inevitable . . . The coming year will bring
> with it many serious problems to those responsible for the Party
> Organization. One can foresee in a number of constituencies diffi-
> culties which will have to be handled with great tact and discretion.

Topping sympathised with the candidates who were defeated and with
those 'who were deprived of the privileges of conducting a contest by
reason of the withdrawal of their candidate', but he offered them little
hope that things would soon change.

At the constituency level Conservative Party organisers were loathe
to cultivate a national spirit, particularly where it was felt that at the
1931 election they and they alone had made sacrifices in the national
interest. The attitude of the Yorkshire agents, expressed at an area
meeting on 2 December 1931, was not untypical:

> They now had more than 41 Conservative MPs for Yorkshire as
> against 15 in 1929. Three seats had been won for the first time ever.
> Four more had their last taste of victory in 1900. Three others had
> never been won since the redistribution of 1918.[38]

With this sort of result the Yorkshire Conservatives might well have been pleased with co-operation in a national government. But this was not the case, as the meeting made clear:

> The Liberal Party had increased their representation from one to six. In five divisions they were given a clear run, and there is little doubt that in each case they owed their victories to strong Conservative support. Their attitude as a Party, however, had been the reverse of 'National'. They had made a great show of withdrawing candidates in divisions where they had not the remotest chance of success, and had then expressed righteous indignation because Conservative candidates had not withdrawn to make way for their eleventh hour nominees in other seats. They did their best to upset us in South Leeds, Penistone, Keighley, and Holderness . . . They were at the bottom of the Poll in the first three cases.

Such ill feeling towards the Liberal Party, however well founded, was not conducive to the replacement of party spirit by a national spirit. Nor was this attitude restricted to Yorkshire. In the same issue of the *Conservative Agents' Journal* there appeared the first of many articles in which the merits and demerits of changing the party's name were discussed. One of these was written by H.C. Nazer, the agent for North Hackney (since 1914 a safe Conservative seat). At the 1931 general election, the normal Conservative majority was greatly increased by the decision of the Liberals not to contest the seat. In these circumstances one would have thought that Nazer would favour changing the party's name; but the reverse was true. He argued that if there was ever a swing of the pendulum against the National Government, there should be an alternative government other than a Socialist one; and in his opinion this should be a Conservative Government. The implication of this view was that propaganda and so on should be Conservative rather than national in character; as such, it was not conducive to the creation of a national rather than party spirit, as Central Office sought.

Indeed, Stonehaven's appeal to constituency organisations to cultivate a national rather than a party spirit while preserving separate Conservative organisations, had not been well received in many constituencies. For example, at the meeting of the Lancashire, Cheshire and Westmoreland agents on 17 February 1932, Topping was compelled to speak against a well-supported motion calling for the abandonment of the title 'Conservative Party'. He told them that he felt sure that agents would be doing good work if they directed their attention to the enrolment of members in their various Associations who had supported Conservative candidates for the first time at the last Election.[39]

At the Western agents' meeting on 12 March Topping again had to ask for the Conservative character of their organisations to be kept intact. 'There was no indication,' he stated, 'of the formation of a "National Party".[40] But there were many who hoped that it would soon be otherwise.

Conservative Party organisers were being told on the one hand that they should cultivate a national spirit and on the other hand that they should keep their organisations intact as separate entities, and should even endeavour to recruit new members from other political groups to the Conservative standard. Not surprisingly this was found to be difficult to put into practice, especially as Central Office's advice on the nature of future political conflict stressed the importance of retaining Conservative ideology — as Sir Patrick Gower told a luncheon of the Northern agents on 18 February 1932:

> it seems likely that the conflict will, to a large extent, centre around [the] clash of Conservative and Socialist principles, and intensive propaganda will be needed if the Socialists are to be defeated at the next election.[41]

He did not explain how Conservative organisations could expect to attract former Liberal and Labour voters if the propaganda they were expected to issue was to stress Conservative ideology; and this was the cause of much disquiet among party workers. Indeed, the desire to see a change in the party name intensified. As a contributor to the December issue of the *Conservative Agents' Journal* wrote:

> It is quite certain that there are a number of constituencies, won at the last election, where a change (of name) is absolutely essential if they are to be held.

Discontent with national government was not confined to party workers. It was apparent at the national level as well. In March 1932 the Samuelite Liberals rebelled against the government's decision to introduce tariffs, though a formula was found which enabled them to remain in the government with the minimum loss of face.[42] In the

autumn of 1932, however, after MacDonald, under pressure from the
Conservative leaders, refused to suspend the Ottawa Agreements until
the World Economic Conference had met later in the year, they
resigned from the government. The effect of their decision was to bring
the parliamentary Liberal Party into closer agreement with Liberal
organisers who, since March, had been conducting an open war with the
Conservatives at successive by-elections — at Henley, Dulwich and
North Cornwall. From the Conservatives' point of view, the departure
of the Samuelites was a mixed blessing: it jeopardised the future of the
Conservative MPs who had benefited from Liberal support at the last
election, though as will be shown in Chapter 3 many Liberal voters
continued to support the National Government; at the same time, for
constituency organisations which in 1931 had withdrawn Conservative
candidates, it meant a return to normal party political activity.

While relations between the Samuelite wing of the Liberal Party and
the Conservative Party were now clearly defined, relations between the
Conservatives and the followers of Simon were in need of clearer defini-
tion. Simon was now well placed to extract from the Conservatives an
even higher price for continued Liberal co-operation, for if the Conservatives refused to meet his demands he could threaten to resign and
thereby reduce to untenable proportions the national character of the
National Government. Since March when Samuel rebelled against the
introduction of tariffs, Simon had striven to present his group as the
true representatives of Liberalism in the country. Shortly before the
summer recess the Simonites formed an independent Liberal National
Council, which had as its president Lord Wimborne, Leslie Hore-
Belisha as chairman of its General Committee, and Lord Hutchison as
chairman of its Executive Committee. The council was to co-ordinate
the efforts of Liberal Nationals and Conservatives at the electoral level,
to publicise the role of the Liberal Nationals in the National Government and to raise the money needed to finance Liberal National candidates at by-elections and the next general election.[43]
    In line with this administrative thrust the Liberal Nationals seized
on the departure of the Samuelites in order to consolidate their own
position within the National Government. Even before the Samuelites
resigned, Simon was being warned by his followers that the price of
severing the umbilical cord with the Liberals should be firmer guarantees
from Baldwin about policy (particularly a more energetic unemployment policy), Liberal National candidatures at by-elections and the
general election, and increased Liberal National representation in the

Cabinet.[44] Once he received assurances that all but a handful of the Liberal National MPs remained loyal to him,[45] he addressed himself in strong terms to Baldwin:

> I spoke to you yesterday of the prospective electoral position of the 35 Liberal Nationals who have taken the same line as Runciman and myself, and who represent a large body of Liberal opinion convinced that the National Government should receive continued support from all sides. Now that Samuel and co. are withdrawing, the position of these friends of mine in their constituencies will be much more difficult and they will very soon be exposed to every sort of attack and pressure from the organizations who approve Samuel's demarche.
>
> At the same time, they sincerely desire to show themselves, as they have shown themselves in the past, amongst the stoutest defenders of the National Government, which I am sure is what you wish. Yet, unless they can be assured that they are going to have, so far as official Conservatism is concerned, a free run in their constituencies at the next election, they stand to be shot at from both sides. You said to me yesterday that their situation was much like that of the Liberal Unionists in 1886, and I agree. Now can you in the interests of national unity and of resistance to subversive forces which will otherwise undermine any administration inspired by the same spirit which binds us together, authorise me to give these men an assurance? It seems to me that it would be only fair to tell them that the division on the Second Reading of the Ottawa Bill will be regarded as the test occasion, and the Liberal Nationals who support the Second Reading and maintain the same general helpfulness to the Government that they have shown in the past, may feel assured (1) that there will be no official Conservative candidate against them in their constituencies when this issue is joined at the election, and (2) that if a local association showed signs of independent opposition you and your Central Association would actively discourage it.
>
> I write plainly, because the case is one which seems to me to call for plainness of speech. I know of course that an exchange of letters on such a point only amounts to a gentleman's agreement, but then I know who I am dealing with and that makes all the difference.

Baldwin kept the Liberal Nationals in suspense for nearly one month before replying. He delayed for two reasons. In the first place he wanted to see if the Liberal Nationals were holding as firmly to the

National Government as Simon was leading him to believe, and the touchstone for the loyalty issue was the second reading of the Ottawa Bill. Secondly, he wished to sound out opinion within his own party, and he could do this most satisfactorily at the party's annual conference to be held in the first week of October. Satisfied on both fronts, Baldwin replied to Simon late in October, though he was unable to give the firm guarantees asked of him, as the following extract makes clear:

> The assurance that I gave [to the party conference] that none of those who supported the Ottawa Bill right through should suffer was received with enthusiastic cheers by the great audience – a large proportion of which were accredited representatives of the Conservative Party drawn from practically every constituency. While I can can give no guarantee that will bind individual constituencies, for democracy is a reality in the Conservative Party and each constituency is a law unto itself, I believe that I am entitled to assume that support will be forthcoming for those Liberal members of Parliament who are prepared to give consistent support to the Government. On that basis I can assure you that I, as Leader of the Party, and the Chairman who directs the Conservative Party Headquarters, will exercise all the influence and authority we possess to see that those who play a patriotic part receive the full support of our party in the constituencies they now represent.[46]

It was as firm a commitment as Baldwin could make at the time, and Simon seems not to have pushed the issue further. For the moment, all was sweetness and light between the two. It was otherwise for the Conservatives and their National Labour allies.

The relations between the Conservative Party and the National Labour Group had always been uncertain and tinged with suspicion on both sides. MacDonald, as we have seen,[47] was intensely annoyed by what he regarded as Central Office intransigence over the distribution of seats at the 1931 general election: he felt that the Conservatives had exploited the crisis for their own ends, and at the expense of MacDonald himself and his colleagues. In order to break down the widely held belief that he was the prisoner of the Tories, he was determined to increase National Labour's representation in the House of Commons.

Things had come to a head following the defeat of Sir William Jowitt, the Attorney General in the National Government, in the Combined English Universities constituency. MacDonald wanted the Conservatives to find Jowitt a seat, and in January he sent his private secretary, H.B. Usher, to Central Office to demand this of Stonehaven. Stonehaven, despite his belief that Conservatives should act in a national rather than a party spirit, received the request coolly. He informed Baldwin that he had told Usher:

> (1) that our information points to any such attempt resulting in a repetition of Montrose Boroughs, or something very like it, and (2) that on general grounds a Bye-election ought to be avoided at all costs, and (3) on personal grounds Jowitt would be singularly unpopular candidate wherever he tried to stand.[48]

In a frank and rather surprising admission that neither he nor Baldwin could influence constituency politics, he added:

> I pointed out to Usher that though S.B. could probably persuade a Conservative Organization to refrain fron adopting a Conservative candidate, it would split the Party and Jowitt would probably be beaten by a local Tory candidate, or one run by Beaverbrook.

A few days later, MacDonald himself wrote to Stonehaven about the matter.[49] He said that while he appreciated Stonehaven's difficulties and, like him, wished to avoid another Montrose Boroughs incident, a seat had to be found for Jowitt, or else:

> The fact would be published to the world that the National Government could not secure the election of one of its own Ministers because he was not a Conservative, and because not one local Conservative Association, despite the immense representation of Conservatism in Parliament, would consent to put the interests of the Government first, and its own local party advantages second.

He added that the position was also unfair to Jowitt personally because he was in his present position at his, Macdonald's, request. Stonehaven sent this letter on to Baldwin, with the following note accompanying it:

> The P. M.'s attitude to the Conservatives is neither fair nor compatible with the debt of gratitude which he has incurred towards it. The Party opened its throat very wide to swallow his 13 followers, who would have had no chance of getting in otherwise — or very little —

but really to follow that up by asking them to swallow Jowitt is overdoing the thing!

Nevertheless, Stonehaven did make enquiries among the constituency organisations, and in the following week he informed MacDonald that the South Nottingham Conservatives might be persuaded to support Jowitt if the incumbent National Labour MP, G. Holford-Knight, could be persuaded to stand down.[50] But the issue was not quite as clear-cut as this implied, for the next day Topping received a report on the situation from the Conservative agent for the East Midlands who warned him that while the local association was prepared to open negotiations with Jowitt or Central Office, its Executive Committee was divided over the matter, and strong terms were being sought; namely that the future of the Conservative Party in the division be safeguarded; that Jowitt should not be allowed to 'dig himself into' the division; and that should the National Government come to an end, Jowitt would have to resign at once. Stonehaven warned MacDonald not to intervene while preparations were in hand or else 'a disagreeable situation might arise as it did in Montrose'.[51] Then the unforeseen occurred: Holford-Knight refused to stand down, thus putting South Nottingham out of consideration. Stonehaven could not find another constituency to take Jowitt, who was then forced to resign his office as Attorney General. MacDonald, who one might have expected to have been annoyed with Holford-Knight, was intensely annoyed with Central Office for not finding a seat which was held by a Conservative rather than one held by one of his own supporters: it might even be surmised from this that MacDonald himself supported Holford-Knight's decision not to stand down.

After this incident, and with the introduction of a general tariff and the subsequent threat of the Samuelite Liberals to resign from the National Government, MacDonald's fear of being a captive of the Tories reached almost hysterical proportions. The incident which brought him near to breaking point was the selection of the National Government candidate to contest the Wednesbury by-election late in July. When it became apparent that the Wednesbury Conservatives intended to select one of their own people rather than a National Labour man, De La Warr at once wrote to Stonehaven expressing his hope that Central Office would intervene and force the local association to take a National Labour man.[52] He reminded Stonehaven that the seat had been held by Labour from 1918 to 1929, and that there were several National Labour ex-MPs for whom seats should be found.

He added that as there could be 'little doubt that there must be at least
over 150 members who owe their seats to the PM', it was unfair that he
should have only 13 followers in the House of Commons.

In his reply, Stonehaven wrote that De La Warr's letter had amazed
him.[53] Both he and Captain Margesson, he argued, had tried very hard
to get the Wednesbury Conservatives to support a National Labour
candidate; but they had proved obdurate. He also drew De La Warr's
attention to the constituency point of view, which was that the constituency organisations themselves felt that it was unfair that if they did
support a National Labour man, they were expected to finance him and
hand over the party machine to him. On the general question of
co-operation, Stonehaven asserted that it was his wish to see the present
combination maintained, but he thought that De La Warr should face
up to some facts about the character of that combination:

> the main factor which gave a really national character to the
> Election campaign was the withdrawal of a large body of Conserva-
> tive candidates and the transfer of their support to Labour and
> Liberal candidates supporting the National Government.

And, he added, if Baldwin and the Conservatives had not rallied round
MacDonald, he could not have remained Prime Minister of the National
Government: 'All this you appear to have forgotten.'

De La Warr showed this letter to MacDonald who, not unnaturally,
took an unfavourable view of it.[54] He appears to have wondered
whether it was the beginning of a movement in the Conservative
Party to get rid of him. He may have contemplated slipping out of the
National Government with the aura of Lausanne still about him, and
thus avoiding the disappointment or unpopularity that might arise from
the results of the Ottawa Conference, which Baldwin was then
attending. If he did intend to resign he could easily have put the blame
for breaking up the National Government on to the Conservative Party
because of its unreasonable attitude in the constituencies; even Stonehaven recognised that MacDonald could do this with telling effect.[55]
Nor would such a course necessarily bring an end to his long political
career. De La Warr thought it was conceivable that MacDonald could
place himself at the head of a body of MPs representing progressive
opinion, of whom there were possibly 150 in the House of Commons.
Stonehaven tended to agree that MacDonald's natural affinity was still
with the left. In the event, MacDonald took no more drastic step than
refusing to send a message of support to the Conservative candidate at

Wednesbury. Stonehaven held talks with Lady Londonderry and with MacDonald's personal physician and friend, Dr Horder, at which he reassured them that he and every other responsible member of the party, and Baldwin most of all, would regard it as a calamity if MacDonald resigned.

If Stonehaven meant to appease MacDonald he did not succeed, for a luncheon talk with De La Warr the day after the Wednesbury by-election (at which the Conservative candidate was defeated) revealed an almost unbridgeable gap between the two parties.[56] Stonehaven told De La Warr that it was his impression that MacDonald was not in favour of a National Party but wished to see the three (four, if the Samuelites were included) different parties which supported the National Government each retaining its own identity. Stonehaven thought that this was bound to cause difficulties:

> From my knowledge of the constituencies not represented by National Labour, I foresee that, in the event of a bye-election occuring in almost any of them, it would be difficult in most cases to persuade our people to adopt again their self-denying attitude during the General Election. In cases like Wednesbury, where the place of a Conservative member had to be filled, it was simply hopeless to expect a Conservative organization to adopt a Socialist as their candidate.

He then stated bluntly that:

> The real fact was that the National Labour Party did not exist; there were individual members of the Labour Party who were supporters of the P.M. but they had no organization in the constituencies. Consequently a National Labour Candidate would have to run simply as a MacDonaldite, and trust to securing enough general support to win.

De La Warr of course regarded the latter part of Stonehaven's observations as irrelevant to the central issue: as long as MacDonald was Prime Minister, he contended, the National Labour Group existed and should have some representation in the House of Commons. As to the earlier remarks, he sympathised with Stonehaven's dilemma but hoped that Stonehaven could keep the local Conservative Associations in line. He hoped also that he and Stonehaven could meet more frequently in order to forestall the occurrence of incidents like that at Wednesbury. To this Stonehaven was agreeable, and in fact the two men met a short while later to discuss the nomination for the vacant Kilmarnock seat. Stonehaven's continued belief in the efficacy of the National combination was expressed in the memo sent to Baldwin in August.

> I am . . . convinced of the necessity to face the fact that the dissolution of the political combination which gave the National Government its majority is only a question of time, unless some action is taken to prevent it. Whether the maintenance of the combination is desirable and if so what steps should be taken to achieve that object are matters for the leaders of the Parties to consider and decide. I am certain that if things are allowed to drift the decision will come automatically, and it will take the form of a break-up. My opinion is that the combination, or at least an adequate part of it, can and ought to be maintained, and that it is in the national interest (which, of course, includes the Conservative Party's interest) that the leaders should decide on the necessary steps to maintain it at an early date.

Not until Baldwin's return from Ottawa was any action taken; but thereafter things moved rapidly. When Samuel left the National Government on 28 September 1932, Simon, as we have seen, asked Baldwin for, and received, an assurance that things would remain as they were: that is, the parties supporting the National Government would retain their separate identities, and Baldwin would safeguard to the best of his ability the fortunes of the Liberal National MPs. Baldwin's hand was strengthened when at the Conservative Party Conference in Blackpool in October a resolution urging the Executive Committee to consider the desirability of adopting a new name for the party was defeated on a show of hands, while at the same time the conference reaffirmed its support of the National Government.[57]

Following the departure of the Samuelite Liberals the remaining components of the National Government became obsessively conscious of the need to publicise the national aspect of National Government. This concern, coupled with their anxiety to avoid a repetition of the Wednesbury affair, produced a meeting between Stonehaven, Hore-Belisha and De La Warr, held early in November, to discuss the formation of a National Coordinating Committee.[58] A memorandum was then circulated among the leaders which gave as the objective of the proposed committee:

> To avoid triplication of essential tasks common to the three parties,

and to review National propaganda for by-elections in conformity
with the views of the three component parts.

Further discussions between November 1932 and March 1933 focused
more on the need for the Committee to meet regularly and discuss
rationally problems concerning national co-operation, particularly the
selection of candidates, than on the publicity objective; though it seems
clear that MacDonald viewed the committee as a propaganda instrument
of the National Government. In March the committee received the
blessing of Baldwin, Simon and MacDonald, and was launched in a
blaze of publicity.[59]

Public interest in the future of the National Government had been
stimulated by Baldwin a short time earlier when in a speech he had
referred vaguely to the events of 1886, the eventual fusion of the Conservatives and Liberal Unionists, and the relevance of this development
to the present situation. Coming in the train of this speech, the
announcement of the establishment of the National Coordinating Committee was seen by a number of people to be the first step towards the
formation of a National Party.[60] But this in fact was not the case.
Rather it was a reaffirmation of the status quo in institutional
terms.

This can be clearly seen when the formation of the National Coordinating Committee is considered in relation to the organisational
changes undertaken by the Liberal Nationals at about the same time. In
March 1933 the Liberal National Council announced that it had taken a
suite of rooms in Old Queen Street, close by to Westminster, which
would provide a focus for Liberal National activities throughout the
country. A memorandum released to the press by the council stressed
that

> The maintenance of the very closest relations between the constitu-
> encies represented by the Liberal National MPs and the Central
> Headquarters in London is and must be the hub of any reliable
> machinery.

It urged that

> What is required . . . is some method of extending the spheres of
> Liberal National influence and interests outside those constituencies.

To achieve this end the Liberal National Council intended to establish area committees, which were to co-operate with local Conservative and National Labour organisations over the selection of candidates, publicity and so on.[61]

Earlier, in October and November 1932, at a meeting of the Executive Committee, the idea of publishing a newsletter had been floated. The party had sufficient funds for such a venture, and the energetic head of Liberal National organisation, Lord Hutchison, was keen to see the newsletter published on a monthly basis.[62] But Simon, approached on the matter late in December, was lukewarm. He was afraid that the magazine would fail and thereby create an unfavourable impression of the party's viability. He was also concerned that the magazine would be interpreted by his coalition colleagues as an act of partisanship by the Liberal Nationals. With this consideration in mind he suggested that Hutchison should use a photograph of Ramsay Mac-Donald on the front of the first issue, rather than one of himself.[63] The magazine eventually appeared, but thereafter was produced only sporadically and was in no sense central to the party's publicity and organisational activities. Nevertheless, it seems clear that the Liberal Nationals had no intention of allowing themselves to be absorbed into the Conservative Party as Baldwin had suggested that they might. The National Coordinating Committee was no more than its title claimed; and its formation was most certainly not the first step towards the formation of a National Party.

Had the Liberal Nationals been financially embarrassed, it is conceivable the idea of a National Party would have been more attractive to them; but in fact the party was in ample funds to continue as an independent entity. After the bills from the general election had been paid, the party still had £3,500 in the kitty.[64] Before the 1931 election Simon had issued a letter to likely subscribers to the Liberal National election fund, which had been well received. The largest contributor to the Liberal National chest was Lord Nuffield, who gave £10,000 to Leslie Hore-Belisha to be used in the Liberal National interest. Others who contributed substantial sums were Lord Inchcape (who gave £1,000 to each of the minor coalition parties), the firm of Layard Brothers (through F.G. Bonham Carter) and Sir Frederick Lewis.[65] Offers of money continued to flow in after the election, and in October 1932 Hutchison was able to inform the Executive Commitee that he had sufficient guarantees for 'an annual income during the lifetime of this Parliament to justify them going on with this Organization'. No less than £1,200 per year had been promised so far and it was expected that a further £300 per year would shortly be available; and this income was separate from the general election and by-election fund, which was also in a healthy condition.[66] It was sufficient for the Liberal Nationals to consolidate themselves as an independent organisation and indeed to extend the range of their activities.

The Conservatives were in less happy circumstances. Constituency propaganda was hesitant; and agents were uncertain as to whether they should issue purely Conservative Party propaganda or propaganda for the National Government, and, as often as not, they produced nothing at all. Throughout 1933 articles in the *Conservative Agents' Journal* referred to the widespread desire among agents for some positive direction from Central Office on the question of publicity, especially as it was thought that the Labour Party was rapidly regaining the ground it had lost at the last election. Most of the area meetings were addressed by Gower, the Chief Publicity Officer, but the best that he could advise them was to concentrate their propaganda on anti-Socialism. Though sound as far as it went, this suggestion sidestepped the issue of concern to the agents; namely whether they should propagandise for the Conservative Party alone or for the Conservative Party in a national government.[67] It was small wonder that Conservative agents were noting sadly that 'The Conservative Party often missed the opportunity of advancing their cause by a reluctance to take advantage of the many chances presented of advertising the Party's interests.'[68] Almost without exception, the June meetings of the area agents called on Central Office to give a clear lead as to the character of the propaganda to be issued.

Allied to this plea was a growing concern about the party's finances. Co-operation in the National Government had affected party finances in two ways: first, those people who wished to see a purely Conservative administration withheld funds for as long as national government lasted; secondly, those who supported the Conservative participation in the National Government wanted a guarantee that the National Government was in no danger of breaking up; without such a guarantee, which few if any associations were prepared (or indeed able) to give, this group too tended to withhold its funds.

This state of affairs, coupled with a reduction in income because of the depression, brought many organisations to the edge of bankruptcy.[69] So desperate was the plight of the Yorkshire Conservatives, for example, that in June they called on Baldwin to make a public appeal for funds for the party; a plea to which, as a Minister in the National Government, he could not respond.[70] Nor were the finances of Central Office in a healthy state. When in June the Middlesex agents asked

Central Office to issue a broadsheet to counter the influential Socialist broadsheet, *Citizen*,[71] their request had to be refused; indeed throughout this period Central Office was itself in severe financial difficulties.[72] If the party was to effectively fight the next general election, it was clear that something drastic would have to be done to place the party on a sound financial basis.

Meanwhile the party had become embroiled in an internecine war over the National Government's India policy. At a meeting of the Central Council held early in 1933, Winston Churchill put forward a resolution which declared that independence for India was injurious to both India and Britain. After an acrimonious debate, the resolution was lost by 189 votes to 165.[73] An even greater debate took place at the meeting of the Central Council held on 28 June. Once more Churchill and his colleagues in the 'India Defence League', Sir Henry Page Croft, Lord Lloyd and others, were defeated, on this occasion by a greater margin; but as the vote indicates − 838 to 356 − the support they enjoyed was not inconsiderable. This large and vocal minority group believed that Baldwin and his fellow Conservative Ministers had surrendered to the Socialist and Liberal elements in the National Government; that long-established Conservative principles were being departed from in the interests of 'national unity'. This angered them and made them anxious to see an early return to party government or at least a reconstructed national government, one less amenable to non-Conservative influence.[74]

Discussion about India and the character of the National Government was not confined to the politicians. As *The Times* observed:

the results of [Churchill's] efforts has already been to make the Indian problem a sort of yardstick for local associations in measuring the precise degree of party spirit which animates their members or their candidates; and it is a process which is likely to grow.[75]

This was particularly true of the selection of Conservative candidates for by-elections. At Hitchin in June, for example, the local association selected Sir Arnold Wilson, a well-known opponent of the Government's India policy. Although on most of the other issues Wilson was impeccably loyal, Central Office refused to give him financial assistance[76] and thereby exacerbated an already dangerous situation. At about the same time, Central Office intervened in the Altrincham by-

election by foisting on the local selection committee a well-known
advocate of Indian independence, Sir Edward Grigg.[77] This intrusion
was bitterly resented by many of the local Conservatives, and it was
only with difficulty that they were restrained from nominating an independent Conservative candidate. Thus, to many party organisers the
National Government came to be equated with an unwelcome dictation
from Central Office, and was resented in that measure. The by-election
reverses which the party suffered late in 1933 confirmed them in their
view that co-operation in the National Government was not furthering
the interests of the party; unless the leadership took steps to prevent it,
it was only a matter of time before discontent in the constituencies
would manifest itself more vehemently.

While many of the Conservative constituency organisations were
becoming disillusioned with the National Government, Baldwin's belief
in its virtues was strengthening. At the 1932 party conference he had
informed the delegates that it was their duty to continue 'to carry our
share in the letter and spirit of the National Government; our aims
must be national and not party; our ideals must be national and not
party'.[78] By mid-1933 it was clear that the National Government had
achieved the purpose for which it had been formed; namely to meet the
financial crisis and to head the country in the direction of prosperity.
At about the same time Baldwin began to justify the continued existence of the National Government in terms of the growing menace of
dictatorships of the right and left at home and abroad, and of the con-
comitant danger of war. Aided by the extremist nature of the resolutions adopted by the Labour Party at its Hastings conference, he told
the nation that:

> The Socialist Party is turning more and more to extremism, and the
> defence against that menace is a continuance of the cooperation on
> which the National Government is based.[79]

At his own party's conference he said that the country need Disraelian
Conservatism, that is, the Conservative Party had to be national or it
was nothing. In short, the National Government must be allowed to
continue its work.[80] Not even the final rupture with the Samuelite
Liberals in November, or the by-electoral reverses of October and
November, caused him to waver:

> The hearts of some have waxed cold, but ours have not, neither our

hearts nor our feet. We may have vaguely wondered at the time how long the combination would last. It was for the duration. When the duration will be over I do not know, but I am not bothering my head about it. It will be a long time before there is an election, and there is a great deal to be done.[81]

Here was a clear sign to the party workers that 'like it or lump it' they were stuck with the National Government for some time to come; but far less certain was whether Baldwin and MacDonald intended to fight the next election as a National Government or on traditional party lines.

Although Baldwin did not lose faith in the National Government as a result of the by-election reverses of October and November, he was spurred into realising that the government's publicity machine was woefully inadequate, and that the government's policies — particularly its international policy — were being subjected to severe criticism from not only the Labour and Samuelite Liberal Parties but also from within the Conservative Party.[82] Accordingly, the National Coordinating Committee was authorised to conduct a great propaganda campaign in the first three months of 1934.[83] This was launched by the Prime Minister at Leeds in January; and on 15 February Baldwin addressed a huge demonstration at Preston, in the course of which he appeased the diehards by saying that he did not believe that a National Party was compatible with British political traditions. 'But,' he added, 'I believe that cooperation among men from different schools is not only possible but desirable. It is being obtained today.' He then went on to speak of the loss of traditional British democratic liberties in the revolutionary programmes of Cripps and Mosley, and he reassured his audience that the National Government stood as a bulwark against alien influences and as the defender of constitutional democracy in Britain and of peace in the world.[84] In a subsequent speech, delivered to the party faithful at Bewdley, he gave Conservative organisers a hint of the likely character of the next election. He was confident, he said, that at the next election the voters would look less to the record of the government and more to its future actions.[85] This appeared to confirm the view that Topping had expressed in his New Year message to the Conservative agents, namely that

> if the next election is to be fought on National lines as is at present indicated then our propaganda between now and the next election must be of a National character. This does not mean . . . that there

will be no more party warfare. There must be warfare with the Socialist Party and there must be warfare with the supporters of Sir Herbert Samuel, and in that warfare we shall have as our allies the National Labour and Liberal National supporters of the National Government.[86]

Encouraged by the remarks of Baldwin at Bewdley, Topping reiterated his view at area meetings throughout the country. But to many Conservatives the prospect was anathema and the more likely it became the more vehemently did they voice their criticism.

For the Conservatives the difficulties of co-operating with the Liberal Nationals and the National Labour Group remained great throughout 1933 and 1934. In the first place the National Coordinating Committee made no striking advances following its creation in March 1933. It had been intended that the Liberal Nationals and the National Labour Group should set up regional bodies which would act in concert with Conservative organisations to secure unanimity over the selection of candidates for by-elections. The theory was that whenever a by-election occurred the chairman for the area in question would immediately get into touch with his two colleagues representing the Liberal National Party and the National Labour Group, and they in turn would get in touch with the local leaders of the government's supporters in the constituency where the by-election was taking place, with a view to securing co-operation in support of the National Government's candidate. But as Stonehaven reported to Baldwin in December 1933, neither of the Conservatives' allies had succeeded in developing any effective organisation in the constituencies, and so the burden of support for the government lay almost entirely with the local Conservative Associations.[87] In view of the fact that the Coordinating Committee was shortly to make a review of constituencies throughout the country in order to discover openings for members of the Liberal National Party and the National Labour Group in constituencies at present held by Conservatives or Samuelites, the failure to develop regional organisations not only reduced the credibility of National Government, but also intensified the reluctance of Conservative associations to persist with co-operation. Despite these difficulties, Stonehaven discounted the idea of creating a National Party. He felt that if the leaders favoured this course they might well precipitate a split in the Conservative Party; and in any case, because of the presence of the Samuelite Liberals, the issue was not simply one of Socialism and anti-Socialism, as those who desired a National Party argued, and both MacDonald and Simon still favoured co-operation between, rather than fusion of, the parties. 'The best course,' he informed Baldwin, 'seems ... to be to pursue the policy of collaboration, notwithstanding its obvious difficulties, to the utmost possible extent, and to await further developments.'

But at the constituency level, agents continued to be unable to find a solution to the dilemma of making a national appeal from a party base. At a meeting of the agents of western England in February 1934, the agents complained that all anti-Socialist groups were seeking from the Conservatives organisational and financial aid which, in many cases, they felt constrained to provide: 'the effect of this was reduced subscriptions to the Party Funds and a falling off of support at meetings'.[88] At a meeting of the south-eastern agents in May, the area secretary, F. Walter, reported that although the government was doing quite well at by-elections, there were unfortunate repercussions which could adversely affect the party's future, for 'all the credit for success went to the National Government and not the Conservative Party'. Furthermore, the propaganda was now being directed by the National Government itself. The effect of this, Walter claimed, was to make it

> exceedingly difficult to maintain a purely Conservative organization, and he was afraid the Conservative Party was developing an inferiority complex for the next Election.[89]

The best that Topping could do by way of reply was to state that they would have to solve their problems somehow because it seemed certain that the next election would be fought on national lines. This was of no comfort whatsoever, and throughout 1934 agents in all parts of the country reported that there was a decline in party membership and a general loss of morale.[90]

Some of this discontent came to the surface at meetings of the Central Council. At the meeting of 28 March, Stonehaven was called on to rebut a press comment that he and Captain Margesson had been 'handing over seats' to the Liberal Nationals and the National Labour Group through the agency of the Coordinating Committee.[91] Stonehaven explained that the committee had been making a review of the constituencies, but that the notion that he was handing over seats was little short of fantastic. He stressed that the Coordinating Committee did not possess seats, which, of course, belonged to the constituency organisations. All that was happening, he added, was that in cases where a member announced that he was not going to stand again, and it appeared that it was more likely that the National Government would hold the seat if it was represented by a National Labour or a Liberal National candidate, then the constituency organisation concerned was being notified of this; but in the end it alone made the selection. Stonehaven denied a further accusation that he took his orders from the Co-ordinating Committee: if this were true, he said, it would mean that he had 'manifestly gone mad and ought to be removed rapidly'.

But his remarks failed to completely reassure the Central Council, which passed by an overwhelming majority a resolution which declared that while placing on record support for the National Government in fulfilment of the mandate of the electors, it was essential that the Conservative Party, 'the one great force in the country which was a bulwark against Socialism', should maintain its organisation intact, and take immediate steps to rally its supporters throughout the country. It also declared that

> a reaffirmation of the major principles of the Conservative faith by the Leaders is in the National interest, more especially with regard to adequate defence, the preservation of the Empire . . . the strengthening of the second chamber, and the determination to grant security to Industry, Agriculture and Shipping.

It is highly significant that this comprehensive resolution was carried, for at the same meeting Churchill and his friends were once again outvoted on the India issue. In short, while many Conservatives, though by no means a majority, thought that the National Government had abandoned traditional Conservative policy regarding India, far more were concerned with the character of the National Government and the direction in which Baldwin was leading it. 'National' government itself was being questioned, rather than any particular policy of the National Government.

In June the party leadership again came under fire at a meeting of the Central Council. During the debate on the report of the Executive Committee it was urged that the Publications Department of Central Office ought to identify itself more closely with purely Conservative policy. An angry Stonehaven replied flatly that propaganda had necessarily to be for the National Government, and that a further aim of Central Office was to capture the support of people who at present did not belong to any political party. But the meeting was characterised by a persistent demand for a restatement of Conservative policy and a barely disguised hostility towards the leadership.[92]

But it was from the Conservatives who wished to see the creation of a National Party that the next move came. To the surprise of everyone, a call to this effect came from a Minister in the National Government — the new Attorney General, Sir Thomas Inskip. In a speech delivered to the United Club on 24 April, Inskip declared that:

> He was very doubtful indeed whether they could put the new wine of this political generation into old bottles, and he did not know whether the measures or the policies which must be supported by the next Government could possibly be contained within the four corners of the old Conservative Party ... He did not think that any of them ought to be afraid to face the permanent constitution of a National Party because in 1931 they thought the National Government was only a temporary arrangement for an emergency.[93]

Central Office at once issued a statement to the effect that Inskip's views were personal, and that the Conservative Party had no intention of changing its name;[94] and the political correspondent of the *Daily Telegraph* was 'authoritatively informed' that the government intended to go to the country in 'the Spring of 1936, as a National Government, with a joint appeal by Conservatives, Liberal Nationals, and the National Labour Party'.[95] But unfortunately for Central Office, it had not heard the last of the Inskip's view. In mid-June there appeared in the press a manifesto, signed by over 100 Conservative MPs, which declared that:

> the existing cooperation between the parties in the system of National Government has been so fruitful and is so promising, that every possible step should be taken to make it, for all practical purposes, a permanent ideal in British politics.[96]

All but about ten of the signatories had been returned to the House of Commons for the first time in 1931[97] and stood to lose their seats if there was a reversion to traditional party politics at the next general election. Caught between this group and those who wished to see an early return to party politics, Stonehaven saw that the only way in which he could prevent a split in the party was to pursue the course on which they had been embarked since 1931: unpopular though it was, it was the least unpopular of the three possibilities open to him, and at the Central Council meeting of 27 June he managed to secure the adoption of two resolutions which gave the impression that things were going to continue along the same lines as before.[98]

But Central Office had been markedly unsettled by the volume and the intensity of the criticism it had received. In July Stonehaven conducted an exhaustive inquiry on the subject of future relations between the supporters of the National Government, and early in August he sent a detailed memorandum to Baldwin.[99] As he diffidently explained in an accompanying note, he was 'rather inclined to tear it up — for there is nothing new in it, and nothing that is not very obvious'. He recognised that from by-election results it was clear that the National Government no longer enjoyed the support of all those who had voted for it in 1931, and that at the next general election it would be difficult to counter the likelihood that the electors would desire a change. It was his opinion, nevertheless, that:

> it certainly looks as if the Government would stand a better chance of obtaining a majority in the next Parliament if it goes to the country in alliance with its present Liberal & Labour associates rather than if the combination were broken up and it appealed for a purely Conservative majority.

He ruled out an amalgamation of the three sections of the National Government's supporters in a National Party — despite its attraction as a long-term course and despite the strong support for the idea from within the Conservative Party — because in the short run it would still further split the Conservative Party, and because it was not acceptable either to the Liberal Nationals or to National Labour. He thought that relations between the government parties stood pretty much as they had at the end of 1933; from the Liberal Nationals and National Labour there was a standing demand for more seats, but little progress had been made by either of them in creating a viable electoral organisation, and 'they themselves are unable to assess the strength of the support on which they can count among the electors'. A further complicating factor was the apparent reluctance of both to attack openly the official Labour Party and the Samuelite Liberals:

> In the case of the Liberal Nationals this reluctance is so pronounced that they refuse either to run a candidate against a sitting Samuelite Liberal or even support Conservative or National Labour candidates standing against them. The result is a standing demand by the Liberal National and National Labour members of the Coordinating

Committee for seats now held by Conservatives.

This led in turn to a marked hostility on the part of the Conservative Party to any suggestion that seats were to be handed over to Liberal Nationals and National Labour. Only by 'treating groups of seats as a unit, e.g. Sheffield with seven Conservative Members', might it prove possible to do a deal, and on this point Stonehaven was none too optimistic. In short, his advice to Baldwin was the same as it had been in 1933, namely 'to pursue the policy of collaboration, notwithstanding its obvious difficulties, to the utmost possible extent, and to await further developments'.

The events of the next few months confirmed the wisdom of the course suggested by Stonehaven. At the party conference in October, Baldwin had to face some criticism over the selection of candidates, as well as a general charge that the National Government in its present form was hardly a viable electoral force. On the latter point, Baldwin replied that he regretted the losses sustained at by-elections, especially as defeats 'always had a morale effect and always depressed the political workers in those constituencies'. But to those who questioned his leadership, he stated that 'I am Leader and I am going to lead', and the direction in which he was leading them was towards a general election in association with the National Government.[100] Three weeks after this, he again threw down the gauntlet to his critics, this time at the annual solidarity meeting of the National Government leadership, the National Labour luncheon at the Trocadero Restaurant.[101] He spoke of the National Government as Britain's guarantee of peace in Europe, and he insisted that it must continue its work:

> I do not see myself — it is impossible to look far forward — I do not see in the near future, with which we older men are concerned, any prospect of going back to the party dog-fight of the old days.

By now he was well and truly roused, and indeed he needed to be for the tide of affairs was beginning to move sharply against him. At the Putney by-election held late in November, the Conservative candidate, fighting on the record of the National Government, almost lost a seat which since 1922 had had Conservative majorities of 8,000 or more. In a fight similar to those of 1929 and 1931 — that is, a straight fight between the Conservatives and Labour — the National Government share of the total vote fell from 81.6% in 1931 to 54.7%. This was the

only occasion between 1931 and 1935 when the government's share of
the total vote fell below that polled by the Conservative candidate in
1929. In December Baldwin once again routed Churchill over India,
but in the same month there was severe criticism of the government's
new unemployment regulations, which to many Conservatives seemed
unnecessarily harsh and their introduction singularly ill-timed.[102]
Furthermore, many of the younger Conservatives — such as Harold
Macmillan, Robert Boothby and W. Ormsby-Gore — felt that the
National Government had lost its momentum, and indeed its credibility, and was incapable of dealing with the problems of the day;
they wanted the National Government to be reconstructed, with
Simon and perhaps Runciman removed from their present positions,
and with Baldwin taking over the premiership from MacDonald.[103]
This was a challenge which could be met, and Baldwin himself was
inclined to agree that some changes were necessary.

But the real threat was still from the right, and to it Baldwin was
uncompromising. He made his position perfectly clear in his New Year
meassage to the Primrose League:

> During 1935 we shall be thinking about and preparing for the next
> appeal to the country. At the next election we will have to make a
> decision that may well determine the fate of the British Empire.
> They will have to choose between the constructive policy of the
> *National Government* and the destructive policy of the Socialist
> Party.[104]

The Queens Hall vote in December had ended the extra-parliamentary
attck on the government's India policy, but dissatisfaction with the
National Government was still widespread. Fortunately for Baldwin it
was spearheaded by the diehards who in February overplayed their
hand and drove the malcontents back into Baldwin's arms. At the
Wavertree by-election an all-out attack on the National Government
was launched by the right wing of the Conservative Party. Its candidate,
Randolph Churchill, was extraordinarily successful, splitting the
Conservative vote so evenly that the Labour Party candidate won the
seat with a small minority vote.[105] But the reaction within the party
was the reverse of that desired by the critics of the government, for
many Conservatives now realised that if they persisted in attacking the
National Government it was likely that the Socialists would win the
next general election. That this was a prospect which was abhorrent to
them became clear at the Lambeth Norwood by-election in March when

once more a right-wing Conservative candidate stood against a National
Government Conservative; but on this occasion he lost his deposit, and
his campaign lacked the influential backing which Churchill had enjoyed
at Wavertree.[106] Perhaps Baldwin himself had played a decisive part in
this change of heart, for at Chelsea just prior to the Norwood by-
election, he had warned the party that he did not believe that it alone
could win a clear majority if an election was held, 'with the amount of
split votes there would be between itself'.[107] Events at Norwood
appeared to indicate that his warning had been heeded.

While Baldwin was busily engaged in convincing his party of the need to
prolong the life of the National Government, Central Office was
proceeding on the assumption that the next election would be fought
by the Conservative Party in alliance with the Liberal Nationals and
National Labour. Since the series of adverse by-election results late in
1933, Stonehaven had turned his attention to publicising the work of
the National Government. In December of that year the National
Coordinating Committee extended the range of its activities to embrace
publicity, but up to the end of 1934 it had proved to be singularly in-
effective. In December 1934 rumours appeared in the press to the
effect that the National Coordinating Committee was being superseded
for the purposes of the next general election by a new body. According
to the *Manchester Guardian*:

> It consists of the famous National Coordinating Committee with the
> addition of Sir Robert Topping, chief of Conservative Central Office,
> Mr. W.G. Spofforth of the National Labour Organisation, and Dr.
> J. Hunter, the Simonite organizer. The Committee is to have a
> central fund, to be devoted exclusively to the electioneering and
> propaganda purposes of the National Government, and Sir Kingsley
> Wood, the Postmaster General, is to act as liaison officer between
> the Prime Minister and the Committee.[108]

At about the same time, A.J. Cummings of the *News Chronicle* warned
his readers that there was a danger of Kingsley Wood becoming a Minister of Propaganda *à la* Goebbels.[109] Substance was given to these
rumours some time later when Central Office announced that the
National Government was going to launch a publicity campaign in February; and this duly took place. Then in March it was officially
announced that a National Publicity Bureau had been formed to publicise the work of the National Government.[110] With offices close to

Westminster, and an organising secretary, Col. E.H. Davidson, who had been a member of Lord Northcliffe's propaganda committee in the Great War, it promised to be an efficient instrument of propaganda. The important members of the bureau were Kingsley Wood; Lord Hutchison, head of the Liberal National Council; and Malcolm Mac-Donald, the son of the Prime Minister and member of the National Labour Committee. Some time later the Chief Publicity Officer of the Conservative Party, Sir Patrick Gower, was co-opted in order to co-ordinate the work of Central Office and the National Publicity Committee. At the same time it was rumoured that the monthly broadsheet issued by Central Office would be taken over by the new organisation.[111]

Press reactions to the creation of the bureau were varied.[112] The *Morning Post* regarded the step as an abdication of responsibility, indeed sovereignty, on the part of the Conservative Party; and other right-wing Conservative papers like the *Daily Mail* and the *Daily Express* were equally unenthusiastic; so too was the organ of moderate Conservative opinion, the *Daily Telegraph*. *The Times* regarded it as a logical and valuable development, while the *Daily Mail* regarded it as logical only.

Nor was comment confined to the press. A number of dissident Conservatives held several meetings at which they resolved to send a memorandum to Baldwin in protest against the way the party was being led.[113] In the memorandum five things were asked of Baldwin. First, that he comment on rumours that when in 1933 the party was in dire financial straits, Central Office refused donations from those people who made their offers conditional upon the maintenance of true and independent Conservative principles, but accepted donations from Sir Julian Cahn, Israel Sieff and others, who had made their offers on the condition that the Conservative Party remained committed to its present unqualified support of the National Government. Secondly, that if there was a Cabinet reconstruction, would Conservatism be more adequately represented? Thirdly, would genuine Conservative propaganda, bearing the name of the party, be available from Central Office? Fourthly, would the Coordinating Committee's activities be restricted to propaganda, or was it proposed to extend its powers further? The fifth question concerned the government's trade policy.

It appears that Baldwin did not reply to the memorandum;[114] but some of the queries were raised and dealt with by Stonehaven at the meeting of the Central Council of 27 March. He explained that the bureau was a purely temporary organisation whose activities would cease at the general election:

> the Bureau will have no authority whatever over the Central Office, and our propaganda department will remain completely free to issue any propaganda it requires, including broadsheets, pamphlets, leaflets, and posters, and the same is true of the other parties supporting the National Government.

In reply to criticism that even before the creation of the new bureau Central Office propaganda had been non-Conservative, Stonehaven agreed that 'there had been some sort of alteration in the film propaganda so as to stress the National Government'; but, he declared, 'If they had a National Government, they had got to pay for it, and if they were going to face a General Election with two other parties they had got to do so.'[115] The force of his reasoning was not lost on the majority of those present, particularly as it was now recognised, thanks to Churchill and the result of the Wavertree by-election, that the alternative to the course adopted by Stonehaven would lead to the defeat of the Conservatives at the next general election. Stonehaven had his way, supported strongly by Neville Chamberlain, and thereafter, indeed for the first time since it took office, [116] the National Government had its work fairly effectively publicised.

At the constituency level, party organisers and voters had seen little of direct Conservative propaganda for several years; and, especially after the by-electoral reverses late in 1933, they had taken part in an increasing number of demonstrations addressed by members of the National Government. The creation of the National Publicity Bureau was followed by a massive propaganda campaign in the constituencies which lasted for most of the summer and was generally thought to be a run-up to a general election.[117] No less than eleven daylight cinema vans toured the country, and some comedians including Arthur Prince and Stanley Holloway were employed to sing the praises of the National Government, the strategy being, apparently, that if you can't solve unemployment, at least you can try to keep the unemployed amused.

Constituency organisations were by no means reconciled to Central Office intervention in the selection of candidates which a Central Office proposal in March increased still further;[118] but almost without exception they were now resigned to the fact that the general election was going to be fought on national lines. The party's finances were in a far sounder state than they had been in 1933, and from July onwards all was in readiness for an election.

By July also the parliamentary Conservative Party had begun to close its ranks. Cabinet reconstruction in June had increased Conservative representation: in particular, Baldwin's accession to the premiership in place of the ailing MacDonald, and the replacement of Sir John Simon as Foreign Secretary by Sir Samuel Hoare, gave great satisfaction to the Conservative Party. Perhaps of equal importance was the passage of the India Bill, for with its enactment, diehards like Churchill buried the hatchet and fell into line behind Baldwin for the first time since 1930. The party conference at Bournemouth in October was merely an exercise in party unanimity and goodwill. There was even the extraordinary sight of Winston Churchill complimenting Baldwin on his leadership of the party.[119] Even when disunited, the Conservative Party had fared quite well at by-elections; united, it could expect to do far better at the general election .

Notes

1. The history of the Liberal National Party has not yet been written. Simon's autobiography, *Retrospect* (1952) is distinctly unhelpful; and Roy Douglas's *History of the Liberal Party from 1895 to 1970* (1971) treats the Liberal Nationals rather cursorily. The National Labour Group has been better served. There is David Marquand's *Ramsay MacDonald* (1977), which is an excellent portrait, and there is an authoritative life of National Labour's most ardent publicist, Clifford Allen, by Arthur Marwick, *The Open Conspirator* (1964), as well as the witty observations of Harold Nicolson in his *Diaries and Letters 1930-39* (1966). Robert Blake's *The Conservative Party from Peel to Churchill* (1970) is regrettably thin on the early 1930s, though it does provide the historical perspective necessary for a detailed study of Conservatives in the 1930s. Biographies and autobiographies of Conservative politicians abound as do studies of various aspects of Conservative policy in the 1930s; but for the internal history of the party one must still turn with gratitude to the work of a former member of the staff of Central Office: Percy Cohen, 'Disraeli's Child: a history of the Conservative and Unionist Party Organization', unpublished typescript, Conservative Research Department Library.
2. The only detailed account of the 1931 crisis and general election is R. Bassett, *Nineteen Thirty-One: political crisis* (1958), pp. 246-350. The background to the crisis is fully explored in R. Skidelsky, *Politicians and the Slump* (1967). Also valuable is an older work: C.L. Mowat, *Britain Between the Wars 1918-1940* (1955), pp. 386-412.
3. This is clear from the following quotations: MacDonald, in a statement issued from Downing Street shortly after the formation of the National Government, 24 August: 'The specific object for which the new Government is being formed is to deal with the national emergency that now exists. It will not be a coalition Government in the usual sense of the term, but a Government of cooperation for this one purpose. When that purpose is achieved the political parties will resume their respective positions.' Also his broadcast on 25 August: 'The election which will follow [when the work of the Government is

complete] will not be fought by the Government.'

Baldwin, in an address to a meeting of the Conservative Party, 28 August: 'It [the National Government] is not a coalition — it is a cooperation of individuals of different parties who joined together temporarily for the purpose of passing legislation necessary to effect economy and to balance the budget.'

Samuel, in an address to a Liberal Party meeting, 28 August: 'The new Government is not intended to be a long continuing combination, still less a permanent coalition.' Of the three-party conference of 20 August, he said: 'There was complete agreement further that no disservice to the country would be greater than to have an immediate election.' Even people like Lord Hailsham, who hoped for and expected an early general election, anticipated that it would be on traditional party lines. (Speech to the Conservative Party meeting, 28 August; *The Times*, 29 Aug.; also letter to the *Daily Express*, 3 Sept.)

4. Not until Britain went off the Gold Standard on 21 September was there a general Conservative demand for an immediate election to be contested by the National Government: at a meeting of the 1922 Club (which represented a substantial body of Conservative backbench opinion) on the evening of 21 September, party whips present were instructed to inform the leader that the party was in favour of an immediate appeal to the electorate as a National Government and with a tariff platform (*The Times*, 22 Sept.). The next day Baldwin told Snowden that he could no longer withstand his party's demand for a national appeal by a National Government under MacDonald (P. Snowden, *Autobiography* (1934), vol. 2, p. 989). MacDonald was the next leader to agree to an election, prompted by the need to reassure the world that the British people endorsed his government's decision to go off the Gold Standard, a genuine desire not to see the National Government broken up, and a recognition that the Labour Party's decision (taken on 28 September) to expel him meant that he had no future in politics outside the National Government. Simon, supported by about thirty Liberal MPs, also agreed to an election, and in the House of Commons expressed his willingness to see 'some block in the way of free imports' (House of Commons Debates (HCD), vol. 256, col. 279, 15 Sept.); and on 5 October he and his followers formed a separate organisation for the purpose of contesting the election in alliance with the Conservative Party and the National Labour Group (*The Times*, 5 Oct.). Samuel was the last leader to agree to an election: Lloyd George was opposed to an election, as was the NLF and the Women's NLF; but by 5 October Samuel and his parliamentary followers had agreed to an election by a National Government appealing for a free hand to deal with the emergency (H. Samuel, *Memoirs* (1945), p. 180). The date of the general election was announced on 6 October, and Parliament was dissolved a day later. As nominations closed on 16 October, there was less than a fortnight for the National Government parties to make arrangements regarding the distribution of seats.

5. K. Middlemas and J. Barnes, *Baldwin: a biography* (1969), p. 640.

6. Baldwin Papers, vol. 45, MacDonald to Baldwin, 7 Oct. MacDonald noted that three National Labour MPs who were changing their seats were still unprovided for: 'There is also a group of very good men who have been turned out of constituencies, several of which provided excellent prospects, and no arrangement has been come to regarding them although negotiations have been going on for days, and the tone of your Head Office representatives yesterday was very forbidding.' MacDonald was also concerned about the Liberal Nationals: 'You will also remember that I spoke to you about Runciman.' (In 1929 Runciman had won St Ives very narrowly from a Conservative. Not unnaturally the local Conservative Association was keen to contest the seat in 1931; eventually, however, it was persuaded to allow Runciman a straight fight with Labour.)

7. The thirteen constituencies were Finsbury, Central Southwark, Ilkeston,

Seaham, Forest of Dean, Central Leeds, South Tottenham, Ormskirk, Bassetlaw, Lichfield, Central Cardiff, Kilmarnock and South Nottingham; on the basis of the 1929 figures and a reasonable assessment of swing to the Conservative Party, the last-named eight seats would probably have returned Conservative candidates had they been in the field.

8. Baldwin Papers, vol. 45, undated note from MacDonald, referring particularly to the situation at Louth, where a Liberal (Ramsay Muir) and a Conservative (Col. Heneage) both claimed to represent the National Government. In this instance, MacDonald's 'rule' would have favoured the Conservative.

9. Ibid., vol. 45, Stonehaven to MacDonald, 23 Oct.

10. If Baldwin thought kindly of MacDonald (Middlemas and Barnes, *Baldwin*, p. 640), Stonehaven most certainly did not. Shortly after the general election, Stonehaven was reported to have said that 'we have a National Government with a mandate to carry out Tory policy' (*The Times*, 3 Dec.). This, not surprisingly, drew a retort from MacDonald. Publicly Stonehaven retracted a little, but in a note to Baldwin (Baldwin Papers, vol. 46) written on 6 December, he stressed that the election free hand did not exclude Tory policy. He added that in his opinion MacDonald was 'floating in the clouds', and that before he attacked a Conservative again he should 'remember that it was 5000 Tory voters who put him in for Seaham'.

11. Baldwin Papers, vol. 45, L. Amery to Baldwin, 17 Oct.: 'You will remember that at the business committee and at the Emergency Party meeting [6 Oct.] it was made quite clear that all candidates duly adopted by a Conservative Association were entitled to the support of the Party and, presumably, therefore, of its leader. At both meetings too, it was made clear that while it would hardly be decent for actual members of the Government to attack others, all the rest of us were free to do so, and your speech at the latter meeting was clearly taken by everyone to mean that you hoped that Samuel would be ousted.' (He then went on to ask Baldwin to assist Graham at Darwen and Williams at North Cornwall.) It might be thought (as Middlemas and Barnes consider, *Baldwin*, p. 648) that Amery's account of the meetings was less than objective; but it is in fact confirmed from a more reliable source. Shortly after the election a conference at Central Office was 'held to consider requests for advice which have been received from organizations throughout the country as to whether they are at liberty to use the word "National" in the titles of constituency associations' (Baldwin Papers, vol. 46). The report of the conference is worth quoting at some length as it clearly explains Central Office's appreciation of the course of events from the formation of the National Government to the election: 'The General Director [Topping] gave a brief outline of the course of events within the Party Organization since the formation of the National Government at the end of August, when at a Party meeting the Leader had explained that when they had succeeded in balancing the Budget each Party would proceed once more with its own plans in its own way. In the middle of September, however, a general Election became inevitable and negotiations took place between Simon Liberals, National Labour and this Office on the assumption that the Government would appeal to the country on a definite and declared policy, but when the Dissolution was announced it was understood that the Prime Minister was asking for a doctor's mandate, and that each Party was at liberty to suggest its own remedies. Except in a few constituencies where it was found impossible to arrive at an agreement, no difficulties arose between the respective central offices of the Conservative, Simon Liberal and National Labour Parties, but it was definitely understood that we were in conflict with the Samuel Liberals' (Baldwin Papers, Report of Central Office Conference, 27 Nov.). The report was accepted by Lord Stonehaven, Sir Patrick Gower, Sir Robert Topping, Lord Ebbisham, Miss Maxse

and Sir George Bowyer, the Conservative Party's principal officers.

12. The report continues: 'until the Leader's speech at Birmingham, which was taken as an indication that the Conservative Party would not force a contest in any Division where the Liberal had declared himself to be a supporter of the National Government.'

13. Baldwin Papers, vol. 45, Gower to Baldwin, 15 Oct. Part of the letter reads as follows: 'I know all the difficulties, but I am really anxious in regard to the feeling which exists in the Party as the result of what you said in your speech in Birmingham, combined with the attitude which Herbert Samuel has since adopted. It is not only a Die-hard stunt. I have met some of your most loyal supporters who are really disturbed because they feel that you were holding up an individual [Graham, at Darwen] candidate, who was placed in a very difficult poisition, to obliquy and condemnation . . . the feeling is far more widespread, and it has been intensified by the literature which the Samuel crowd have pushed out, combined with the attitude of the Free Trade Liberals in various constituencies . . . Our Party is getting tired of being told in the Press that they are not playing the game, when they are making sacrifices in every direction, and when they see Liberals here, there, and everywhere up to their old party tricks.'

14. Ibid., vol. 45, Samuel to Baldwin, 17 Oct.

15. Ibid., vol. 45, Samuel to Baldwin, 22 Oct.

16. Ibid., vol. 45, transcript of telephone message, 23 Oct.

17. Ibid., vol. 44, correspondence concerning the candidates at Mid-Bedfordshire, 20 and 21 Oct.

18. Ibid., vol. 45, note attached to transcript of telephone message from Samuel, 23 Oct. See also M. Stocks, *Ernest Simon of Manchester* (1963), pp. 89-91.

19. Baldwin Papers, vol. 45, Stonehaven to Baldwin, 23 Oct. Stonehaven also enclosed a draft of a letter to Samuel about the Liberal Notes, which he wanted Baldwin to send to Samuel. On the same day he wrote to Snowden reprimanding him for sending a message of support to the Liberal candidate at Colne Valley.

20. Ibid., vol. 45, manuscript note, 24 Oct. It is possible that at no time did Baldwin consider sending a message of support to McLean. As early as 17 October he knew that Central Office was sending Leo Amery to North Cornwall to speak against McLean (Amery to Baldwin, 17 Oct.: 'Central Office . . . have asked me to go down to N. Cornwall to speak for Williams against Donald McLean. I have accepted.'), and he made no attempt to discourage Amery.

21. Ibid., vol. 45, Samuel to Baldwin, 26 Oct. He merely notes what Baldwin has done: 'I do not make a grievance of it.'

22. Bassett, *Nineteen Thirty-One*, p. 302.

23. Middlemas and Barnes, *Baldwin*, p. 649.

24. Stonehaven was misinformed about Western Isles; and at Gateshead and Barnsley, Conservative candidates withdrew after he had issued his statement to the press. The corrected list of Conservative withdrawals in favour of Liberals is as follows (L — Samuelite Liberal; LN — Simonite Liberal): East Birkenhead (L), West Leicester (L), Isle of Ely (L— however, Lord Beaverbrook sponsored an independent Conservative candidate: *Evening Standard*, 19 Oct.), Bodmin (L), Banffshire (L), Caithness and Sutherland (L), Dumfries (L), Orkney and Shetland (L), North Lambeth (L), East Middlesbrough (L), East Swansea (L), Wrexham (L), Gower (L), Shoreditch (LN), North Southwark (LN), Durham (LN), Huddersfield (LN), East Newcastle-upon-Tyne (LN), Walsall (LN), Luton (LN), Eddisbury (LN), St. Ives (LN), South Molton (LN), Harwick (LN), Huntingdon (LN), Bosworth (LN), Holland with Boston (LN), East Norfolk (LN), Eye (LN), Denbigh (LN), Flint (LN), Montgomery (LN), East Fife (LN), Barnsley (LN), Gateshead (LN), Great Yarmouth (LN), Norwich (LN), Devonport (LN),

Southampton (LN), West Swansea (LN), Greenock (LN), Leith (LN), Ross and Cromarty (LN), Montrose Burghs (LN) and Inverness (LN). To these should be added Whitechapel and St Georges (L), South Bradford (L), Dewsbury (L), South Shields (L), East Edinburgh (L), Paisley (L), Consett (LN), Bishop Auckland (LN) and Dunfermline (LN).

25. Great Yarmouth, Southampton, Eddisbury, Harwich, Holland-with-Boston, Walsall, Dunfermline, Durham, East Middlesbrough and South Bradford. Only in the last two did Conservatives withdraw in favour of Samuelites.

26. The four constituencies where there were clashes between Conservatives and Simonites were East Dorset, Ashford, Nuneaton and Western Isles.

27. The two Simonites defeated by Conservatives in 1931 were A.E. Glassey (East Dorset) and R.M. Kedward (Ashford); the defeated Samuelite Liberals were M. Gray (Mid-Beds.), P.M. Oliver (Blackley), W.N. Birkett (East Nottingham), L.S. Jones (Camborne), H.F. Owen (Hereford), J. Scott (Kincardine and Western) and E.D. Simon (Penryn and Falmouth) — at Galloway the Liberal MP, C.R. Dudgeon, did not stand in 1931, but E.M. Campbell contested the seat in the Liberal interest.

28. This number includes 112 Samuelites, 41 Simonites and 6 followers of Lloyd George.

29. *The Times*, 29 Oct. 1931.

30. *Liberal Magazine*, Nov. 1931.

31. Most of them later signed a manifesto which called on the leadership to change the name of the party to 'National' (*Manchester Guardian*, 13 June 1934).

32. *The Times*, 17 Oct. 1931.

33. Ibid., 9 Oct. 1931.

34. Baldwin Papers, Report of Central Office Conference held on 27 November 1931.

35. This seems to have been the view of two of MacDonald's closest associates, his personal physician, Dr Horder, and the secretary of the National Labour Committee, Lord De La Warr (Baldwin Papers, Stonehaven to Baldwin, Aug. 1932).

36. As will be shown later in the chapter, Usher and De La Warr were anxious to increase the parliamentary representation of the National Labour Group.

37. See *Conservative Agents' Journal* (CAJ), Jan. 1932.

38. Ibid., Jan. 1932.

39. Ibid., Mar. 1932.

40. Ibid., Apr. 1932.

41. Ibid., Mar. 1932.

42. See Chapter 3.

43. Statement issued to the press, 11 July; for detailed summary of proposals see *Liberal Magazine*, Aug. 1932.

44. Simon Papers, G. Shakespeare to Simon, 23 Sept. 1932.

45. Ibid., notes of a meeting between Ramsay MacDonald and Shakespeare on 27 September. Simon was in Geneva throughout the domestic crisis, but on his instructions a meeting of the Liberal Nationals was held on 26 September. Following this meeting Shakespeare reported to MacDonald that 90% of the Liberal Nationals favoured the continuance of the National Government.

46. Baldwin Papers, vol. 46, Simon to Baldwin, 28 Sept. 1932; Simon Papers, Baldwin to Simon, 26 Oct. 1932.

47. See pp. 17-18.

48. Baldwin Papers, Stonehaven to Baldwin, 5 Jan. 1932.

49. Ibid., MacDonald to Stonehaven, 8 Jan. 1932.

50. Ibid., Stonehaven to MacDonald (copy), 13 Jan. 1932.

51. Ibid., Little to Topping, 14 Jan. 1932.

52. Ibid., De La Warr to Stonehaven, 5 July 1932.

53. Ibid., Stonehaven to De La Warr, 7 July 1932: 'I read your letter with so much astonishment that I decided to let 24 hours pass before replying to it.'

54. Ibid., Stonehaven to Baldwin, 9 Aug. 1932: 'The PM wants my head.'

55. Ibid., memorandum prepared by Stonehaven and seen by Baldwin at Ottawa.

56. Ibid. The memorandum contains a full account of the talks; also Stonehaven to De La Warr (copy), 9 Aug. 1932.

57. *Liberal Magazine*, Nov. 1932.

58. Simon Papers, notes of a meeting held in Hore-Belisha's rooms in the House of Commons on 4 November 1932.

59. Baldwin Papers, vol. 46, MacDonald to Baldwin, 8 Mar. 1932; note in Baldwin's hand, dated 29 Mar. 1932. See also P. Cohen, 'Disraeli's Child', p. 370.

60. See for example, the correspondence columns of *The Times* following the announcement of the formation of the National Coordinating Committee.

61. *CAJ*, May 1933. Also Simon Papers, which contain a list of the area committees and secretaries. The West Midlands, East Midlands, Eastern Counties, Metropolitan Area and Wessex, were each to have two full-time officers; Northern, Yorkshire, Sheffield, Barnsley, Spen Valley, Lancashire-Cheshire-Westmorland, South Wales and Devon-Cornwall-Somerset, one officer each.

62. Simon Papers, Report of a meeting of the Executive Committee of the Liberal National Party, 31 Oct. 1932.

63. Ibid., Simon to Hutchison, 30 Dec. 1932.

64. Ibid., Hutchison to Simon, 14 Jan. 1932.

65. Ibid., telegram from Lord Inchcape to Simon, 7 Oct. 1931; Hackney (party organiser and publicity agent) to Simon, 13 Oct. 1931; Shakespeare to Simon, 14 Oct. 1931. Also Simon to Lord Nuffield, 10 July 1934. (Lord Nuffield gave the money to Hore-Belisha in the belief that he would pass it on to Hutchison and Simon. It appears from the correspondence between Simon and Lord Nuffield in mid-1934 that Hore-Belisha gave £2,500 to Hutchison for election expenses, and then returned £5,000 to Nuffield, much to his surprise. Nuffield later sent back the money to Hore-Belisha. Pressed by Simon to put all monies with Hutchison and the Liberal National Council, Nuffield replied that he thought that he had already done this through Hore-Belisha. Both Simon and Nuffield were perplexed as to the fate of the £7,500. In his note to Simon of 14 January 1932, Hutchison was confident that he was to receive a further £5,500 from Hore-Belisha; but from the later correspondence between Simon and Lord Nuffield it seems clear that the money had not been passed on to the Liberal National Council. In the absence of further correspondence on the matter in the Simon Papers one can only speculate as to the outcome of the affair; and from the plenitude of funds available to the Liberal Nationals at the 1935 election it would seem that Nuffield's money eventually found its way into the coffers of the Liberal National Council.)

66. Ibid., Hutchison to Simon, 14 Jan. 1932.

67. Central Office advice was often too vague to be useful: for example, at the Metropolitan Agents' meeting in January 1933, Topping 'urged combination and cooperation, but at the same time they ought not to allow the identity of their Party to be confused or blurred. They would eventually again split into separate parties and still be good friends.'

68. *CAJ*, June 1933.

69. Ibid., Mar. and July 1933; also Feb. 1934.

70. Ibid., July 1933.

71. *Citizen* was published in London in 52 localised editions, each of 10,000

copies; almost every issue of *CAJ* carried an article on the strength of Labour's organisation in London. See for example, *CAJ*, July 1933.

72. Information conveyed to the writer by Percy Cohen, 25 Sept. 1969.

73. Minute Book of the Central Council, held at Conservative Central Office.

74. Ibid.

75. *The Times*, 25 May 1933.

76. *CAJ*, July 1933.

77. *The Times*, 25 May 1933.

78. Ibid., 5 Oct. 1932.

79. Ibid., 13 Oct. 1933. This would seem to be at odds with Ramsay MacDonald's diary entry for mid-October 1933: 'Discussed with Mr Baldwin the future alignment of parties with reference to position at election. Was not forthcoming.' Cited in Marquand, *Ramsay MacDonald*, p. 745.

80. *Daily Telegraph*, 7 Oct.

81. *Daily Express*, 7 Nov.

82. See C.T. Stannage, 'The East Fulham by-election, 25 October 1933', *Historical Journal*, vol. 18, no. 1 (Mar. 1971).

83. *The Times*, 2 Dec. 1933.

84. *Daily Telegraph*, 15 Feb. 1934.

85. *Manchester Guardian*, 16 Apr. 1934.

86. *CAJ*, Jan. 1934.

87. Baldwin Papers, vol. 46, memorandum on the Conservative Party and its relations with the National Government, 12 Dec. 1933.

88. *CAJ*, Mar. 1934.

89. Ibid., June 1934.

90. Ibid., Apr., July, and Sept. 1934. In 1932 and 1933 Central Office issued five leaflets inviting the public to join the Conservative Party, and these were on the lines that the Conservative Party was a National Party which stood for national prosperity and the well-being of all classes; in the same period it issued five leaflets on the National Government. In 1934 it issued no leaflets on party membership, but at least fourteen on the National Government; while in 1935 it issued only one on the Conservative Party, and about seventeen on the National Government (Conservative Party leaflets and pamphlets 1932-5, with subject index, Conservative Research Department). The disproportionate character of Central Office publications was not lost on constituency organisers.

91. Minute Book of the Central Council.

92. Ibid.

93. *Liberal Magazine*, May 1934.

94. Statement issued to the press, 29 Apr. 1934.

95. *Daily Telegraph*, 26 Apr. 1934.

96. *The Times*, 13 June 1934; also *Manchester Guardian*, 14 June 1934.

97. *The Times House of Commons 1929, 1931*.

98. The resolutions were as follows:
'That this Council strongly urges on all Conservative Associations the paramount necessity of concentrating their propaganda and efforts towards the retention of the interest and loyalty of all those voters who supported the National Government at the last General Election' and 'That this Council is of the opinion that more definite and active measures should be taken by Constituency Associations to combat the menace of Socialism, and urges better organization of propaganda during the coming months.'

99. Baldwin Papers, vol. 46, memorandum on the Conservative Party and its relations with the National Government, 1 Aug. 1934.

100. *Manchester Guardian*, 6 Oct. 1934.

101. *The Times*, 30 Oct. 1934.

102. Criticism had also come from friends and allies; in the Baldwin Papers, vol. 47, there are letters on the subject from as early as May 1934. See for example, Ormsby-Gore to Baldwin, 10 Feb. 1935: 'The rot has set in strong in the House and in the country.'

103. See H. Macmillan, *Winds of Change 1914-1939* (1966), p. 300 ff.

104. *Daily Telegraph*, 28 Dec. 1934.

105. See Appendix 2. 1.

106. Even the India Defence League took no part in the campaign (letter from its Executive Committee to *The Times*, 6 Mar. 1935). In the course of the campaign, Randolph Churchill declared that as soon as the by-election was over, he intended to form a Conservative Union, 'whose object will be to revive Conservative principles within the Conservative Party'. The government's India policy, he added, 'is but a symptom of the disease which is today destroying the very soul of the Party' (*Daily Mail*, 25 Feb. 1935). Coupled with the reaction to the Wavertree result, the Lambeth Norwood campaign and result effectively put an end to his plan.

107. *Manchester Guardian*, 6 Feb. 1935.

108. Ibid., 20 Dec. 1934.

109. *News Chronicle*, 28 Dec. Cummings was not being entirely fanciful. In the Baldwin Papers, vol. 48, there is a C.O. memorandum, dated about mid-1934, in which gradual and legal control of the mass media by the National Government is envisaged as a practicable policy. The first step was to purchase cinemas and use them as propaganda cells. See also Stonehaven to Baldwin, 8 May 1934.

110. *Manchester Guardian*, 28 Mar. 1935. See also *Politics in Review*, April-June 1935.

111. *Morning Post*, 21 Mar. 1935.

112. See *Daily Mail*, *Daily Telegraph*, *Daily Express*, *The Times* and *Daily Herald* for last week of March 1935.

113. Baldwin Papers, vol. 47. The memorandum is several pages long, and although it is undated, from internal evidence it can be put at some time between 14 and 27 March.

114. In the letter to the writer, Percy Cohen stated that he had never seen the memorandum; but he denied that Central Office had accepted money from Cahn and Sieff. He could not say whether the National Publicity Bureau was financed by donations from Cahn or Sieff; but he asserted that the finances of the NPB were independent of Central Office. It should be noted that Cahn was honoured with a baronetcy around this time on Baldwin's recommendation. See Marquand, *Ramsay MacDonald*, p. 747.

115. Minute Book of the Central Council.

116. Baldwin Papers, vol. 48. In an accompanying note to a memo on the subject prepared by Gower for Stonehaven and forwarded to Baldwin, Stonehaven wrote of his concern that 'the whole of the so-called popular press is closed to us'. The memo paid particular attention to the role of film propaganda (Stonehaven to Baldwin, 10 May 1934). See also Chamberlain Papers, Chamberlain to Hilda, 18 May 1935: 'I must say that I was immensely impressed with their propaganda value.'

117. *The Times*, 5 Apr. 1935.

118. At the March meeting of the Central Council it was announced that a Standing Advisory Committee on the selection of parliamentary candidates had been established. It had an unenthusiastic reception. In the words of one of the delegates, 'If we are going to have further interference by a central advisory council it is going to do a great deal of harm in the constituencies.' See also the complaints registered in *CAJ*, June 1935.

119. *The Times*, 5 Oct. A fuller account of the events of summer and autumn of 1935 is given in Chapter 4.

2 THE LABOUR PARTY, 1931-35

At the 1931 general election the parliamentary Labour Party was almost completely annihilated. Approximately 250 Labour MPs were defeated; and of the 52 remaining in the House of Commons, six were ILPers whose candidatures had not been endorsed by the National Executive Committee (NEC) of the Labour Party. Among those missing from the Labour benches were the former leaders who now graced the National Government front bench. Other prominent men such as Henderson, Clynes, Dalton, Morrison, Greenwood, Johnston and Alexander had lost their seats at the general election. Indeed of the Cabinet Ministers of the 1929-31 administration only Lansbury had survived the holocaust; and there were also two former junior ministers, Attlee and Cripps. Supporting them was a small group of trade unionist MPs, most of whom represented mining constituencies. It was a piteous remnant from the great garment woven in 1929. What follows here is a survey of the ways in which the party strove to recover from the trauma of 1931.[1]

The first task facing the NEC was to establish the causes of the party's abysmal showing at the general election. At its initial meeting after the election the NEC considered a report prepared by the party secretary and leader during the election, Arthur Henderson.[2] Henderson isolated several factors, the most important of which was the charge that the party was composed of men who had 'run away' from the financial crisis; in contrast, he noted, with MacDonald, Snowden and Thomas, who 'were regarded by many people as having stood by the ship of State whereas their colleagues had put Party first'. He thought that the means by which this was so effectively done was the National Government's political broadcasts, notably Snowden's. He also deplored the unequal distribution of political broadcasts which had favoured the National Government.

Henderson stressed that the party had been caught unawares by the general election and had lacked sufficient funds to contest it effectively:

> the response of the Trade Unions was both prompt and generous, but individual contributions were not as good as in previous appeals. We had to fight the most formidable opposition ever experienced

with nearly £20,000 less available than in 1929.

In consequence of this the party had been able to contest only 490
seats, or 80 less than in 1929. And even apart from lack of finance, the
suddenness of the election had made it extremely difficult to find
candidates, especially for those constituencies where the incumbent
Labour MP was a follower of MacDonald. The suddenness of the
election had created another problem. Henderson noted:

> The material being prepared for a normal general election had had to
> be scrapped and new material produced at very short notice: the
> Party publicity machine had found this a difficult task.

Other causes of Labour's rout were the Post Office Savings 'slander'
and the fear that inflation would follow the return of another Labour
Government, the fact that the national and provincial press (apart from
the *Daily Herald*, the *Manchester Guardian* and *Reynolds' News*)
supported the National Government, and the charge that the Labour
Government had done nothing to assist the unemployed. In relation to
this last point, Henderson noted that at by-elections between 1929 and
1931, the Labour Party had on an average polled nearly 3,000 votes
below the 1929 figure. He took this to mean that had the general election taken place in normal circumstances the party would still have
done badly. In short, he concluded, the party was in poor shape, and
'the work of rebuilding must cover policy, organization, education and
propaganda'.

At the meeting at which Henderson's report was discussed, the NEC
took the first steps towards resuscitating the Party.[3] First, it rehired
two lecturers for propaganda purposes. Secondly, it decided to launch
a new membership campaign called 'A Million New Members and
Power'. Shepherd, the party's principal agent, was provided with
£1,000 to get the campaign under way, which he did early in
December.

Later that same day the NEC met representatives of the General
Council of the Trades Union Congress (TUC) at the request of the latter
in order to discuss the future relationship of the two bodies.[4] The
meeting opened with formal expressions of mutual goodwill. For the
NEC, George Latham said that

> He was convinced of the absolute necessity of the closest possible
> harmonious working of the two bodies

and Bromley, the chairman of the General Council, thought that

> It was time for straight conversations, fearless analysis, and a kindly understanding of each other.

They were followed by Walter Citrine, the secretary of the TUC, who took his cue from the first part of his chairman's remarks. 'They must examine,' he said, 'the extent to which it had been possible for three men whom they trusted most, to contribute to the disaster which had befallen.' He stated that under no circumstances would the TUC tolerate the return of MacDonald, Snowden and Thomas, and then observed that the root of the problem had been

> a manifest reluctance on the part of the late Labour Government to have contact with the General Council . . . The National Joint Council had hardly ever functioned.

The TUC was determined to prevent a recurrence of this, and Citrine warned the NEC that while the General Council

> did not seek in any shape or form to say what the Party was to do, they did ask that the primary purpose of the creation of the Party should not be forgotten. It was created by the Trade Union Movement to do those things in Parliament which the Trade Union Movement found ineffectively performed by the two-party system.

While the NEC may not have been in full agreement with Citrine's analysis, with its implied criticism of some NEC members, it was prepared to regularise its link with the TUC by agreeing that the National Joint Council (NJC) should meet monthly. As Henderson wrote of the proposed constitution of the NJC, it

> would enable Labour to speak with one voice on all questions of national importance, and to pursue one policy in support of its common ends.[5]

At subsequent meetings of the NJC, the TUC attempted with limited success to assert an authority over the NEC and the parliamentary Labour Party (PLP). At the 7 December meeting of the NJC, Bromley expressed the view that while the TUC General Council could reasonably claim to function without consultation on a purely industrial and trade union matter, the political side of the labour movement could not be quite as free, as the interest of the workers was bound up with political action. Replying for the NEC, Morrison thought that there were certain spheres where the party too should create its own policy. The meeting didn't go beyond these general statements, but it was agreed that each body should define its point of view for later meetings. At the next meeting, held late in January 1932, the NEC was confronted with a detailed memorandum of TUC views prepared by Citrine.[6] Most of the points raised were in relation to the situation where Labour was in a position to form a government, points such as whether the leader of the party should automatically become the Prime Minister, or whether the party should take office while having no parliamentary majority, and so on. Of more immediate concern was the TUC's demand that it be given the right to raise any matter upon which it felt it had a common interest with the NEC and PLP (this right it also guaranteed to the NEC and the PLP), and a demand that the secretary of the TUC should have a standing on the NJC equal to that of the secretary of the NEC. The latter demands were agreed to by the NEC; the former were deferred for later discussions, and, while they did cause some friction between the two bodies through this period, there was the closest possible co-operation between them on electoral matters including party organisation.

On one issue of particular significance for by-election contests, namely the Means Test, the TUC, the NEC and the PLP were soon in agreement. In the last months of the Labour Government, the Cabinet and the NEC had favoured the introduction of a Means Test for the unemployed, a suggestion which was strongly objected to by the TUC. The government fell before a final decision had been taken, and the Means Test was instituted by the National Government. The TUC promptly called for its abolition, and raised the matter at a meeting of the NJC in February 1932.[7] The NEC was at first reluctant to commit itself, and at a meeting held the following day Morrison argued that while the party should deplore the National Government's Means Test, the PLP should not be committed to the view 'that payments from public funds (apart from insurance) to the unemployed should totally ignore the income of the applicant'. His resolution to this effect was amended by Ben Turner and Leah Manning to read:

> That the policy of the Parliamentary Party should be to move for the abolition of the Means Test.[8]

Their amendment was carried by twelve votes to six, thus bringing the policy of the NEC and the PLP into line with that of the TUC and providing by-election candidates (like Arthur Greenwood at Wakefield) with a weapon with which to attack the National Government.

Throughout 1932, however, the legacy of 1931 hung heavily over the Labour Party. Up to the time of the general election the year's income had balanced the year's expenditure, but thereafter the party was in difficulties. The estimated income for 1932 was £38,000 (£33,350 from the trade unions, £4,000 from divisional Labour parties (DLPs), and £600 from Socialist societies) while the estimated expenditure was £45,000.[9] It was clear that on the one hand economies would have to be effected, while on the other a great effort would have to be made to raise money. All members of the Transport House staff were asked to accept a 5% reduction in their salaries,[10] and other departmental economies, such as the amalgamation of the *Labour Magazine*, the *Labour Bulletin* and the *Industrial Review*,[11] were made: it was hoped that these economies would reduce expenditure by about £6,000.

Many constituency organisations were in desperate straits as a result of economies at the national level. The South Tottenham DLP, for example, wished to employ a full-time agent and was prepared to contribute to his expenses; but it was informed that Transport House could not afford to subsidise the appointment and so presumably no appointment was made.[12] Quite a large number of constituency organisations had fought the general election on credit and now, finding themselves unable to pay their debts, turned to Transport House for assistance, only to be told that money for grants of this sort was simply not available.[13] In this situation it was extremely difficult for DLPs to purchase the party literature which the national body had to sell in order to balance its own books. And lack of finance caused the Eastbourne, Richmond and St Marylebone DLPs to withdraw from by-elections in the divisions.[14]

The NEC was deeply concerned about this problem. It recognised that if the party was to make an electoral impact it was imperative that most by-elections should be contested. It decided therefore to grant up to £50 to selected constituencies.[15] However, this was found to be an excessive burden on the finances of Transport House, and towards the end of 1932 a central By-Election Insurance Fund was created, which was to operate in the following way: each DLP was to contribute about 7s 6d per by-election into the fund, while unions contributed in proportion to the size of their memberships (e.g. trade unions with over

50,000 members (8), £9 7s 6d per by-election; under 5,000 members
(52), 15s per by-election); in return, constituencies having by-elections
could be subsidised from the fund to the value of £375. It was hoped
that the scheme would ultimately be self-supporting and would leave
other funds untouched.[16] The scheme's success or failure depended on
the ability of the DLPs and the unions to squeeze the few pounds extra
from their members, but in the short term Transport House expected to
subsidise the fund from other sources. It remained to be seen whether
the scheme would prove successful in the long term.

    Lack of finance hindered the party's recovery in other ways.
Shepherd's 'A Million New Members and Power' campaign had made
some headway — 32 regional and local conferences had been held and had
been well reported in the *Daily Herald*,[17] and by the end of the year
Shepherd was able to inform the NJC that membership had increased
by 100,000 and that an autumn and winter campaign had been
launched to build on this.[18] But it was also noted that DLPs not
employing a full-time agent (there were only 131 full-time agents)
showed little or no progress, and some, like Islington, Putney and Stoke
Newington, actually regressed;[19] and as there was no money available to
appoint new agents this fact produced some disquiet. Membership gains
were most striking in London and in industrial centres like Sunderland,
Stockton-on-Tees, Barrow-in-Furness, Wallsend, Coventry, Oldham and
St Helens; also in Swindon, Leek, and Nelson; but in predominantly
agricultural constituencies like Saffron Walden gains were at a
premium.[20]

    The financial condition of the party was not improved by
Henderson's decision, announced at the Leicester conference, to vacate
the party leadership in order to chair the forthcoming meetings of the
Disarmament Conference. He retained the party treasurership but only
acted in a part-time capacity, and throughout 1933 the party's financial
condition continued to deteriorate. Early in January an Economy Committee reported to the Finance and General Purposes Sub-Committee of
the NEC that to remain solvent in 1932 the party had had to draw on
reserves in special funds to the value of £12,800; the Economy Committee warned that this could not be repeated without greatly damaging
the party. It recommended further staff salary cuts, the dismissal of
some members of the already undermanned national organisation, and
the continuation throughout 1933 of existing departmental budget
restrictions. The Economy Committee thought that the party's parlous
financial condition could be blamed on the

continued and increasing trade depression, with consequent unemployment which has dried up sources of income, whilst so far as the Trade Unions are concerned there has been little to encourage the hope of an increase in the 'contracting in' membership . . . The additional income from increased individual membership is not overlooked, but this so far has not been sufficient for requirements.[21]

In an endeavour to assist the party (as well as itself) the *Daily Herald* told the NJC that if trade unions and local Labour parties could secure for the paper an additional 100,000 readers, the paper would give the party a film van and provide funds to cover the cost of an operator for one year.[22] This offer was particularly welcome since the National Government already had several film vans touring the country and the Labour Party had no effective means of countering this form of propaganda. The van actually commenced work in June 1933. But at best it was only a palliative, and the financial condition of the party remained bad throughout 1933. In May the Finance and General Purposes Sub-Committee reported that trade union membership was declining and that this meant that the estimated income from that source would not be reached.[23]

Furthermore, the by-election fund, created late in 1932, had not become self-supporting as had been hoped. By the end of 1933 some 13 constituencies had benefited from the fund, and £4,626 had been paid out in grants; but only £4,029 had been received in premiums, and 185 DLPs and several of the smaller unions had paid nothing into the fund.[24] In February 1934 the NEC issued a statement saying that if they fell eight weeks in arrears in their payments they would be deemed to be 'out of benefit', that is, ineligible for a grant.[25] It was further decided that contribution to the by-election fund should be a condition of affiliation.[26] As the fund had been created to enable all constituencies to contest by-elections without touching the resources of Transport House, it was clear that on both counts it was not an unqualified success. In brief, as the Finance and General Purposes Sub-Committee reported to the NEC in February 1934, 'The Party had not yet reached a stage where income balanced liabilities'. A deficit of £2,900 was estimated for 1934.[27]

Despite the severe financial handicap, the party contested every by-election and performed creditably at most. In February 1933 Rotherham was recaptured from the National Government in such a convincing manner that Shepherd, in his by-election report to the NEC, claimed that:

> Dobbie's victory, his total vote and his majority are the first indica-
> tions of a definite move towards the Labour Party.[28]

By-elections at Ashford in March and at Hitchin in June tended to confirm this impression, as on both occasions the party's share of the total
vote rose above the figure for the 1929 general election and was, of
course, much higher than the figures for the 1931 general election;
and traditional Labour seats like East Rhondda were held easily, though
an embarrassingly large number of electors were now voting for the
Communist Party.

In high summer Henderson forsook the Disarmament Conference
and contested the Clay Cross by-election, which he won easily. During
the campaign he made the issue of peace and disarmament his principal
platform, and the apparent success of this tactic and the drift of events
in October prompted other Labour candidates to follow suit, again with
apparent success. At the six by-elections held in October and November, the party's share of the total vote was consistently higher than at
previous elections. East Fulham was won for the first time ever;
Kilmarnock was lost only through the intervention of an ILP candidate;
at Skipton the Labour vote was higher than ever before; at Rutland and
Stamford, despite financial difficulties and an indifferent campaign,
the seat was almost won; and at Rusholme, as at East Fulham, the party
attracted a great number of Liberal votes.[29] The other side of the coin
was that the need for more money was heavily underlined; the breach
with the ILP was electorally dangerous for the party; and if places like
Skipton were to be captured, the party would have to intensify its
membership campaign and other activities in rural areas. The NEC was
aware of and concerned about these factors, but was nevertheless well
pleased with the results of the by-elections and, if electoral strategy
thereafter is any guide, with having found in peace and disarmament an
issue which appealed to the electorate.

The Labour Party's by-election successes late in 1933 were due in
part to an ability to poll the full Labour vote, and this itself was partly
due to the enthusiasm created by the various membership campaigns
conducted by the party throughout the year and in all types of constituencies. Shepherd's initial campaign, 'A Million New Members and
Power', had proved quite fruitful, and once its momentum slackened it
had been replaced by a series of 'Propaganda Weeks' in the great conur-
bations and a more general campaign launched under the title of 'Call

to Action'.[30]

In May 1933 at the instigation of Dr Addison, the party launched an agricultural campaign limited at first to Norfolk and Cambridgeshire and later extended to cover the entire country. Addison himself donated £100 for this effort, and the *Daily Herald* (now that its circulatin had reached two million) provided a film van, an operator and propaganda leaflets.[31] In November the Agricultural Campaign Committee decided to concentrate on 82 constituencies which for those purposes were divided into three groups according to their promise.[32] This appears to have been done rather haphazardly and may have been characteristic of the campaign as a whole. Of the 37 constituencies listed in the first group, two did not exist; 17 had been won by the Labour Party in 1929, but doubt is cast on the effectiveness of the campaign by the fact that of these only three were regained by the party at the 1935 general election. None of the constituencies in the second group was won at the 1935 general election; yet, surprisingly, two constituencies in the group regarded as least promising *were* won at the 1935 general election. Not until the 1945 general election did the work of Addision bear fruit.

But in other than agricultural divisions the party made some headway. In his General Organization Report to the NEC for January 1934, Shepherd stated that as a result of the various campaigns 307 constituency organisations (mainly in the North-West, Wales, London and Greater London) had shown a membership increase in 1933. On the other hand 110 (30 of which were in Scotland) had shown a decrease, and a further 162 had remained static. (Most of the last group were in Scotland, London and the Midlands.) On the basis of these figures he thought that the position of the party was much improved, but that more would have to be done before the next general election.[33]

In their membership and propaganda campaigns, Shepherd and the Publicity Department were hampered by the fact that on many issues the party had no clearly stated policy, and on any single issue no two speakers appeared to say the same thing: in short, it was difficult to publicise Labour's policies if those policies were not uniform. Since the 1931 crisis the Labour Party as a whole had taken a leftward turn, but some groups had moved further to the left than others, and this showed up clearly at the annual conferences. The NEC, while critical of previous election programmes (including 'Labour and the Nation') on the grounds that they were too vague and 'failed to commit leaders to

a specific course of action', was less inclined to break completely with
the past than were elements among the rank and file. At the Leicester
conference in October 1932, the NEC submitted four important policy
resolutions relating to banking and finance, agriculture, transport and
electricity. The first of these proposed that the Bank of England should
be turned into a central bank under state control. This was acceptable
to the conference, though there were some who wondered whether the
change would mean much in practice. From the conference itself came
the demand that public ownership and control should be extended to
the Joint Stock Banks; the NEC was hesitant but conference swept
objections aside and voted for an amendment to this effect. The resolutions on transport and electricity also came under attack. In proposing
that these industries should be nationalised, the NEC had not provided
for worker representation on the new boards and for this reason the
conference referred back the resolutions for further consideration.
Also from the conference came a resolution, moved by Charles
Trevelyan, that

> the leaders of the next Labour Government and the Parliamentary
> Labour Party be instructed by the National Conference that, on
> assuming office, either with or without power, definite Socialist
> legislation must be immediately promulgated, and that the Party
> shall stand or fall in the House of Commons on the principles in
> which it has faith.

Though opposed by Henderson, the resolution was carried by conference.[34]
   Much of the opposition to the NEC had come from members of the
newly formed Socialist League, which was composed principally of
former members of the ILP who had opposed that body's decision to
disaffiliate from the Labour Party, among them E.F. Wise and H.N.
Brailsford and other radical socialists like Stafford Cripps. In the words
of its constitution the Socialist League was

> pledged to work within and through the wider movements, and to
> place all their talents, their energies and their devotion at the
> disposal of the movement for one specific purpose, the making of
> Socialists.[35]

So impeccable were these sentiments that the conference ruled that the
new body did not contravene the rules of the party, and that its

application to affiliate with the parent body should be ratified.[36] In conference, it was the alliance of this body with the trade unions which caused the NEC so much discomfort; and the effect of the breach was to produce uncertainty at the constituency level as to the policy of the party, a state of affairs which did not improve in the course of 1933.

The rise to power of Hitler early in 1933 forced the Labour Party to adopt an attitude not only towards fascism, but also towards the leftist fringe groups. This was because the Communist Party, the ILP, and the Socialist League sought NEC participation in united activity against fascism. The TUC and the NEC rejected their overtures however, and in March jointly issued a manifesto entitled 'Democracy versus Dictatorship' which denounced both fascist dictatorships and dictatorships of the left. The workers of Great Britain, it asserted, 'should strengthen the Labour Party – the spearhead of political power against dictators Fascist or Communist'.[38] Predictably the NJC manifesto was regarded by the Socialist League as mistaken; but before any further action was taken by either side, the issue was blurred by renewed discussion on the party's general international policy.

At a meeting of the NEC early in September 1933 it was decided that 'simplified policy proposals should be drawn up to form the platform for a Campaign leading up to the next General Election'. This was done, and just prior to the annual conference a policy leaflet called 'Victory for Socialism' was circulated among the constituency organisations.[39] On foreign policy it reaffirmed the party's intention to pursue international disarmament and its belief in the efficacy of the League of Nations. At the Hastings conference it emerged that the party wanted something more radical than this, and at the instigation of the Socialist League a resolution was carried unanimously pledging the party 'to take no part in war and to resist it with the whole force of the Labour movement . . . including a General Strike'.[40]

At the time the resolution was accepted by the NEC; but shortly afterwards reservations were expressed as to the wisdom of such a course, and the NEC determined to reopen the debate. In January 1934 the Advisory Committee to the NEC on international questions issued a memorandum on the subject in which it was claimed that if sanctioned by Parliament, a Labour Government could proceed to measures of military coercion in co-operation with the League (under Article XVI of the Covenant of the League of Nations).[41] Early in February Henderson was authorised by the Policy Committee of the NEC to prepare a draft of a general statement of the policy of the party which, if acceptable to the Policy Committee, would be sent to the

NEC for ratification. Henderson took advantage of this opportunity to reverse the Hastings decision on resistance to war and restated the party's traditional allegiance to the League of Nations and the obligations implicit in this, short of advocating rearmament. At the end of the month his policy statement was considered by the NEC.[42] Henderson explained to its members

> that owing to the difficulty of the rank and file of the Movement in keeping abreast with the large number of Policy Reports that had been issued and were in contemplation, it had been considered advisable to issue a Statement on the General Policy of the Party. This would take the form of a document similar to 'Labour and the New Social Order' or 'Labour and the Nation' and would ultimately form the basis of the General Election Manifesto.

It would also be discussed at the annual conference of the party to be held at Southport in October. Clearly Henderson was intent on forcing a showdown with the proponents of a resistance to war policy and in this he had the support of the TUC which had declared that a general strike would be illegal. Having won the full support of the NEC and the TUC, Henderson issued the policy statement, now called 'For Socialism and Peace', in July; and at the Southport conference in October it was endorsed with an overwhelming majority.[43] This vote was more than a reversal of the resistance to war policy: it was a declaration in favour of moderation, of a gradualism less slow than that in the years up to 1931, but gradualism nevertheless and therefore anathema to the radical pretensions of the Socialist League.[44] Henderson's aims had been to give the constituency organisations a lucid and coherent statement of policy. In this he met with only limited success, and the continued alienation of the Socialist League was to be electorally embarrassing to the party right up to the general election.

While at the national level the party was embroiled in policy disputes, at the constituency level party organisers were trying in a succession of propaganda campaigns to increase party membership and convince a wider public of Labour's fitness to govern. But they were meeting with only limited success. After the Hastings conference a 'Peace and Freedom' campaign had been launched with meetings addressed by Labour's foremost spokesmen. Since the autumn of 1933 Baldwin had taken every opportunity to identify the Labour Party with 'totalitarianism (the Hastings conference resolutions providing him with additional

evidence of Labour's revolutionary and 'unBritish' intentions), a charge
so forceful in its impact that party organisers went to great lengths to
disprove it. Late in Janaury 1934 the NEC issued a statement to the
press which read:

> The attitude of the Labour Party towards Dictatorship has recently
> been subject to grave misrepresentation by supporters of the
> National Government. The Labour Party, as has repeatedly been
> made plain, in its official declaration, stands for Parliamentary
> Democracy. It is firmly opposed to Individual or Group Dictator-
> ship, whether from the Right or from the Left.[45]

Attempts to get this message and general policy over to a wide public
through the medium of campaign meetings were not successful. Successful 'Peace and Freedom' meetings were held in Burnley, Lincoln,
Reading, Huddersfield, Newport and Swansea; but elsewhere the
response was dismal: Glasgow 'disorderly', Southampton 'no marked
enthusiasm', Bristol 'small', Leeds 'attendance disappointing', Hull
'cancelled', Newcastle-upon-Tyne 'complete fiasco', Nottingham 'can-
called', Bradford 'poor meeting', Plymouth 'meeting quite good but
poorly attended', Birmingham 'meeting very unsatisfactory' and
Swindon 'meeting poorly attended'. All these were in areas where it was
imperative that the party should make progress if the general election
was to be won, and the NEC was now really deeply alarmed.[46] Only the
very real success of the London Labour Party's victory in the LCC
elections in March and the reasonable performances of Labour candidates at the Cambridge and Lowestoft by-elections gave it any comfort;
and even these successes were tempered by by-election disasters at North
Portsmouth and Basingstoke.[47]

In addition, the party continued to be plagued with financial
problems. It wanted to launch a spring campaign on Henderson's new
policy statement, but the money for such a campaign was simply not
forthcoming. At least £5,000 were required before the campaign could
get off the ground, and by mid-March only £3,500 had been received,
and this included an offer from J.S. Elias of Odhams Press Ltd to print
free of charge one million leaflets (a gift valued at £1,000). Constituency organisations were asked to contribute £1 15s per month for literature for the duration of the campaign, but of 581 organisations circul-
arised by mid-March, 366 had not even replied, and of the 215 which
had, only 85 were prepared to pay the full £1 15s per month, and no
less than 56 flatly refused to join the scheme.[48] This was hardly an

auspicious start to a campaign which was intended to increase Labour's
voting strength at the next general election to more than 15 million, or
twice the number which had supported the party in 1931.[49]

The campaign finally got under way late in April, but with only 156
DLPs participating in the scheme on a financial basis:[50] not even by-
election victories in North Hammersmith and West Ham Upton could
disguise from the NEC that the party was in an unhealthy state. The
'Victory for Socialism' campaign met with the same lack of enthusiasm
as previous campaigns and nowhere was this more marked than in Scotland, a region where Labour hoped to recapture 23 seats lost at the
1931 general election.[51] However, there was little the party could do
but to persevere with the campaign and, once the conference had
endorsed the NEC's policy statement with some show of enthusiasms, to
intensify it. Wtih the assistance of a second film van (also a gift from
the *Daily Herald*) it was planned to hold a further 50 demonstrations,
'to rally the Party membership and to generate enthusiasm for the
Campaign and Party work up to the Election' and a Conference of the
PLP, NEC and 'prominent political and industrial spokesmen' was convened to plan for the general election.[52]

From November 1934 the party was preparing in earnest for a
general election. It was anticipated that this would probably take place
in the autumn of 1935, and propaganda campaigns and finance drives
were planned to reach a peak at that time. Henderson was authorised
to open a General Election Fund, and Greenwood's Research and
Publicity Committee issued a memorandum on 'General Election Literature Preparations' in which it was argued that such preparations should
have reached an advanced stage by July 1935.[53] In January 1935 the
NEC reported to the NCL that

> The signs of an approaching General Election render it essential to
> make preparations . . . Constituency Parties, where no selection of
> candidates has taken place, have been pushed along a bit. And a
> series of meetings with County Federations and the Candidates and
> Agents in big divided boroughs has begun with a view to securing
> their assistance in bracing up the Party machine.[54]

The key to these preparations was Henderson's General Election Fund;
if this failed the party would have to contest the election almost bank-
rupt. The Southport conference had called on the NEC to provide extra
resources for those rural and urban divisions where organisation and
finance were weak; but the NEC, after due consideration, was forced to

reject the resolution on the grounds that no money was available;[55] the implication being that the party's effort in non-self-supporting constituencies would be severely restricted.

Indeed, overall, the party's finances remained very weak. In the first place the by-election fund, which had now been in operation for two years, was still not self-supporting. Despite threats of disaffiliation, no less than 65 constituency parties and 14 borough parties had not yet made their first contribution to the fund, and a further 20 had indicated that they would be unable to make up arrears. In the second place, the party's income for 1934 was nearly £3,000 below the income for 1933, which had also been regarded as a very bad year.[56] In these circumstances it was imperative that Henderson's appeal for funds to fight the general election should succeed. To the delight of the NEC the initial response was encouraging. In December Henderson had sent out over 500 personal letters, and by the end of February 1935 he had received £1,400 in cash with promises of £750 more.[57]

By the spring of 1935 the party was more ebullient than it had been at any time since the 1931 general election. It had spearheaded an attack on the National Government's new unemployment regulations and in particular on the decision to reduce the scales of payment; and the government had been forced to suspend the new regulations and restore the old scales of relief. Partly due to the unemployment question, the party had almost captured Wandsworth Putney late in November, had succeeded in capturing Liverpool Wavertree in February 1935, and had done quite well at the Lambeth Norwood by-election in March.[58] Towards the end of March Shepherd reported to the NEC that many more candidates were now coming forward, and that about 470 had already been adopted.[59] Even the long-lived 'Victory for Socialism' campaign, boosted by the unemployment agitation, seemed at last to be achieving some of its objectives. In 1934 individual party membership was only 380,000, an increase of 14,000 in the year, which compared poorly with the increase of over 100,000 in 1933.[60] While in the first few months of 1935 there was no striking further increase, the NEC was able to report to the NCL that several very successful demonstrations had been held and that 'there was a growing confidence on the part of the rank and file'.[61] Furthermore, the General Election Fund was proceeding satisfactorily.[62] In short it appeared to the party hierarchy that its foreign policy of peace and disarmament and its continuing demand for the abolition of the Means Test were returning high dividends in the form of by-election successes and an enthusiasm among the rank and file which augured well for the party at the forthcoming election.

Events in May and June, however, caused some of this new-found
confidence to dissipate. By-elections in Scotland in May caused
concern, for at both West Edinburgh and South Aberdeen the party's
share of the total vote was considerably lower than it had been in 1929,
results which did little to suggest that the 23 seats lost by the party in
Scotland in 1931 would be recovered.[63] And the report prepared for
the NEC by Arthur Woodburn, the secretary of the Scottish Labour
Party, made uneasy reading.[64] Woodburn noted that some local issues
(such as sectarianism at West Edinburgh) might have affected the result,
but that national factors were also very important. In particular, he
noted that the recent budget and the Jubilee celebrations had increased
the prestige of the National Government; the party's intention to
nationalise the banks frightened many people, particularly the poor;
there was a general lack of faith that the Labour Party was a viable
alternative government to the National Government; and, most
ominous of all, the 'growing war atmosphere was shaking people's faith
in the ability of the League of Nations to guarantee security'. At
Aberdeen especially the Conservative candidate had campaigned on the
platform of 'Peace by Preparedness' — by which was meant an increase
in armaments — an appeal which had proved extremely popular.
Woodburn concluded that

> the positive passion for Peace which gave us such a powerful plea in
> earlier elections was not so effective under the shadow of Hitler's
> threats.

He also offered a general comment on the party's standing in Scotland:
compared with 1929 the Scottish movement now suffered from
Socialist critics (he seems to have had in mind the ILP and the Socialist
League) who were constantly deprecating Labour's achievements and
pouring scorn on its ability to govern:

> People would not have believed our enemies — they did believe our
> own people.

Woodburn's perceptive analysis of the situation in Scotland was discussed by the NEC and possibly confirmed it in its resolve to keep to
the path of moderation; but in the critical area of foreign policy it
could only have exacerbated existing tensions. At the Southport conference the party had rejected the policy of resistance to war; but there

was still a great deal of uncertainty as to the conditions under which a Labour Party would condone Britain's participation in a war or indeed Britain's rearmament; and the pacifist element in the party was still vocal. Woodburn's report, with its clear statement that disarmament was no longer electorally popular, may have been used by Hugh Dalton and others against the pacifist views of Lansbury;[65] but it was not until the party conference at Brighton in October, and then under the shadow of the Abyssinian conflict and its repercussions, that the party thrashed out its international policy, and then with such vehemence that the leadership split into factions and the party found itself in the anomalous position of supporting collective security through the League of Nations while pressing for disarmament at home and abroad. Woodburn's warning, though heeded by a few of the Labour leaders, was ignored by the majority — with dire electoral consequences.[66]

Throughout the summer the party had great difficulty in maintaining popular interest in politics, but preparations for the general election continued apace. By the end of June Henderson's general election fund stood at £8,450.[67] By July the party's preparation for the election were almost complete. Head Office had been reorganised in readiness for an election. Shepherd had told the NCL that plans were being made

> to hold a series of Mass Conferences and Demonstrations to rally the Movement in September and October in anticipation of the dissolution of Parliament.[68]

In June MPs and candidates attended a two-day conference in London which amounted to a briefing on the party's strategy and tactics at the election: Shepherd addressed them on 'Organization and Tactics', Willie Henderson spoke about 'The Press and Publicity', Greenwood discussed 'The Emphasis on Propaganda in Preparation for the General Election', and Dalton reported on 'Labour's Foreign Policy in Relation to the International Situation'.[69] The same month the Research and Publicity Committee recommended that

> six basic leaflets, four pictorial posters, one letter press poster, one canvassers' handbook, and twelve pamphlets be put in hand at once as General Election propaganda.

Propaganda and organisation at the national level were more necessary than ever for at the constituency level in many places the party was in considerable disarray. The Eastern Counties had been without an area organiser since 1934, and some marginal constituencies like Rushcliffe in Nottinghamshire had to be managed from offices outside the division.[70] Furthermore, the party had fewer full-time agents than it had in 1924 — 150 in 1924, 169 in 1929 and only 136 in October 1935[71] — and the burden to be shouldered by Transport House was heavier to that extent. But it was not only organisation which made Labour vulnerable at the election. It was also the nature of the party's reaction to international affairs between August and October.

Notes

1. While there is no detailed history of the Labour Party for the 1930s, there are general accounts in H. Pelling, *A Short History of the Labour Party* (new ed., 1968), G.D.H. Cole, *A History of the Labour Party from 1914* (1948), and D.É. McHenry, *The Labour Party in Transition, 1931-1938* (1938). Labour's foreign policy is the subject of a detailed study by J.F. Naylor, *Labour's International Policy: the Labour Party in the 1930s* (1967). Also valuable is A. Bullock, *The Life and Times of Ernest Bevin*, vol. 1 (1960), and M. Foot, *Aneurin Bevin*, vol. 1 (1962).

2. The report is attached to the minutes of the NEC meeting, 10 Nov. 1931. (The minutes are in the care of the Librarian, Transport House.)

3. Minutes, NEC meeting, 10 Nov. 1931.

4. Minutes, joint meeting of the NEC and the TUC, 10 Nov. 1931.

5. From a circular prepared by Henderson for the NJC meeting, 7 Dec. 1931, and attached to the minutes of that meeting.

6. Minutes, NJC meeting, 26 Jan. 1932.

7. Ibid., 23 Feb. 1932.

8. Minutes, NEC meeting, 24 Feb. 1932.

9. Financial Statement attached to minutes, NEC meeting, 16 Dec. 1931.

10. The salary cuts took effect from July 1932. Report of the Economy Committee to the Finance and General Purposes Sub-Committee, attached to the Minutes of the NEC meeting, 17 Jan. 1932.

11. Minutes, Research and Publicity Committee meeting, 16 Mar. 1932.

12. Minutes, Organization Sub-Committee meeting, 17 Feb. 1932.

13. Minutes, Finance and General Purposes Sub-Committee, 17 Mar. 1932.

14. By-Election Report prepared by Shepherd, attached to minutes of NEC meeting, 27 Apr. 1932.

15. Recommendation of the Elections Sub-Committee, considered and endorsed by NEC, 27 Apr. The NEC report to the 1932 annual conference stated that 'The NEC feels that more and more importance must be attached to by-elections' (report, p. 52).

16. The By-Election Insurance Fund was opened on 1 Jan. 1933.

17. Minutes, NJC meeting, 22 Mar. 1932.

18. Minutes, NJC meeting, 22 Nov. 1932.

19. 'The Collection of Individual Members' Contributions', paper read by Hinley Atkinson, area organiser for London, to the Annual Staff Conference, 30 Sept. 1932. The paper is attached to minutes, NEC meeting, 26 Oct. 1932.

20. Ibid.

21. Report attached to minutes, NEC meeting, 17 Jan. 1933.

22. Minutes, NJC meeting, 21 Feb. 1933.

23. 'Statement on the Financial Position of the Party', prepared by Finance and General Purposes Sub-Committee; attached to minutes, NEC meeting, 31 May 1933.

24. Report on the first year of the By-Election Insurance Fund, prepared by Shepherd; attached to minutes, NEC meeting, 24 Jan. 1934. The amount owing was £1,450.

25. Report of the monthly activities of the TUC, PLP and the NEC, attached to minutes, NJC meeting, 27 Feb. 1934.

26. Minutes, Finance and General Purposes Sub-Committee meeting, 21 June 1935; it was resolved that DLPs and unions in arrears in their By-Election Insurance Fund contributions should be debarred from representation at the annual conference. A memorandum on the By-Election Insurance Fund, prepared by Shepherd on 30 July stated categorically: 'Payments to the Fund now form a definite part of the basis of affiliation to the Party.'

27. Minutes, Finance and General Purposes Sub-Committee meeting, 21 Feb. 1934. This was partly brought about by the decision of the Transport and General Workers' Union to withhold over £2,000 in affiliation fees as a formal expression of the union's loss of confidence in the NEC and the officers of the party with respect to the promotion of the political interests of the union. (The TGWU's decision was prompted by the decision of the Clay Cross DLP, under some pressure from Transport House, to overlook the claims of the nominees of affiliated bodies in favour of Arthur Henderson, who was elected for the division at a by-election in September 1933. An NEC Enquiry Committee reported in March 1934 that the Elections Sub-Committee of the NEC had been at fault; but relations between the two executives remained uneasy.)

28. Report of the monthly activities of the TUC, PLP and the NEC, attached to minutes, NJC meeting, 21 Mar. 1933.

29. See Appendix 2.1.

30. Report of the monthly activities of the TUC, PLP and the NEC, attached to minutes, NJC meeting, 23 May 1933.

31. Ibid.

32. Minutes, Agricultural Campaign Committee meeting, 21 Nov. 1933, attached to minutes, NEC meeting, 20 Dec. 1933.

33. National Agents' General Organization Report for 1933, considered at NEC meeting, 21 Jan. 1934.

34. Report of the Annual Conference of the Labour Party, Leicester, Oct. 1932, p. 204. James Jupp has examined these confrontations from the point of view of the left in 'The Left in Britain, 1931-1941', unpublished MSc (Econ.) thesis, London School of Economics, 1956.

35. A copy of the Constitution of the Socialist League is appended to the minutes of the meeting of the NEC's Organization Sub-Committee, 19 Oct. 1932.

36. Annual Conference Report, 1933, p. 31.

37. Minutes, NEC meeting, 22 Mar. 1933.

38. *Daily Herald*, 24 Mar. 1933.

39. Minutes, NEC meeting, 6 Sept. 1933.

40. Report of the Annual Conference of the Labour Party, Hastings, Oct. 1933, p. 186. Dalton accepted the resolution on behalf of the NEC.

41. The memorandum is appended to minutes, NEC meeting, 27 Feb. 1934. (The memorandum is dated Jan. 1934.)

42. Minutes, NEC meeting, 27 Feb. 1934.

43. Report of the Annual Conference of the Labour Party, Southport, Oct.

1934, p. 165. The voting was 2,146,000 for the NEC's policy, and 206,000 against.

44. A Policy Committee memorandum on the 'Victory for Socialism' campaign had recognised this: 'If the Campaign is to have its maximum effect, Speakers at the Conferences and Meetings must concentrate on a common policy . . . Whilst the Party has a Socialist objective, it cannot ignore ameliorative and remedial measures.' (Memorandum dated Apr. 1934, attached to minutes, NEC meeting, 25 Apr.)

45. *The Times*, 24 Jan. 1934.

46. Report of the monthly activities of the TUC, PLP and the NEC, attached to minutes, NJC meeting, 27 Mar. 1934.

47. See Appendix 2.1.

48. Minutes, NEC meeting, 1 Mar. 1934.

49. Ibid., 16 May 1934.

50. Policy Committee memorandum, April 1934; see Note 44.

51. Between August 1933 and August 1934, membership of the Scottish Labour Party increased by only 565 – from 24,521 to 25,086. Minutes of meeting of the Executive of the Scottish Labour Party, 15 Oct. 1934. (A copy of the minutes is held at Transport House.)

52. Report of the monthly activities of the TUC, PLP and the NEC, attached to minutes, National Council of Labour meeting, 27 Nov. 1934.

53. Minutes, NEC meeting, 28 Nov. 1934. Part of the Research and Publicity Committee's memorandum (dated 22 Nov.) reads: 'It seems safe to assume that the General Election will not be delayed beyond the Spring of 1936. It is unlikely to occur earlier than, but it may take place during, the autumn of 1935. Commonsense dictates, therefore, that our preparations should be based upon the possibility of an autumn election next year.' This should be placed alongside the party's claim, made after the 1935 general election, that it had been caught unawares by the timing of Baldwin's decision to go to the country.

54. Report of the monthly activities of the TUC, PLP and the NEC, attached to minutes, NCL meeting, 22 Jan. 1935.

55. Minutes, Finance and General Purposes Sub-Committee meeting, 16 Nov. 1934.

56. Financial Report for 1934, attached to minutes, NEC meeting, 23 Jan. 1935. In May 1934, the Birmingham Borough Labour Party found that it had to call in monies owed by DLPs; these in turn petitioned the NEC for money, but none was available. Lack of finance may in part account for the failure of the Labour Party to recapture the six Birmingham seats lost to the National Government in 1931.

57. Minutes, NEC meeting, 27 Feb. 1935.

58. See Appendix 2.1.

59. Minutes, NEC meeting, 17 Apr. 1935.

60. Minutes, Finance and General Purposes Sub-Committee meeting, 20 May 1935.

61. Report of the monthly activities of the TUC, PLP and the NEC, attached to minutes, NCL meeting, 16 Apr. 1935.

62. Minutes, NEC meeting, 17 Apr. 1935.

63. From 38.6% to 33.9% at West Edinburgh; from 39.2% to 34.0% at South Aberdeen.

64. 'By-Election Report by Arthur Woodburn, Scottish Secretary', attached to minutes, NEC meeting, 26 June 1935.

65. Dalton, in particular, was determined to force the PLP to see the light, as entries in his diary at this time show: 'We are in a bad political recession. Three by-elections in Scotland have gone badly, all below the 1929 level. Combination

of the Jubilee, Hitler, and poor leadership in the House of Commons. Hitler's Air Force, now greater than ours, is helping the Government. The past four years' errors in foreign policy are apt to seem secondary. The primary question tends to be "Are you, or are you not in favour of Hitler having four or more aeroplanes to your one?" If one opposes the Government's rearmament policy, one is in a difficult position, as indefensible as disarmament by example. If one does not oppose it, one loses one's initiative of attack on the Government' (undated entry, mid-May). At the NCL meeting on 14 May, Dalton, Citrine, Bevin and Walker warned the PLP of the dangers of voting against the increases in the Air Force. The following day the PLP, led by Henderson, did vote against the increases: thereafter, Dalton styled the PLP leaders as 'political cripples' (entry, 31 May). Dalton Papers, British Library of Political and Economic Science.

66. See Bullock, *Ernest Bevin*, vol. 1, pp. 565-74 for an account of the Brighton conference and its aftermath.

67. Minutes, Finance and General Purposes Sub-Committee meeting, 21 June 1935.

68. Report of the monthly activities of the TUC, PLP and the NEC, attached to minutes, NCL meeting, 25 June 1935.

69. Ibid.

70. Minutes, NEC meeting, 24 July 1935.

71. Report of the monthly activities of the TUC, PLP and the NEC, attached to minutes, NCL meeting, 25 Feb. 1936.

3 THE LIBERALS IN DISARRAY, 1931-35

If the period 1923 to 1931 can be regarded as the denouement of the
tragic history of organised liberalism, then the years 1931-35 form an
epilogue which is not without interest or importance but which lacks all
nobility. It is a story marked by internecine warfare, moments of
promise, by electoral disaster and ultimate despair.[1]

For the Liberals 1929 was a false dawn. At the election in that year
the party gained more votes than at any time in its illustrious history.
To achieve this it had fielded over 500 candidates who, under Lloyd
George's leadership, had presented a united front to the country. It was
true that only 59 candidates had been elected, but this was a marked
advance on the 1924 result; and Liberal efforts at the election had been
responsible for making unemployment the principal issue of the
campaign. The drift into oblivion appeared to have been arrested and
once more the party seemed to be a potent electoral force.

Co-operation with the Labour Government between 1929 and 1931,
and the crisis of August-October 1931, altered the situation. In June
1931 the parliamentary Liberal Party split into several loose factions,
ostensibly because of the government's Land Tax which Lloyd George
supported but which some Liberals opposed. But a deeper cause was
the dislike felt by some Liberals for co-operation with a Socialist
government, especially one which was manifestly failing to deal with
the problems of the day.[2] When in August 1931 the Labour Government fell, all the Liberal groups supported the formation of the
National Government.[3] But their relations deteriorated again when the
National Government decided to hold a general election. The dissident
Liberals, of whom Sir John Simon was now the acknowledged leader,
formed a new organisation for the purpose of co-ordinating their
electoral effort with that of the Conservative Party.[4] The official
Liberal Party also co-operated with the Conservative Party, but with far
less zeal, and with considerable suspicion of the intentions of its allies.
The split was taking on a rather more permanent character.

But of even greater significance for the historic Liberal Party was
Lloyd George's decision to oppose the general election and to deny the
resources of his fund to the main body of the Liberal Party; his action
made it impossible for the Liberal Party to contest as many seats as it
had fought in 1929. As has been shown in Chapter 1, the Samuelites

were able to field only 112 candidates while the Simonites fielded 41 and Lloyd George 6; at the election 35 Simonites, 33 Samuelites and 4 followers of Lloyd George were returned. Compared with 1929 the Liberal share of the total vote fell from 23.6% to 10.9%,[5] though this was hardly surprising as so few seats were contested in 1931.

Of even greater significance was the failure of the Samuelite Liberals to improve much on the average vote per constituency contested, even though on this occasion they contested only those seats which on the 1929 results looked winnable. In 1929 the average Liberal vote was 10,348 per constituency (of the 513 seats contested, at least 200 were quite hopeless). In 1931 the average Liberal vote per constituency was 15,194, which at first sight seems a substantial increase, particularly as the total vote cast at the election was one million less than in 1929. But the figure is deceptive. The average Liberal vote cast in Simonite-contested seats was 19,731; in Lloyd Georgite-contested seats, 17,255; while in Samuelite-contested seats it was only 12,527, an increase over 1929 but a marginal increase only, and in the seats which on the 1929 figures the Liberals had thought that they had stood a good chance of winning. Furthermore, as was shown in Chapter 1,[6] in the 88 contests the Liberal and Conservative Parties (80 of them between the Samuelites and the Conservatives) the size of the Liberal vote declined in 51 cases and was similar to 1929 in another 16: that is, the average increase in Samuelite-contested seats in 1931 was achieved on an actual increase in only 45 seats at most, and in many of these the gain came from the fact that Conservative voters, in the absence of candidates of their own party, cast their votes for Liberal candidates, a situation without beneficial long-term significance for the Liberal Party. In comparison with 1929 the general election in 1931 was a catastrophe for the Liberal Party.

As soon as the election was over the Liberals, like Labour, began to try to put their house in order; but in this task they met with even less success than did Labour. The crux of the problem was that while the Labour Party could survive, indeed flourish, without its former leader, Ramsay MacDonald, the Liberal Party could make no headway whatsoever without its nominal but estranged leader, Lloyd George. Shortly after the election Samuel wrote to Lloyd George to ask him whether he intended to stand again for the party chairmanship. Lloyd George replied that he had no such intention; he also clearly stated his attitude to the Samuelite Liberals (and the NLF):

As you are aware, I am completely at variance with the disastrous

course into which the Party has recently been guided . . . I am
hoping that by the New Year my health will be fully restored. I am
looking forward then to the pleasure of cooperating with all those
who have at heart the advancement of those ideas to which so many
millions rallied hopefully in 1929. For the moment these courses
have been overwhelmed by the calamitous folly of October, and
any attempt to revive them will be met for some time by impatience
and ridicule. That phase will soon pass and all true progressives can
then resume the task out of which they were so regretfully man-
oeuvred.[7]

To a reporter from the *Manchester Guardian* he attacked both Simon
and Samuel for deserting the 1929 Liberal programme as outlined in
the Yellow Book:

they are glad of this opportunity of throwing it over. They are now
on top of the midden, buzzing like flies, as if at last they had
recovered the old farm. It is their Indian summer, a quite
unexpected piece of luck to them.[8]

His refusal to co-operate with Samuel had two effects on the party,
both of the utmost significance. First, it left the Liberal Party leadership in the hands of the far from charismatic Samuel. In the 1920s
Samuel had proved himself to be a capable adminstrator and organiser,
as well (since 1929[9]) as an able parliamentarian; but he had never
shown those qualities of initiative and inspiration which the party now
so desperately needed. Secondly, it deprived the Liberal Party of its
principal source of income. Sinclair stated the extent of the party's
dependence on the Lloyd George fund in a letter to Samuel written
shortly after the election — Party Headquarters, he said, needed £3,000
per annum:

Towards this total the Liberal Central Association has an income of
slightly less than £1000 a year. The remaining £2000 has hitherto
been found by grants averaging £500 a quarter from Mr. Lloyd
George's Trustees.[10]

Even this did not exhaust the extent of the party's dependence on
Lloyd George, for by-elections too had been financed from his fund.
Furthermore, though less seriously, the split had caused the party to
lose its ablest organiser, Colonel Tweed, who had remained loyal to

Lloyd George.[11] Thus, apart from the electoral disaster, the historic
Liberal Party went forward into the 1930s bereft of its only really
inspiring leader, with an income reduced by two-thirds, with no by-
election fund, without its ablest organiser and with the constituency
organisations in disarray.

Shortly after the election it became clear that Lloyd George and not
Samuel had accurately calculated the cost of co-operation with the
Conservative Party. During the campaign the former had warned
Liberals that although Lord Snowden had told them that a second
general election would have to be held before a tariff could be introduced, Neville Chamberlain had said otherwise, and that after the
election Chamberlain and not Snowden would be in a position to
enforce his views.[12] Liberals had not heeded his warning, and, perhaps
lulled into a false sense of security by Baldwin's promise to establish a
permanent non-political commission on tariffs, had overwhelmingly
supported the Samuelite position. Within two months of the election,
however, no less than three tariff measures had been enacted. In
November the Samuelites accepted, though reluctantly, an Abnormal
Importations Bill, and in December they voted against a Horticultural
Products (Emergency Duties) Bill. In December also the Liberals got
the 'impartial inquiry' promised by Baldwin: a Cabinet Committee on
the Balance of Trade which was composed principally of known proponents of the introduction of a general tariff. It was hardly surprising
that this committee recommended the immediate introduction of a
general tariff. Samuel and his followers refused to endorse the recommendation; but, as at the general election, a face-saving formula was
found, and on 22 January 1932 the following statement was issued
from Downing Street:

> The Cabinet has had before it the report of its Committee on the
> Balance of Trade, and after prolonged discussion it has been found
> impossible to reach a unanimous conclusion on the Committee's
> recommendations.
> The Cabinet, however, is deeply impressed with the paramount
> importance of maintaining national unity in presence of the grave
> problems that now confront this country and the whole world. It
> has accordingly determined that some modification of usual
> ministerial practice is required, and has decided that Ministers who
> find themselves unable to support the conclusions arrived at by the
> majority of their colleagues on the subject of import duties and

cognate matters are to be at liberty to express their view by speech and vote. The Cabinet being essentially united on all other matters of policy believes that by this special provision it is best interpreting the will of the nation and the needs of the time.[13]

One month later an Import Duties Bill was enacted, thereby placing a 10% tariff on a large range of goods. It was supported by the Simonite Liberals and opposed by the Samuelites who, however, remained in the government. The miscalculation had proved to be costly but the price was still worth paying.

But if the parliamentary Liberal Party remained committed to the National Government, extraparliamentary Liberal organisations did not. As early as 16 December 1931 the executive of the National Liberal Federation (NLF) had passed a resolution deploring the measures of protection taken by the National Government and calling on the Liberal MPs to remember their responsibilities to the millions of Liberal voters who had cast their votes for Conservative candidates in the belief that tariffs would not be introduced.[14] The *Liberal Magazine*, which represented the opinion of the Central Liberal Association, fulminated against the government's failure to keep its promise to set up an independent tariff commission,[15] and it stressed that there was widespread Liberal concern over an observation made by the chairman of the Conservative Party Organization, namely that 'We have a National Government with a mandate to carry out Tory policy.'[16]

Liberals were divided, however, over whether Samuel should leave the National Government. The so-called 'agreement to differ' was approved by, among others, Lord Grey of Fallodon and the Yorkshire Liberal Federation, but not by Ramsay Muir, the chairman of the NLF who, nevertheless, was reluctant to censure the Liberal Ministers.[17] Some Liberals went beyond Muir's position: for example, at the annual meeting of the Union of University Liberal Societies held late in March, the delegates passed a resolution calling on the Liberal Ministers to resign; and, taking their cue from Lloyd George, they called on Liberals to join other progressive forces in the formation of a Radical Party.[18] In March, too, the General Council of the Scottish Liberal Federation[19] and the Executive Committee of the Welsh Liberal Federation[20] also called on the Liberal Ministers to leave the National Government. And of course there was Lloyd George.

Shortly before the annual meeting of the NLF, which was to be held at Clacton on 28-29 April, Muir tried to dissuade Lloyd George from attending the conference and from heaping execration on the Samuelite

Ministers. In an earlier letter Lloyd George had threatened to do this:

> I am convinced that unless Liberalism declares its complete detach-
> ment from the Government at an early date, and takes actual steps
> to emphasise its independence we shall miss the greatest oppor-
> tunity that has come the way of Liberalism since the war. The
> Labour Party has not yet recovered the confidence of even its own
> supporters, and if the Liberal Federation were to raise the standard
> and bring out a resounding policy at Clacton, millions of those who
> formerly looked to the Labour Party with hope, would rally to that
> standard. Would you kindly let me know whether the Executive
> mean to frame an amendment which will make it quite clear that we
> are no longer hooked to the chariot of this reactionary crowd. If
> they cannot see their way to do so, I am afraid that I must come
> down and support the Welsh resolution.[21]

He was appeased only when Muir wrote to tell him that the executive
intended to declare the independence of the party as a whole, while
leaving it to the Liberal Ministers themselves to judge the extent to
which their support of the government should be carried.[22]

In his efforts to achieve some sort of consensus within the party,
Muir also asked Samuel to stay away from the Clacton conference,
as his attendance 'might smack of dictation and drive many delegates
into rebellion'; it might also, he added, induce Lloyd George to 'kick up
a shindy'. As to the state of opinion in the party, Muir estimated that
only about 5% of the delegates would express their support for the
National Government; perhaps a further 20% would not censure the
government until Samuel had decided one way or the other:

> Probably 25% will demand your immediate resignation and would
> repudiate you if you refused. The remaining 50% want the Party to
> be clearly dissociated from the Government, but also want to avoid
> any criticism of or attack upon Liberal Ministers. This is also the
> Executive line.[23]

In the event, both Lloyd George and Samuel stayed away. Muir's estimate proved to be correct, and the executive's resolution was carried
fairly comfortably but with a vocal minority in dissent. An interesting
feature of the Clacton conference was that the free trade resolution was
supported by most of the constituencies which were represented by
Liberal National MPs. Quite clearly they had accepted their MPs'

explanation that tariffs were to be temporary only and were to be used as a bargaining counter to bring about an all-round reduction of other countries' tariffs. Encouraged by what it believed to be a reasonable show of party unity, the NLF a month later launched an appeal for £100,000 and organised area conferences and demonstrations for the summer.[24]

In March Samuel had emphasised that it was in the interests of the party to contest all by-elections, at least where local circumstances permitted; but participation in by-elections only exposed the disunity within the Liberal Party and the paradoxes inherent in the character of national government. At the Dulwich by-election in June the Liberal candidate received messages of support from Lloyd George who advocated withdrawal from the National Government, and from Samuel who stressed the unanimity of the National Government on a range of matters of importance and the value of continued Liberal participation in it.[25] To complete a rather confused picture of Liberal activity at the by-election, Cooke-Taylor's Conservative opponent received a message of support from Simon. At the North Cornwall by-election the picture was equally confused. The Liberal candidate, Sir Francis Acland, acknowledged the leadership of Samuel and approved of the course taken by him since the 1931 crisis.[26] By refusing to agree that the Liberal Ministers should withdraw from the National Government, he forfeited the goodwill of the NLF.[27] Samuel sent him a message of support, and Isaac Foot, also a Minister, addressed several of his meetings.[28] Simon also intervened to the extent of writing an open letter to the North Cornwall electors in which he regretted that the Liberal candidate was not a wholehearted supporter of the National Government.[29] Baldwin, on this occasion, also supported the Conservative candidate although he had not done so in 1931.[30] The facade of electoral co-operation, so laboriously constructed at the 1931 general election, was rapidly crumbling, and the tensions between the Liberal spokesmen increased as a result. With Acland's victory at North Cornwall, Sinclair, the party's deputy leader and the Secretary of State for Scotland, expressed satisfaction at what he regarded as a vindication of the Samuelite position. He told Samuel:

> The Simonites and the NLF sink into their proper place, at least for the time being.[31]

'At least for the time being' — that was the operative part of his observation, for throughout the country Liberals continued to call on their parliamentary representatives to withdraw from the National Government. Events were soon to force Samuel to a decision.

The catalytic event was the Imperial Economic Conference held at Ottawa late in the summer of 1932, when agreements were signed between Britain and the Dominions whereby the preference scheme for foodstuffs from the Dominions was continued. In return, British exports to the Dominions were to receive preferential treatment, 'but chiefly by increasing the tariff against foreign goods, leaving untouched the rate against British goods, already impossibly high in many cases'.[32] These agreements incensed the Samuelite Liberals, as well as Snowden who was now on close terms with Samuel. In a letter to Samuel, Snowden outlined their dilemma:

> As far as I understand the Report [on Ottawa] we have given up entirely our fiscal autonomy, and surrendered our power to use the new tariffs as a bargaining weapon to get foreign tariffs down, which was the main defence of the tariffs used by Runciman and Baldwin . . . We are now pledged to maintain the existing tariffs and to increase them in some circumstances . . . my own feeling at present is that I cannot be dragged along this road any farther without loss of all honour and self respect.[33]

Samuel too was inclined to think that he and the other Liberal Ministers should withdraw from the National Government; but unlike Snowden, he had to take into account the opinion of the parliamentary Liberal Party. Accordingly, on 29 August, he issued a circular to all Liberal Ministers and MPs in order to establish a consensus of opinion as to the course they should adopt.[34] His task was complicated by the fact that most of his colleagues were away on vacation, with several holidaying on the Continent; but by 8 September he had seen or been in contact with enough of them to be able to come to a decision, which he outlined in a letter to Walter Rea, the Liberal Chief Whip, who was out of England at the time.

> There is a general consensus of opinion that it is impossible for us to remain in the Government, but also that we should not cross the floor of the House or regard ourselves as an Opposition Party.[35]

At least three factors of importance brought about this compromise resolution of the dilemma. In the first place at least eight of the

Samuelite MPs owed their seats to the fact that the Conservative Party
had withdrawn candidates at the 1931 general election. Not surprisingly, several were unwilling to commit political suicide by antagon-
ising the Conservatives — even for the principle of free trade.[36]
Secondly, the arguments and personal influence of Lord Lothian, one
of organised Liberalism's foremost publicists, may have been decisive.
Lothian had impressed on Sinclair, as he did later on Samuel, that
while he was at one with them over Ottawa, he was doubtful of the
value to the party of resignation on a 'mere negative', especially with
the Lausanne Conference on Reparations and the World Economic Conference in sight, the India question as yet unresolved, and international
crises looming: in short, he had argued, 'it would be fatal if we
weakened Liberal forces in the Government or the prestige of the
country at Geneva'.[37] With Lothian and a number of his House of
Commons colleagues on one side, and the NLF, the WLF, the SLF and
a similar number of parliamentary colleagues on the other, as well
probably as his own reluctance to admit that Lloyd George had been
right about the effect of continuing to work in alliance with the Conservatives, Samuel once more agreed to a formula which satisfied few of
his followers and ultimately proved to be unworkable. Despite a rather
pathetic plea from MacDonald not to leave him to the not-so-tender
mercies of the Tories,[38] Samuel and his colleagues resigned from the
National Government on 28 September and took up seats on the
government backbenches — as critics but not opponents of the National
Government.

Samuel's decision to leave the National Government only succeeded
in widening further what was already an unbridgeable gap between
himself and the Simonites. The gap had been widening steadily since
August 1931. In November 1931 Simon had refused to meet Samuel to
discuss the future of the party;[39] and in June 1932, while the Simonites
had supported the Finance Bill (one clause of which authorised the
Treasury to remove certain articles, including meat, from the free list),
the Samuelites had abstained.[40] In June and July 1932 *The Times*
published an acrimonious exchange of letters between Simon and the
president of the NLF, A. Brampton. The subject in contention was a
statement issued by the Executive Committee of the Liberal National
Party expressing its regret that Acland, the Liberal candidate at North
Cornwall, had refused to declare that he supported the National
Government unreservedly.[41] Also in July 1932 the Simonites formed a
council, which in the first instance was to appeal for funds and then, if
the appeal was successful, to appoint a full-time secretary, rent offices

and launch a publicity campaign.[42] Thus when in September Samuel
left the National Government, Simon merely issued a statement in
which he referred to the election mandate, the 'agreement to differ'
and the present unanimity of the Cabinet on a 'large collection of vital
issues' apart from tariffs:[43] in short, he and his followers had no intention of joining Samuel on the backbenches.

   Among the rank and file of the Liberal Party, Samuel's decision to
leave the government but not move into outright opposition to it, met
with a mixed reception. The Executive Committee of the Liberal
Council and the NLF welcomed the decision, though the latter regarded
it as only a first step towards the complete independence of the Liberal
Party from the National Government;[44] the SLF gave its unqualified
approval of the course taken by the Ministers;[45] but Welsh Liberals
remained critical.[46]

   And, as in 1931, there was the problem of Lloyd George and the
considerable following he enjoyed among the Young Liberals, the
Women's National Liberal Federation and the Welsh Liberals. The NLF
invited Lloyd George to attend a meeting in Queen's Hall, London, on
12 October, to welcome back the Liberal Ministers. Of the Liberal
spokesmen, Muir in particular was keen to see the Samuelite and
Lloyd Georgites reunited, though on his rather than Lloyd George's
terms;[47] and the NLF intimated to Lloyd George that he was not
expected to address the meeting. This snub so enraged Lloyd George
that he replied with an open letter in which he expressed his regret at
not being consulted about the decision to leave the government and his
annoyance with the NLF for not allowing him to speak at the Queen's
Hall meeting, which he now refused to attend. He added that in his
opinion the Liberal Ministers had done nothing of particular merit in
leaving the government over Ottawa:

> I am particularly curious to learn why, having put up with trough
> after trough of husks, they drew the line at swallowing this last feed
> of exactly the same provender.[48]

If this did not completely close the door to an early reconciliation, his
subsequent comments certainly did so. In a press interview on his seven-
tieth birthday, which took place a few weeks after the Queen's Hall
incident, Lloyd George urged Liberals to break with what he described
as the 'flaccid, oleaginous Whiggery of Samuel'.[49] His use of such
emotive language stifled hopes of an early reconciliation.[50]

   By refusing to move into outright opposition to the National

Government, Samuel left the constituency organisations much as they
had been since the 1931 general election: that is, being critical of the
National Government while not wishing to repudiate Samuel and his
colleagues. If Samuel had heeded only the opinion of the constituency
organisations he would have moved into open opposition to the
National Government much earlier than he did. At the East Fife by-
election in February 1933, the local Liberal Association nominated a
Liberal National in succession to the former MP, also a Liberal
National. However, a minority of the local association decided to
nominate an independent Liberal candidate to oppose him, the first
time since 1931 that such a thing had occurred. This had the effect of
exposing as false the Liberal National claim to represent the mainstream
of Liberal opinion, for David Keir, the independent Liberal candidate,
received letters of support from no less than 200 Liberal Associations in
England, several in Scotland, as well as from the NLF, the SLF, Lloyd
George and Snowden.[51] In East Fife itself a clear majority of the Liberal
voters remained loyal to the Liberal National standard, but the importance of Keir's intervention lay outside East Fife. At the Rotherham by-
election shortly afterwards, the secretary of the local Liberal
Association declared that Samuel should move into a stance of outright
opposition to the National Government;[52] and at the Ashford by-
election in March, Lloyd George was given a tumultuous reception
when he spoke on behalf of the independent Liberal candidate.[53]

In Parliament meanwhile the position of the Samuelite Liberals as backbench supporters of the National Government was rapidly becoming
untenable. From March the Samuelites' attack on the government's
economic policy broadened. They opposed the Agricultural Marketing
Bill which Samuel described as 'by far the most Socialistic Measure that
has been brought before Parliament in recent years'.[54] They then gave
their qualified support to the government's White Paper on India, but in
May they opposed the government's embargo on the export of goods to
Russia, the tax on Cooperative Societies and the Rent Restrictions
Bill.[55] In June a full meeting of the parliamentary Liberal Party condemned the government's proposals for the World Economic Conference.[56] In July the Liberals voted against the estimates of the Board of
Trade, a revolt which led to their being rebuked by Captain Margesson,
the government Chief Whip. The situation was becoming intolerable
and many of the Samuelites, perhaps influenced also by the annual
meeting's decision to call on them to move into opposition, had come to
favour, at least in theory, such a course.

Foremost among these was the deputy leader of the party, Sir
Archibald Sinclair. In mid-July Sinclair forwarded to Samuel a lengthy
and detailed analysis of the Liberal dilemma.[57]

> It seems to me that our support of the Government is becoming
> more and more nominal and that the front of our opposition in the
> House of Commons is constantly widening . . . We are agreed that
> when we do cross the floor it must be on a large issue of our own
> choosing; the longer we stay on the Government side and the more
> persistently and forcibly we criticise them, the greater the danger
> that they may deprive us of the initiative.

For a number of reasons Sinclair thought that it would be unwise to
cross the floor until November or December. In the first place, Samuel
was to spend the summer in Canada and would not be back in England
before the end of October. Secondly, the House was dispersing for the
holidays, obviously a poor time to make a 'big gesture such as crossing
the floor':

> more particularly is this the case when a mood of optimism seems to
> be prevalent accompanied by a minor boom on the Stock Exchange
> and a substantial reduction of the figures of unemployment.

He was confident, however, that this state of affairs would have
changed by the end of the year:

> The situation in the winter, however, is likely to be different. Un-
> employment figures will again be rising, and the demand for a moder-
> ate policy of expansion, of which there was ample evidence in the
> recent debate on the World Economic Conference in the House of
> Commons and which is reflected in newspapers of all shades of
> opinion . . . will probably grow.

Sinclair recognised that much could happen between July and
December — in particular he thought that Churchill's agitation over the
government's India policy could produce a new political crisis — but he
thought that Samuel should arrange for a series of conferences of the
leading Liberals with a view to publishing a 'forward' policy statement
in December. Sinclair hoped that this would lay less emphasis on free
trade and more on a positive policy for dealing directly with unemployment than had previous Liberal policy statements. As he observed to

Samuel:

> I am informed that when the Secretaries of the Women's Federations
> from all over the country met in London last week they were almost
> unanimous in expressing the opinion that we were making too much
> of free trade in our speeches and that the demand in the country was
> for a positive policy for dealing directly with unemployment.

Samuel was inclined to agree that he should move into opposition
and at the annual meeting he had spoken in favour of the party's modified fiscal policy; but he was reluctant to do more than talk about it. In
an address to the annual meeting of the NLF, he appeared to assume
that his party would be opposed to the National Government in the
near future, for he noted that:

> those responsible for the organization in the constituencies fully
> anticipate that when the next election comes (and he thought it
> could come late in 1933), with the cooperation of the local associa-
> tions, not less than 400 Liberal candidates, and probably many
> more, will be nominated, so that the country may definitely have
> the chance of returning a Liberal Government as an alternative.[58]

Beyond saying this he took no action. Shortly afterwards the summer
session came to an end and Samuel left for Canada without calling a
meeting of the parliamentary Liberal Party or arranging for the series of
policy-making conferences which Sinclair, his deputy leader, and others
desired.

At the annual meeting of the NLF held two months later, the executive failed to carry a resolution which was neutral in tone and did not
censure the Ministers for not going into outright opposition to the
National Government; instead, the meeting carried an amendment
calling on Samuel to 'cross the floor'. The executive had more success
with a resolution calling on the government to form a Union of Free
Trade or Low Tariff (10%) Countries should the outright abolition of
tariffs prove impossible: this was carried by 254 votes to 210 and could
be regarded as support for Lloyd George's plea for a realistic Liberal
fiscal policy. Also carried were resolutions condemning the government's unemployment, fiscal and international policies.[59] In short,
Samuel and his group were rapidly becoming even more unrepresentative of majority Liberal opinon.

While Samuel was away in Canada the state of the party deteriorated still further. Sinclair wrote to him shortly before his return:

> I only hope that after sojourning in the splendid palaces of Liber-
> lism in Canada you will not find its hutments here at home too
> squalid and depressing. Quite frankly the situation of the Party is
> bad.[60]

Sinclair believed that although the National Government was benefiting
from falling figures of unemployment and improved trade returns, its
stock in the country was not particularly high owing to the unfavourable impact of the Ottawa agreements and a vapid foreign policy. He
thought that the Labour Party had not recovered from 1931, and that
the antics of the Socialist League would prevent it from doing so.
Nevertheless, he argued that this did not necessarily mean that the
country regarded the Liberal Party as an alternative government:

> As far as I can gauge public opinion there is no anxiety among the
> great mass of people to return to party politics or any faith that any
> particular party possesses the secret of prosperity.

This however could not be the operative factor determining the party's
future course, for

> On the other hand the keen Radicals are becoming increasingly
> hostile to the Government and, as Ramsay Muir assures me,
> impatient with and violently unfriendly towards the Liberal Parlia-
> mentary Party.

After due consideration he concluded that:

> The longer we remain in our present position the more inglorious,
> embarrassing and insignificant it becomes.

Sinclair further impressed on Samuel the party's need for a statement of
immediate objectives, an appeal for money (without which the party
could neither contest the six by-elections scheduled to be held before
December nor prepare itself for a general election) and an early decision on a move into opposition, whether or not there arose a 'great
issue' on which to make such a move.

Samuel returned to England on 18 October. He was determined to
canvass the opinion of his followers as to a possible move into opposi-

tion to the National Government. He contacted each of the Liberal MPs and found that most of them were keen to take the step even without a great issue as a *cause de la raison*. Acland, for example, did not think that a big issue would arise; the party, he thought, should move into opposition using the government's disarmament failures as its main reason.[61] Sinclair still hoped that they would not have to cross the floor on a general grumble at the government's policies but, if no big issue arose, Samuel would have to justify their decision by making a particularly forceful speech in the Commons.[62] His hand strengthened by the support of all the outstanding Liberals, apart from Lothian, Samuel formally crossed the floor on 13 November. Of the 33 Liberals who had followed him since 1931, 29 followed him now; four — W. McKeag, R.H. Bernays, J.P. Maclay and J.A. Lockie — refused to move into outright opposition to the National Government and remained in the position occupied by Samuel from September 1932. Most of them ultimately joined the Liberal National Group. At least three of the four defectors represented constituencies where electoral success turned on the distribution of Conservative votes, a factor which may have weighed with them when they were deciding whether or not to follow Samuel. Samuel also recruited one Liberal National supporter, namely A.C. Curry, the MP for Bishop Auckland.[63] The move into opposition was applauded by the NLF, the SLF, the WLF and all the area federations.[64] But it did not herald a Liberal revival.

Prior to the move into outright opposition to the National Government, Liberal candidates at by-elections had performed fairly creditably, in most cases equalling the Liberal share of the total vote in 1931;[65] thereafter, however, the Liberal vote slumped disastrously. Shortly after the Liberal move, Muir (despite the death in October of one of the party's principal benefactors, Lord Cowdray), stated confidently that 'We at headquarters see our way to fighting at least 400 seats' at the next general election,[66] but events in the next six months forced him to reassess the situation. In the last by-election held before the Liberals crossed the floor, at Skipton on 7 November, the Liberal candidate's share of the total vote was 23.6% which compared fairly favourably with the 29.3% in 1929. At the first by-election held after the party had moved into opposition, at Rusholme on 21 November, the Liberal share of the total vote was only 9.3% whereas in 1929 it had been 32.9%. At Rutland and Stamford a by-election was held on the same day, but owing to lack of finance the Liberals did not contest it, although in 1929 they had performed creditably in securing 24.8% of the total vote. They did contest the next by-election, at Market Harborough on 29 November, but their share of the total vote was only 16% whereas in 1929 it had been 26%. The by-elections held early in 1934 were even more disastrous. At Cambridge on 8 February the Liberal share of the total vote fell from 25% to 7%; while at Lowestoft a week later there was an equally catastrophic collapse of the Liberal vote — from 31% to 10%. In an address to the National Liberal Club in January 1934 J.A. Spender had spoken the mind of the party leadership when he said:

> We must get into the minds of the public some clear idea of Liberal policy as distinguished from both Toryism and Socialism.[67]

But on the evidence of the results of the by-election the Liberals were either not getting this message across or it was being rejected, and some Liberals began to question whether there was any future for an independent Liberal Party.

Some Liberals turned to a revived form of Lib-Labism, but this did not recommend itself to the leadership, and was soon dropped. The principal proponents of Lib-Labism were the Liberal and Radical Candidates' Association, which at its April meeting carried a resolution (the voting was 20 for and 13 against the resolution) calling for a Lib-Lab electoral alliance,[68] and the former Liberal newspaper, the *News Chronicle*, which since 1931 had been disaffected with official liberalism. Among some of the younger Liberals, too, the idea was not without its attractions. At the Oxford Summer School for Liberals held in August, Megan Lloyd George chaired a meeting which was addressed by A.L. Rowse, a young research fellow at All Souls College and a Labour candidate in 1931, whose theme was Lib-Lab electoral co-operation. His proposals, however, were received coolly by the school.[69] And the idea of formal Lib-Labism was repudiated by the Liberal hierarchy and by the *Manchester Guardian*. At the meeting of the Liberal and Radical Candidates' Association just referred to, Muir spoke against the resolution, and Samuel, while not speaking directly to the resolution, left the meeting in no doubt that he endorsed Muir's view.[70]

While denouncing Lib-Labism, Muir was himself compromising independent Liberalism in a way endorsed by Lloyd George but not by Samuel. In the 8 April issue of the *Westminster Gazette*, he called on Liberal voters to support 'progressive' candidates at by-elections where no Liberal was in the field: his criterion for 'progressiveness' was that the candidate concerned must be sound on free trade, India and the League of Nations; and as an example of a progressive Conservative he mentioned Vyvyan Adams, and as a progressive Labour man, Norman Angell. This advice was almost identical to that given by Lloyd George to Liberal voters at the North Hammersmith by-election; but despite this there was no *rapprochement* between the two men. Like Muir's position Samuel's was rather ambiguous. In the one speech he could say: 'If there are any ready to cooperate on these lines [a positive unemployment policy and a defence of 'freedom'] let them all come', and follow this by: 'Our present task is clearly to build up again a powerful and united Liberal Party.'[71] Unlike Muir, however, he refused to endorse Liberal support for any but Liberal candidates, and he was absolutely set against any accommodation with the Labour Party. For its part, the Labour Party was also opposed to any form of electoral cooperation with the Liberal Party, as Lansbury, Morrison and others were always at pains to make clear.[72]

There were two other manifestations of Liberal discontent with Samuel's version of the creed. The first was the insistence of some Liberals that Lloyd George held the key to the recovery of the Liberal Party as a major political force. It was a view with which Samuel was reluctant to concur. For a brief period after Samuel crossed the floor in November 1933, it did appear that the two leaders might again cooperate to the benefit of their party, though when Samuel returned from Canada in October he had not brought Lloyd George into discussions about the party's future, nor had he personally informed Lloyd George that he intended to lead the Liberals into outright opposition to the National Government. It was only through the mediation of Lord Snowden that the leaders were made aware of each other's position. One week after the Liberals crossed the floor, Snowden wrote to Samuel to let him know of Lloyd George's reaction to the decision and his general assessment of the situation.[73] Lloyd George, he wrote, thought that there was no chance

of a sufficient revival of the Liberal Party to give it much representation in the new Parliament. From his analysis of the prospects he has come to the conclusion that it is not likely to get more than a dozen seats at the next election. He thinks that this is largely attributable to the divisions which still exist in the Party.

Lloyd George, he went on,

spoke without the slightest feeling of bitterness about your action in
'crossing the floor', but he felt rather sorry that you had not taken
advantage of that occasion to hold out the hand of fellowship to
him. He thought it would have been a generous thing if you had
written to him to tell him what you intended to do, and had said:
'Now let byegones be byegones. Let us bury our differences and all
work together to try to resuscitate the Liberal Party.'

In brief, Snowden felt that Lloyd George was in a conciliatory mood.
It was also his belief that Samuel should take advantage of this, particularly in view of the fact that Lloyd George appeared to command a
considerable following in the Liberal Party.

Samuel heeded Snowden's advice. The next day he sent a note to
Lloyd George which read:

Now that the political situation is somewhat cleared, I should be
glad of an opportunity to talk over the position with you.[74]

It is likely that meetings between the two did take place, but unfortunately neither of them kept a detailed record of what transpired at
the meetings.[75] What seems to have happened is this: at an initial
meeting in November it was agreed that Lloyd George should see a
draft manifesto of the Liberal Party's policies and future course of
action, and his comments on it would form the basis for further talks.
Lloyd George appears to have seen the manifesto early in February
1934, and a meeting to discuss it was arranged for a week or so later.
What occurred at this meeting must be open to conjecture, but there
can be no doubt that they found themselves unable to agree on the content of the manifesto. They may also have disagreed about its form,
and there may have been a conflict over the role which Lloyd George
would play in a reunited party. From the evidence of later activities it
can be deduced that Lloyd George tried to radicalise the Liberal Party
in a way unacceptable to Samuel.

Soon after these meetings Lloyd George again tried to rally liberal
opinion to a standard less exclusively Liberal than the one raised by
Samuel. In a message of support to John Foot, the Liberal candidate
at the Basingstoke by-election in April, he declared that he was ready to

support any Government, Party, or combination of Parties that
showed the disposition, capacity and courage for dealing effectively
with our share of the world emergency.[76]

And he confirmed this in a message he sent to a Liberal voter at the North Hammersmith by-election some days later. As there was no Liberal candidate, he advised his correspondent, Liberals should vote for the Labour candidate:

> Mr. West may go further in some directions than you would care to travel. But the point he wishes ultimately to reach is a long way off. Meanwhile he is on the right road and walking steadily our way . . . Concentrate on the practical questions with which we are and shall for some years be confronted in Britain, our Empire and the world.[77]

Samuel did not intervene in the North Hammersmith by-election, but a split in Liberal opinion was nevertheless apparent for the chairman of the local Liberal Association advised Liberals to vote for the National Government candidate. In the event Foot did well at Basingstoke and West recaptured North Hammersmith for the Labour Party.

These results were not achieved solely or even largely because of Lloyd George's intervention, but to many Liberals it seemed that he rather than Samuel was giving a clear lead to them — one which could return electoral dividends. Of course Lloyd George's appeal was greatest in Wales, where in February 1934 the North Wales Liberal Federation called on him to lead a 'great campaign throughout the country';[78] but it was not restricted to Wales. In May the League of Young Liberals made a similar plea,[79] and, as the number of by-electoral disasters multiplied, responsible politicians like Sinclair and Harcourt Johnstone began, albeit reluctantly, to entertain thoughts of approaching Lloyd George about some sort of co-operation.[80] Nothing came of this, possibly because Samuel was still smarting from the rebuff Lloyd George had given him earlier in the year, and possibly because Lloyd George himself thought that official Liberalism had lost all chance of again becoming a viable electoral force.[81] And there the matter rested until Lloyd George announced his New Deal proposals early in 1935.

A further manifestation of discontent with official Liberalism was the increasing frequency of defections from the party. In the course of 1934 the party lost one MP, H.L. Nathan, to the Labour Party, a defection of considerable importance since it was recognised that no Liberal candidate could wrench Nathan's seat from him.[82] Other prominent Liberals to defect were Basil Murray, a Liberal candidate for St Marylebone in 1928 and Argyll in 1929, and Moelwyn Hughes, a Liberal organiser in Wales. Others who seem to have been thinking of doing so included Sir Ernest Simon, Liberal Minster in the first National Government, and Arthur Salter, who was later to represent Oxford University as an Independent.[83] These actual and imminent defections were bound to discredit the claim of Samuel that at the next election the Liberal Party was capable of nominating sufficient candidates to be an alternative government.

By the end of 1934 the Liberal leadership was deeply concerned with the party's failure to make an impact on the electorate. When the Liberals had crossed the floor in November 1933, Sinclair had stressed to Samuel that it was imperative that all by-elections should be contested by Liberal candidates. They started off well by contesting four out of the first five by-elections, but thereafter their record was less sound. On the twelve contested by-elections held between April and December of 1934, the Liberals failed to contest seven, principally due to lack of finance. They fared well at Basingstoke and Merthyr; but at Weston-super-Mare their share of the total vote slumped from 37% in 1929 to 22%, at Rushcliffe from 23% to 13%, and at North Lambeth from 42% to 27%.

Apart from lack of finance, the party suffered from not being able to present itself as an opposition party markedly different from the Labour Party. Early in 1934 Spender had noted that there was in the country a definite 'Drift to the Left' which was affecting the Liberals adversely: people wondered why the Liberals bothered to put up candidates at all — 'we need', he urged, 'a Liberal policy clear and distinct from Labour'.[84] While this was quite easy to formulate, it was extremely difficult to put into practice. For example, late in 1933 the Liberals voted against the government's Marketing and Unemployment Bills; but so too did the Labour Party. In February 1934 the Liberals voted in favour of a motion against the private manufacture of arms; but the motion had been put forward by the Labour Party. In March the Liberals published an 'Address to the Nation' which, while differing in some respects from Socialist statements (it was opposed, for example, to the nationalisation of industry and the Bank of England), was remarkably similar in other respects, particularly in its resolute support for the League of Nations and general disarmament, its desire to see freer trade and the restoration of cuts in unemployment pay, as well as a forward housing policy and national development schemes; on India too, its policy was broadly in line with that of the Labour Party.

This, however, was only one half of the Liberal Party's problem: the other half was to find a policy distinct from that of the National

Government, and this proved to be equally difficult. The National
Government leaders, especially Baldwin and MacDonald, also spoke of
tariffs as an expedient only, and they too hoped to see a return to freer
trade. The National Government also claimed to believe in the efficacy
of the League of Nations, and its India policy was impeccably Liberal.
And in the budget of April 1934 the National Government restored the
cuts in unemployment pay. The National Government in fact had the
middle seat to which Samuel aspired, and try as he might he could not
dislodge it.

Yet he continued to be optimistic about the future, at least publicly.
At the Oxford Summer School for Liberals, held in August 1934, he
told delegates that at the next general election there could well be a
position where there were 200 Conservatives, 200 Labour MPs and
200 Liberals in the House of Commons.[85] In private, however, the
other Liberal leaders despaired of seeing such a situation. Organisation
and morale were at a low ebb and finance was still a major problem. The
summer school itself was perhaps symptomatic of the condition of the
party. Only 120 delegates attended: most of them were elderly, most
were wedded to pre-war free trade, and none was in favour of electoral
co-operation with the Labour Party.[86] Even Muir had become pessimistic. In October 1934 he wrote to Lothian putting the NLF point of
view:[87]

> I take a most gloomy, almost a despairing, view of our prospects. We
> are beaten in advance by the public's idea that we are done for, and
> this affects our own people ... If we put up 400 candidates (which I
> think impossible), we shall forfeit at least 200 deposits.

Muir went on to write that 'when the Liberal Party is destroyed, as it
soon will be,' it might be a good idea to form a Liberty League, which
would be a non-party organisation for the propagation of Liberal principles. Such was the spirit animating the NLF.

Nor was the feeling at Liberal Party Headquarters in Abingdon
Street any less pessimistic, as an exchange of letters between Harcourt
Johnstone and Lothian shows. In reply to Johnstone's invitation to
address the Midlands Liberal Federation, Lothian wrote:[88]

> My difficulty about accepting your proposal that I should speak to
> the Liberal Federation on Jan. 19th [1935] is that at present
> advised, I think the policy of trying to put 400 candidates in the
> field is doomed to hopeless failure. I believe the Liberal vote, if it

can be officially organized, may be a decisive factor at the next election.

Lothian estimated that there were between 200 and 300 constituencies where the outcome of an election would be affected by the distribution of the Liberal votes. He believed that the party should formulate a set of questions on five or six fundamental issues and submit it to all candidates where there was no Liberal standing. 'Holding these views,' he went on, 'how can I go down and attempt to rouse the Midland fraternity to putting up candidates in two-thirds of the constituencies?' Furthermore, Lothian was inclined to think that the Liberal Party had outlived its usefulness: many of its objectives had been achieved, and those remaining were part and parcel of the policies of the National Government, or at least of the progressive Conservative group within the National Government.

In reply Johnstone agreed that in theory Lothian's outline of the course which the party should pursue was probably correct; but he asked him to consider the effect on the constituencies if the Liberal leadership announced that the party intended to contest only 100 or so seats. There would be, he wrote,

> a scream of rage from all the Party Organizations and an immediate collapse of the Associations which had been told that it was not intended that they should contest the election. Then you would have to undertake a sort of educational campaign on your Questionnaire and you must remember that even in a well organized constituency not more than a few hundred Liberals are known by name . . . I agree that it is most improbable as things are now going, that we shall be able to run 400 effective candidates at the General Election, but I think we must try to keep up the bluff until the last moment, or decide here and now to disband the Liberal Party as an organized political entity.[89]

If the Liberal leadership was so pessimistic about the party's future, it was hardly surprising that the rank and file should clutch at any and every straw. One such straw was now proffered by Lloyd George.

After the breakdown of his talks with Samuel in the weeks following the Liberals' move into outright opposition to the National Government, Lloyd George, as we have seen, took a highly individual course. He expressed his general attitude to the official Liberal Party in a letter he wrote to Goronwy Owen, who on behalf of the North Wales Liberal Federation had asked him to lead the Liberal Party out of the wilderness. This Lloyd George refused to do, principally because he felt that 'would lead to an unseemly and unprofitable wrangle in the Party about personalities'. 'I think,' he wrote,

> the Party has missed its opportunity as far as the present generation is concerned . . . Recent by-elections show that the Party is disintegrating rapidly.

He believed that 'the fight for Liberal ideals seems to have passed to the Labour and Socialist sector of the battlefront'. He thought, for instance, that at the 1931 general election only the Labour Party had raised the standard of free trade; that the Liberals' 1929 housing programme had been left entirely to Labour; that Labour alone was protesting about 'economy-minded financiers'; and that since 1931 the League of Nations and disarmament issues had also been left to Labour.[90] While these charges were less than just to the Samuelite Liberals, they seem to have been believed by Lloyd George; they certainly motivated his later course of action, and in that sense are important.

In November and October he again intervened in by-elections in support of Labour candidates where no Liberal was standing. Dr Christopher Addison, a former coalition colleague and now the Labour candidate at Swindon, was described by him as a 'wholehearted and sincere Progressive',[91] and Dr Edith Summerskill, the Labour candidate at the Putney by-election, was recommended by him to Liberal voters because of her outstanding personal qualities, her peace platform and her record of attempting to improve conditions of life for the underprivileged.[92] That she was also a member of the Socialist League was apparently a matter of indifference to him.

Lloyd George did not, however, think that the Labour Party should have things all its own way; nor did he ever subscribe to the Socialist ideal of the Labour Party. And early in 1935 he launched his New Deal campaign, which was intended to draw under one standard all elements dissatisfied with the performance of the National Government over a range of subjects.[93] It was essentially an educative programme designed to ensure that after the next election MPs with 'progressive opinions' would predominate in the House of Commons.[94]

The Liberal Party welcomed Lloyd George's proposals and campaign, but it did not formally ally with him. Some Liberals, notably

Lothian and Walter Layton, had assisted Lloyd George in formulating his proposals, and not surprisingly they thought that

> There is everything to be said for an appeal to the country for an all-party effort towards greater expenditure on public works.[95]

According to Lothian, Lloyd George claimed to have considerable support from within the Liberal Party, especially among the Welsh and Scottish Liberals (including Sir Daniel Stevenson on whose beneficence the Scottish Party depended). Lothian himself had spoken to William Baird, the chairman of the Scottish Liberal Federation, who had thought that most Liberals

> would be glad to see a prominent leading Liberal making a stir on the lines of a policy with which most of them broadly agreed. In short, he thought that Lloyd George's campaign would attract a good deal of friendly support and interest in Scotland.

Lloyd George had probed Lothian about the line Sinclair and Samuel proposed taking: he was certainly keen to have their support. Sinclair was inclined to agree with Lothian's and Layton's view, particularly as Lloyd George's programme seemed to accord

> with the Liberal Address to the Nation and with the policy which the Liberal Party has been advocating since we crossed the floor. Lothian and I also agreed that it might well be — for I entered into no commitment — a good plan for me to make some friendly reference (in my address to the National Liberal Club) to the fact that Lloyd George would be speaking the following day.[96]

Sinclair must have been under the impression that Samuel was not fully alive to the seriousness of his party's plight, for a few days after Lloyd George had launched his campaign Sinclair again wrote to Samuel, this time pointing out that the party was in dire straits and that Lloyd George could not be ignored. His report on the state of the party certainly made gloomy reading, containing as it did sentences like:

> There is a real danger that the Liberal Party may cease to be regarded as an effective fighting force — James Scott, for example, tells me that he is finding difficulty in getting people to stand, and other

people tell me that they know Liberals who were candidates in 1929 and remain Liberals but say that they would not stand again at the next General Election because they would feel that they would have no real chance of winning;

and,

Much curiosity is manifested about the number of candidates which the Liberals could put into the field. One or two Liberals whom I should have thought to be well informed have told me of their conviction that we have only 50 or 60 candidates definitely adopted.

Sinclair thought that the time was rapidly approaching when the party would have to make a 'big effort to arrest public attention and to arouse the fighting spirit of Liberals in the country by dramatic announcements and skilful publicity'. He also thought that it would make a considerable impact if Samuel could announce that the Liberal Party was certainly going to fight at least 400 seats, that it had a number of candidates adopted already, and that it intended to fight every by-election; 'Of course,' Sinclair went on,

the obvious difficulty of fighting bye-elections is that of finance, but it was suggested to me that if we were to make a fighting declaration about the number of candidates we had now in the field [he was hopeful that there were more than 60], the number we intended to have at the General Election, and our resolve to fight bye-elctions we could at the same time make a special public appeal for a fighting fund to be expended only at candidatures at bye-elections or at the General Election.

As far as Lloyd George was concerned, Sinclair thought that they should bide their time and see what response was aroused by his campaign; but they could not afford to delay much longer an appeal of their own.[97]

At the meeting of Liberal ex-Ministers held three days later (24 January), Sinclair's policy towards Lloyd George was endorsed; but it appears that no steps were taken to make preparations for a Liberal appeal along the lines he had outlined to Samuel as essential.[98] Nearly three months after this meeting Spender again appealed to Samuel to authorise the publication of a manifesto signed by the Liberal leaders;[99] but Samuel merely passed on the letter to Sinclair a fortnight later.

Sinclair, who was fighting hard to preserve independent Liberalism in Scotland, also tried to tear Samuel out of the web of inertia which he had spun round himself. 'We suffer badly,' he wrote, 'from our press and from the fact that we present the appearance of hopeless disunity.'[100]

Despite Sinclair's plea in January that it was essential for the party to contest all by-elections, none in fact were contested until May, when Sir George Paish stood for West Edinburgh. The by-election was disastrous for the party, for the Liberal share of the total vote fell from 29.7% in 1929 to 13.1%, and its actual vote was 8,000 below the figure for 1929. Sinclair wrote despairingly to Lothian that

> The West Edinburgh election is only the most recent and most striking of the portents which seem to show that we are unlikely to make much headway on our present lines.

All he could suggest was that the party should play for time and try to prevent an early general election, perhaps by delaying the passage of the government's India Bill.[101] Late in May the parliamentary Liberal Party altered its defence policy, bringing it more into line with that of the National Government.[102] But by voting in favour of an increase in defence expenditure the Samuelites became even less distinguishable from the government, and the problem of creating a viable and separate electoral identity became even more acute.

To add to their woes the Samuelites lost control of the Scottish Liberal Federation for the critical period April-October 1935. In April the chairman of the SLF, William Baird, and a number of the SLF's other principal office bearers, many of whom had welcomed Samuel's decision to move into outright opposition to the National Government in November 1933,[103] decided that the SLF needed the financial support of the Simonites, and that the party's quarrel with the National Government was minor and restricted to domestic issues only, and that some sort of *rapprochement* was needed: and this change of heart they announced in the SLF's annual report, released early in April. Outraged to find in Baird a fifth columnist, Sinclair strove to discredit him, and through James Scott presented to the SLF's Executive Committee a counter-report in which the independence of the SLF from the Liberal Nationals and the National Government was reaffirmed. The counter-report was endorsed by the Executive Committee, but Baird retained his office.[104] This stalemate was broken in July when, following the abject failure of the independent Liberal candidate, Sir George Paish, at the

West Edinburgh by-election in May, and the decision in the same month of the Samuelite MPs to support the government's defence policy, Baird felt strong enough to issue to all SLF office bearers a memorandum advocating 'genuine (if to some extent qualified) co-operation with the National Government, especially at the coming general election'.[105] The memorandum was signed by Baird, by the chairman of the Eastern and Western Committees, and by several of the SLF vice-presidents, including C.M. Weir who had had angry words with Sinclair as long ago as 1932.[106] Sinclair protested at once, and at his suggestion a special meeting was convened to consider the memorandum. At the meeting Sinclair succeeded in getting the matter referred back to the chairman's committee which indeed met that same afternoon and decided to delay further action concerning the proposals contained in the memorandum. It was stalemate once more.

And so it might have remained right up to the general election had it not been that some of Sinclair's followers, if not Sinclair himself, wished to bring Baird to heel.[107] They prepared a counter-memorandum which was debated by the Executive Committee at its September meeting, when the whole matter was referred to a special meeting of the General Council, called for 17 October. Sinclair was perturbed by his turn of events, particularly as he was certain that the parliamentary Liberal Party would support the government in the Abyssinian crisis; but, as he wrote to Samuel, he was also unwilling to damp down what he regarded as the sparks of general Liberal enthusiasm manifest in the nature and intention of the counter-memorandum.[108] At the meeting of 17 October the principal speakers were SLF office bearers, the Liberal National MP and Secretary of State for Scotland, Sir Godfrey Collins, and Sinclair. After an acrimonious debate Sinclair and Scott triumphed and the counter-memorandum was approved by 166 votes to 102.[109] Baird and the other signatories to the memorandum resigned their offices, and Scott was elected to the chair. At the conclusion of the meeting of the General Council, Sinclair convened a meeting of the new Executive Committee, at which the Liberal Party's manifesto 'A Call to Arms' was approved and it was resolved to mount a political offensive in the constituencies. But in fact the initiative had passed to the Liberal Nationals, who for the first time established a separate electoral organisation in Scotland.[110] The Samuelites, their difficulties increased by the unexpected turn of events in Scotland, were feeling the chill of electoral despair well before Baldwin announced that the election would be held on 14 November.

Notes

1. There is as yet no substantial study of the Liberal Party in the 1930s. The best available accounts are R. Douglas, *History of the Liberal Party from 1895 to 1970* (1971) and the Epilogue in T. Wilson, *The Downfall of the Liberal Party, 1914-1935* (1966). For the party's parliamentary history, C.L. Mowat, *Britain Between the Wars 1918-1940* (1955) is still valuable. Also useful are J. Bowle, *Viscount Samuel: a biography* (1957) and Viscount Simon, *Retrospect* (1952). Most recently there is Chris Cook's *A Short History of the Liberal Party 1900-1976* (1976).

2. *Observer*, 28 June 1931; *Manchester Guardian*, 29 and 30 June 1931.

3. R. Bassett, *Nineteen Thirty-One: political crisis* (1958), p. 189.

4. See Chapter 1.

5. The 10.9% includes Liberal Nationals (3.7%), the National Liberals (6.7%) and the Lloyd George Liberals (0.5%).

6. See pp. 23-4.

7. Samuel Papers, Lloyd George to Samuel, 3 Nov. 1931.

8. *Manchester Guardian*, 2 Nov. 1931.

9. Samuel had been defeated at the 1918 general election. He did not return to Westminster until 1929, when he won the Darwen seat at the general election.

10. Samuel Papers, Sinclair to Samuel, 3 Nov. 1931.

11. Tweed had masterminded the various Liberal campaigns since 1926, including that for the 1929 general election. For details of his resignation see *The Times*, 10 Oct. 1931.

12. Transcript of speech recorded for gramophone, *Manchester Guardian*, 23 Oct. 1931.

13. *The Times*, 23 Jan. 1932.

14. *News Chronicle*, 17 Dec. 1931.

15. See the numbers for Dec. 1931, and Jan., Feb. and Mar. 1932.

16. *Liberal Magazine*, Jan. 1932. For Stonehaven's speech see *The Times*, 3 Nov. 1931.

17. *Liberal Magazine*, Feb. 1932.

18. *News Chronicle*, 23 Mar. 1932.

19. *The Times*, 31 Mar. 1932.

20. *News Chronicle*, 23 Mar. 1932.

21. Lloyd George Papers, Lloyd George to Muir, 13 Apr. 1932.

22. Ibid., Muir to Lloyd George, 16 Apr. 1932.

23. Samuel Papers, Muir to Samuel, 22 Apr. 1932.

24. *News Chronicle*, 31 May 1932.

25. *The Times*, 7 June 1932.

26. Ibid., 6 June 1932.

27. *Manchester Guardian*, 22 June 1932.

28. *The Times*, 15 July; *Manchester Guardian*, 21 July 1932.

29. *The Times*, 15 July 1932.

30. Duff Cooper, a close friend of Baldwin and the hero of the famous St George's by-election in March 1931, spoke on behalf of the Conservative candidate. *Manchester Guardian*, 21 July 1932.

31. Samuel Papers, Sinclair to Samuel, July 1932.

32. Mowat, *Britain Between the Wars*, p. 418.

33. Samuel Papers, Snowden to Samuel, 23 Aug. 1932.

34. Ibid., A/89. This file contains a copy of the circular.

35. Ibid., Samuel to Rea, 8 Sept. 1932.

36. For example, R. Bernays at North Bristol.

37. Samuel Papers, Sinclair to Samuel, 2 Sept. contains an assessment of

Lothian's attitude; also Lothian Papers, Lothian to Samuel (copy), 25 Sept. 1932.
38. Samuel Papers, MacDonald to Samuel, 10 Sept. 1932: 'If you go I am no longer head of a combination.'
39. Bowle, *Samuel*, p. 285.
40. HCD, vol. 266, cols. 2347-51, 10 June 1932.
41. *Liberal Magazine*, Aug. 1932, published all the correspondence relating to the incident.
42. See Chapter 1.
43. *The Times*, 29 and 30 Sept. 1932.
44. *Manchester Guardian*, 1 Oct. 1932.
45. *The Times*, 14 Oct. 1932.
46. *Manchester Guardian*, 24 Oct. 1932. In September the Welsh Liberals invited Lloyd George to speak on behalf of an independent Liberal candidate at the Cardiganshire by-election. Lloyd George accepted without consulting Samuel beforehand.
47. Samuel Papers, Muir to Samuel, 1 Oct. 1932.
48. *Daily Express*, 11 Oct. 1932. The letter was addressed to W.R. Davies, the secretary of the NLF.
49. *News Chronicle*, 16 Jan. 1933. Lloyd George told A.J. Cummings that 'Liberalism is in an advanced state of creeping paralysis. The world is whirling towards a catastrophe, and the Liberal Party stands staring on incanting phylacteries.'
50. That same day Lloyd George received and replied to a letter of birthday greetings from Samuel. His reply read: 'Thanks for your kindly message. It was very kind of you to send it. You may rest assured that when I criticise it is from no sense of personal opposition to you or to any of my old colleagues. I wish the occasion had never arisen.' That this was merely 'good form' was shown in his press interview (Samuel Papers, A/155 (VIII), Lloyd George to Samuel).
51. *News Chronicle*, 20, 23 and 31 Jan. 1933; *Manchester Guardian*, 18 and 28 Jan. and 1 Feb. 1933; *The Times*, 27 Jan. 1933.
52. *Daily Herald*, 16 Feb. 1933.
53. *Manchester Guardian*, 13 Mar. 1933.
54. HCD, vol. 276, col. 72, 20 Mar. 1933 .
55. *Liberal Magazine*, June, contains a useful summary of speeches and divisions on these matters in the House of Commons.
56. *The Times*, 21 June 1933.
57. Samuel Papers, Sinclair to Samuel, 18 July 1933.
58. *The Times*, 19 May 1933.
59. *Manchester Guardian*, 19 and 20 May 1933.
60. Samuel Papers, Sinclair to Samuel, 14 Oct. 1933.
61. Ibid., Acland to Samuel, 31 Oct. 1933.
62. Ibid., Sinclair to Samuel, 2 Nov. 1933.
63. *Manchester Guardian*, 17 Nov. Most of them wrote to Samuel to explain their positions. See Samuel Papers, A/95.
64. *Manchester Guardian*, 21 Nov. 1933.
65. See Appendix 2.1.
66. In a speech delivered at Glasgow on 9 Nov. 1933.
67. Speech delivered on 24 Jan. 1934, printed in *Liberal Magazine*, Feb. 1934.
68. *Daily Herald*, 17 Apr. 1934.
69. *News Chronicle*, 4 Aug. 1934.
70. For Muir's position, see also his letters to *Manchester Guardian*, 8 and 14 May 1934. In these he claimed that while co-operation might be possible on a limited and temporary policy, long-term co-operation was impossible because no

Liberal could accept the Socialist objective, because the Labour Party was in favour of internal trade barriers, and because many Liberal organisations would simply ignore a directive from Headquarters to co-operate with the Labour Party: 'Especially since the Hastings Conference of the Labour Party I have thought that the differences between the outlook of the two parties were now too wide to be bridged.'

71. *Daily Telegraph*, 5 May 1934.

72. See for example, *News Chronicle*, 7 May 1934.

73. Samuel Papers, Snowden to Samuel, 20 Nov. 1933.

74. Ibid., Samuel to Lloyd George, 21 Nov. 1933.

75. In his reply to Samuel's initial approach, Lloyd George, on 21 Nov., agreed to meet Samuel on 'Monday'; presumably this meeting took place. The only other letter which refers to the meetings is dated 3 Feb. 1934, in which Lloyd George asked Samuel to send him the 'draft' a few days before they next met. Both letters are in the Samuel Papers.

76. *The Times*, 14 Apr. 1934.

77. *Manchester Guardian*, 14 Apr. 1934.

78. The text of the resolution was forwarded to Lloyd George on 10 Feb. 1934. See Lloyd George Papers, G/17/7/4.

79. *Manchester Guardian*, 21 May 1934.

80. Samuel Papers, Johnstone to Samuel, 26 July 1934. The Central Association even selected a Radical Liberal, Victor Evans, to contest the Merthyr by-election in June.

81. It was only with some difficulty that his friend and devotee, W. Salathiel, the secretary of the WLF, persuaded him to send a message of support to Evans at Merthyr; and even then the message was uncompromising: 'Official liberalism threw away its chances in 1931 by sheer cowardice in a crisis. Stick to your independent attitude.' Lloyd George Papers, G/17/7/10.

82. Samuel Papers, Johnstone to Samuel, 26 July: 'As an individual we gain by his departure, but I fear he will take his seat with him.' Nathan had consulted Lloyd George about his move, and it appears that he received Lloyd George's blessing. Lloyd George Papers, Nathan to Lloyd George, 31 July 1934. See also H. Montgomery Hyde, *Strong for Service: the life of Lord Nathan of Churt* (1968), pp. 111-13.

83. Lloyd George Papers, A.J. Sylvester (who was Lloyd George's spy in the lobbies of Westminster) to Lloyd George, 6 Aug. 1934.

84. Lothian Papers, Spender to Lothian, 29 Jan. 1934.

85. *News Chronicle*, 4 Aug. 1934.

86. An even more pessimistic description of the summer school is given in a letter from Sylvester to Lloyd George (Lloyd George Papers, 6 Aug. 1934). Sylvester quotes Tweed as saying: 'He was depressed by Liberalism before he went to the Summer School, but left feeling that the whole thing was not worth worrying about.'

87. Lothian Papers, Muir to Lothian, 29 Oct. 1934.

88. Ibid., Lothian to Johnstone (copy), 13 Nov. 1934.

89. Ibid., Johnstone to Lothian, 19 Nov. 1934.

90. Lloyd George Papers, Lloyd George to Goronwy Owen, Feb. 1934.

91. *Manchester Guardian*, 23 Oct. 1934.

92. *The Times*, 26 Nov. 1934.

93. Lloyd George launched his New Deal campaign at Bangor on 17 Jan. 1935. This and his subsequent speeches had an exceptionally good press coverage. For his New Deal proposals see M. Thomson, *David Lloyd George: the official biography* (1949), pp. 417-18.

94. Lloyd George Papers, Lloyd George to Sir Edward Grigg, 13 Jan. 1935:

'I have always told you that I thought nothing could be done until after the next election. The result will force drastic changes in policy and personnel. S[tanley] B[aldwin] will then be faced with a new situation.' Grigg was acting as an intermediary between Lloyd George and Baldwin on the subject of possible talks between the two about the former's New Deal proposals. For a sketchy account (none other is available) see K. Middlemas and J. Barnes, *Baldwin: a biography* (1969), pp. 808-10. There is a fuller account in C.T. Stannage, 'Lloyd George and the Politics of "Agreement" 1931-1935', unpublished seminar paper, Beaverbrook Library, Jan. 1970.

95. Samuel Papers, Sinclair to Samuel, 11 Jan.1935, in which Sinclair reports on his talks with Lothian and others. See also Minute Book of the Eastern Organizing Committee of the SLF, Jan. and Feb. 1935.

96. Samuel Papers, A/155 (IX).

97. Ibid., Sinclair to Samuel, 21 Jan. 1935.

98. *Liberal Magazine*, Feb. 1935.

99. Samuel Papers, Spender to Samuel, 15 Apr. 1935.

100. Ibid., Sinclair to Samuel, 4 May 1935.

101. Lothian Papers, Sinclair to Lothian, 8 May 1935.

102. HCD, vol. 302, cols. 483-6, 22 May 1935. In the course of the debate Sinclair had said guardedly: 'I agree with deep reluctance – I would even say with repugnance –that a case for an expansion in our air armaments has been made out' (cols. 393-4).

103. *Liberal Magazine*, Dec. 1933.

104. Samuel Papers, Sinclair to Samuel, 8 May 1935.

105. The contents and subsequent history of the memorandum are contained in the Minute Book of the Liberal Party in Scotland for 1935.

106. See *News Chronicle*, 14 Mar. 1932; *Manchester Guardian*, 16 Mar. 1932. Weir, then chairman of the Dumbartonshire Liberal Association, resented Sinclair's intervention into the Dumbartonshire by-election.

107. The leading figure seems to have been Dr J. Fraser Orr, a member of the Executive Committee of the SLF and the Liberal candidate for Linlithgow at the 1929 general election. In the official records of the party the counter-memorandum is referred to as the 'Requisition'.

108. Samuel Papers, Sinclair to Samuel, 16 Sept. 1935. In fact between 11 Sept. and 17 Oct. several of the signatories of the Requisition withdrew their objections to Baird's memorandum, and Baird was moved to ask one of the Requisition's sponsors whether it was being proceeded with (Minute Book of the General Council of the Liberal Party of Scotland, Sept. 1935).

109. From Sept. the *Scotsman* and the *Glasgow Herald* reported the split fully. See particularly *Scotsman*, 12 Sept., 11 and 18 Oct. 1935; *Glasgow Herald*, 18 Oct. 1935. Both newspapers approved of Baird's memorandum.

110. *Scotsman*, 24 Oct. 1935.

4 THE TIMING OF THE ELECTION

At the time of the 1931 general election it was thought by most people
that once the National Government had taken steps to deal with the
economic crisis Parliament would dissolve and the ensuing election
would be fought on traditional party lines. A few people, most of them
Conservatives, hinted that the life of the National Government ought
to be prolonged for some time after the immediate crisis had been met,
if only to deal satisfactorily with the problem of the adverse balance
of trade.[1] No one suggested that the National Government should
last beyond the life of a full Parliament; and it was generally agreed that
the following election would be conducted on traditional party lines.
In the event, however, these expectations were not realised. Parliament
was not dissolved immediately the financial crisis was met and the
trade balance restored; and the election, held near the end of the life of
a full Parliament, was not fought on traditional party lines.

There were several reasons for this unanticipated development. From
October 1931 to June 1935 the right to dissolve Parliament lay with
Ramsay MacDonald who was set implacably against both an early
election and one on traditional party lines. From press reports and the
results of by-elections held early in the life of the 1931 Parliament it
was clear to him that his National Labour Group was fast losing credibility with the electorate;[2] he had to gamble that the effluxion of time
might bring about a reversal of this unfortunate trend. Furthermore, his
own eviction from Seaham would almost certainly follow a return to
party politics.[3] When eventually the general election was held Mac-
Donald did not shirk the contest at Seaham even though he expected to
be defeated.[4] But it does not seem unreasonable to suggest that it was
a prospect which he wished to defer for as long as was possible. Less
negative grounds for not calling an early general election could be
found in the performance of the National Government. At the Ministry
of Agriculture Walter Elliot was beginning to introduce legislation of at
least a quasi-Socialistic character; at the Foreign Office Simon was conducting affairs in a manner which by and large met with MacDonald's
approval; and at the India Office Hoare's policy was sufficiently Liberal
to be in accord with MacDonald's own.[5] While he was head of a government, some of whose policies mirrored his own views, he was hardly
likely to rush precipitately into a general election.

Nor was he pressed to do so by Baldwin, though the latter was motivated by rather different considerations. In the first place the continued existence of the National Government was a convenient prop to his leadership of the Conservative Party. In 1930 and 1931 he had faced and defeated challenges to his leadership from Winston Churchill and from the press lords: it had been a 'damned near thing'.[6] By greatly swelling the number of Conservative MPs whose political survival was dependent on the continuation of 'national' government[7] the 1931 general election had placed Baldwin in an unassailable position, one he was unlikely to jeopardise by forcing MacDonald to call an early general election. For the same reason Baldwin was keen to see the next election fought by the Conservative Party under the aegis of the National Government.

Like MacDonald he saw no pressing reason why an election should be held early. By-elections in 1932 and for much of 1933, while showing some swing to Labour, were not unduly depressing; the government's India policy owed much to him; and industry was showing clear signs of recovery, which happy trend could be – and was – attributed to the government's tariff and cheap money policies.[8] There were also considerations more personal in character, notably his admiration for and friendship with MacDonald. Baldwin simply was reluctant to force MacDonald into the political wilderness.[9] All the factors considered here increased the odds against an early general election.

In public, of course, Baldwin justified the continued existence of the National Government in terms other than those considered in the previous paragraph. Until about September 1932 he argued that it would be irresponsible of the National Government to hold an election until the effects on the economy of the introduction of tariffs could be gauged satisfactorily.[10] Prompted, however, by the resignation of the Liberal Ministers in September and the obvious need to paper over the cracks in the facade of national government,[11] Baldwin began to incorporate in his speeches certain new lines of justification, notably 'the increasing difficulties of the world situation'.[12] The strength of this new position – *vis-à-vis* one based on something as specific as the impact of tariffs – lay in its vagueness; the 'difficulties of the world situation' were legion and there would be no end to them.

The resolution carried by the Labour Party at its annual conferences in 1932 and 1933 provided Baldwin with yet another rewarding line. In his own words, the real fight now was against 'crude, rank Socialism', and no political force was better equipped to conduct the fight than the National Government. Baldwin later expanded this line of reasoning into something rather more high-sounding and less specific; namely that the National Government was Britain's bulwark against dictatorships of the right and of the left.[13] Set against a background of European unsettlement this reasoning seems to have struck a responsive chord in the British electorate.

The aspect of government policy with which Baldwin was most concerned was that dealing with India.[14] His determination to legislate for constitutional reform in India undoubtedly was an important reason why he did not want to make an early appeal to the country. Early in 1933 the government issued a White Paper on the subject, and in June a Joint Select Committee of both Houses was set up to examine the White Paper and to make recommendations. The committee deliberated for the next eighteen months, and reported in December 1934. An India Bill was drafted, and in February 1935 it was given a first reading in the House of Commons. Due to the spirited opposition of the parliamentary spokesmen of the India Defence League its passage thereafter was very slow; indeed it was not until July that the Bill was enacted. Baldwin's insistence that the problem of India should be settled in the lifetime of the1931 Parliament, and his difficulty in achieving that end speedily, determined that the election would not be held in the first half of 1935.

Without so firm an objective Baldwin might have succumbed to the vicissitudes of the winter of 1934-5 and called an early general election. Certainly the events of these months brought the awkward colossus of the National Government to its knees — down, if not out. In the first place there was a succession of adverse by-election results, notably at Putney where a Conservative almost succeeded in losing one of the safest government seats in the country.[15] Secondly, much of the government's energies had to be diverted into beating off the continuous barrage of criticism from Churchill and his India Defence League colleagues. Thirdly, the government found itself in the centre of a storm following the release of its new unemployment regulations, criticism coming as strongly from within the Conservative Party as without.[16] Finding himself beset upon from all sides Baldwin grumbled to Lord Salisbury that it was 'The worst mess I have ever been associated with.'[17] But there was more trouble to come. A number of the younger Conservative MPs, notably Harold Macmillan and Robert Boothby, were anxious to see the public image of the government improved through the inclusion in the Cabinet of some dynamic youngsters like themselves; still other Conservatives wished to see proportionately more of their number in the Cabinet, with a corresponding reduction in the representation of Liberal Nationals and National Labour.[18] Furthermore, that thorn in the side of all governments since 1922, Lloyd George, was active again.[19] In short the difficulties of the National Government were such that at the turn of the year political commentators began to suggest the likelihood of a Cabinet reconstruction probably followed by an early election.

In mid-January MacDonald tried to still the rumours. He told a meeting of electors in his own constituency that he would return to Seaham when the next election was held, which in his opinion would not be in the immediate future.[20] Nevertheless the rumours persisted and reached a peak of intensity in the second and third weeks of February, following the disastrous showing of the government at the Wavertree by-election. A snap election with a Labour victory was widely predicted, and panic in the city saw War Loan, Conversion Loan 2 and Consols fall sharply.[21] It needed the massive authority of the Chancellor of the Exchequer to restore order. From Edgbaston Neville Chamberlain spoke reassuringly to supporters of the government:

> Don't worry about elections. There won't be any election yet awhile . . . The Government had so far not even considered the date of the general election.

This impression he confirmed in a speech delivered at Bradford a week later.[22] Other government spokesmen hastened to offer similar reassurances, and the rumours were dispelled, albeit slowly.[23]

Public debate about the timing of the next general election was not renewed until April when the rumours began again in a modified form when the press publicised a circular, issued by Conservative Central Office, which ordered constituency organisations to begin preparations for an election.[24] In the first weeks of May the celebrations of the King's Jubilee created so widespread a feeling of goodwill that it was thought by many people, and feared by some, that Baldwin and MacDonald could not fail to be alive to the electoral implications, and respond by calling an election in June.[25] It was also widely rumoured that MacDonald and Baldwin would change places before such an election was held. Substance was given to the rumours when the government did extremely well at two by-elections in Scotland. But the one factor which militated most against a June election was the slow passage of the India Bill, particularly through the House of Lords; and there is no evidence to suggest that MacDonald and Baldwin were so attracted to the idea of taking immediate advantage of the general feeling of bonhomie created by the King's Jubilee celebrations that they were prepared to hold over the India Bill until an election had been held. And by the time the Bill was read for a third time in the Lords the moment for a snap election had passed, and members dispersed at once for the summer vacation.

With a summer election now out of calculations it was confidently predicted that an election would take place in the autumn,[26] though government spokesmen, particularly Central Office officials, stressed that the following spring was also a likely time for the election. In June MacDonald at last retired and Baldwin became Prime Minister. The main change in his Cabinet was that Sir Samuel Hoare replaced Simon at the Foreign Office. Self-seekers like Sir Edward Grigg were not obliged, and the 'young Turks' of the Conservative Party were still left queuing for ministerial tickets; and the diehard right of the Conservative Party continued to lack representation at the Cabinet level.[27] From the nature of the Cabinet reconstruction it was clear to all that Baldwin intended to fight the next election under the aegis of the National Government.[28] Perhaps encouraged by the very few Conservative defections during the later stages of the India Bill debate,[29] he seems to have gambled (successfully as it turned out) that the exigencies of a general election would force the dissidents to toe the leadership line. He was now in a position to call an election at a time of his own choosing; but he was anxious initially to keep speculation to a minimum and 'invited his colleagues to avoid references in public speeches to the possible dates of the next General Election'.[30]

In private, however, Baldwin had begun to give serious thought to the date of the election. Early in June he noted that the new electoral register would come into force in mid-October, and at one private meeting he seems to have discussed the possibility of going to the country on a limited rearmament programme.[31] Certainly some time in July he held a meeting of the Cabinet 'Big Six' (Baldwin, MacDonald, Chamberlain, Runciman, Simon, Hoare) to discuss the date of the next general election. At this meeting there was general agreement that an early election should be held, perhaps in October or November. Baldwin, however, refused to commit himself, saying that 'he did not intend to take any decision (even provisional) until after he returned from Aix'. Neville Chamberlain, who recorded this meeting, added that Baldwin 'is now in the condition that usually overtakes him at this time of year, when he is quite unable to set his mind to anything or even to listen to what you say'.[32] Nevertheless, Baldwin mustered the energy to instruct Sir Patrick Gower, the Chief Publicity Officer at Central Office, to prepare a brief on the pros and cons of various dates for the election, at the same time giving Gower to believe that in his view the choice lay between November 1935 and January 1936.[33] Before he had time to consider Gower's reply, however, he left for Aix-les-Bains for his annual holiday. It was reported in *The Times* that Baldwin intended to 'think about' the election while on vacation.[34]

If Aix-les-Bains was good for Baldwin's constitution, reflection from there on recent events at home could not have been otherwise than good for his soul. Much of the previous winter's unrest over the government's unemployment regulations had dissipated with the decision to restore the old scales of payment. The merry month of May had ushered in a clearly discernable by-electoral swing back to the National Government, attributable in part to the timely removal of the last of the 1931 salary restrictions and a measure of tax relief in the April budget. Furthermore, each month now brought news of marked improvement in trade and unemployment figures.[35] And the King's Jubilee, celebrated in a sunny May, had produced a national mood which was not conducive to division and strife, even of a traditional party character. Within his own party, now that the India question had been settled, there was sweetness and light; even that redoubtable duo Sir Henry Page-Croft and Winston Churchill were on record as saying that they were prepared to see the party fight the election under the aegis of the National Government.[36] Finally, in the last session of Parliament the Samuelite Liberals had voted for the government's defence proposals, thereby making it even easier than previously for the National Government to claim that it was the embodiment of Liberalism in the country. Reflection on this timely conjunction of events must have added to the pleasures of Baldwin's holiday at Aix-les-Bains.

Nevertheless, Baldwin seems to have arrived back in London with an open mind about the most suitable date for a general election. While he was away several leading Conservatives had advocated an autumn election, among them Winston Churchill and Lord Ebbisham;[37] but the National Coordinating Committee had issued a list of speakers and dates for the period 1 October to 6 December, apparently on the assumption that an election would not be held until the New Year.[38] Labour and Liberal spokesmen were fairly confident that Baldwin would opt for an autumn election. And Baldwin now had before him Gower's memorandum on the subject.

The choice as Gower understood it lay between early November and January 1936, for late November and December could be ruled out because of the unpopularity of any disruption to the Christmas trade; and he told Baldwin that his preference was for January. There were several reasons for Gower's choice. He contended that the electors needed to see a few more months of improvement in trade and employmet: what was lacking at present, he thought, was a 'psychological feeling of slow and steady progress'. He argued that the Christmas employment figure was usually high, that a January election would involve no interference with parliamentary business, and that for most people January was a 'pretty dull month'. Gower believed, as did many a government supporter, that the Cabinet should settle the vexed question of unemployment assistance before going to the country. He reasoned that if nothing was done

> Our Members and Candidates might be accused of running away from a difficult task just as the Socialists did in 1931.

There were also organisational factors to consider. Gower explained to Baldwin that for some time past constituency organisations had done little in the way of propaganda on behalf of the government. He acknowledged that the 'excellent work' of the National Publicity Bureau had improved the situation; 'but', he added, 'even so I do not feel that a three months campaign after a long period of stagnation is sufficient to create the desired effect'. And he doubted whether any statements of party policy had been drawn up with a view to an election, and this, he thought, would take some time.

The area of greatest concern to Gower was international affairs. He thought that developments in Abyssinia were fraught with danger for the continued existence of the National Government, for if Italy felt compelled to withdraw from the League of Nations, and thereby reduce its viability as a peace-keeping instrument, then almost certainly the blame would fall on the National Government. In particular, it seemed clear to Gower that any apparent weakening of the League would result in the redirection of the critically important Liberal vote away from the National Government. In short, Gower deprecated

> the holding of a General Election until some time had elapsed in which to explain the position to the country and counter the misrepresentations in which our opponents would inevitably indulge in order to discredit the Government.

Gower concluded his memorandum by noting that while there was a
good deal of quiet support for the government there was not any wave
of enthusiasm which would sweep it back into office. He added that it
was necessary to create 'a real national feeling', particularly as

> the policy of frightening the electors may not be entirely successful.
> It is not easy to frighten the electorate twice running, and one's
> efforts in this direction may be made difficult owing to the fact that
> the Socialists have spent three years in trying to persuade them that
> the fears that were created last time were largely due to scaremon-
> gering. If we are to win the next election it will be on a positive not
> a negative policy.[39]

Baldwin was similarly advised by Alan Chorlton, MP for the Platting
division of Manchester.[40] Chorlton believed that the election should be
held in February because in the cotton areas the government's unpopularity over the Spindles Bill was still a great deal stronger than Baldwin
realised. He also argued that as yet there was not anything with which
to scare the people, and 'fear is the only way to make a great many
people go to the poll'. Chorlton recognised, however, that a February
election would mean that the question of the unemployment regulations would have to be faced again,[41] and remembering the outcry on
the previous occasion he thought that this could be an unpleasant task
for the government.

There was one point common to both memoranda which must have
weighed heavily with Baldwin. If he went to the country as late as
January or February 1936 he would find it hard to delay the immediate
introduction of a new set of unemployment regulations, and with the
memory of the previous winter's vicissitudes fresh in his mind it seems
reasonable to suggest that he did not wish to raise the subject again,
especially as since February his 'standstill' policy on unemployment
regulations had not appeared to be unduly harmful to the public image
of the National Government. If, as Neville Chamberlain recorded in
August,[42] Baldwin did think that unemployment would be an
important election issue, he may well have reasoned that there was less
risk attached to a policy of not introducing new regulations and being
charged with 'running away' from the problem, than of introducing new
regulations which, because of the public's sensitivity on the subject,
were bound to be controversial, even within his own party. If Baldwin
did reason along these lines it follows that he would prefer an autumn
election to one in the spring.

The other points put by Gower and Chorlton seem also to have left
Baldwin unconvinced that a spring election was preferable to one in the
autumn. Both advisers had been concerned that there seemed to be
nothing at hand with which to scare the electors. But Baldwin may well
have argued that the 'something required' could arise in a very short
time, as had occurred in 1924. Baldwin may have been disturbed by
Gower's gloomy report on the state of party organisation in the constituencies. On the other hand he may also have believed that the
National Publicity Bureau was having a greater impact on the electorate
than Gower thought: certainly he was aware that the bureau's activities
had discomfited the government's opponents.[43] And concerning
Gower's view that it would be wise to wait until improved trade and
employment were more permanent features of the economy, Baldwin
may well have believed that the recovery indicated in the figures of the
previous few months was already having the psychological effect
desired by Gower. He may also have been advised by the Treasury that
the present trend would continue, and that he need not fear a slackening
in the rate of recovery.[44]

Baldwin was alive to the electoral implications of any development
in international affairs which reduced the credibility of the League of
Nations as a peace-keeping instrument. The importance of the distribution of the Liberal vote to the continued electoral success of the
National Government had not been overlooked at any time since 1931,
but an incident in March 1935 brought the question into particularly
sharp focus. Shortly after the Lambeth Norwood by-election in that
month, Baldwin had received a report from Lloyd George in which it
was claimed that at recent by-elections National Government candidates had not received any Liberal votes. This news probably discon-
certed Baldwin, but a rejoinder, prepared by Sir Reginald Topping, the
Conservative Party's principal agent, showed that at least one in three
Liberals were still voting for the National Government.[45] Topping's
paper probably went some way to reassure Baldwin, but the incident
could only have increased his sensitivity to the need to appease Liberal
opinion. There seems no reason to doubt, therefore, that Baldwin, like
Gower, was concerned that the Abyssinian affair might have unfortunate consequences at Geneva and in Britain.

Nevertheless, he seems to have been a little less pessimistic about
the future than was Gower; or rather, his course of action from August
would suggest that he thought that the state of affairs postulated by
Gower might be forestalled were the government to take steps to mini-
mise the worst effects of a crisis at home and abroad. Indeed some-

thing along these lines had been under way for some time. In June, with an eye to the public image of the government, Baldwin had appointed Anthony Eden, the government's 'blue-eyed boy' as regards disarmament and the League of Nations, to the post of Minister with special responsibilities for League of Nations affairs, with a seat in the Cabinet.[46] He had been urged to do this by Hoare, whose analysis of the international situation and likely repercussions at home closely approximated Gower's.[47] However, the public reaction to the announcement of the result of the Peace Ballot seemed to indicate that further insurance cover should be sought, perhaps in the form of a 'big speech' at Geneva.[48] If this succeeded in rallying public opinion, particularly Liberal opinion, to the support of the National Government, there would be no need to postpone an election until January or February. From July until the election in November it would appear that the foreign policy of the National Government was conditioned by electoral considerations, and vice versa.

The relationship of foreign affairs and the timing of the election merits further consideration, particularly as it has exercised Baldwin's biographers. Baldwin's official biographer, G.M. Young, suggests that his subject was keeping an eye on the impending election while forming his foreign policy; but Middlemas and Barnes, writing nearly twenty years later, are less certain. Baldwin, they write, 'was an old and genuine supporter of the League who had never succumbed to the obvious myths prevalent among its more natural allies'. For this reason they are reluctant to agree with the suggestion that Baldwin 'allowed electoral expediency to outweigh his natural caution'.[49] But such would appear to be the case.

By mid-June 1935 the implications of Mussolini's Abyssinian venture had put the Cabinet on its mettle. At the Cabinet meeting of 19 June the new Foreign Secretary, Sir Samuel Hoare, proposed to approach Mussolini with the suggestion that Abyssinia should be partitioned — Mussolini to have Ogaden, and Abyssinia to get a strip of coastline with a corridor through to it. In support of his proposal Hoare cited the opinion of Sir Eric Drummond, British Ambassador in Rome, that any other course of action would be futile. After a short discussion the Cabinet agreed to Hoare's proposal.[50] Between this and the next meeting the result of the Peace Ballot was announced. At the next meeting the Cabinet did not refer to the possibility of partition, but considered a proposal to invoke Clause XVI of the League Charter against Italy.[51] In typically muddled fashion it also concluded that as yet there was no question of sanctions being applied, and that a possible meeting of the signatories of the 1906 Agreement (that is, further circumvention of the League of Nations) should not be ruled out. But a change in direction was becoming apparent.

At the Cabinet meeting of 22 July the Ministers were still vaguely hopeful that the signatories to the 1906 Agreement might meet to discuss the affair; but, as at the previous meeting, no mention was made of the possibility of partitioning Abyssinia. Furthermore, Ministers now referred openly to the climate of opinion within Britain. The meeting resolved that Eden should hold talks with Laval, the French Foreign Minister, and impress on him that Britain would honour its League obligations, as this was the 'present trend of development of public opinion in this country'.[52] Sanctions were still thought of as a last resort, but the change of direction was now readily apparent nevertheless.

In August the Abyssinian affair continued to hold the stage. On 20 and 21 August Hoare tested the climate of opinion by holding talks separately with Herbert Samuel, Austen Chamberlain, Lloyd George, Lord Robert Cecil and perhaps others, on the future direction of British foreign policy, especially with reference to the Italian question. Without exception they advised him that collective action through the machinery of the League was the only possible policy. Hoare quickly came to the conclusion that

> if the Government edged out of collective action of this kind, a great wave of public opinion would sweep the Government out of power ... this view is confirmed by the Press Department of the Foreign Office, the foreign editor of the *Yorkshire Post* declaring that 75% of the north of England is behind the Covenant.[53]

Hoare conveyed his views to his colleagues at the meeting of the Cabinet of 21 August. He concluded by asserting that

> It was abundantly clear that the only safe line for His Majesty's Government was to try out the regular League of Nations procedure.

His colleagues did not demur.[54] The government's course was now firmly set, and all obstacles were swept away, including an observation from Drummond — whose advice had been cited approvingly only several weeks earlier — that Mussolini's course was also firmly set, and that nothing the League might do would deter him.[55] Thus after nearly five years of pursuing a foreign policy which had appeared to lack appeal to public opinion, the National Government reached for and tasted the fruits of popularity in this sphere; and it hoped to continue to enjoy them.

The commitment was duly made at Geneva where on 11 September Hoare made a notable declaration of the intention of the National Government to fulfil its obligations under the Covenant.[56] His statement was given a rapturous reception in Britain, and for the government it seemed that at long last the sun was shining.[57] It hardly mattered that the sanctions question had still to be settled or that sanctions when applied might fail or drive Mussolini into war with Britain and France. The National Government could calculate that these things would not occur overnight; better in the circumstances to get an election over before the storm clouds appeared on the horizon; and that meant, in effect, an autumn election. Had the decision to hold the election rested with Chamberlain or Hoare it would probably have been taken in September;[58] but it rested with Baldwin, and was not taken until October.

Baldwin delayed a decision for several reasons. In part he did so because it was his way to ruminate upon new developments:[59] in this case the sun seemed to be shining but was it really and truly shining? This was true of his response to the rapturous applause which greeted Hoare's Geneva speech. It was equally true of his response to the signs, so obvious since July, that the Conservative Party was once more a cohesive political force. As late as 28 September *The Times* was permitted to publish an official list of speeches to be delivered by Ministers between 1 October and 10 December, which seemed to indicate that there would be no election until the New Year. But in the first week of October, at its annual conference, the Conservative Party carried what amounted to a unity resolution, and Baldwin even received a kindly note from Churchill who urged him to go to the country at once, as did influential newspaper editors Dawson and Gwynne.[60] In the same week it emerged that the Labour Party was divided deeply over policy and leadership, while the August unemployment figures showed a fall to be below two million for the first time since 1930; the trade figures were also favourable. Furthermore, although his National Labour colleagues wanted a spring election, Simon and the Liberal Nationals were known to be in favour of a November election.[61] Even Baldwin could see that the sun was really shining at last; and yet he continued to hesitate, or at least he gave the appearance of doing so. On 15 October Neville Chamberlain wrote to his sister that 'In spite of all you see in the papers the Cabinet have never discussed, much less decided the date of

the election.' Chamberlain himself had already delivered what
amounted to the government's opening election address (at Glasgow)
but at the Cabinet meeting of 16 October Baldwin refused to be drawn
as to the date of the election, even though an election programme was
discussed. It was understood by Ministers that an announcement was
only a matter of days away.[62]

Opinion outside Cabinet had already decided that an election would
be held in November. Late in September the Liberal Party had arranged
for area conferences to be held 'as part of an election campaign'.[63] On 8
October *The Times*, whose editor Geoffrey Dawson was on the closest
possible terms with Baldwin, claimed that an early election was not
generally anticipated: it suggested – partly on the basis of the contents
of a letter from Sir John Simon to his constituents – that 14 November
was the most likely date. The *Manchester Guardian* agreed with *The
Times*' assessment, as did several other newspapers. And by mid-
October several Liberal and Labour spokesmen had stated that Baldwin
would almost certainly go to the country before the end of
November.[64]

On the morning of 18 October there was another meeting of the 'Big
Six', at which it was decided that the election should be held on 14
November. Later that day Baldwin requested the King to dissolve
Parliament on 23 October. At a Conservative Party rally in Worcester
on 19 October Baldwin announced that

It was only yesterday that I made up my mind that in the present
circumstances it would be impossible to delay the election now and
that it must come very quickly.

The actual date, he added, would be announced when Parliament re-
assembled on 23 October, but it would be the earliest possible; and this,
as everyone knew, was 14 November.[65] Apparently as an afterthought,
though perhaps really as a gesture calculated to win him a vote of
sympathy or gratitude at the election, he said that it was unlikely that
he would ever contest a general election again.[66]

The final scene of the final act took place in the House of Commons
on 23 October, when Baldwin announced that he had decided to hold
the election on 14 November.[67] In the course of his speech he referred
to Macaulay's observation that a wise Prime Minister will dissolve Parliament a year before the legal date; he had taken the trouble to find out
if this happened in practice, and he reported that it was customary,
especially when the government of the day had a large majority and was

well supported in the country. He then outlined some of the standard reasons why only the autumn and the first six weeks of the year were suitable for an election. Having whittled the choice down to January or November, he informed the House — which had just taken the serious step of endorsing the League's decision to impose sanctions on Italy — that he 'detected signs coming of a lull in international affairs' which would leave November free for an election. He added that 'he could not say the same in January'. Shortly after, the 1931 Parliament was dissolved and members dispersed to prepare for the election.

Notes

1. See for example, the manifesto issued by Baldwin to the press on 9 Oct. 1931.
2. For National Labour's decline in popularity see the following press reports on by-elections: *Manchester Guardian*, 17 Mar. 1932 (Dumbartonshire); *Daily Herald*, 13 Apr. 1932 (Wakefield); *The Times*, 18 Feb. 1933 (Rotherham).
3. At Seaham at the 1931 general election MacDonald had defeated an obscure Labour candidate by the relatively narrow margin of 5,000 votes. Between that time and the commencement of the election campaign in 1935 MacDonald visited Seaham twice, and on both occasions met with a hostile reception, especially from the miners who formed the larger part of the electorate. For the comments of a partial witness (MacDonald's conqueror in 1935), see E. Shinwell, *Conflict Without Malice* (1955), p. 128.
4. See for example, Baldwin Papers, vol. 47, MacDonald to Baldwin, 13 Nov. 1935: 'You must not be surprised if the result is not what we would like it to be.'
5. These assertions are made on the basis of a general appraisal of the Cabinet Minutes for 1932-5.
6. There is a pithy account of the attacks on Baldwin in R. Blake, *The Conservative Party from Peel to Churchill* (1970), pp. 233-4.
7. See Chapter 1.
8. For Baldwin's part in the formation of the government's India and foreign policies, see K. Middlemas and J. Barnes, *Baldwin: a biography* (1969), Chs. 26 and 28; see also *The Times* 31 May 1933, 3 Dec. 1934, and 22 July 1935 for some of his speeches on industrial recovery and agriculture.
9. Middlemas and Barnes, *Baldwin*, p. 640. Also R. Rhodes James (ed.), *Memoirs of a Conservative: J.C.C. Davidson's Memoirs and Papers 1910-1937* (1969), p. 378: 'He seemed to feel that MacDonald was the Prime Minister, and that he [Baldwin] was not going to be the cause of his removal.'
10. In March he told a meeting of Conservatives that Britain was about to turn the corner into prosperity: but, he added, 'we have yet much to do, so do not look for a general election for another four years' (*Daily Express*, 16 Mar. 1932). At a later meeting at Caernarvon he countered criticism on the tariff issue with: 'As leader of the largest party I honestly can say that I have not yet begun to think about the next election. There is too much work to be done now which I am going to face, and I ask Liberal friends to pull at the oars as I am pulling, and not to bother about the election, the policy, the party, or anything else' (*Daily Express*, 16 Apr. 1932). Late in April he informed the Conservative Women's Conference that the government had introduced tariffs not as a matter of prin-

ciple but as an expediency made possible by the mandate of the 1931 election; and until tariffs had begun to have an effect on the economy he was prepared to court possible losses at by-elections rather than hold a general election. Referring to a recent by-election he added: 'I am prepared to lose a dozen Wakefields for the ultimate good of the country.'

11. Following the resignation of the Liberal Ministers in September the daily newspapers ridiculed the claim of the government to the title 'National'. See *Daily Mail, Daily Express, Daily Herald, News Chronicle* and *Manchester Guardian* for 29 and 30 Sept. 1932. Only *The Times* and the *Daily Telegraph* rallied to the support of the government.

12. *Manchester Guardian*, 1 Oct. 1932, report of Baldwin's wireless address to the nation. In the course of this address Baldwin made quite clear his attitude to the question of the continuance of the National Government: 'A little over a year ago the Ship of State was heading for the rocks. The skipper had to change his course suddenly, and many of his officers and most of his crew deserted. It was a case of all hands to the pumps, and I signed on with my friends, not for six months or a year. I signed on for the duration be the weather fair or foul and I am going to stick to the ship whether it goes to the bottom or comes into port and I think the latter is a good deal more likely.'

13. Report of his speech to the annual conference of the Conservative Party (*The Times*, 8 Oct. 1932). In the same speech Baldwin noted that in his view there would be no election 'for some years yet'. See also *The Times*, 26 June 1933; *Daily Telegraph*, 7 Oct. 1933.

14. Middlemas and Barnes, *Baldwin*, Ch. 26, particularly p. 698: 'There could be no doubt that after 1930 Baldwin had made up his mind irrevocably that India was to be his great mission, perhaps the last, because for it he was prepared if necessary to go out of politics altogether.'

15. See Appendix 2.1.

16. Baldwin Papers, vol. 6. For example, Irene Ward to Baldwin, 4 Apr. 1935.

17. Middlemas and Barnes, *Baldwin*, p. 809.

18. H. Macmillan, *Winds of Change 1914-1939* (1966), p. 300 ff. Also Baldwin Papers. vol. 47.

19. See Chapter 3.

20. *The Times*, 18 Jan. 1935.

21. Ibid., 12 and 13 Feb. 1935.

22. Ibid., 16 and 23 Feb. 1935.

23. Ibid., 14 and 16 Feb. for reports of speeches by Sir T.V. Bowater, MP for the City of London, and Cunliffe-Lister, Minister for Colonies.

24. See *Daily Herald, The Times* and *Manchester Guardian*, 23 Apr. 1935.

25. For Lloyd George's fear that Baldwin would hold a summer election see T. Jones, *Lloyd George* (1951), p. 146. Also Lloyd George Papers, G/141/24/4. The Labour Party was less fearful, but leaders such as Henderson thought that a summer election was a possibility. See Henderson's address to the National Conference of Labour Women (*The Times*, 17 May 1935).

26. See for example, *Spectator*, 14 June: 'There is little doubt that as soon as Parliament reassembles after the Whitsun recess, the pressure will increase for an election in the autumn. All the indications are that the appeal to the country will be made in November at the latest.'

27. Baldwin Papers, vol. 47, contain some correspondence relating to Cabinet reconstruction. See also Neville Chamberlain Papers, the political diaries and journals, entries for 8, 18 and 29 Apr., 3 and 17 May, and 3 June 1935.

28. Baldwin had in fact made this clear as early as December 1934 in a New Year message to the Primrose League. See *Daily Telegraph*, 28 Dec. 1934. But the events of January and February 1935 had given rise to hopes that he might be

persuaded to change his mind. Certainly Ramsay MacDonald was relieved to be able to enter in his diary for 11 February 1935, 'Definite statement from Baldwin and Neville [that] they were not in favour of Party Government either by reconstruction nor by change before the General Election' (cited in D. Marquand, *Ramsay MacDonald* (1977), p. 767).

29. At least five Conservative MPs asked that the party whip be withdrawn from them but the revolt spread no further. See Baldwin Papers, vol. 107. Even this revolt was not due entirely to the India question. See the correspondence between the Duchess of Atholl and others and Baldwin in May 1935.

30. Cab. 23/82, 26 June 1935.

31. A. Baker, *The House is Sitting* (1958), p. 38. Also Jones, *Lloyd George*, p. 152.

32. Neville Chamberlain Papers, the political diaries and journals, entry for 2 Aug. 1935.

33. Baldwin Papers, vol. 47, Gower to Baldwin, 1 Aug. 1935.

34. *The Times*, 30 July 1935.

35. In June the number of unemployed declined by nearly 45,000 and in July fell to below two million for the first time since 1930 (*Ministry of Labour Gazette*, 1935). After an uncertain first quarter the volume of exports was again increasing; the volume of imports remained steady for the second and third quarters (*Board of Trade Journal*, 1935).

36. For Page-Croft's announcement see *The Times*, 11 June; for Churchill's *The Times*, 25 July. Even the Junior Imperial and Constitutional League now supported the National Government – see *The Times*, 6 May. Perhaps the best source for evidence of growing Conservative unity is *The Times Index* for 1935. In the quarterly volume for January-March there are nearly twenty lines of references to dissensions within the Conservative Party; for April-June, only two lines; and for July-September, none. *The Times* made the new-found unity of the Conservative Party the subject of two editorials at this time: 4 May and 10 June 1935.

37. *The Times*, 25 July and 15 Aug. 1935.

38. Ibid., 13 Aug. 1935.

39. This observation casts some doubts upon the validity of Bassett's assertion that at the 1931 general election the government did not indulge in scaremongering (R. Bassett, *Nineteen Thirty-One: political crisis* (1958), pp. 311 and 327). One reason why Neville Chamberlain wished to see the 1935 election fought on the rearmament issue was that it had overtones of 'fear' about it (I. MacLeod, *Neville Chamberlain* (1961), p. 182).

40. Baldwin Papers, vol. 47, A. Chorlton to G. Lloyd, 1 and 26 July 1935.

41. It was widely held that the government would have to deal with the question of unemployment regulations before it called a general election. See *The Times*, 17 June; *Spectator*, 14 June 1935.

42. Neville Chamberlain Papers, political diaries and journals, 2 Aug. 1935: 'S.B. and the C.O. have been talking on the assumption that it [the election] would turn on unemployment and especially the depressed areas.'

43. Tom Jones (Jones, *Lloyd George*, pp. 146-7) reported to Baldwin in May that Lloyd George was intensely annoyed that the bureau was 'covering the country with paper propaganda while he, Lloyd George, was silent'. The Labour Party was trying frantically to match the bureau in its cinema van work.

44. Treasury opinion is difficult to discern, but Neville Chamberlain certainly favoured an early election. Indeed as late as 2 October he was still desperately trying to get Baldwin to commit himself to an early election. See Neville Chamberlain Papers, political diaries and journals, 2 Aug. and 2 Oct. 1935.

45. Lloyd George Papers, vol. G141, memorandum on the Lambeth Norwood by-election prepared by Henderson Livesy (copy). Baldwin Papers, Topping to

G. Lloyd, 8 Apr: 'the writer says that the Liberals did not vote, but we had a telephone canvass of every elector in the Division whose name appeared in the telephone directory. Two-thirds of the Liberals so canvassed promised to vote for the Conservative candidate, and our records show that most of them carried out their promise. At bye-elections held within the last couple of years, the votes polled indicate that of the Liberals who voted in 1929, one-third of them support the National Government to-day, and two-thirds of them vote against the Government. I think that is probably what happened at Norwood. We polled the type of individual who was likely to be found in the telephone directory; those with more left-wing tendencies voted against us.' Late in May the Samuelite Liberals made an about-turn and henceforth (i.e. up to the general election) supported the government's defence policy. In May also there was a pronounced swing back to the National Government at the West Edinburgh and South Aberdeen by-elections: of the former by-election, the *Spectator* commented (10 May) that 'Herr Hitler has rallied Left Centre opinion here to the side of the Government to an extent that would have seemed incredible even six months ago.' These developments may have reassured Baldwin while making him conscious of the need to retain this new-found support.

46. Whenever the government felt constrained to reply to the criticism that it was not wholeheartedly behind the League of Nations and the Disarmament Conference, it referred to Eden's work and the speeches he made, and at particularly awkward moments such as the fortnight after East Fulham he was sent into the constituencies as the 'walking talking' embodiment of government policy. See *The Times*, 6 Nov. 1933. (Eden spoke on behalf of the Conservative candidate at Skipton.) For a comment on Eden's role see *Spectator*, 31 May 1935.

47. Baldwin Papers, vol. 47, Hoare to Baldwin, 31 May 1935: 'the more I think of it the more sure I am that it is essential, if we are not to run great risks, that Anthony Eden should retain his position in the Foreign Office. I see signs of the position becoming very dangerous if he refuses. From one angle you will be attacked for preferring the old men to the young, from another angle you will be charged with pushing out the champion of the League of Nations Union. If, then, anything goes wrong – and many things may and will go wrong – for instance Mussolini may annexe Ethiopia, and the French may be truculent with Hitler – it will be put down to the fact that you excluded Eden and preferred me. This being so, I greatly hope that you will induce Anthony to stop.'

48. In the Peace Ballot the public was asked to record its vote on the following questionnaire: –

1. Should Great Britain remain a member of the League of Nations?
2. Are you in favour of an all-round reduction in armaments by international agreement?
3. Are you in favour of an all-round abolition of national military and naval aircraft by international agreement?
4. Should the manufacture and sale of armaments for private profit be prohibited by international agreement?
5. Do you consider that, if a nation insists on attacking another, the other nations should combine to compel it to stop by
a) Economic and non-military measures?
b) If necessary, military measures?

'On June 27th, 1935, the results were announced. The total votes cast reached the impressive figure of 11,559,165. Over eleven million answered the first question affirmatively. Over ten million did the same for questions 2, 4 and 5a, while the affirmative vote on no. 3 was not much lower. There was, however, a highly significant drop in the answers to 5b, and those who approved military sanctions were only 6,784,368, though even this showed a striking majority over the negative vote of 2,351,981' (G.M. Gathorne-Hardy, *A Short History of International Affairs 1920 to 1939* (1942), p. 406). It was not the result alone which was important: in fact, the final result was similar to the preliminary findings which had been published as early as March (*New Statesman and Nation*, 30 Mar. 1935), and was known at ministerial level in February (Cecil of Chelwood Papers, Eden to Cecil, 4 Feb. 1935). It was also the reaction to the publication of the results, which seemed to suggest that the feeling of December 1934, the month in which the Peace Ballot was conducted, was still dominating public opinion. See *Liberal Magazine*, July; *Politics in Review*, July-Sept. These contain summaries of press and party reactions to the Peace Ballot.

49. G.M. Young, *Stanley Baldwin* (1952), pp. 200-12; Middlemas and Barnes, *Baldwin*, pp. 837-8.

50. Cab. 23/82, 19 June 1935.

51. Ibid., 3 July 1935. Article XVI of the Covenant referred specifically to sanctions against an agressor nation.

52. Ibid., 22 July 1935.

53. Hoare Papers, box VIII, file 1. See also file 3: on 24 August, Hoare wrote to Ambassadors Clerk (Paris) and Drummond (Rome) informing them that at home 'now everyone important is for the Covenant'.

54. Cab. 23/82, 21 Aug. Only three days before this Cabinet meeting Sam Hoare had written despairingly to his close friend Neville Chamberlain that 'As you may imagine ! have received little or no help from other quarters. Stanley [Baldwin] would think about nothing but his holiday and the necessity of keeping out of the whole business almost at any cost' (Neville Chamberlain Papers, Hoare to Chamberlain, 18 Aug. 1935).

55. Hoare Papers, Drummond to Hoare, 27 Aug. and 3 Sept. 1935.

56. See Gathorne-Hardy, *A Short History*, p. 405.

57. See *Spectator*, 13 and 20 Sept.; *New Statesman and Nation*, 14 Sept.; *The Times*, 12 Sept.; *Manchester Guardian*, 12 Sept.; *Daily Herald*, 12 Sept.; even the Beaverbrook press and the *Morning Post* approved of Hoare's address. The only discordant note was sounded by the *Daily Mail*, which called the speech 'humbug'.

58. Hoare himself has recorded how amazed he was at the 'universal acclamation' which greeted his speech (Viscount Templewood, *Nine Troubled Years: 1931-1939* (1954), pp. 169-70). He was also at a loss as to what to do next — as he wrote to Eden, 'Somehow or other we must now avoid an anti-climax. Give me your suggestions' (Hoare Papers, Hoare to Eden, 15 Sept.). Hoare caught the rays of the sun squarely; Baldwin, obliquely.

59. See Middlemas and Barnes, *Baldwin*, p. 1075.

60. Baldwin Papers, vol. 47, Churchill to Baldwin, 7 Oct.: 'I think you ought to go to the country at the earliest moment, and I hope you will do so.' See also Middlemas and Barnes, *Baldwin*, p. 860.

61. For National Labour see Baldwin Papers, vol. 47, M. MacDonald to Baldwin, 14 Oct. For the Liberal Nationals see Simon Papers, diary entry, 22 Oct.: 'There should be a general election at once. Neville Chamberlain and I strongly take this view: MacDonald seems against it: Baldwin kept his counsel to the end.'

62. Neville Chamberlain Papers, Chamberlain to Hilda, 15 Oct. 1935; Hoare Papers, Hoare to Eden, 15 Oct. 1935.

63. *The Times*, 21 Sept. 1935.

64. See the comments of Herbert Morrison and J.R. Clynes in *The Times*, 12 and 14 Oct.; both were, of course, critical of the likely decision to hold an early general election. For the similarly critical comments of Liberal spokesmen see *Manchester Guardian*, 12 Oct.

65. See Neville Chamberlain Papers, political diaries and journals, 19 Oct. 1935. Also Middlemas and Barnes, *Baldwin*, p. 863; *The Times*, 21 Oct.
66. He had foreshadowed this decision in a note to Tom Jones as early as February 1932.
67. HCD, vol. 305, cols. 153-7, 23 Oct. 1935.

5 THE COURSE OF THE CAMPAIGN

Well before 23 October, the date on which Baldwin announced that the election would be held on 14 November, the first shots in the campaign had been fired, mostly by the opponents of the National Government; and predictably they were in relation to the question of whether an election was necessary when the nation was so obviously united behind the government on the most important issue of the day, namely collective action through the League of Nations and the imposition of sanctions against Italy. On 8 October Herbert Morrison fired Labour's first shot: Baldwin, he declared, was being urged by his party managers

> to exploit the international situation in the interests of his party, and to have a snap general election in the hope that the Coalition may repeat the scare victory of 1931.[1]

This theme was developed by Attlee, the newly elected leader of the Labour Party, at a party demonstration at Harwood on 15 October. Attlee asserted that the Tories were using the moment to divert attention away from the unemployment question. At the same meeting Clynes protested against what he perceived to be

> a partisan use of a disturbing international situation, and it will be unpardonable if the Prime Minister exploits for party ends the national backing given to the League of Nations.[2]

The opposition Liberals were equally disturbed by the prospect of a snap election. On 10 October Samuel spoke of such an election as a

> Conservative attempt to exploit the international crisis, which has created a unity in the nation, in order to secure power for the Conservative Party for the next five years.[3]

And shortly after, he accused the government of 'running away' from their promise to produce revised scales of unemployment assistance before the next election.[4] In the same period the *Manchester Guardian* devoted a number of editorials to what it described as 'The Indefensible Election'. In one it commented:

The Cabinet's decision to have an election next month seems to be a piece of sharp practice. One does not know which to condemn the most — the levity with which the country is plunged into an election in the middle of a grave international crisis, or the effrontery of the arguments to excuse it.

And in another:

There is only one opinion in Liberal and Labour headquarters about the reason for an immediate general election. It is assumed that the motive is to snatch a new lease of power for the Conservative Party by a 'khaki' election.[5]

The government also drew the fire of a number of prominent political figures who did not have formal links with any party. On 14 October Lord Allen of Hurtwood, who supported the idea of national government but was concerned by what he regarded as an abuse of the idea by the Conservatives, sardonically expressed his desire to know what the election could possibly be about. In his view it couldn't possibly be about the League and sanctions as the country was already united on the issue: it must therefore be to secure a mandate for rearmament and a trick to give the Conservatives a renewed term of office.[6] Lord Snowden was more forthright. On 16 October he told the National Liberal Club that an election would be a 'spurious appeal to patriotism'.[7] Lloyd George was as emphatic as Snowden; he also raised the spectre of an arms race like that preceding the 1914-18 war if the election was held and resulted in a Tory victory.[8]

Criticism of the government was threefold. It was argued in the first place that as there was already a national consensus on the issue of most vital concern there was no need for an election. Secondly, it was thought that the Conservatives wished to exploit the worsening international situation in order to turn attention away from the question of the reintroduction of unemployment regulations and the general failure of the government to solve the unemployment problem. Thirdly, it was feared that the Conservatives intended to use the national consensus on collective security as cover under which they could gain a mandate for a an armaments build-up. This three-pronged criticism was put cogently and with passion, and government supporters felt obliged to reply to it.

Somewhat to the embarrassment of the Baldwin ministry, its foremost champion was Winston Churchill, since June 1935 a defender of the government if not of all its works. Churchill stirred the passions of the opponents of the National Government (and perhaps raised the blood pressure of its leaders) by declaring roundly that an early election should be held and that the government should seek a mandate for large-scale rearmament; without arms, he contended, Britain's influence in international affairs would fade away. In an indirect reference to Neville Chamberlain's address at the recent Bournemouth conference of the Conservative Party, Churchill asserted that Ministers were now openly admitting that words would have to be supported by weapons.[9] In a marginally less provocative vein he claimed that because the government was entering the final year of its constitutional life, the trading world was in a state of uncertainty which could best be removed with an early election and the comfortable return of the National Government. Other Conservative backbenchers joined the fray, but it was not until 14 October that the critics of an early election could draw a reply from a Minister.

Among the Ministers the most strenuous advocate of an early election was Neville Chanberlain and it was he who, in the course of an address to the annual conference of the Scottish Conservative Party in Glasgow on 14 October, replied to the government's critics. Referring to the international situation he made an observation which was to provide a theme for the government's election campaign:

we are not at the end but at the beginning of what might be a long period of difficulty, doubt, and anxiety, during which there might be recurring crises of a most serious character. That is one reason why the general election should be held at a time when there was no danger of immediate trouble in Europe.

He then stated bluntly that the country needed more arms and that a mandate to this effect would be sought at the election; and, with a keen sense of location, he added that increased armaments meant more hope for the depressed areas in that the unemployed could secure employment on cruiser, aircraft and small-arms construction projects. Indeed by linking rearmament and unemployment in this way, Chamberlain went some way towards taking the edge off the unacceptability of the former and at the same time giving the impression of active ministerial concern about the latter. In all, Chamberlain's Glasgow speech was a fine piece of electioneering on behalf of the government, something it had been sorely in need of.[10] It was recognised as such by *The Times* which, much heartened by Chamberlain's performance, urged that no one need be disturbed at the prospect of an early election, particularly as the 1931 mandate had almost expired, and:

> The postponement of an election cannot make for and must detract
> from the weight and efficacy of British policy.[11]

The pronouncements of *The Times* and the air of authority which
pervaded Chamberlain's Glasgow address seemed to indicate that the
government had resolved to go to the country in November. In his
speech at Worcester on 19 October the Prime Minister more or less gave
the game away, and did so completely in his House of Commons
address four days later: the election date was set for 14 November.
Baldwin's announcement intensified the debate of the preceding
several weeks, particularly as the reasons he gave for going to the
country at such short notice seemed open to question. The Labour
Party, saddened by the death of Arthur Henderson on 20 October, but
no less determined to make a fight of it, greeted Baldwin's announcement with derision and anger. Lansbury wanted the government to
name the enemy against whom the increased armaments were to be
used, and Attlee again denounced Baldwin for calling another 'scare'
election:

> He gathered that the election campaign was for the purpose of piling
> up armaments.[12]

In a characterisically spirited response Lloyd George ridiculed Baldwin's
use of the phrase 'lull in international affairs':

> We have just commenced economic warfare and he calls that a lull.
> What an amazing statement.

He congratulated Baldwin for getting in his election before it became
apparent that economic sanctions against Italy would not work.[13]
Lloyd George's venom was not unrelated to the cool press reception
given to his booklets on *Peace and Reconstruction* a few days earlier —
The Times, for example, had expressed its utter boredom with Lloyd
George and his Councils of Action.[14] Nevertheless, Lloyd George's
attack on Baldwin's decision to hold an early election drew notice to
himself and ensured that he, if not his organisation, would play a prominent part in the election campaign.

Comment on the timing of the election received formal expression
with the publication of the party manifestos between 24 and 27

October.[15] Despite their administrative and financial problems the Liberals were first in the field, with a manifesto signed by all the party organisations and by the leaders of the parliamentary party. The first paragraph asserted bluntly:

> A General Election is being held at a moment of acute international crisis. After long delay the Government have lately been taking definite action at Geneva. All parties support that action. An election is therefore unnecessary.

The manifesto contained no surprises, was short, and was given a tepid welcome by the press — indeed the *Morning Post*, the *Daily Herald* and the *Daily Mail*, among the national dailies, did not even refer to its publication. And other than the *News Chronicle* no national daily newspaper honoured it with an editorial. Furthermore, most Labour and Conservative spokesmen ignored it in their speeches. It was an unhappy opening to the Liberals' election campaign.

The following day the Labour Party issued its manifesto. This too was short and contained little that was new to the electors. It also opened by deploring the 'snap election', though it did so less concisely:

> Four years have passed since the National Government obtained a swollen majority in the House of Commons on a campaign of fraud, misrepresentation and panic. The Government has now decided to plunge the nation into an electoral struggle in the midst of an international crisis. The Labour Party deplores this attempt to exploit for partisan ends a situation of grave international anxiety.

But despite being good knockabout election material, the manifesto failed to generate much discussion in the newspapers. In part this was due to the publication the same day of the manifesto of the Communist Party, which had wished to demonstrate its solidarity with the Labour Party. At a meeting of the Communist International in August, the secretary of the British Communist Party, Harry Pollitt, had declared that the principal task of his party was to promote the return of a Labour Government. To this end the party's election manifesto announced that

> The Communist Party of Great Britain calls on all working men and women to vote down this wage-cutter Government and return a Labour Government pledged to improve the conditions of the

masses. In the interests of unity, the Communist Party has withdrawn all its candidates with the exception of Comrades Harry
Pollitt (Rhondda East) and William Gallacher (West Fife).

Publication of the Communist manifesto undermined the efforts of the
Labour Party to avoid being identified with the Communists. For the
remainder of the campaign, though especially on 26 and 27 October,
the Conservative and National Government spokesmen and press made
much with what was termed a 'natural alliance' and Labour Party
spokesmen, instead of being able to expand on the policies outlined in
their manifesto, had to reply to this criticism.

But even without the complication of the publication of the manifesto of the Communist Party, it is doubtful whether the press would
have devoted much space to consideration of the manifesto of the
Labour Party, for on the evening of 25 October Baldwin delivered the
first election broadcast of the campaign, which dominated the
following morning's news. Indeed even Labour spokesmen and the
Daily Herald were far more energetic in replying to Baldwin's speech
than in commenting on their own manifesto.[16] It was an inauspicious
opening to Labour's election campaign.

The Labour Party was driven still further on to the defensive by the
publication on 27 October of the National Government's manifesto. It
was signed by Baldwin and MacDonald, was nearly three times as long
as the manifestos of the other parties and, unlike them, did not open
with a comment on the timing of the election; rather it pointed to the
marked improvement in the state of the nation's affairs since 1931:

> The broad issue is whether the stability and confidence which the
> National Government have built up are to be preserved in a period of
> special difficulty and anxiety.

It concluded a long and detailed account of its stewardship and its
proposals for the future by warning that

> The advent to power of the Labour opposition, pledged to a
> number of revolutionary measures of which the ultimate results
> could not be clearly foreseen, would inevitably be followed by a
> collapse of confidence . . . The international situation reinforces the
> same lesson. The influence of Britain among the nations, now so
> conspicuous, could never be maintained under an Administration
> drawn from a party whose leaders of experience in foreign affairs no

longer cooperate with it, and which is hopelessly divided on the
most important points in foreign policy.

The government's manifesto drew the fire of opposition spokesmen.
In particular, Lansbury and Morrison denounced the government for
failing to bring forward a coherent unemployment policy; they also
poured scorn on the charges that the leadership of the Labour Party
was disunited, and that the introduction of Socialism would precipitate
a loss of confidence.[17] Arthur Greenwood tried to turn the criticism
back on the National Government by pointing to the dissensions within
the Conservative Party; he noted in particular the differences in emphasis
between the speeches of Churchill and of Baldwin on the issues of rearmament and the League of Nations.

It was the *Daily Herald*, however, which succeeded in upsetting the
government's equanimity. It accused Baldwin of attempting to scare the
electors into believing that the Navy was obsolete and incapable of
defending the country. The Navy, it asserted, was well capable of
defending Britain, and it cited the word of an expert on the subject, a
Labour spokesman, Lord Strabolgi, in support of its case.[18] Support
was also forthcoming from A.V. Alexander, former First Lord of the
Admiralty in the Labour administration of 1929-31. Alexander contended that the British Navy was still the best in the world and was
quite capable of sustaining an air attack, a contention he made with
supporting evidence about its composition.[19] This eventually drew a
rebuke from the present First Lord, Sir Bolton Eyres Monsell, who
asserted that Alexander was guilty of releasing 'secret knowledge'.[20] But government spokesmen were in a difficult position for
they could not reply that the Navy was insufficiently strong to defend
the country and therefore should be strengthened: to admit this would
be to play into the opposition's hands. A formula was found by the
Morning Post. It agreed with Strabolgi that the Navy was sufficiently
strong for present needs, but this, it claimed, was beside the point,
which was to be prepared for Britain's needs in the future.[21] Spokesmen
for the extreme right wing of the Conservative Party did not observe
the niceties of the situation, and one of their number, Lord Lloyd,
thundered that

> The situation in regard to the Navy has never been so serious since
> the days of the Stuarts brought the Dutch up the Medway. Never
> since then has our security been so imperilled.[22]

It was a splendid piece of electioneering, and ensured that the debate over the Navy would continue to rage for a good part of the campaign.

While this debate was producing many a flushed cheek, the election issues on a broader front were being canvassed extensively by the party leaders. It was Baldwin who once again stole the scene from Labour. On 28 October Attlee delivered the first of Labour's broadcasts; but at Wolverhampton on the same evening Baldwin gave the first of what was to be a series of set-piece speeches in the National Government's 'target zone', namely the North of England and the Midlands. Baldwin's Wolverhampton speech was widely reported in the press the following morning while Attlee's broadcast was indifferently received. The only part of Attlee's speech to gain much notice was his proposal to nationalise the Bank of England. The *Morning Post*, for example, urged that the Bank should not be allowed to become 'a mere adjunct of the National Council of Labour and the TUC'.[23] A number of commentators pointedly drew a contrast between Attlee's assertion that the government's 'appeal is for a blank cheque for armaments' and Baldwin's quietly reasoned assurance that

> There has not been, there is not, and there will be no question of big armaments or materially increased forces. What we do want, and what we must have, is to replace our pre-war construction in ships in the Navy with modern ships. It does not mean increasing the Navy.

It was also easy to draw a contrast between the relaxed and confident style of Baldwin, with his personal identification with the people of the Midlands and his references to 'my old friends the steelworkers', with Attlee's stilted delivery and apparent unease with — or alienation from — the provinces of Britain; and this despite the fact that Attlee addressed himself to the 'ordinary family'.

On 30 October campaign interest focused briefly on Lloyd George. His Council of Action held a well-attended rally in London, at which there was considerable speculation as to the progress of the council's questionnaire to the parliamentary candidates. But favourable press comment was rare. Indeed the council had been dubbed very early on the 'Council of Inaction', a tag it found difficult to shake off in the run-up to the election.

Of far greater significance to the course of the campaign was Lord Snowden's broadcast address in the evening. Delivered ostensibly on behalf of the Liberal Party, he spoke as an Independent, acknowledging as he did so his thanks to the Liberals for giving him this opportunity.

As in 1931 his speech dripped with vitriol. The National Government, he contended, was masquerading under that title: what the people really had was a Tory Government, pure and simple. He then claimed responsibility for the balanced budget of 1932, and went on to denounce the government's decision to go to the country with such an appalling domestic record. He warned the electors to be wary of Baldwin's assurances about the government's intentions concerning rearmament: he himself was confident that Baldwin wanted a mandate to rearm. He concluded his speech by urging the electors to vote against the government — for Liberal candidates where such were standing, for Labour candidates where such was not the case. As to the latter, however, Snowden was under no illusions. He noted that it was safe to vote Labour on this occasion because Labour could not hope to win the election.[24]

With the memory of Snowden's immense influence at the last election fresh in their minds, and by no means as confident as he that the result of the election was a foregone conclusion, the government's supporters strove to discredit him. First in the field was Churchill, who at a meeting later in the evening described Snowden's address as 'mischievous'. He urged his hearers to ignore the advice of 'so soured a mind'. The following day Chamberlain and Simon joined the attack on Snowden. In the course of a speech in the City, Chamberlain denied the validity of Snowden's assertion that the 1932 budget owed little to the post-1931-election National Government. He also accused Snowden of irresponsibility in advising the electors to vote for Labour when it was clear that Labour's return could only result in a financial crisis of the first order. Chamberlain further speculated as to whether Labour could be entrusted with the nation's foreign policy now that Henderson was dead. It was Chamberlain's first weighty intervention into the campaign.

That same evening Simon delivered the third of the National Government's broadcast addresses. So seriously did the government view Snowden's allegations and his possible electoral impact, that Simon devoted nearly three-quarters of his time to giving a considered reply. In the course of his address he asked the electors to note Snowden's *volte face* since 1931; he denied that the National Government was not truly national in character; and he dealt efficiently with Snowden's criticisms of the National Government's handling of domestic and foreign affairs. He also referred to Snowden's 'bitter character' and political instability.

On Thursday 31 October major speeches were delivered by Attlee,

Greenwood and Clynes for the Labour Party, and by Simon, Kingsley Wood and Duff Cooper for the National Government. At his home base in Limehouse, Attlee did not venture beyond the confines of the party manifesto; that is, he criticised the record of the National Government at great length, but gave few details of Labour's programme of Socialist reconstruction:

> The Government invented and enforced the Means Test, which has broken up many homes. It has failed to deal with the most serious aspects of unemployment, has cut down educational facilities, handed over housing to private profit, and neglected the social services,

and now, to cap it all off, the government was asking for a blank cheque for armaments. In his broadcast address Clynes argued along similar lines. He denounced the government for seeking 'Peace by millions of bayonets'. Only in his concluding remarks did he refer to Labour's programme, and even then only in the vaguest way possible:

> So long as our country is in private ownership under private control, public content and well-being are impossible.

Greenwood was roused by Chamberlain's suggestion that Labour in office would leave the country undefended: he warned the electors to be wary of National Government scaremongering.[25]

While the Labour spokesmen were saying as little as possible about their party's schemes, National Government spokesmen were seizing on what offerings there were. With the weight of Treasury opinion behind him, Kingsley Wood proclaimed that Labour's pension schemes were financially unsound: he cautioned the electors not to be taken in by promises which no government could implement. Duff Cooper launched an attack on Attlee, charging him with irresponsibility and hypocrisy for supporting sanctions while opposing rearmament:

> What would you think of a man who would lightly go to war and send out soldiers and airmen to fight on behalf of his policy, but would allow them to be slaughtered by their enemies because they were not provided with as modern equipment as their enemies?

After his trenchant reply to Snowden the previous evening, Simon spoke in a lower key: 'I advise you,' he said, 'to put your trust in Mr

Baldwin.'

But as so often occurred during the campaign the day belonged to Baldwin, and the Friday newspapers gave full coverage to his address to the Peace Society: by comparison, Clynes's broadcast went almost unrecorded. In his speech at Wolverhampton on 28 October Baldwin had defined the peace question as 'a subject of the utmost importance'. His speech to the Peace Society three days later, while ostensibly apolitical, was on the 'subject of the utmost importance' and must be seen as an integral part of the course of the campaign. One line from this speech became the focus of discussion for the remainder of the campaign and, indeed, for well after the election: he said, 'I give you my word there will be no great armaments.'[26] Labour spokesmen urged the electors to disbelieve Baldwin's 'word'. Morrison stated bluntly that 'The National Government is seeking a mandate for swollen armaments.'[27] The right wing of the Conservative Party was also sceptical. Churchill argued that the present state of international relations — 'more dangerous now than it was in 1914' — demanded that the defences should be built up.[28] But all speakers felt constrained to respond in one way or another to Baldwin's speech.

Friday 1 November was the day of the municipal elections. It was generally thought that the results of the municipal elections would indicate the likely results of the parliamentary elections. Hence interest in the municipal election was far greater than was usual. Only a few results were known by the time the national dailies went to press for Saturday's edition. Among these, however, was Leeds, which for the first time since 1932 showed a Conservative gain over Labour. The Sunday newspapers carried the full results, and it became quite clear that after the lean years of 1933 and 1934 the Conservatives were now rallying strongly. Among the important towns showing Conservative gains were Stoke-on-Trent, Stockport, Dudley, Oldham, Leeds and, above all, Birmingham, in all of which it had been anticipated that at the general election the government could fare badly. Overall there was no spectacular turnover of seats, but the results could only have disquieted Labour. The Conservatives were jubilant, and their estimates of the size of their likely parliamentary majority rose accordingly. Labour spokesmen tended to refrain from mentioning the results; but where they were discussed it was only to note that overall there was no decisive movement one way or the other, and that anyway the municipal elections should not be taken as a guide as to what was likely to take place at the parliamentary elections.[29]

On the Friday evening Lloyd George had delivered his broadcast address which, though fairly well reported in the national press, was jostled for space by early reports of the municipal elections. Lloyd George had expressed his concern that

> Our prestige in the world has been hopelessly impaired by the two feeble attempts we made to lead the nations over Manchuria.

As for the government's handling of the most recent international crisis, Lloyd George had nothing but contempt: sanctions against Italy, he said, had been imposed at too late a date and were too mild to be effective. He then urged the electors to cast their votes not for the National Government but for those candidates who signed the Council of Action's questionnaire. While delivered with his usual wit and gusto, his speech offered the same loaf which he had been hawking around since January, and for many people it had grown rather stale as a purchasing proposition.

When Chamberlain broadcast on the following evening, he not only replied to Lloyd George's criticisms of the National Government but also offered the electors some news items. In the first place he was able to announce that unemployment for October was 40,000 down on the September figure: this was a trend which, he reasoned, could be reversed if the National Government was not permitted to continue with its sound work of the past four years. His second item of news was equally cheering. He announced that in the next five years the government proposed to spend £100 million on road construction. He stressed that this would mean employment for many more people. Having created the impression of government bustle and concern, Chamberlain turned on Lloyd George. He poured scorn on Lloyd George's criticisms of the government and ridiculed him as an unrepresentative political figure. Surely, he asked, Lloyd George did not represent the Liberal Party, for the Liberals had approved of the course taken by the government at Geneva. He insisted that Lloyd George represented no one but himself and should not be taken seriously by the electors. Chamberlain's speech was authoritative in tone, exuding a sense of reliability and competence; it brilliantly complemented the breezy humanitarianism of his leader's speech, delivered a few nights earlier.

Chamberlain's speech took a lot of the wind out of Labour's (and Lloyd George's) sails for the remainder of the campaign. Until then most Labour spokesmen had impressed on the electors that the government was opposed to expenditure on public works as a means of relieving unemployment, but following his address this line of attack had to be reshaped. Sunday was a rest day, but on Monday evening Arthur Greenwood broadcast to the nation. He complained that for most of the life of the last parliament Chamberlain had opposed public works. Only in this year, an election year, had he come to view them more favourably. Similarly, the government had only decided to support the League of Nations after the Peace Ballot had shown that it was electorally expedient to do so. He denied that the Labour Party was split over foreign policy, and he pointed to divisions on the Government side, notably the differing attitudes of Eden on the one hand and Amery and Churchill on the other. It was a workmanlike performance but seems to have done little to counter the impact made by Chamberlain two evenings earlier.

Greenwood had the added misfortune to have to share newspaper space with two items with greater popular appeal than his broadcast address. The first of these was the disappearance of the popular aviator, Kingsford Smith, while making an attempt on the speed record for a flight between Britain and Australia. Kingsford Smith was reported to have crashed somewhere between Ceylon and Indonesia. The other, and less exciting, news item was Baldwin's speech at Liverpool. Baldwin was now talking less about defence than he had before the dissolution and in the first week of his campaign. Instead he concentrated more on Britain's record of support for the League of Nations and on the extent of economic recovery at home. In particular he discussed the revival of international trade, the worldwide problems of the cotton industry, improvements in the coal industry and so on. As usual he was not merely content to defend his government's record: he also attempted to undercut the Labour Party's claim to represent the working man. He put himself in the place of 'the ordinary working man' and speculated on what 'nationalisation' meant to him – it was all rather 'vague', he concluded. He felt confident that the good sense of the British workers would prevail at the election, and that they would vote for substance rather than shadow – the National Government rather than Labour. Received enthusiastically in Liverpool, his speech also stole columns from Labour in the national dailies the next morning, and dictated the pattern of the following days' campaigning.

On 4 November nominations closed and the election campaign entered its last phase. On the same day Lloyd George announced the results of the Council of Action questionnaire. These were roughly as had been anticipated by the press. Of the 365 candidates who signed the questionnaire, only about 20 were supporters of the National Government: about 200 Labour candidates signed, as did the great majority of Liberal candidates. Lloyd George expressed his satisfaction with the result, and urged the electors to cast their votes for the candidates listed as being signatories to the questionnaire.[30] But 365 out of more than 1,300 candidates was a meagre return, and the popular press, as well as *The Times*, devoted some space to pointing this out. Their amusement at Lloyd George's expense was increased further when several candidates, whose names had been listed as being signatories to the questionnaire, denied that they had replied affirmatively to the questionnaire.[31] It seemed that Lloyd George's desperate attempt to influence the result of the election could not meet with success.

On the evening of 5 November Ramsay MacDonald broadcast on behalf of the National Government. He had had a hectic week in Seaham and was now convinced that he could not hope to retain the seat.[32] Nevertheless, he gave a spirited broadcast which exuded confidence that the government would win the election. He roundly declared that the return of Labour would precipitate a crisis, while the National Government had done a great deal of good for the country in the past four years. He added that there were signs of improvement even in the depressed areas. In conclusion he issued a warning to the electors:

> Go back to party now and you will return to a political condition when everything to be proposed by the one side has to be opposed by the other. A Nation cannot afford that with all the uncertainties and risks that surround it.

Momentarily he succeeded in drawing the fire of Labour's leaders away from Baldwin: indeed the following day Attlee, Greenwood and Lansbury all fired a few shots in his direction.[33]

But the campaign was rapidly losing its impetus owing to a number of factors. In the first place it was conceded on all sides that there was not the remotest possibility that the government would suffer defeat at the hands of Labour.[34] Conservative organisers were moderately agitated by the possibility that the government's supporters would be so confident that the result of the election was a foregone conclusion that they would not take the trouble to turn out on polling day: otherwise Central Office was elated by the apparent popularity of the government.[35] Furthermore, there was little new to interest the electors. The issues of the campaign had been debated at great length, indeed to the point of tiresomeness, in the preceding three years. Throughout the campaign the Stock Exchange remained rock steady in expectation of a comfortable government victory. With a week still to

go to polling day it seemed that only a scare on the scale of the
Zinoviev Letter could revive the flagging interest in the campaign.

But no scare came. Since the commencement of the campaign the
Daily Herald had been predicting, almost daily, that a 'Tory Scare',
perhaps similar to the Bank Scare of 1931, was imminent. On 2
November Attlee had warned the electors that

> This election is being run as a stunt. The method is to put the wind
> up you, to build on fear, for fear is the potent weapon in the Tory
> armoury. Now they tell you there will be a financial crisis if ever a
> Socialist Government comes in, but that again is a stunt. It is a scare
> for those who do not know.

The *Daily Herald* had likewise referred to this scare, but it seized even
more avidly on the contents of a Conservative pamphlet (published on
9 November), where it was predicted that if Labour won the election, a
wholesale confiscation of private houses would follow. The pamphlet
carried the lurid title of 'Your House to Go! Your Building Society
Too! If Socialism Comes!' Labour spokesmen were so outraged by what
they regarded as a blatant misrepresentation of their housing policy
that they demanded that Conservative Central Office issue an
apology.[36] Central Office did in fact issue an apology, but one which
was double-edged. It apologised for having apparently misrepresented
Labour policy, but at the same time pointed out that the source of the
'error' was G.R. Mitchison's Socialist novel *The First Workers' Government* (1934). But it was an issue of peripheral interest only, and hardly
amounted to a 'scare'.

On 6 November Herbert Samuel delivered a broadcast on behalf of
the Liberal Party. His theme was that over the past three years (that is,
since the Liberals had left the ministry) the government had erred and
strayed like lost sheep — especially over foreign affairs — but was now
back in the fold — or almost: a few sheep, labelled Means Test, unemployment and Ottawa Agreements, were still at large. He advised his
followers to vote for the Liberal candidate where one was standing, and
otherwise for the candidate who had signed the Council of Action's
questionnaire. In the 300 or so constituencies where there was neither a
Liberal nor a Council of Action candidate, Liberal voters were presumably to abstain; on this Samuel offered no advice. Samuel's speech
was well reported in the national dailies, but the reports were accompanied by very little critical comment; and on the evidence of special
correspondents' reports, there was hardly a flicker of interest in the

constituencies.

Of far greater importance to the campaign was Herbert Morrison's speech at Dartford on 5 November. Morrison promised the electors of Dartford that if Labour was returned, it would construct a tunnel under the Thames at Dartford. Morrison was thought by many people, particularly the Conservatives, to be the most authoritative spokesman for the Labour Party, despite the fact that Attlee had defeated him for the leadership of the party. Indeed, alone among the Labour leaders, he was feared by the Conservative hierarchy, if only because of his brilliant successes as leader of the London Labour Party. One measure of Conservative respect for Morrison was that the cartoonist of the *Morning Post* invariably used Morrison rather than Attlee in his portrayal of the Labour Party.[37] Throughout the campaign the Conservatives had striven to discredit Morrison, but with little success. His Dartford speech, however, seemed to provide them with the opportunity to score a direct hit. In a speech widely reported in the government press. Neville Chamberlain accused Morrison of mass bribery; he urged the electors to have nothing to do with such a person. Other Conservative leaders, including Hoare, said much the same thing.

Conservative apprehension about Morrison's influence increased when he delivered the final and easily the most effective of Labour's broadcasts. Morrison skilfully contrasted Labour's handling of foreign affairs with the record of the National Government; and with considerable subtlety he shed doubt on whether Baldwin really led the Conservative Party on policy matters, particularly defence matters. He deplored the failure of the government to advance social services; and while noting the improvement in unemployment, he attributed this to developments in the world economy rather than to the actions of the National Government. Perhaps fortunately for the National Government, Morrison had to share news space with Baldwin, who on the same evening had delivered an important speech at Leeds.

Baldwin enjoyed an enormously successful evening at Leeds. His speech was of the usual mixture — some discussion of the League of Nations, next to nothing on defence, and a great deal of time on the economy, with special reference to the plight of the coalmining areas and the government's assistance to them. The impact of Morrison's speech was further blunted when on the following evening Baldwin delivered the last of the government's broadcasts. It was one of his greatest set-piece addresses, designed to lift politics above the level of everyday inter-party squabbles. His central theme was that

The whole world is watching this Election, because in this Election democracy itself is on trial.

By way of comparison Attlee's speech at Middlesbrough seemed parochial and divisive and carping — and this comparison was drawn in the press and by many candidates as well.[38]

The campaign now lost any momentum it had possessed. For the past week most newspapers had been devoting much space to the marriage of Lady Alice Scott to the Duke of Gloucester (celebrated on 7 November), while a number of popular papers were describing in detail the full horror of the Ravine Murders. Newspaper reports of the campaign suggest that candidates were tiring of discussing issues and were resorting to personal abuse of opponents. Conservative candidates referred to Attlee as a *locum tenens* leader, who lacked authority even in his own party (the phrase was Churchill's; the sentiment that of all National Government candidates). Morrison, the most persuasive of the Labour spokesmen, was reduced to rather weak slogans: 'A vote for the Government is a vote for war and bankruptcy.' And even Lloyd George could offer no more than 'the National Government is sham Tory; it is sham Liberal; it has got sham sanctions'. And there were still several campaigning days left.

Mercifully the final days of the campaign were enlivened by two incidents. The first concerned the defection of the Free Church leader, Dr Scott Lidgett, from the Council of Action. On 8 November, having since June supported Lloyd George's attack on the National Government, Scott Lidgett backed down and instructed his flock to vote for the National Government and against the Socialists. He gave as his reasons for defecting his belief that Baldwin's speeches showed 'some affinity' with the objectives of the Council of Action, while Labour's proposals would precipitate a crisis of severe proportions.[39] His defection dealt a cruel blow to Lloyd George's campaign to mobilise the nonconformist vote against the National Government.[40]

The second incident revolved around the unlikely person of Lord Hailsham. Probably at the instigation of Central Office, which was concerned with the extent of apathy among National Government supporters, Hailsham on 9 November raised again the spectre of a Moscow-dominated Labour Government. He pointed to the apparent electoral co-operation between the Communists and Labour. Other Conservative spokesmen followed his lead, with the result that for much of the last few days of the campaign Labour was driven even further on to the defensive.

The campaign finished as it had begun: namely with Baldwin calling the tune. At Newcastle on 12 November he wound up his northern tour with yet another outstanding meeting. Drawing on the memories of national sacrifice and unity aroused by the celebration of Remembrance Day, Baldwin stressed the dangers inherent in the present international situation, and the need for a renewal of the National Government's mandate to both keep the nation safe from war and to restore her prosperity. *The Times* editorial the following day was entitled simply, 'Mr. Baldwin's Final Message'. Baldwin's was indeed the final word.

On the eve of the election the newspapers, the candidates and the party organisers made their predictions as to the outcome. It was agreed on all sides that the National Government would win the election; but there was little agreement as to the size of the majority. At the time of the dissolution the government's majority over the opposition was 405. In the final week of the campaign the chairman of Conservative Party Organization, Lord Stonehaven, was reported to have said that he expected that the government would lose about 120 seats, leaving it with a clear majority of 165.[41] Other Conservative predictions were only slightly less optimistic. The *Daily Mail* quoted a Central Office source as predicting a government majority of 159; while on the final day of the campaign *The Times* claimed that in government circles a majority of between 110 and 140 was anticipated. Predictions made in the Conservative press varied between 120 and 170 as the size of the government majority. The *Daily Mail* predicted a government majority of 169; the *Daily Telegraph* 153; the *Morning Post* 123 and the *Scotsman* 120. The most optimistic prediction, and the one closest to the final result was in *Truth* (appropriately enough) – a majority of 210.[42] For the Liberal Nationals Lord Hutchison predicted a government majority of 127, though Lord Runciman thought the majority would be twice as great.[43] Lord Snowden and Lloyd George had predicted a government victory on a reduced majority, though on the eve of the poll Snowden seems to have believed that the combined total of Liberal and Labour MPs would be very close to the size of the National Government contingent.[44] Naturally enough Labour was more reticent about making its predictions known publicly. In his diary Dalton recorded his belief that Labour could gain between 150 to 200 seats, leaving the government with a majority of between 75 and 126.[45] The *Daily Mail* printed a prediction, purportedly emanating from Transport House, which gave the government a majority of 113, which seems consistent with Dalton's diary entry. This figure is confirmed by

H.L. Nathan, since 1934 a Labour politician, who reported to Lloyd George that the Labour Party only hoped 'for something between 150 and 225'.[46]

The punters at Ladbrokes had also been active. It was reported that most bets had been placed on government majorities of between 160 and 210, with the average being about 185, or considerably higher than allegedly more informed political circles, though one must take into consideration that National Government spokesmen may have predicted a small majority in order to encourage government supporters to turn out on polling day. In the event even the Ladbroke punters underestimated the size of the government victory, for on 14 November the government was returned with a majority of 240. As with the East Fulham by-election it is the size of the majority, not the victory itself, which requires explanation.

Notes

1. *The Times*, 9 Oct. 1935.
2. Ibid., 13 Oct. 1935.
3. Ibid., 11 Oct. 1935.
4. Ibid., 20 Oct. 1935.
5. *Manchester Guardian*, 10 and 11 Oct. 1935.
6. *The Times*, 13 Oct. 1935.
7. *Manchester Guardian*, 17 Oct. 1935.
8. Ibid., 21 Oct. 1935.
9. *Morning Post*, 9 Oct. 1935.
10. *Scotsman*, 15 Oct. 1935. Chamberlain was immensely pleased with his own speech, for it gave a 'lead to our people', which Baldwin, in his view was failing to do. He quoted approvingly the *Daily Herald*'s report of the address: 'Chancellor Dresses Election Window' – 'That was precisely what I was after' (Neville Chamberlain Papers, Chamberlain to Hilda, 15 Oct. 1935).
11. *The Times*, 15 Oct. 1935.
12. Ibid., 21 Oct. 1935.
13. Ibid., 24 Oct. 1935.
14. Ibid., 22 and 23 Oct. 1935.
15. The manifestos are reprinted in *The Times House of Commons 1935*; also in F.W.S. Craig (ed.), *Election Manifestos 1918-1945* (1970). See also Chapter 7.
16. Newspapers consulted include *The Times, Daily Telegraph, Daily Mail, Daily Herald, Morning Post, Daily Express, Manchester Guardian, News Chronicle* and *Daily Worker*. For election broadcasts see *The Listener*.
17. *The Times*, 28 Oct. 1935.
18. *Daily Herald*, 26 and 28 Oct. 1935.
19. *Reynolds' News*, 27 Oct. 1935. Alexander reiterated his views in speeches at Sheffield on 31 Oct. and at Dudley on 7 Nov.
20. At Ilford on 8 Nov. 1935.
21. *Morning Post*, 29 Oct. 1935.
22. *Daily Mail*, 2 Nov. 1935.

23. *Morning Post*, 29 Oct. 1935.
24. *The Times*, 30 Oct. 1935.
25. *Daily Herald* and *The Times*, 1 Nov. 1935.
26. See for example, C.L. Mowat, *Britain Between the Wars 1918-1940* (1955), p. 553.
27. In a speech in his home district of Hackney (*The Times*, 20 Nov. 1935).
28. *The Times*, 2 Nov. 1935.
29. *Reynolds' News*, 3 Nov. 1935; *Daily Herald* and *Daily Mail*, 4 Nov. 1935.
30. *News Chronicle*, 5 Nov. 1935.
31. *The Times*, 6 and 7 Nov. 1935.
32. Baldwin Papers, vol. 47, MacDonald to Baldwin, 13 Nov. 1935.
33. *Daily Herald*, 6 and 7 Nov. 1935.
34. See end of this chapter.
35. *The Times* periodically issued Central Office warnings to this effect, as did the special correspondents in the constituencies. See also Baldwin Papers, vol. 47, G. Lloyd to Baldwin, 8 and 11 Nov. 1935.
36. *Daily Herald*, 11 Nov. 1935.
37. *Morning Post*, 8 Nov. 1935.
38. Ibid., 9 Nov. 1935. For a partisan though not unrepresentative view of the reception given to Baldwin's broadcast see correspondence in Baldwin Papers, vol. 41.
39. *The Times*, 9 and 11 Nov. 1935.
40. That Scott Lidgett got cold feet over the Council of Action is evident from a comparison of an article he published in the September number of the *Free Church Chronicle* with his letter to Lloyd George on 11 Nov. (Lloyd George Papers, G 141/27/1).
41. Unless indicated otherwise, predictions come from newspaper reports for 12, 13 and 14 Nov. 1935.
42. The leading weekly journals *Spectator* (25 Oct. 1935) and *New Statesman and Nation* (19 Oct. 1935) also anticipated a comfortable victory for the government.
43. Baldwin Papers, vol. 39, Runciman to Baldwin, 15 Nov. 1935.
44. *News Chronicle*, 14 Nov. 1935.
45. H. Dalton, *The Fateful Years: memoirs 1931-1945* (1957), p. 74.
46. A.J.P. Taylor (ed.), *Lloyd George: a diary by Frances Stevenson* (1971), p. 318.

6 THE PARTIES AND THE ISSUES

It is difficult to state with any confidence which of the many issues of the campaign weighed most heavily with the electors. The student of elections of the post-World War II period can turn to opinion polls to provide him with additional information about the mind of the electorate, and since 1964 the BBC's Election Forum has assisted him still further. The student of pre-World War II elections does not possess these aids. His only direct source of information about the issues of interest to the electors is press reports of questions asked by them at campaign meetings, and such reports are infrequent and reflect more the bias of the particular newspaper than the views of the meeting. They form too unreliable a basis from which to generalise. Even more, therefore, than the student of post-World War II elections, the student of interwar and earlier elections must rely on the ability of press and politicians to interpret and influence the public mind. Indeed it is likely that as a source for understanding the public mind interwar politicians are more reliable than their post-war counterparts, if only because the voters of the latter period are exposed to a wider range of influence, among them (since the 1950s) television. This chapter concerns itself with the ways in which the politicians dealt with the issues which they considered were of interest to the electors. The principal sources for the chapter are the party manifestos and election addresses, though where incidents of speeches in the course of the campaign led to clarification or modification of views expressed earlier, these have been noted.

On 16 October 1935 the Cabinet agreed to set up a committee composed of Neville Chamberlain (chairman), Thomas, Malcolm MacDonald, Hailsham, Elliot, Percy, Wood, Simon and Brown, which was to 'make recommendations as to the items to be included in the Government's Election Programme'.[1] On 23 October this committee reported to the Cabinet that the manifesto

> should deal with the following subjects in the order in which they are here set out. We have discussed and are agreed upon the way in which each of these subjects should be presented in the Manifesto, and in particular we attach importance to the document being kept on broad and general lines with as little reference as may be to the details of the programme.

(1)   The position in regard to the League of Nations and the policy
       which the Government were pursuing
(2)   The defence programme
(3)   Imperial policy
(4)   The export trade
(5)   Agriculture (including land settlement) and Fisheries
(6)   Employment
(7)   Special Areas
(8)   Social Reform
       a. Housing
       b. Extension of contributory pensions scheme to classes such
          as clerks, small shop-keepers and others now outside that
          scheme
       c. Education
       d. Raising the National standard of health
(9)   Scotland. It is proposed to include a paragraph to the effect
       that while the programme is generally applicable to the whole
       of the United Kingdom it is recognized that in Scotland
       certain problems (the Highlands, Agriculture, and Housing)
       call for special treatment. These matters will receive the
       sympathetic attention of the Government.

At the meeting of the Cabinet on 23 October Chamberlain spoke for
the report, which was accepted with a recommendation that a further
committee consisting of Chamberlain, MacDonald, Simon and Wood
should draft a manifesto for publication on the 28th:

> The Committee was asked to invite the attendance of the Secretary
> of State for Scotland in connection with Scottish Affairs.

The Cabinet made several other recommendations, among them that
coal policy (including unification of mining royalties) should be dealt
with under Export Trade, that Baldwin should be asked to consider a
suggestion that he should deal comprehensively with the question of
the government's coal policy in the speech he was to make at Wolverhampton on 28 October, and that in his forthcoming statement on the
wireless broadcast he should give a hint of his intention to do so.
    Labour's manifesto was primarily the work of Arthur Greenwood
and was based on the 1934 policy statement. At the meeting of the
Elections Sub-Committee of the NEC on 16 October, 'Discussion took
place upon the general lines of the Election Manifesto, and there was a

consensus of opinion that it should be short, and should not take the form of a list of items on Party Policy as in previous Elections.' Arthur Greenwood was deputed to draft the manifesto. His draft was discussed at the full meeting of the NEC on 22 and 23 October and, in substance, was approved. Several apparently minor changes were effected by a subcommittee consisting of Greenwood, Attlee, Dalton and Morrison.[2]

Throughout the life of the 1931 Parliament, and particularly in 1935, foreign affairs had been in the forefront of political discussion. It had also been the subject of the only national referendum — albeit an unofficial one — in British history, commonly called the 'Peace Ballot'. The result of the Peace Ballot, coupled with the widespread interest in the progress of the Italo-Abyssinian affair (which reached crisis proportions in the months preceding the election, and remained newsworthy for much of the campaign), made certain that foreign affairs would be a central issue at the election.

Behind the rhetoric all parties were roughly in agreement about present and future policy, while in considerable disagreement about the effects of the policy pursued by the National Government since 1931. Not surprisingly the extent of agreement took some of the edge off the keenness with which the issue might otherwise have been debated. The National Government manifesto declared boldly that

> The League of Nations will remain as heretofore the keystone of British foreign policy. In the present unhappy dispute between Italy and Abyssinia there will be no wavering in the policy we have hitherto pursued. We shall take no action in isolation, but we shall be prepared faithfully to take our part in any collective action decided upon by the League and shared in by its members . . .
> Our attitude to the League is dictated by the conviction that collective security by collective action can alone save us from a return to the old system which resulted in the Great War.

Support for the League of Nations was then linked with the need for national armaments:

> The Covenant itself requires that national armaments should be measured by the needs of national defence and by the duty of fulfilling international obligations.

It was then stated that

our influence can fully be exerted only if we are recognized to be strong enough to fulfil our obligations which, jointly with others, we may undertake.

The purpose of this careful build-up was made clear in the next paragraph:

The fact is that the actual condition of our defence forces is not satisfactory. We have made it clear that we must in the course of the next few years do what is necessary to repair the gaps in our defences, which have accumulated over the past decade. The defence programme will be strictly confined to what is required to make the country and the Empire safe and to fulfil our obligations towards the League.

To which was added the rider:

And we shall not for one moment relax our efforts to attain by international agreement a general limitation of armaments by every possible means, whether by the restriction of numbers or by prohibition of weapons and methods of warfare.

The National Government manifesto opened with the League of Nations and armaments; but the Labour Party gave first place to the government's record in domestic affairs. Nevertheless, two of the three section headings were about foreign affairs. Unlike the National Government's manifesto, Labour's discussed at some length the record of the government in international affairs over the past four years. It was claimed that the government had

a terrible responsibility for the present international situation. It did nothing to check the aggression of Japan in the Far East, and thus seriously discredited the League of Nations and undermined the collective peace system. It has wrecked the Disarmament Conference by resisting all the constructive proposals made by the other States . . . has helped restart the arms race, and it failed to make Signor Mussolini understand that, if he broke the peace in Africa, Britain would join with other nations in upholding the authority of the League. To late to stop the war, the Government ranged itself at the eleventh hour behind the Covenant at Geneva. Even now its action has been slow and half-hearted.

The government's intentions, so it was charged in the manifesto, were
as despicable as its record:

> Whilst paying lip service to the League, it is planning a vast and
> expensive rearmament programme, which will only stimulate similar
> programmes elsewhere.

'This Government,' it was roundly declared, 'is a danger to the peace of
the world and to the security of this country.'

The Labour Party then offered its alternative programme:

> The Labour Party calls for a reversal of this suicidal foreign policy. It
> seeks whole-hearted cooperation with the League of Nations and
> with all States outside the League which desire peace. It stands
> firmly for the collective peace system. It demands speedy action
> through the League to bring the war in Africa to an end, to be
> followed by an immediate resumption of negotiations for all-round
> disarmament.

The manifesto was briefer on defence:

> Labour will efficiently maintain such defence forces as are necessary
> and consistent with our membership of the League.

It was stated clearly, however, that

> The best defence is not huge competitive national armaments, but
> the organization of collective security against any aggressor and the
> agreed reduction of national armaments everywhere.

In the course of the campaign all the national leaders stayed well
within the brief of the respective manifestos, though from each side an
attempt was made to show that certain leaders diverged from the
policies outlined in the manifestos. The National Government
exploited to the full the obvious division of opinion in the Labour
Party which had led to the resignations of Lansbury, Cripps and
Ponsonby from the NEC, while Labour spokesmen did their best to
demonstrate that Baldwin was merely the puppet of men of immod-
erate views like Churchill and Lord Lloyd. In several of his speeches
Baldwin linked the need to repair defence gaps to the 'changed situation in Europe' subsequent to the rise of Hitler, but more often he

related defence needs to the obligations of membership of the League and of national security. That is, the lack of a sense of urgency in the phrasing of the manifesto was also characteristic of the speeches of Baldwin and those of his colleagues who had collaborated in the prepa- aration of the manifesto. On Labour's side, Attlee and Morrison carried on to the hustings the emotional language of the party's manifesto, the platform slogan being 'A Vote for the Tories is a Vote for War', but both also drew attention to the fact that

> the Labour Party is pledged to maintain our defence forces in a state of efficiency and at a strength sufficient to fulfil our obligations at home and abroad.

The Liberal Party manifesto was the work of a committee composed of representatives of the parliamentary Liberal Party (for example, Sinclair), elder statesmen (Crewe), the NLF (Muir) and the SLF (James Scott). It stated that 'After long delay the Government have lately been taking definite action at Geneva', and made very little comment about the government's record in international affairs. Instead it commented that

> Upon the success or the failure of the League of Nations in its effort to penalise aggression must depend our own future policy in foreign affairs, and as to armaments. If the League succeeds we shall take one course; if it fails, another. The issue is now in the balance. Until we know we cannot judge. This is precisely the moment when the nation ought not to be asked to give a mandate on these matters for the next five years.

Nevertheless, the party's aims were clearly defined:

> Our aim is to maintain the peace of the world and to preserve our own security. Armaments, on however vast a scale, will not bring security or stop war. The national defences must be kept efficient and large enough for the needs of the time; but a colossal, panic expenditure in arms is not the road to peace.

On the hustings, Samuel, who since May had supported an increase in arms expenditure, appeared almost to be participating in the govern- ment's campaign. At Manchester on 28 October he said that

The Government manifesto spoke of strengthening our defences, and it was clear that in present circumstances they needed strengthening.[3]

While he continued to denounce the government for holding what he regarded as an 'unnecessary' election, the policy he propounded was similar to that of his opponents. In this he differed from Lloyd George and Lord Snowden, both of whom, despite giving election broadcasts ostensibly in the Liberal interest, strenuously denied that Britain was ill equipped to defend herself.[4]

Without exception the politicians regarded unemployment as the principal domestic issue of the campaign. Allied to the unemployment question were issues such as the Means Test, public works schemes, Special Areas, and the government's tariff policy. Nearly two of the five pages of the government's manifesto dealt directly or indirectly with unemployment, a reflection perhaps of Conservative Central Office's (and maybe Baldwin's) belief that the result of the election would turn on the issue.[5] In general terms the government congratulated itself on its fine record of bringing about a substantial reduction in the number of unemployed, and reassured those still unemployed that it intended to treat them humanely:

The remarkable fact that more persons are now employed in this country than ever before in its whole history has not sprung from accident or the unfettered operation of natural laws. It has been the result of the deliberate policy of the Government in protecting the home market and in creating a regime of cheap money, which has facilitated enterprise and stimulated industrial expansion (especially in housing).

Nor was that all:

The Government are constantly working on all kinds of plans by which they may make use of the present favourable circumstances to initiate new enterprises, thereby creating additional employment by the use of credit or other resources of the State. The building of the Queen Mary, the subsidy to tramp shipping, the production of oil from coal by the hydrogenation process, and the great scheme of London Transport improvements at a cost of between £30 and £40 million are instances in point.

For those on unemployment assistance the government manifesto offered less, at least in concrete terms. The government was giving the arrangements under the Unemployment Assistance Scheme 'prolonged and anxious' consideration. The present ('present' that is since February) standstill arrangements were to continue until the spring of 1936 when they would be replaced by 'permanent arrangements, which must remedy certain abuses and at the same time avoid hardship to applicants'. With the memory of the previous winter's row still fresh in their minds, the framers of the manifesto had added that

> Any action must be gradual, and must be carried out in full associa-
> tion with local opinion, so as to give effect to reasonable differences
> in the localities.

Details concerning the 'permanent arrangements' were not given, nor were they as much as hinted at subsequently in speeches.

Concerning the Means Test, it was observed in the government manifesto that 'the question is not whether there should be a Means Test, but what that test should be'. This, those concerned were reassured, was a matter

> now under close examination, but in any scheme great importance
> will be attached to maintaining the unity of family life and, in
> addition, provision will be made to meet any cases of proved hard-
> ship.

The manifesto also addressed itself directly to the people in the distressed areas. The government, it was claimed, had already revealed its willingness to grapple with the problem by appointing special commissioners with £2 million at their disposal for public works, with more finance available if and when it was required. Furthermore, the government recognised that the cause of the depression in the special areas was largely the contraction of the coalmining industry. It declared, therefore, that through the unification of mining royalties and the creation of a Royal Commission, the industry should come under the closer scrutiny of the state.

On unemployment, Labour's manifesto was more aggressive in tone. Under a section heading, 'Four Barren Years', it proclaimed that after four years of National Government

The country faces the grim spectacle of 2 million workless, with an army of well over 1½ million people on the Poor Law, and with the deepening tragedy of the distressed areas. The Government has robbed the unemployed of benefit and subjected them to a harsh and cruel household means test. It withdrew, under a storm of public indignation, its new Unemployment Regulations, and after nine months of reconsideration of this burning question it has ignominiously failed to produce any policy for the proper care of the unemployed.

Only in one other paragraph did the manifesto refer directly to unemployment:

Labour in power will attack the problem of the distressed areas by special steps designed to deal with the root causes of their troubles as part of a vigorous policy of national planning. Labour will sweep away the humiliating means test imposed by the 'National Government' and will provide adequately for the unemployed, but will seek above all to reabsorb idle workers into productive employment by far-reaching schemes of national development.

In the course of the campaign there were several developments on the government side. The most important of these was Chamberlain's broadcast announcement of a road construction programme of £100 million, which he confidently predicted would substantially reduce unemployment. A few days prior to the release of the manifesto, it was announced in the press that the Cunard White Star liner *Olympic* was to be towed to and broken up at Jarrow, where the earlier closure of Palmer's shipyard had left 90% of the workers without employment.[6] The *Olympic* project would, it was claimed, keep the town's workers employed for eighteen months, and inject into the economy about £100,000 in wages.[7] On 31 October it was also announced that Richard Thomas Company had acquired the long-closed Ebbw Vale steelworks. The company intended to reopen the works immediately, thereby providing employment for 6,000 steelworkers and 4,000 iron-ore miners. On the same day the Admiralty announced its 1935 construction programme of one leader and eight destroyers;[8] and, in a reversal of government policy, the dockyards contracted to build the ships were those with the heaviest unemployment (among them Clydeside, Tynemouth and Birkenhead), rather than those with the lowest tenders.[9] Announcements of this kind, so fortuitously timed, lent credibility to the government's manifesto promise not to rest on its laurels.

Throughout the campaign government spokesmen defended the principle of the Means Test, directing their remarks to that majority of the voters who contributed through taxation to the monies made available for the sustenance of the unemployed. It was implied in government speeches that by voting for the abolition of the Means Test, electors would be voting in favour of an increase in taxation.[10] By appealing to the economic sensibilities of the electorate and at the same time promising reform of the administration of the Means Test, Baldwin took much of the sting out of Labour's most potentially damaging attack on the government. Labour was further handicapped by the widespread belief that in 1931 the Labour Government was itself going to introduce a Means Test. The party's spokesmen strenuously denied this accusation, and throughout the campaign continued to call for the abolition of the test, some more vociferously than others. Among the former was Greenwood who at Leeds said:

> The position of the Labour Party is that the humiliation, injustice, and hardship resulting from the Means Test can be removed only by its entire aboliton.[11]

On one point of criticism the government offered no reply; namely Labour's assertion that even if unemployment was going down, the number of people subjected to the Poor Law was increasing, and increasing rapidly.

The Liberal manifesto also referred to unemployment, linking it to the 'disastrous reduction in the volume of world trade' along with

> the unrelieved misery of the depressed areas; the low wages of the miners of the farm workers, and of many others; the immensely reduced figures of our export trade compared with a few years ago; the plight of our shipping industry.

All this, it claimed, was due to the erection of tariff barriers by many governments, the British among them. For the Liberals it followed from this analysis that the basic solution to the unemployment problem was to rid commerce of hindrances like tariffs, subsidies, quotas and so on. It was also proposed to employ 'idle capital and idle labour upon a great number of enterprises which are urgently needed'. It was also stressed that 'the present Government has stubbornly rejected that policy'. On the subject of the Means Test, the Liberals hedged a little. It condemned the Means Test regulations, and considered that it was wrong to treat the household as a unit for Means Test purposes. The government was also denounced for failing to issue revised regulations, promised as long ago as February. But the manifesto did not call specifically for the abolition of the Means Test, and in subsequent speeches Liberal leaders did nothing to clarify their party's policy on this point. By laying stress on the need for national development schemes, the Liberals clearly wished to fire the imagination of the electorate as they had succeeded in doing in 1929; but on the hustings they met with little of the enthusiasm of that year.

Under the National Government the agricultural industry had experienced a variety of marketing innovations, inspired by the energetic Minister, Walter Elliot. The farmers were far from being happy with Elliot's schemes — indeed some influential Conservatives doubted whether they were well-advised.[12] But farmer discontent did not take the form of voting against the government, for the alternative source of marketing arrangements was the Labour Party, the schemes of which were far more radical than those put forward by Elliot. Furthermore, the government had offered subsidies to sectors of the agricultural industry, and these were very popular. Early in 1935 Lloyd George had revived interest in large-scale agricultural settlement schemes; he hoped to see at least 500,000 people put on the land under such a scheme, and in part because of his advocacy of the idea it formed part of the agricultural issue at the election. The agricultural issue was largely of concern to the Conservative and Liberal Parties; it played little part in Labour's campaign.

The National Government recognised that 'A prosperous countryside is an essential foundation of national well-being.' It also recognised that agriculture was not one but many industries, each working under different conditions and requiring different treatment for its improvement. Accordingly the government had made use of import duties, levies, or combinations of these devices according to the circumstances of each case:

> The producers have played their part by organization and cooperation, and this we have encouraged and helped. So bold a treatment was bound to raise some problems not yet solved, but we can claim that, broadly speaking, our efforts have met with success.

The manifesto reminded the farmers that the prices they were receiving at present were 15% higher than the low point of two years ago, while the agricultural worker had also benefited and his wage now stood at its highest for ten years. Nor had these benefits been made at the expense of the customer, who, it was claimed, had been able in 1935 to buy more food for 19s than could be bought for £1 when the government took office. Nor was the government resting on its laurels:

> It has also been announced that the Government have accepted the principle of unemployment insurance for agricultural workers, and it is our intention, if returned, to introduce legislation to that end.

As a concession to the likely popularity of Lloyd George's settlement scheme, it was observed that

> In all branches of agriculture our policy has been and will remain one of expansion of the home market. As the market expands, home production can expand with it, and in this way only can a real opportunity be afforded for new men to make a career on the land.

The manifesto concluded with a word for the Scots, who were assured that the government would attend to the needs of rural housing and rural repopulation, as well as the needs of Scottish agriculture.

The Labour manifesto gave less space to the requirements of the farmers, and rather more to the plight of the consumers, than did the government manifesto. The National Government, it was noted,

> has imposed new burdens on the people through increased taxes on food and the necessaries of life and the organized restriction of supplies.

Labour's solution for the problems of the agricultural industry lay partly in the international control of raw materials and partly through its policy of Socialist reconstruction:

> It . . . declared for public ownership of land in order that the community should profit by its value and proper use, the reorganization of agriculture, the introduction of unemployment insurance for farm workers, the abolition of the tied cottage and the provision of cheap cottages in the countryside.

In the course of the campaign party leaders stayed well within the brief of their respective manifestos, though indeed the issue was little

discussed on the hustings outside the counties where the farming
interest was dominant. Some Labour spokesmen, however, were
reluctant to stress the party's declared policy of immediate nationalisation of the land. In an article in the *Daily Herald*[13] Herbert Morrison
first restated this policy but added:

> we are not preparing a wholesale scheme for the socialization of
> farming. We recognize that the great bulk of agricultural production
> must, for a long time, be the responsibility of the individual.

In the main, however, Labour spokesmen adhered to the brief of the
manifesto when the agricultural issue was debated.

In view of their past commitment to agricultural reform, it is surprising that the Liberals devoted little space to the subject in their
manifesto. The low wages of farm labourers were referred to briefly,
and reference was made to 'a wide and detailed programme' (presumably *The Liberal Way*, published late in 1934) which dealt with the
ownership and use of land and the development of agriculture. While
expressing the party's interest in agriculture the Liberal manifesto
offered no observations on the state of the industry or the government's
record since 1931.

When party spokesmen referred to the social services they used the
term to embrace unemployment assistance, housing, education, health
(including 'maternal mortality') and pensions. Unemployment has
already been discussed and the rest, apart from housing, merit only
scant attention as issues in themselves, though they are important as
elements in the abstract issues of the campaign, namely 'democracy'
and 'Socialism', which are discussed later in this section. Housing,
however, was an important issue.

In the manifesto of the National Government it was claimed that the
'phenomenal growth' of the building industry had been brought about
by the government's cheap money policy. Since 1931 one million
houses had been built:

> On the foundations which sound financial policy has laid, new and
> rapid progress in social reform has again become possible.

In order to counter the criticisms of the Labour Party that most of the
new homes were beyond the means of those who most urgently
required them, and that the slum clearance programme should be
speeded up, it was claimed that

A very considerable proportion are small houses, and a substantial number that are being erected today are houses to let. The slum clearance campaign is actively proceeding. Already 420,000 occupiers have been actually rehoused, and transfer to new and well-built homes is now proceeding at the unprecedented rate of over 200,000 persons a year. The first steps have already been taken to deal with the problem of overcrowding in accordance with the provisions of the Acts which have been placed upon the Statute Book. We shall proceed vigorously with all these efforts.

While the figures were constantly used by government speakers throughout the campaign, the most popular slogan was simply 'One Million Houses Built'.

Labour could not, of course, dispute the accuracy of the government's figures, but it refused to agree that the houses were intended for or were going to those who most needed them. The government, it was asserted in the manifesto, 'has retarded the building of houses to let'. Rather strangely, the government's record on slum clearance was not referred to, nor was any promise given as to the number of houses which a Labour Government might build in the lifetime of a Parliament. It was, however, promised that a Labour Government would

go ahead with the provision of healthy homes for the people at reasonable rents until the needs of the nation are fully met.

In the course of the campaign Labour spokesmen denounced the government for handing over housing to private profit, a charge which government speakers strenuously denied. The Liberals took a middle position. They welcomed the improvements in the housing situation, but they wished to see the work done more rapidly and more systematically. People interested in the Liberals' proposals for the future were referred to 'the wide and detailed programme . . . already laid before the country'.

The National Government was sensitive to the charge that during its term of office it had not introduced any substantial social reforms. Just prior to the election it rushed through Parliament an increase in the child allowance, and announced that the school-leaving age should be increased to 15 years. Through its manifesto the government explained that a number of social reforms had been delayed 'by the necessity of first restoring the national finances', which had now, however, been accomplished. The reforms now proposed were threefold in character, dealing with pensions, education and the health of the nation. On the subject of pensions the government did not envisage any radical structural changes. It did, however, propose to extend the pensions scheme to black-coated workers like clerks, as well as shopkeepers, who could participate on a voluntary basis.

'Consolidation' was also the keynote of education and health reforms. 'Education,' it was declared in the manifesto,

> must always take a foremost place in social progress, and for some time past the Government have been engaged in drawing up a comprehensive scheme of reform.

This included raising the school-leaving age to 15 years (though if a child could find employment before he turned 15 years he was encouraged to take it), increasing by means of grants the accommodation available and so on. And concerning the health of the nation the government recognised the need to raise standards still higher, especially among 'the younger generation'.

> We must further improve our maternity services and make provision for medical assistance at points where there is a gap in the existing services. We must continue to extend our child welfare services and the provision of nursery schools.

In short the government promised to consolidate and extend existing services rather than initiate radical reforms. This was in keeping with Baldwin's declaration that he would sooner go out of office than see the government make rash promises.

The Labour manifesto was only marginally more radical. Labour believed that the government had actively discouraged the development of the social services and that as a consequence reforms were urgently required. The party stood for

> a big move forward in education, including the raising of the school-leaving age with adequate maintenance allowances.

It also promised to

> vigorously develop the health services and in particular . . . treat as one of its immediate concerns the terrible and neglected problem of maternal mortality.

Labour's pensions proposals were rather more controversial, for they included not only an increase in the value of the old age pension, but also a lowering of the qualifying age from 65 to 60 years. Furthermore, Labour pledged itself to

> a comprehensive programme of industrial legislation so as to secure reasonable hours and conditions of employment for all workers, and adequate compensation for the accidents of working life. It would restore the freedom of trade unions lost through the Trades Disputes and Trades Union Act.

Finally, Labour pledged itself to remove the government's tax on Cooperative Societies, imposed in the 1933 budget and retained in 1934 and 1935. It was hardly an ambitious programme of social reform but it went somewhat further than the government.

In the course of the campaign speakers of all parties expanded on their respective manifestos. Labour accused the government of having neglected social services for four years and then, as sops to the electors, introducing the increase in child allowances and announcing the raising of the school-leaving age, both of which proposals had been in Labour's programme for several years. The *Daily Herald* was moved to comment that 'The school-leaving age decision marks the beginning in the dressing of the Government shop window.'[14] Attlee urged the electors not to be taken in by the government's election 'tricks', for in the past four years educational facilities had actually been cut down and the social services badly neglected.[15] The National Government counter-attacked very strongly. The Minister of Health, Kingsley Wood, asserted that Labour's pensions proposals were financially unsound: he warned the voters to greet with scepticism promises which in the present circumstances could not possibly be implemented. Wood also denied that the black-coated worker had been neglected by the Government, and he pointed to the benefits accruing from his government's housing programme and the fact that in the last budget there had been taxation relief for lower-salaried workers.[16] Government spokesmen, when called upon to defend the tax on Cooperative Societies (which happened most frequently at constituency meetings), did so on financial grounds: they contended that the revenue produced from this tax would be channelled into the social services. Labour speakers doubted whether this would occur, and speculated on the likelihood of the money being spent on armaments instead. In his final broadcast address Baldwin categorically denied this charge.

As with housing and agriculture, the Liberal manifesto referred electors to their earlier programme for details of their social services scheme. The manifesto merely mentioned in passing that the Liberals were in favour of raising the school-leaving age and expanding the educational system. It also referred vaguely to 'the inclusion of other classes in National Insurance'. Alone among the manifestos of the major parties, the Liberals mentioned temperance and 'the extension of leisure and greater facilities for its use'. Nor during the campaign did Liberal speakers develop their own ideas for the reform of the social services. Instead they preferred to attack the government's failure to improve social services and to cast doubt on its promises for the future.

One of the subjects most discussed at the election was 'Socialism' and its corollary 'nationalisation'. Shortly after his election to the leadership of the Labour Party, and at a time when an early election was widely forecast, Attlee told the party faithful that 'We have got to make the issue at that Election Socialism.'[17] This appeared to imply that the Labour Party intended to fight the election on domestic rather than foreign affairs. In the manifesto, however, it was foreign affairs which figured most prominently, while Socialism was squeezed into half a paragraph midway through the manifesto, and in a line or two at the end. Though brief, the comments were unequivocal about the party's commitment to Socialism:

At home the Labour Party will pursue its policy of Socialist reconstruction. Labour has already put before the country boldly and
clearly schemes of public ownership for the efficient conduct in the
national interest of banking, coal and its products, transport, electricity, iron and steel and cotton. It has also declared for the public
ownership of land in order that the community should profit by its
value and proper use.

The final paragraph of the manifesto was forthright on the subject of political reform:

Labour seeks a mandate to carry out this programme by constitutional and democratic means, and with this end in view, it seeks
power to abolish the House of Lords and improve the procedure of
the House of Commons. Labour asks the nation for a Parliamentary
majority in order to promote Socialism at home and peace abroad.

The National Government manifesto placed Labour's Socialist proposals alongside what it regarded as the 'broad issue' of the election, namely

> whether the stability and confidence which the National Government have built up are to be preserved in a period of special difficulty and anxiety . . . The advent to power of the Labour Opposition pledged to a number of revolutionary measures of which the ultimate results could not be clearly foreseen, would inevitably be followed by a collapse of confidence.

In the course of the campaign the relatively restrained language of the manifesto — 'collapse of confidence' — was replaced by more emotive language like 'immediate financial crisis' which reminded voters that the crisis of 1931 had been precipitated by the Labour Government. This charge Labour denied strenuously, and in support of their denial they cited a speech of Neville Chamberlain's in the course of which he had appeared to exonerate Labour of any blame for the 1931 crisis. Fairly early in the campaign, however, Chamberlain issued a press statement categorically denying that he had never blamed the Labour Government; and for good measure he restated his belief that the Labour Government's policies had been a cause of the crisis of 1931 and would precipitate another crisis if Labour won this election.[18] Earlier he had informed the City that bank savings would be placed in jeopardy if Labour was returned.[19] Other government Ministers said much the same thing. Sir John Simon said that the country would be ruined if another financial crisis occurred, and this would certainly follow the return of a Socialist government.[20] Lord Hailsham equated Socialism with revolution and totalitarianism, and Anthony Eden was convinced that the return of Labour would cause an upheaval at home and have disastrous effects internationally.[21] As usual Baldwin took a line far more subtle than that of his colleagues. He put himself in the place of a workman and wondered exactly what 'nationalisation' meant — it was all very vague and did not appear to offer any immediate relief for the people.[22] This was a throwback reference to a speech made two years earlier in which he said that he trusted the British working man, but that the working man was no longer in control of the Labour Party, which was being run by Socialist intellectuals. In his final broadcast Baldwin emphasised to his listeners that 'the whole world is watching this Election, because in this Election democracy itself is on trial'. This was a line of argument which he had been developing since the formation of the Socialist League in 1932, the rise to power of Nazism in Germany, and the extremist resolutions of the Hastings conference of the Labour Party in October 1933.[23] Socialism, so his argument ran, was as unBritish as communism and fascism – or, as he put it, as un-British as totalitarianism of the left and the right.

Government speakers identified Socialism with misgovernment and incompetence. Indeed so often was this charge made against Labour that the question of Labour's 'fitness to govern' emerges as one of the central issues of the campaign. Almost without exception government candidates quoted from speeches made by Cripps, Attlee (especially from the years 1932 and 1933) and Lansbury to show that even Labour's leaders anticipated that a tremendous upheaval in the economic and social life of the people would follow the return of a Labour Government.[24] There was another aspect of the 'misgovernment' charge, namely, that the party was not fit to govern because its leaders were hopelessly divided on the important issue of international affairs. An allied charge was that Labour did not have any experienced and proven administrators among its leaders. As Attlee had been elected to the leadership on the eve of the election campaign, and as he had never held a Cabinet portfolio this charge was difficult to rebutt. Attlee did claim, however, that lack of a powerful leader was nothing new for Labour. At a Lancashire meeting he told the party faithful not to be

led astray by talk of splits and schisms. Our movement has never depended on leaders. It has depended on the rank and file. We do not need a wonder worker in a pink, red or blue shirt.[25]

He was quite wrong. Only with such a wonder worker could Labour have convinced the electors that it was fit to govern.

While the form and content of the manifestos provide clues as to the popularity rating of election issues, this can be done more precisely through the use of election addresses. Table 6.1 is a précis of the content of the election addresses.[26]

The worth of election addresses to the student of elections is in the information they provide about the attitudes of the candidates themselves and the stress which they lay on the various issues of the campaign. Of course in large measure they 'echo the themes of the centre', but they do so selectively, stressing those issues which are attractive locally.[27] Hence, for example, as in 1945, election addresses of candidates in Scottish and Welsh constituencies tend to emphasise domestic rather than international issues, whereas for the nation as a whole the two types of issue are quite finely balanced as of concern to

Table 6.1: Candidates' Election Addresses: The Top Ten Issues

National Government		Labour		Liberals	
1. Pro League of Nations	90%	Pro League of Nations	90%	Pro League of Nations	90%
2. Prosperity, recovery	80%	Rearmament, fear of	85%	Anti-Tariffs, trade down	93%
3. Employment	86%	Means Test	84%	Unemployment	83%
4. Rearmament, modernisation of services	86%	Unemployment	82%	Pro Public Works	70%
5. Pro Tariffs, trade up	77%	Education	76%	Agriculture	65%
6. Housing, one million homes built	72%	Pro Disarmament	71%	Means Test	63%
7. Education	61%	Pro Nationalisation	67%	Pro Disarmament	48%
8. Pensions	53%	Housing	67%	'National' government	45%
9. Anti-Socialism	52%	Pensions, at 60 years	62%	Anti-Socialism	40%
10. Slum Clearance	51%	Distressed Areas	60%	Rearmament/ Distressed Areas	38%

the candidates.

Little more can be said about election addresses for it is impossible to determine with precision the number of electors who read the addresses, and equally impossible to determine whether electors were influenced by what they read. Gallup polls suggest that in the 1950s and 1960s about 50% of the electors read election addresses.[28] It seems likely that for the interwar years addresses were read by a rather higher percentage than this, if only because there were then fewer rival sources of information about the character of an election. In particular, there was of course no television. But even if it could be demonstrated that up to 75% of the electors read the addresses, no assessment would be possible as to the impact made upon electors. The value of election addresses lies therefore in the indications they offer as to what the election was about in the eyes of the contestants.

At the 1935 election, as for other elections, the addresses were drafted on the eve of the campaign; but unlike some other twentieth-century elections, the campaign in 1935 was fought from start to finish on a broad front — issues did not ebb and flow as, for example, at the

1910 elections.[29] Hence in 1935 the election addresses reflect quite accurately the matters of concern to the contestants right through to the eve of the poll.

The more recent of the Nuffield studies of British general elections have compared the content of election addresses for various elections.[30] The content of election addresses for the 1935 election can be compared very roughly with addresses for the 1929 and 1945 elections.[31] Rowe's analysis of the election addresses for the 1929 election suggest that employment and social reform were about as important as they were in 1935.[32] On the other hand, international affairs seem to have been rather less dominant in 1929, while agriculture and Socialism were rather more important then than in 1935. At the 1945 election housing was by far the most important election issue, and was mentioned by a considerably higher percentage of candidates than in 1935 (over 90% of all election addresses).[33] On the other hand, foreign policy was rather less important (under 80%) and world organisation for peace even less so (under 60%). The Empire question was referred to more often in 1945, the fairly low percentage for 1935 reflecting the 'stillness' following the passing of the India Act. In 1945 less than 40% of candidates referred to trade and tariffs, whereas they had been mentioned in over 75% of the addresses in 1935. Labour percentages for nationalisation were roughly similar for both elections, except for land nationalisation which in 1945 was not referred to.[34]

Notes

1. Cab. 23/82, 16 and 23 Oct. Also Cab. 24/257, memoranda C.P. 193. In his life of Neville Chamberlain, Keith Feiling records that it was Chamberlain who prepared the first draft of the manifesto, and this indeed seems very likely. It is clear, however, that the manifesto cannot be identified completely with Chamberlain because it does not have rearmament as its centrepiece. In August Chamberlain had written that 'we should take the bold course of actually appealing to the country on a defence programme'; but by mid-October he had accepted Baldwin's view that it was wiser to lay stress on the 'long and anxious foreign affairs arguments rather than rearmament *per se*'. See K. Feiling, *The Life of Neville Chamberlain* (1946), pp. 266, 268-9; also Neville Chamberlain Papers, the political diaries and journals, 19 Oct. 1935.

2. Minutes of NEC meetings, 22 and 23 Oct., including the minutes of the Election Sub-Committee meeting on 16 Oct. Members of the subcommittee included Attlee, Dalton, Adamson, Greenwood, Latham, Middleton and Shepherd.

3. *News Chronicle*, 29 Oct. 1935.

4. *The Times*, 21 and 30 Oct. 1935.

5. See Feiling, *Life of Chamberlain*, pp. 266 and 268.

6. The classic account of the effect of the closure of Palmer's on Jarrow is Ellen Wilkinson's *The Town That Was Murdered* (1936).

7. *Morning Post*, 14 Oct. 1935.

8. Both referred to in *The Times*, 31 Oct. 1935.

9. In the early 1930s some members of the Cabinet, notably Ramsay Mac-Donald, wished to use Admiralty orders for the relief of unemployment in stricken dockyards like the Tyne, but their economy-minded colleagues refused to co-operate until the eve of the 1935 general election. See for example, discussions in Cab. 23/80, 31 Oct., 14 Nov. 1934. For the change of mind with an election close at hand see Cab. 23/72, 23 Oct. 1935. For the unheeded pleas of Pearson, MP for Jarrow, see Baldwin Papers, vol. 6, numbered pages 99-119 dealing with correspondence for 1933-4.

10. See for example, *Yorkshire Post*, 8 Nov. 1935.

11. *Yorkshire Observer*, 7 Nov. 1935.

12. See Baldwin Papers, vol. 107, Lord Salisbury to Baldwin, 10 Feb. 1935.

13. *Daily Herald*, 2 Nov. 1935.

14. Ibid., 12 Oct. 1935.

15. *The Times*, 7 Nov. 1935.

16. Ibid., 1 and 6 Nov. 1935.

17. *Daily Herald*, 14 Oct. 1935.

18. *The Times*, 5 Nov. 1935.

19. *Daily Herald*, 31 Oct. 1935.

20. *Morning Post*, 29 Oct. 1935.

21. *The Times*, 1 Nov. 1935.

22. Liverpool speech, *The Times*, 5 Nov. 1935.

23. See for example, *Daily Telegraph*, 7 Oct. 1933.

24. See also the Conservative Party's *Notes for Speakers and Workers* published at the commencement of the election campaign.

25. *Daily Herald*, 14 Oct. 1935.

26. See Appendix 4 for full table and explanatory note.

27. D.E. Butler and M. Pinto-Duschinsky, *The British General Election of 1970* (1971), p. 437.

28. Ibid., p. 311.

29. N. Blewett 'The British General Elections of 1910', D.Phil. thesis, University of Oxford, 1966, Ch. 4.

30. See Butler and Pinto-Duschinsky, *1970 Election*, p. 441.

31. No full-scale study of the 1931 general election has yet been undertaken. Bassett's interesting and perceptive account of the election does not analyse election addresses in a formal way. It is clear, however, that domestic affairs dominated the election. R. Bassett *Nineteen Thirty-One: political crisis* (1958), Chs. 14-16.

32. E.A. Rowe, 'The British General Election of 1929', B.Litt. thesis, University of Oxford, 1959, pp. 193-200.

33. R.B. McCallum and A. Readman, *The British General Election of 1945* (1947), pp. 88-117.

34. I have not touched on the form and style of election addresses at the 1935 election. The differences between those for 1929 and 1945 and those for 1935 are negligible.

7 ELECTORAL POLITICS AND THE MASS MEDIA

It was in the 1930s that the talkie film and the wireless came of age as agencies of political expression. Newspapers had come of age before the Great War, but it was in the 1930s that circulations increased so markedly that it could be said with confidence that

> there can be very few homes in Great Britain where some kind of daily morning newspaper is not seen and the Sunday paper . . . is almost universal.[1]

This chapter deals with the interactions of the mass media, the electors and the politicians. It suggests that the shape taken by these interactions was to the advantage of the National Government rather than to the principal opposition group, the Labour Party.

The Cinema and the Wireless

In the mid-1930s about 40% of the people, or perhaps up to 66% of the electorate, were going to the country's 4,300 or more cinemas at least once a week.[2] The cinema was clearly connected with the working class. As Nicholas Pronay has noted, drawing on contemporary surveys, the largest proportion of 'regulars' (once or more a week) came from lower income groups.[3] He also contends that

> The distinguishing features of this relationship, early conditioning, habitual attendance and communal participation, were especially significant in terms of the potential effectiveness of the media.

What these people saw each week was a newsreel and two features; and it is the newsreel which is of interest here. It was from 1932 on that newsreels with soundtracks were shown. Before that the range of social and political information which could be covered by pictures and monosyllabic captions alone was obviously very restricted.

Soundtracks enabled the newsreels not only to show something but also to interpret it. Pronay underlines this point by writing that

> Between the acquisition of their 'voice' by 1932, and the Second World War, that is during those same difficult years of uncertain

loyalties and leadership, there falls the first period when the news-reels were in a position, technically, to contribute to public opinion.

The newsreels were produced by five companies: Gaumont-British, Movietone, Pathe, Paramount and Universal, the first three of which were jointly or solely owned by British interests, and the last two American-owned. On an average they produced over 500 newsreels per annum, two a week by each of the companies for twice-weekly pro-gramme changes. The owners and editors were not subject to any statu-tory restrictions on 'controversial' topics, but as they had no wish to upset their patrons, in Pronay's words,

> They featured and played up the ordinary, the orderly, the well-arranged aspects of the society around them, rather than the truly sensational. The Newsreels laid stress on the points of similarity, identity of outlook and interest between the world of the govern-ment and that of their working-class regulars. Above all, they stressed the points of consensus rather than the points of conflict. The majority of Newsreel editors, it should be added, did so by inclination as well as necessity . . . In real and practical terms the Newsreels served well their regulars who wanted to hang on to what they believed were the basic decencies of their situation: a belief in the good intentions of their rulers, the belief that things would get better without violence in Britain, and that they should bravely meet their present plight with a laugh.

None of this was conducive to winning converts to the Labour Party; all of it reinforced support for the National Government, the self-proclaimed party of consensus.

The newsreels personalised politics in that of necessity they gave much of their limited time for politics to shots of the party leaders in action, whether delivering speeches, boarding ships, attending the launching of ships, boarding aeroplanes, attending airshows and the like. The activities of the government leaders received by far the greater coverage and the more favourable coverage. When, for instance, on the eve of the 1935 election Stanley Baldwin addressed the Peace Society in a speech not meant to be a contribution to the election campaign, Gaumont-British filmed it and distributed before the election, thereby ensuring that it did play a part in the election campaign in the govern-ment's interest.[4] No film was made of Attlee's speech to the party faithful at Harwood.[5] This imbalance in the scale and favourability of newsreel exposure may well have been a long-term factor conditioning the electors to see their leaders in particular roles; and as such it should not be overlooked as a possible reason for the National Government's comfortable victory at the 1935 election.

Indeed the National Government was alive to the importance of film as a vehicle for political propaganda. In the course of 1934 when public opinion was running strongly against the government, and all newspapers save the *Daily Telegraph* and *The Times* (both of which had small circulations) were closed to the government, it was mooted in government circles that money should be made available for the purchase of cinemas throughout the country.[6] This proposal was not taken up, but the government did encourage its constituent parties to purchase film vans and to make propaganda films for the National Government. During the 1935 election campaign the National Government used fourteen outdoor film units and seventeen vans carrying indoor film equipment.[7] The Labour Party had only two cinema vans.[8] The government units and vans carried films of Baldwin, MacDonald, Simon and Neville Chamberlain making speeches about the achievements of the National Government since 1931, as well as films demonstrating the increased prosperity of all sectors of British industry. One film, called 'The Signs of the Times', showed British workmen enjoying seaside holidays; another imparted propaganda through the humour of well-known comedians Arthur Prince and Stanley Holloway.[9]

The film units seem to have been extremely popular, particularly in remote agricultural areas and in big cities with heavy unemployment like Glasgow.[10] Occasionally a film produced some rowdyism as when a Mancunian was moved to heave a brick through the glass screen;[11] but in general the films were watched attentively and even applauded on occasion. Labour, with only two vans, and apparently with no film of Attlee, was unable to match the National Government in this sphere of propaganda. While it is impossible to gauge whether the films caused any redirection of votes, it is also difficult to resist the conclusion that the National Government benefited from the increased exposure. Certainly Baldwin seems to have been as effective on film as he was over the wireless. A correspondent reported that while she was seated with a working-class audience in a cinema in Wood Green a film was shown of the party leaders addressing rallies; only Baldwin's speech, she noted, was clapped. As she was leaving the cinema she heard a working man say: 'What I likes about Baldwin 'e don't sling no mud!'[12]

The 1930s was 'The Golden Age of Wireless'.[13] In the early part of the decade the introduction of cheap wireless sets led to a marked increase in the number of licence holders: between 1931 and 1935 the number of licences increased from 4 million to 7½ million,[14] and by the latter date about 17% of the population had licences (9% in 1931), and there were probably between 65 and 70 licences for every 100 house-holds in Britain.[15] For Greater London and England south of the Trent the percentage was greater than this, while for Scotland and Wales it was substantially less. However, even in Wales and Scotland the percent-age of licence holders doubled between 1931 and 1935. Penetration of broadcasting was greatest among the middle and upper classes, but by the mid-1930s was also very marked among the employed working class. While political broadcasts were not as popular as other pro-grammes, it would seem from newspaper surveys conducted on the eve of the 1935 election that perhaps up to 40 per cent of licence holders listened to them.[16] In the weeks leading up to the election there was a major rush to buy sets.[17] The number of electors who listened cannot be calculated with any precision, but perhaps between one-third and one-half of the electorate heard political broadcasts during the election campaign, an unprecedented degree of contact between politicians and electors.

It would seem that the introduction of wireless broadcasts had at least two effects on constituency campaigning. At the 1935 election a number of candidates tuned in to the broadcasts before going to mid-evening meetings, where they would then reply to or expand on the content of the broadcasts.[18] That is, the broadcasts not only moulded the election campaign directly, but also indirectly by shaping the character of constituency meetings. Furthermore, in many cases the audiences at constituency meetings would also have listened to the broadcasts and then come to the meeting 'in a spirit perhaps a shade more critical than before of home town oratory'.[19] The second major effect was not so much on the character of local meetings as on their size. In the course of the 1935 election considerable press comment was directed to the decline in numbers attending constituency meetings.[20]

In the confused circumstances of the 1931 general election the parties had been unable to agree among themselves about the alloca-tion of election talks, and J.C.W. Reith, the Director General of the BBC, had himself taken part in the selection of speakers.[21] At the 1935 election the parties managed to agree on quotas of five speeches for the National Government, four for Labour and three for the Samuelite Liberals, an overall increase of three on the 1931 allocations, and six on the 1929 figures. Each of the twelve talks was to be of 20

minutes duration. The BBC itself had to decide upon the claims of
other parties, and arranged to do this on Nomination Day, when it
would be known how many candidates would be going to the polls.
Twenty candidates was taken as the minimum number which would
qualify a party for a broadcast.[22] Perhaps Oswald Mosley was not
informed of this, for it seems unlikely that he would have missed so
golden an opportunity to advance his cause. As it was, Mosley's
decision not to contest the election made certain that the BBC would
not be called on to allocate a broadcast to other than the major
parties.[23]

The government speakers were Baldwin, Neville Chamberlain, Mac-
Donald and Simon, all experienced broadcasters. Baldwin, of all politicians the one most alive to the potential of wireless,[24] not only
opened the wireless campaign for the government, he also took the unprecedented step of closing it with a second broadcast. By doing this
he prevented what could well have been an acrimonious debate about
the selection of the fifth government speaker, for both the Liberal
National and National Labour Groups would have lobbied for a second
speaker (Simon must certainly have been aggrieved at the generous
allocation given to the Samuelite Liberals), while the Conservative
Party would have been keen to get a third broadcast, though selection
of the speaker could have proved difficult. Not only did Baldwin's decision preserve harmony within the National Government, it also enabled
him to give the appearance of dominating the campaign from start to
finish, an impression which the other government speakers reinforced.
In his opening speech Baldwin was authoritative, yet personable, with,
as one writer had put it about an earlier broadcast, 'his feet on our
fenders'; Simon spoke in his clipped and cool way about Liberalism
being more important than the Liberal Party, and that all Liberals could
trust Baldwin; Chamberlain offered a package of goodies to the
electors, hoping to convince them that the government was a dynamic
as well as a stabilising force in British society; MacDonald was suitably
stoical, and he too sang Baldwin's praises; and of course Baldwin himself delivered the last broadcast of the election campaign.[25] Even
Labour Party supporters like Walter Citrine, General Secretary of the
TUC, acknowledged Baldwin's skill as a broadcaster.[26] It was an admirable team superbly led by a master playing-coach.

The Labour Party's wireless campaign was beset by problems. In
the first instance the party had difficulty in the selection of speakers,
which was in the gift of the NEC. One of the obvious candidates, and an
experienced broadcaster, Arthur Henderson, died on the eve of the

election. Attlee, from early October the leader of the party, was the
obvious choice to open the campaign; but he had never before delivered
an election broadcast, and in the order of things would have to follow
Baldwin. Given their high standing in the party hierarchy, Arthur Greenwood and J.R. Clynes could not be overlooked, though the latter had
shown little understanding of the medium in 1931.[27] It was the selection
of the fourth speaker which proved most contentious. The parliamentary Labour Party wanted the recently deposed leader, George
Lansbury, to be the fourth speaker. At the NEC meeting the case for
Lansbury was put by Attlee. However, there was a strong group which
favoured the claims of Herbert Morrison who had won control of the
London County Council for Labour in the previous year, and whose
voice might well be heeded by Londoners at a general election. After a
spirited debate the NEC narrowly carried a motion that Morrison
should be the party's fourth speaker.[28]

Labour's wireless campaign was generally considered to be inept,
especially in comparison with the National Government's skilful display
of teamwork. Attlee, Clynes and Greenwood all said roughly the same
things in roughly the same way. Only Morrison seems to have shown any
skill as a broadcaster; and certainly he attracted more listeners than did
his colleagues, though still far fewer than Stanley Baldwin.[29] Of all the
speakers Attlee had the most difficult task. He was burdened with great
disadvantages even before he spoke into the microphone. In the first
place he was little known to the country at large; even at Labour Party
conferences he was less well known than a half-dozen other men. At
the 1929 general election he had hardly spoken outside his constituency in Stepney; and at the 1931 election, although Londoners got to
know him a little better (though even here Herbert Morrison captured
the imagination of Labour supporters in London), he was not senior
enough to be invited to deliver a broadcast. In the years 1931 to 1935
he consolidated his parliamentary reputation, but outside the House he
was rarely in the limelight; Lansbury and Cripps received far greater
publicity though in the course of 1935 Attlee delivered two political
broadcasts.[30] On his election to the leadership of the party following
Lansbury's resignation, only five weeks before the general election,[31]
the anti-Labour newspapers delightedly asked 'Who is Mr. Attlee?'
Even the *Daily Herald* and *Reynolds' News* gave their readers the
impression that Attlee was merely a stopgap leader who would be
replaced as soon as abler men were available; that is, immediately after
the election.[32] Within three weeks of being elected leader Attlee had to
make the party's first broadcast, and he had to follow what was

generally acknowledged to be a masterly performance by Baldwin. Under the circumstances Attlee did quite well, but it was too much to expect that he could wrest the initiative from Baldwin.

There was really no such thing as a Liberal Party wireless campaign; rather there were three personal campaigns loosely built around the theme of Liberalism. The first of the broadcasts were delivered not by Archibald Sinclair, Samuel's able and dedicated lieutenant since 1931, but by Lloyd George, Samuel's most vigorous opponent for much of the time since 1931. In the course of 1935 Samuel and Lloyd George had gone some way towards composing their differences, but it was a rather surprised Lloyd George who received a formal invitation from Samuel to open the Liberals' wireless campaign. The explanation may lie in the fact that Lloyd George had made it known that candidates who pledged themselves to the programme of the Council of Action — and many of these would be Liberals — were to receive financial assistance; but it seems clear that Lloyd George was not anticipating a *quid pro quo* from Samuel, and that he was genuinely surprised when the offer came.[33] Naturally he grasped this opportunity to further the interests of the Council of Action, while at the same time making it quite clear that he was not a spokesman for the Liberal Party. His address was the usual mixture of aggression, ebullience and wit; but the consensus of contemporary press opinion was that his oratorical style was unsuited to the medium, that his message was substantially that which he had been ineffectually hawking around the country for the past year, and that his attack had scarcely dented the National Government's armour, so skilfully crafted by Baldwin a few nights earlier.

The selection of the second opposition Liberal speaker was no less controversial. Once again the claims of Sinclair was overlooked (as were those of Isaac Foot, who since 1931 had delivered several broadcasts for the Liberal Party), this time in favour of those of Lord Snowden, formerly Chancellor of the Exchequer in the 1929-31 Labour Government, later arch-critic of the Labour Party and spokesman for the National Government, and still later a leading critic of the National Government. He had assumed this last guise in the course of 1932 when the National Government proceeded to demolish the crumbling edifice of free trade, which Snowden himself had helped shore up during Labour's second administration and the first months of the life of the National Government. Thereafter he increasingly involved himself in the affairs of the Liberal Party, and was consulted by Samuel at the time the Liberals decided to move into opposition to the

National Government. He acted closely with Samuel, partly in the role of intermediary between Samuel and Lloyd George, for he was anxious to bring the latter into the Samuelite fold.[34] From Samuel's point of view Snowden possessed an additional virtue; namely that at the 1931 general election Snowden had established a reputation of being a first-rate political broadcaster, whereas none of Samuel's immediate colleagues, save Isaac Foot, had ever before delivered a broadcast. Hence, much to the indignation of the Conservative and Labour Parties, and probably to some Liberals as well, Snowden delivered the second of the opposition Liberal broadcasts.[35] He was as forthright in his criticism of the National Government as he had been in its defence in 1931; but he seemed to be speaking on behalf of no group in particular, and, disconcertingly no doubt for the Liberal and Labour Parties, he stated emphatically that he believed that the National Government was in no danger of defeat.[36]

Samuel himself delivered the final broadcast for the opposition Liberals. Perhaps he should have permitted Sinclair to try his hand, for he at least would have been energetic and forthright in his criticism of the government and would have conveyed an air of commitment to the cause of the Liberal Party. As it was, Samuel gave a rather 'tired' address in which he virtually conceded defeat. And it was his misfortune that the two speakers who followed him – Morrison and Baldwin – delivered what were popularly believed to be the best broadcasts of the campaign.

During the election campaign the National Government clearly won the war on the air. But it is arguable whether this was the full war or merely a final skirmish of a prolonged war whose outcome was not really in doubt when that final skirmish took place. In short, had the BBC's self-proclaimed adherence to a 'middle road'[37] in the inter-election years been a factor consolidating the hold of the National Government on the electorate?

Any consideration of conscious or unconscious political bias in the BBC should have as its starting point the backgrounds of those responsible for BBC policy, the chairman and the Board of Governors, for as W.A. Robson has noted:

> The complexion of the Board will affect the whole trend of administration in an organization like the BBC, not by virtue of their decisions on questions of policy, but by reason of the feeling that executive officials will have as to what line of approach is or is not likely to meet with approval in the Board room.[38]

The BBC was the creation of a Conservative Government (headed by
Stanley Baldwin), and the first chairman of the BBC was Lord
Clarendon, who had been chief Conservative whip in the House of
Lords. His successor was J.H. Whitley, a former Liberal whip, a coalition Liberal, and Speaker of the House of Commons from 1921 to
1928. On Whitley's death early in 1935 the National Government
appointed to the chair Lord Bridgeman, formerly a Conservative MP, a
Minister in successive Conservative Governments, and Stanley Baldwin's
friend and confidant since before the Great War.[39] Bridgeman was
chairman until his death late in 1935, when, in a broadcast tribute, he
was described as a 'typical country gentleman in politics'.[40] The Board
of Governors was similarly composed. Robson grumbled in 1935 that

> During the whole existence of the BBC there has been a strong
> majority on the Board of Governors of persons of pronounced Con-
> servative or Conservative-Liberal outlook. Only the two women
> members of the Board holding office at separate times, are known to
> have any sympathy with the philosophy of the Left. This predomin-
> ance makes the Board highly unreflective of the general outlook of
> the community.[41]

Founded by a Conservative Government headed by Stanley Baldwin,
administered by elderly men of Conservative-Liberal inclining, the BBC
could hardly be otherwise than a weapon in the armoury of the forces
aligned with the National Government against the Labour Party.

While listener response to BBC programmes cannot be gauged with
any certainty for the 1930s,[42] contemporary opinion seems agreed that
the BBC did exercise a considerable cultural, moral and political influence on British society. It is contended here that whatever influence
the BBC did exercise it most certainly was not in the interest of the
Labour Party, the principal opposition party to the National Government. Nor was it in the interest of the Tory diehards. Rather it was
squarely in the National Government's interests.

Hilda Matheson, the BBC's Director of Talks until 1932, and thereafter one of the few well-informed critics of the corporation, observed
in 1934 that

> Any attempt to estimate the political influence or the political
> flavour of broadcasting must take into account the whole front
> along which broadcasting operates, from the Sunday joint to the
> comic turn, must note the thousand and one points at which pro-

grammes make contact with men, women, and children during the
day and night.[43]

Miss Matheson's point is well taken, but here consideration is given only
to the more obvious of her 'thousand and one points': party political
broadcasts, ministerial statements, and talks and news programmes.

Early in 1936 a Broadcasting Committee headed by Lord Ullswater
reported that

> It must be recognized as inevitable that more prominence is given
> to the leaders of the political party in power than to the Opposition.
> There are numbers of occasions on which the Ministers of State are
> called upon to make important pronouncements. These necessarily
> have some political flavour and tend naturally to stress the benefic-
> ence of Government activities.[44]

A glance at the programmes for 1935 confirms the Ullswater
Committee's finding. The year opened with Ramsay MacDonald
'Looking Ahead to 1935'.[45] He was followed by Sir John Simon on 'A
Plan for Air Security'.[46] In April MacDonald again broadcast to the
nation, this time on the triumphs of the 'Stresa Conference'. Shortly
after, Lord Londonderry spoke on 'Britain's Air Policy',[47] and in June
Stanley Baldwin, Prime Minister for the third time and as much a
fixture in British life as George V, delivered a 'Message to the Nation'.[48]
On this occasion the opposition parties were also given an opportunity
to give broadcasts, but not before Sir Bolton Eyres Monsell had spoken
cheerfully of the advantages to Britain of the recently concluded
'Anglo-German Naval Agreement'.[49] On behalf of the Liberals Samuel
then gave a lifeless talk on the minsterial changes and Clement Attlee
gave a rather more vigorous broadcast for Labour. Attlee was followed
by the retiring Prime Minister, Ramsay MacDonald, who thus had the
last word in what amounted to a miniature pre-election debate.[50]
From July through to the general election in November, Samuel Hoare
and Anthony Eden frequently delivered broadcasts on the international
situation, at all times stressing the government's commitment to the
League of Nations.[51] In August Kingsley Wood had news of the
National Health Insurance Scheme; and he noted in passing that
unemployment was declining rapidly.[52] To none of these telling thrusts
could either the Liberals or Labour reply.

But political bias in broadcasting went well beyond direct government pronouncements. In January and February 1935 the BBC ran a

series of talks on India. Of the ten speakers chosen only two — Attlee and Lansbury — were from the Labour Party, and one — Isaac Foot — was from the Liberal Party. The series was far more a debate between National Government spokesmen like Samuel Hoare (Minister of State for India), Sir George Schuster (from 1938 a Liberal National MP) and Stanley Baldwin, and spokesmen for the right wing of the Conservative Party like Winston Churchill and Lord Lloyd.[53] In March Lord Robert Cecil and L.S. Amery debated the merits and demerits of the Peace Ballot, the latter expressing the majority view of the Conservative Party and the National Government, the former speaking for the League of Nations Union.[54] Labour's voice on the subject was not heard. In the spring of 1935 the BBC ran an important series of talks on 'Liberty'. Of the twelve speakers, only two — Herbert Morrison and J. Moore, a mat-weaver from Bradford — spoke from Labour's point of view. George Bernard Shaw, who might have done so, delivered a frivolous talk instead; and G.K. Chesterton spoke from the viewpoint of the Roman Catholic Church. The remaining eight speakers, while differing on points of detail, were in agreement that 'Liberty' and 'Socialism' were incompatible.[55] Coming at the same time as the King's Jubilee celebrations, with their reaffirmation of the virtues of traditional British institutions and values, these supposedly apolitical talks on 'Liberty' could only have redounded to the advantage of the National Government, whose new head, Stanley Baldwin, was also constantly extolling traditional British values and institutions and proclaiming that his government was the nation's bulwark of those values and institutions.

In the autumn of 1935 the BBC commenced a series of talks on 'The Citizen and his Government'. It was intended that the first four of the talks should be 'expositional' in character, rather than 'polemical'. The man chosen to deliver the 'expositional' talks was Captain H. Balfour, a relation of the former Conservative Prime Minister, A.J. Balfour, and himself a Conservative MP.[56] Balfour's first talk, on the subject of 'The Free-Born Briton', was a straightforward account of British 'freedoms' in relation to the unfortunate peoples of Europe, and as such sounded like an echo of the speeches which Baldwin had been making for the past three yers. His second talk, 'Making the Law', included a defence of the House of Lords, which must have caused resentment within the Labour Party. His third talk, 'Putting the Law into Effect', was technical and uncontroversial. In his fourth and final talk he spoke of 'The Responsibility of the Elector'. This was notable only for a savage attack on the idea of proportional representation, so strongly advocated by Liberal oppositionists who would have relished a right of reply.[57] There followed instead three talks by Agnes Headlam-Morley on aspects of government in America and selected European countries. She found no system of government quite as satisfactory as the British.[58] The BBC had intended to follow Headlam-Morley with Oswald Mosley, Harry Pollitt, Herbert Morrison, Isaac Foot and Kenneth Pickthorn,[59] but the series was abandoned, probably due to the general election.

Political bias extended even to programmes less overtly political than those considered so far. Following the dismissal in 1934 of its regular broadcaster on foreign affairs, Vernon Bartlett, the BBC employed several occasional speakers.[60] Throughout 1935 the BBC's radio journalists on foreign affairs were Sir Frederick Whyte and F.A. Voigt, whose views closely corresponded with those of the National Government. In March Whyte commented favourably on the government's White Paper on defence, while Voigt spoke of the dangers to Europe and Britain of a resurgent Germany.[61] In July both men spoke feelingly of the need for collective security, Whyte indeed speaking of Baldwin as 'our representative citizen'.[62] In the same month the BBC broadcast a talk by J. Avenol, the Secretary-General of the League of Nations. In speaking of Britain's strong support for the work of the League, Avenol might have weakened Labour's charge that the National Government had been, and was still, less than full-hearted in its support of the League. A talk on similar lines by the Archbishop of Canterbury may have had a like effect.[63] Late in May, at a time when rumours of a reshuffle of the Cabinet were rife, H.A. Mess gave a talk on 'The Power of Leadership', in which he stressed a nation's need of a tried and trusted leader.[64] A week later, to general rejoicing, Stanley Baldwin replaced MacDonald as Prime Minister.

Throughout 1935 broadcasters on domestic affairs stressed that Britain was recovering rapidly from the economic and social catastrophe of the early 1930s. For instance, the theme of many of John Hilton's popular talks was similar to Baldwin's: 'We're on the road to recovery, but more remains to be done.'[65] Apart from a regular broadcaster like Hilton, a succession of occasional speakers reinforced the message. In July the government's Commissioner for the Depressed Areas, M.P. Stewart, commented that 'The nation is enjoying considerable prosperity';[66] and from early October, in a series entitled 'Ways and Means', the young *Economist* and *News Chronicle* writer, Geoffrey Crowther, spoke of 'three years of steady recovery'.[67] Crowther's talks were so blatantly in the National Government's interest that they drew a sharp rebuke from the General Secretary of the National Council of Labour Colleges who wrote that

> Mr. Crowther's article reads more like a defence of the existing social system than an objective analysis of the unemployment problem.[68]

This bias extended even to book reviews. In the course of a review of *The Next Five Years*, Max Nicholson wrote of the 'historic national revival' since 1931, and of the 'diminishing appeal of party', a statement hardly calculated to appeal to Labour.[69]

The Ullswater Committee noted in its report that:

> The influence of broadcasting on the political life of the country is brought to bear not only by speeches, talks, and reports, but also by the provision of news. It is, therefore, of the utmost importance that the news distributed by the BBC should be a fair selection of items impartially represented.

The committee considered that the existing arrangements were satisfactory, 'on the whole'. Its use of the colloquial qualifying phrase suggests, however, that it had reservations about the impartiality of the BBC's news reports:

> The BBC, it is true, is dependent for the bulk of its news on four commercial agencies which are primarily designed to cater for the Press. It is obviously possible that the selection of news for the BBC may be influenced by the weight of opinion whether political, economic, religious, or social, temporarily predominating in the Press. Fears have been expressed by witnesses on this score, with special reference to the relations of Capital and Labour.

The report concluded lamely that 'it is fair to say that any such suggestion of bias is denied by the News Agencies'. Even so, the nervousness of the committee on this issue can be seen in its recommendation that the BBC should supplement the agency services by sending out its own correspondents.[70] In a reservation appended to the report, Clement Attlee urged the BBC to dispense with agency services altogether.

It is not possible to sift through the daily news bulletins, but the weekly radio newsreels published in *The Listener* provide some evidence of lack of impartiality in the BBC's news presentation. First, all government announcements were given air space in news bulletins as well as news talks, while the opposition's reactions went unrecorded. Secondly, the news about unemployment was invariably good. The BBC seemed to take particular pleasure in recording the launching of ships built in British shipyards, or old ships being sent to places with heavy unemployment like Jarrow in order to be broken up. The government's Unemployment Instructional Centres were also given some publicity. Perhaps more striking was the BBC's news coverage of defence matters. In July and August the BBC paid as much attention to the Air Force and Navy reviews as did a Conservative newspaper like the *Morning Post*; and from August the Abyssinian crisis and the work of the League of Nations dominated the news, along with expressions of concern about the 'warlike appearance' of German troops. In October the Labour Party's split over foreign policy was well publicised, and a photograph was shown of one of the National Government's cinema vans, though not one of Labour's.

A survey of BBC programmes for 1932, 1933 and 1934 suggests that what has been argued above for 1935 applies also to these years.[71] Even in a controversial series like 'Whither Britain?' in the spring of 1934, mavericks who were included tended to come from the right rather than the left — Winston Churchill rather than Stafford Cripps. And there were a number of status quo talks — series such as 'Some British Institutions' (which included a talk on the greatness of the British Navy), as well as a series on 'Agriculture and Marketing' with Walter Elliot, Minister for Agriculture, as one of the speakers. Early in 1934 Stanley Baldwin gave a schools broadcast on 'The English Idea of Political Freedom'. A series on 'The British Empire' was rather more controversial, but the Labour Party's point of view seems not to have been put. On any particular issue the BBC claimed to be concerned to secure adequate representation of as many views as possible, for it recognised 'the potential influence of a broadcast'; but it seemed unconcerned that its 'drift towards long unwieldy symposia' exacerbated rather than reduced the bias against the Labour Party.[72]

While expressing its concern that more prominence was given to the leaders of the political party in power than to the leaders of the opposition, the Ullswater Committee took comfort from what it observed to be

an equally inevitable tendency in the general programmes of the Corporation to devote more time to the expression of new ideas and the advocacy of change in social and other spheres, than to the defence of orthodoxy and stability, since the reiteration of what exists and is familiar is not so interesting as the exposition of what might be. We have been informed by the BBC that criticism on the ground of political, intellectual, and artistic bias comes both from the Right and from the Left.[73]

The Ullswater Committee had been pleased to record that the BBC had informed it that criticism 'on the ground of political, intellectual, and artistic bias comes both from the Right and from the Left'. This was ingenuous. In the Britain of the 1930s the right (the Tory diehards) did not speak for the government, whereas the left did speak for the major opposition party, the Labour Party. It was wishful thinking on the part of the committee to believe that the two sets of criticism cancelled each other out. The validity of this assertion is open to question. It is true that the series 'Whither Britain?' saw some advocacy of change in social and other spheres, and the art interviews of R.S. Lambert, for example, occasionally pitted the traditional against the modern (though, it must be said, often to the disadvantage of the latter). But there were also plays like Arthur Bryant's *The Thin Red Line*,[74] such series as 'Some British Institutions', 'The Citizen and His Government' and the talks on 'Liberty', most of which were defences of orthodoxy and stability. There was also the publicity given to the annual ceremonies like the King's Christmas broadcast, the Lord Mayor's Banquet, Navy Week, the Hendon Airshow, Empire Day, Remembrance Day (used so skilfully in the National Government's interest by the Archbishop of Canterbury in 1935[75]) and so on, all helping to strengthen orthodoxy and stability through the reiteration of what existed and what was familiar. Above all else in 1935 there was the celebration of the King's Jubilee, a great national occasion which underlined the stability of Britain and the British at a time when Europe was in disarray and succumbing to dictatorships of the right and the left, a point taken up by Baldwin in his broadcast 'Message to the Nation', delivered one month after the Jubilee. In 1938 *The Economist* observed of the BBC's news service that

If unbiassed information tends to break down the barriers of party feeling and thereby to make the traditional organization of democracy on a party basis more difficult and uncertain, it has unquestionably helped to consolidate the feeling for democracy itself.[76]

What is said here of the news service applies equally to the general programmes; and in consolidating the feeling for democracy in the mid-1930s the BBC consolidated support for the self-proclaimed bulwark of

British traditions and values, the National Government.

The Press

Press coverage of the 1935 general election was massive in scope. As the result of an acrimonious newspaper war in the early1930s, two morning newspapers had circulations over 2,000,000 by 1935, while three others were close to 1,500,000.[77] In the same period the circulations of class newspapers also increased at a fast rate, though of course their circulation totals were far more modest. Among the Sunday newspapers the *News of the World* and the *People* had circulations in excess of 3,000,000 in 1935, while a further five enjoyed circulations in excess of 1,000,000. In the inter-election period newspaper interest in electoral politics was minimal, aside from fairly extensive coverage of the government's difficulties in the winter of 1934/5 and the immediate aftermath of the East Fulham by-election a year before. But at the general election even the pictorial and Sunday newspapers allotted space for election news, thereby helping the 1935 electors to be the best informed in British political history.

Not only was press coverage of the 1935 general election massive in scope, it was also partisan in treatment. The Labour Party was supported by newspapers whose combined circulation was only about 2,500,000. The newspapers of the Westminster Press Group, with a combined circulation of more than 1,500,000, while opposed to the National Government, did not support the Labour Party; rather they advised readers to vote Liberal where there was a Liberal Party candidate, and a Council of Action candidate — who might be a Labour candidate — where there was not. The National Government was supported, with varying degrees of enthusiasm, by newspapers with a combined circulation of well over 20,000,000. Unlike 1931, much of the National Government's press support in 1935 was lukewarm; newspapers like the *Daily Express* and the *Daily Mail* described the National Government as the lesser of two evils, a description hardly calculated to inspire a large turnout on polling day. But the National Government was not without keen press supporters, and in favourable press exposure certainly enjoyed a considerable advantage over the Labour Party, as Tables 7.1 and 7.2 show.

One of the most striking features of the inter-election years was the extent to which the National Government was villified in the Conservative as well as the Liberal and Labour press. Indeed the government's only consistent support came from the *Daily Telegraph* and *The Times*, both 'class' newspapers with little popular appeal and small circulations.

Table 7.1: Circulations, Proprietors, Political Alignments of London
Morning Newspapers

Name	Type	Proprietor	Circulation in 1935 (approx.)	Alignment at 1935 election
Daily Telegraph	Class	Berry	500,000	Nat. Govt.
The Times	Class	J.J. Astor J. Walter	195,000	Nat. Govt.
Morning Post	Class	Duke of North. Sir P.E. Bates	130,000	Nat. Govt.
Daily Sketch	Popular	Berry*	850,000	Nat. Govt.
Daily Mirror	Popular	Rothermere	1,000,000	Nat. Govt.
Daily Mail	Popular	Rothermere	1,500,000	Nat. Govt. (?)
Daily Express	Popular	Beaverbrook	2,000,000	Nat. Govt. (?)
News Chronicle	Popular	Westminster Press	1,330,000	Council of Action/ Liberal
Daily Herald	Popular	Odhams/TUC	2,000,000	Labour
Daily Worker	Popular	CPGB	100,000	Labour

*The Berrys also published the *Daily Dispatch* which although published in
Manchester had national sales of 390,000.
? indicates lukewarm support for the National Government — also for Table 7.2
overleaf.
Sources: Information for this and the following table compiled mainly from the
following sources: (i) the newspapers themselves, (ii) Kurt von Stutterheim, *The
Press in England* (1934), esp. p. 190, (iii) PEP, *Report on the British Press*
(1938), (iv) Mitchell's Newspaper Press Directory (1936), (v) H. Wickham Steed,
The Press (1938), (vi) Royal Commission on the Press, 1947-49 (Cmd 7700), and
(vii) A.P. Wadworth, 'Newspaper Circulations in Great Britain 1800-1954',
Transactions of the Manchester Statistical Society Journal (1954-5).

Naturally the government was deeply concerned. In mid-1934 Stonehaven wrote to Baldwin:

> Owing to the fact that practically the whole of the so-called popular
> press is closed to us, it is very important that we should give the
> amplest facilities to those papers which are prepared to report
> Minister's speeches adequately.[78]

In practice this meant co-operating closely with the *Daily Telegraph*
and *The Times*. Lack of press support for the government had already
prompted the National Coordinating Committee to extend the range of
its activities to include publicity and propaganda; and it led eventually,
in March 1935, to the formation of the National Publicity Bureau.

In the course of 1935, however, the National Government won back

Table 7.2: Circulations, Proprietors, Political Alignments of Sunday Newspapers

Name	Proprietors	Circulation in 1935 (approx.)	Alignment at 1935 election*
Sunday Times	Berry	250,000	Nat. Govt.
Sunday Graphic	Berry	1,000,000	Nat. Govt.
Empire News	Berry	1,500,000	Nat. Govt.
Sunday Chronicle	Berry	1,000,000	Nat. Govt.
Observer	Lord Astor	200,000	Nat. Govt.
News of the World	Riddell/Carr	3,500,000	Nat. Govt.
Sunday Pictorial	Rothermere	1,500,000	Nat. Govt.
People	Odhams Ltd	3,000,000	Nat. Govt. (?)
Sunday Dispatch	Rothermere	800,000	Nat. Govt. (?)
Sunday Express	Beaverbrook	1,300,000	Nat. Govt. (?)
Sunday Referee	Ostrer	300,000	Nat. Govt. (?)
Reynolds' News	Cooperative Society	400,000	Labour

*The tables under-represent the scale of newspaper support for the National Government. Two of the three London evening newspapers supported the government, as did all but a handful of the regional newspapers; not one evening or regional newspaper supported the Labour Party.

some of the press support it had enjoyed briefly in 1931. This was due primarily to three events: the passing of the Government of India Act, the decision to rearm and the approach of a general election. The second of these won the grudging, partial approval of the *Daily Mail*, the *Daily Express* and the *Morning Post*; the first removed a contentious and divisive issue from public debate; and the third forced all newspapers to choose between the National Government and the Labour Party, most of them preferring the former as the lesser of two evils. Shortly before the election A.J. Cummings, the eminent journalist, wrote that

> When a government of the Right is faced with a real crisis, or is in the actual throes of a General Election, the recalcitrant Conservative newspapers will shed their differences in a single revolution of the globe and re-form themselves on the united front.[79]

In fact it took numerous revolutions of the globe for the recalcitrant Conservative newspapers to re-form on the united front, but it had been more or less accomplished by 14 November 1935.

In the 1930s party leaders sought favourable publicity primarily in the morning newspapers, in the belief that they were more influential among electors than the Sunday or evening newspapers. Yet on a circulation basis alone, the Sunday newspapers were pre-eminent, as the following table indicates.

Table 7.3: Percentage of Families Reading Newspapers

Daily morning newspapers	(popular)	73%
Daily morning newspapers	(class and local)	22%
Daily evening newspapers		57%
Sunday newspapers	(national and local)	130%

Source: PEP, *Report on the British Press*, p. 230, based on the London Press Exchange's 1934 survey, 'The Home Market' (1936).

However, the political content of the Sunday newspapers was low, and it was widely believed that they were read more for general entertainment than for political instruction. In their recent study of the causes and nature of political change Butler and Stokes found, on the basis of surveys conducted in 1963-4, that readers followed election campaigns far more from morning than from evening and Sunday newspapers.[80] This finding is consonant with the result of a more impressionistic survey conducted by Mass Observation shortly after the Second World War, and suggests that the similar impressions of politicans and commentators in the 1930s were well founded.[81] Hence detailed coverage of the evening newspapers has not been attempted, and the Sunday newspapers have received somewhat slighter treatment than the morning newspapers.

The distribution of Sunday newspapers among the income groups is similar to that for the morning newspapers.[82] The affluent classes read more newspapers than the less affluent, and different ones. The less prosperous classes (under £250) read the *People*, the *News of the World*, the *Empire News* and *Reynolds' News*. The middle-income group (£250-500) read the *Sunday Express* and the *Sunday Pictorial*, with the *News of the World*, the *Sunday Dispatch* and the *People* rather less popular. The upper-income group read the *Sunday Times*, the *Sunday Pictorial* and the *Observer*, with the *Sunday Express* and the *Sunday Dispatch* marginally less popular.

On a regional basis the London newspapers declined in strength almost in proportion to the distance from London, until in Scotland they were read by as little as 40% of the adult population. The most truly national newspapers, in the sense that they achieved over 20%

Table 7.4: Newspapers, Income Groups and Family Readership

Income group	Families in group as percentage of total	Percentage of readers within each income group	Newspapers (percentage of family readership within each income group)	
Over £1,000 p.a.	0.9%	100%	*The Times*	54%
			Daily Telegraph/ Morning Post	48%
			Daily Mail	32%
			Daily Mirror	26%
			Daily Express	12%
£500– 1,000	3.4%	100%	*Daily Telegraph/ Morning Post*	36%
			Daily Mail	35%
			The Times	21%
			Daily Mirror	19%
			Daily Express	17%
£250– 500	14.3%	100%	*Daily Mail*	32%
			Daily Express	26%
			Daily Telegraph/ Morning Post	14%
			Daily Mirror	13%
			News Chronicle	10%
£125– 250	57.5%	80%	*Daily Herald*	21%
			Daily Express	20%
			News Chronicle	13%
			Daily Mail	12%
			Daily Mirror	5%
To £125	24.0%	45%	*Daily Herald*	21%
			Daily Express	8%
			News Chronicle	8%
			Daily Mail	5%
			Daily Sketch	2%
	100.0%*			

*The survey actually covered 80,000 visits to private families in urban areas containing 80% of the families in Great Britain. A later survey of four rural villages in Oxfordshire and Gloucestershire, while not conducted on income-group lines, showed that the *Daily Express*, the *Daily Mail* and the *Daily Herald* achieved a 20% penetration, followed by the *News Chronicle* (14%), *Daily Telegraph* (7%) and *The Times* (5%), the percentages for the last three being higher than for the urban centres.
Source: Table compiled from PEP, *Report on the British Press*, pp. 125 and 230-1, based on survey conducted in 1935 by the Incorporated Society of British Advertisers.

penetration in all parts of the country, were the *Daily Express*, the *Daily Herald*, the *News of the World* and the *People*. South of the Trent the class newspapers, the two pictorial newspapers and the *News Chronicle* were also much in favour. In and around London the *News Chronicle*, the *Daily Telegraph* and the *Daily Mirror* were especially strong. Among Sunday newspapers the South of England favoured the class newspapers, the pictorials, and the *Sunday Express*. North of the Trent the Manchester newspapers were very popular, especially the *Empire News* and the *Sunday Chronicle*; while north of the Tweed the national press played second fiddle to the local newspapers. A final distinction between North and South was that the former favoured the *People*, the latter the *News of the World*. The electoral significance of these points will be noted later.

Readers in all income groups saw between 60% and 70% of their morning newspapers, and perhaps more of their Sunday newspapers. The morning newspapers' most popular pages were the Picture Page, Main News Page, Leader Page, Crime News Page, News Page (not Main), and the News-Features Page. As one might expect, reader interest in political news was greater at election than other times. On the whole men read their newspapers more thoroughly than women, and upper-class readers more thoroughly than lower-class readers. Among the morning newspapers only the *Morning Post* and the *Daily Mirror* were read by more women than men. Three of the mass circulation newspapers — the *Daily Express*, the *Daily Herald* and the *News Chronicle* — had nearly two male readers to one female reader. At least three cartoonists — Strube (*Daily Express*), Low (*Evening Standard*) and Dyson (*Daily Herald*) — enjoyed an 80% readership.

As Tables 7.1 and 7.2 indicate, the national newspapers and many of the regional newspapers were owned by great combines like the Westminster and Berry Groups and monopolists like Lords Beaverbrook and Rothermere. With few exceptions they and the so-called independent press supported the National Government at the 1935 general election; but they did so with varying degrees of enthusiasm, and their assessments of the government's and opposition's strengths and weaknesses did not always coincide. Furthermore, even within a combine the editors of the various newspapers were not always in agreement on a particular issue. The remainder of this section takes its shape from these considerations.

Two of the government's strongest supporters at the 1935 general election were *The Times* and the *Observer*. The first was owned by Col. J.J. Astor and John Walter, who had purchased it in dramatic cir-

cumstances shortly after the death of Lord Northcliffe in 1922.[83]
Astor had brought back to the editorial chair Geoffrey Dawson, who
had previously edited the paper from 1912 to 1919, and who was to
remain editor until 1941. Dawson had returned to *The Times* on his
own terms, namely that the editor should be supreme on the editorial
side;[84] and there is no evidence to suggest that in the years that followed the views of editor and proprietors diverged on any major issue.
In the early and mid-1930s Dawson kept *The Times* solidly in support
of the National Government, which, indeed, was in some measure his
creation.[85] Throughout 1935 he was one of Baldwin's closest advisers,
and perhaps it was at his prompting that Baldwin decided to hold the
election before the turn of the new year.[86] During the election campaign, in the face of strenuous opposition criticism, *The Times* upheld
Baldwin's decision to go to the country. It contended that the 1931
mandate had all but expired, and that 'the postponement of an election
cannot make for, and must detract from, the weight and efficacy of
British policy' in international affairs.[87] Barely pausing to notice
Lloyd George or Samuel, *The Times* concentrated its attack on the
Labour Party. It urged the electors to reject a party whose leaders were
so obviously disunited on 'the foremost issue of the day', namely the
Abyssinian crisis;[88] and to turn out in great numbers in support of a
government which inspired confidence, and a leader, Stanley Baldwin,
who could be trusted to act responsibly, unlike Labour leaders such as
Stafford Cripps.[89] From the outset of the campaign, but particularly
after the municipal elections on 1 November, *The Times* was confident
that the National Government would win comfortably and that the
only threat to the Government lay in the possible apathy of its supporters, a view shared by Conservative Central Office, with which *The
Times* was in close contact.[90]

At the 1935 election *The Times'* Sunday partner was not its near
namesake, the *Sunday Times*, which was owned by the Berry family,
but the *Observer*, owned by J.J. Astor's elder brother, Lord Waldorf
Astor, and edited, as it had been since 1908, by the legendary
J.L. Garvin.[91] With approximately the same circulation as *The Times*,
and appealing to much the same people, the *Observer* shared its implac-
able hostility to the Labour Party. Garvin believed that on the three
most important issues of the election, namely 'Prosperity, Security,
and Peace', the Labour Party, on its record and in its present disunited
condition, could not be relied upon to serve the nation well.[92] On international affairs Garvin was less certain than Dawson that the government would not slide into war with Italy, and one of his famous five-

tiered headlines read:

'Keep Out This Time'
'Thus Far and No Farther'
'Sanctions As Suicide'
'Final Truths About the League and Peace'
'No Muddling Into Wider War'[93]

However, by the time the campaign was under way Garvin had realised that the government was as anxious as he to keep out of a war with Italy; and, if the image is not a little inappropriate, he turned his guns on to the Labour Party:

'Defence for Peace'
'Labour and the Jingo Stampede'
'Disarmament With War'
'Vote It Down'[94]

And he was confident that the people would 'Vote It Down', especially as he believed that since mid-1935 the government's popularity had risen markedly in marginal regions like the Midlands.[95]

In terms of circulation figures, a far more electorally important family newspaper empire than that of the Astors was that of the Berrys, whose newspapers had a combined circulation in excess of 6,000,000. In 1935 the Berry family owned seven morning, seven evening, six Sunday and six weekly newspapers, making it by far the greatest of the huge combines. Their newspapers were read by electors in all income groups and in all parts of the country. The three Berry brothers, Lords Camrose, Kemsley and Iliffe, were relative newcomers to the newspaper world, becoming press magnates only from the mid-1920s. Between 1924 and 1927 they had acquired the *Daily Record* in Glasgow, as late as the mid-1930s the most popular morning newspaper in Scotland; the *Daily Dispatch* in Manchester (with Lancashire and elsewhere sales of 390,000 in 1935); the *Daily Sketch*, into which they merged the *Daily Graphic*; the *Daily Telegraph*; and the *Illustrated Sunday Herald*, which they subsequently retitled the *Sunday Graphic*.[96] At the time of the 1935 general election the Berrys acted as a unit, though Lord Camrose was editor-in-chief of the *Daily Telegraph* and Lord Kemsley seems to have been more concerned with the *Daily Sketch* and the Sunday newspapers. All three brothers were strong supporters of the National Government, though none was personally close to Baldwin and his circle.[97]

The showpiece of the Berry Group holdings was the *Daily Telegraph*.
A shaky concern in 1927, with sales of under 100,000, the *Daily Telegraph* by 1935 had become a major newspaper force, with sales
totalling nearly 500,000, due in large measure to Lord Camrose's decision in 1930 to reduce its cost from 2d to 1d. In Arthur Watson, the
Telegraph had an experienced editor whose political views were entirely
compatible with those of Lord Camrose.[98] During the campaign
Watson's editorials were more biting than Dawson's; his language was
less restrained, indicating perhaps that the *Telegraph* took the threat
from Labour rather more seriously than *The Times*. 'Socialism', wrote
Watson, was 'predicated on a faith in mob rule and the suppression of
free opinion'.[99] His final words to the electors were

> A vote for socialism at today's election is a vote for quick industrial
> suicide.[100]

He urged electors to note the TUC's 'close grip on a Labour Government', which would be 'A menace to the liberty of Parliament.'[101]
Unlike *The Times*, the *Daily Telegraph* did not ignore Winston
Churchill's part in the campaign, though like *The Times* it made
Baldwin the centrepiece of its election coverage. Baldwin, indeed,
rewarded the *Telegraph* for its faithful support since 1931 by contri-
buting an article on 'Avoid Another Socialist Crisis Like That of 1931',
a favour not even accorded *The Times*.[102] Like *The Times*, however,
the *Telegraph* was confident that the National Government could withstand Labour's challenge, even in the marginal constituencies of Birmingham.[103]

Of all the popular morning newspapers perhaps none struck the
'national' chord more loudly or more often than the Berry Group's
Daily Sketch. A pictorial daily which carried a minimal amount of
political news, even at election times, the *Sketch* none the less left its
readers in no doubt as to how they should vote at the 1935 election.
Wedged in between articles on the 'Ravine Murder', the spiritual powers
of the well-known medium Estelle Roberts, the trial of Madame
Stavisky and the wedding of the Duke of Gloucester, was the opinion
column of an able ex-*Manchester Guardian* writer, Herbert Sidebotham,
written over the pseudonym of 'Candidus'.[104] Through Candidus the
Sketch conveyed to its largely low-income readers its belief that 'In a
National system of Government all your angles of vision on politics
have a fair chance of satisfaction'.[105] Unlike the *Telegraph* it refrained

from attacking the Labour Party due, perhaps, to Sidebotham's Liberal
sympathies, and prompted by the need not to antagonise working-class
readers. Certainly all the reasons the *Sketch* put forward for supporting
the National Government were positive ones, linked to the government's record and the nation's future needs; at no time did it employ
the 'lesser of two evils' line adopted by the Beaverbrook and
Rothermere newspapers, even though it was appealing to similar groups
of readers. If the *Daily Telegraph* could be described as a right-centre
newspaper, perhaps the *Daily Sketch* could be described as a left-centre
newspaper: if the favourite politician of the former was Stanley
Baldwin, the favourite of the latter was Ramsay MacDonald.

Although the Berry Group owned several influential national
morning newspapers with large circulations, its strength was greatest in
the Sunday and regional newspaper fields. With a combined circulation
in excess of 4,000,000, and with readers from all income groups and all
parts of the country, the Berry's six Sunday newspapers were in a
unique position to influence electors. All of them came out strongly in
favour of the National Government, but some were less virulently anti-
Socialist than others. None of them devoted much space to election
news; even the staid 'class' paper, the *Sunday Times*, over forty pages
long, gave only a half page to election news. Sidebotham, this time in
the guise of 'Scrutator', contented himself with noting that the policies
of government and opposition were remarkably similar, but that
Labour was 'unfit to govern'.[106]

Among the Berry Group's mass circulation Sunday newspapers,
the *Empire News* and the *Sunday Chronicle* (published in Manchester)
were extremely popular in Wales, the West Midlands, Lancashire and
Cheshire, the West Riding of Yorkshire, and the rural North including
Cumberland: in short, in those areas which would decide the fate of
the National Government. The Berry newspapers, conscious that unemployment was still a major issue, accordingly adopted a low-key profile.
They stressed that while all was not yet sweetness and light, Britain
was in fact pulling out of the mire of depression.[107] As Sir John Foster
Fraser, the feature writer for the *Sunday Graphic* and the *Empire
News*, put it:

How am I going to vote? I shall vote National — not because I think
the Government is composed of archangels, but because it has done
better than any other Government of the world during the last four
years. I expect it will keep on doing better.[108]

The Berry newspapers were further rewarded for their faithful support of the National Government when they were given exclusive rights to a homely article by Mrs Stanley Baldwin on 'The Women's Election', which was accompanied by a photograph of Mrs Baldwin and the Prime Minister seated by the hearth at Astley. While most of the Berry morning newspapers forecast a government majority of 150 to 160 seats, the Sunday Manchester newspapers, perhaps more closely attuned to the beat of the industrial heart, forecast a government majority of 250, a remarkably accurate estimate.[109]

As with its Sunday newspapers, the Berry Group's regional newspapers were located primarily in areas most susceptible to a Labour revival. The editors of newspapers like the *Sheffield Telegraph*, the *Daily Dispatch* (Manchester), the *Newcastle Journal*, the *Western Mail* (Cardiff) and the Glasgow *Daily Record*, enjoyed considerable freedom to develop lines of support for the National Government best suited to the local situations. For example, on the morning preceding polling day the *Western Mail*'s editorial headings were 'The Full Tide of Recovery' and 'How the Government Helped Ebbw Vale',[110] while the Glasgow *Daily Record*, which enjoyed the largest circulation of any morning newspaper in Scotland, wrote cautiously that

> If there are jobs to be lost it is more likely to be by getting rid of this Government and disrupting the continuity of policy and progressive advance to prosperity for which it has been largely if not altogether responsible.

It could add that:

> One indication of how confidence has returned and prospects have brightened is provided by the fact that Clydeside ship building and engineering firms booked orders of an aggregate value of about £5 million during the month of October.[111]

Most of the Berrys' regional newspapers were more virulently anti-Socialist than the London dailies and the Sunday newspapers;[112] and several enjoyed themselves by mocking Lloyd George and the Council of Action.[113]

At the 1935 general election the National Government was supported by a number of newspapers which were independent of the great combines and monopolies. The degree of support given varied from newspaper to newspaper. Some like the *Morning Post* and the *Scotsman* were right-centre in political terms; others like the *Sunday Referee* and the *Liverpool Daily Post* were decidedly left-centre: none considered Labour as a likely alternative government.

At the time of the 1935 election the *Morning Post* was rapidly losing ground to the Berrys' *Daily Telegraph*, and its circulation had slipped to under 150,000. Less than two years after the election the proprietors conceded defeat and sold out to the rival organisation. At the time of the election, indeed since 1925 when it had been purchased from the famous Borthwick family,[114] the *Morning Post* was owned by a group of Conservative businessmen, notably the Duke of Northumberland and Sir P.E. Bates.[115] In the early 1930s its policy was perhaps more akin to that of the *Daily Mail* than the *Daily Telegraph*, and even at the election it could state that the National Government had 'departed from some very good Tory principles in the past four years'.[116] But like the *Daily Mail* it was also vehemently anti-Socialist, and inundated its upper-class, mainly female, readers, with reports of the iniquities of the leaders of the Labour Party.[117] However, its particular *bête noir* was Lloyd George, whose electoral organisation was described as 'The Council of Inaction'.[118] As for policy, the Duke and his colleagues were most concerned that the government should receive a mandate to construct a great navy.

The *Scotsman* too was concerned about rearmament, as was its sister newspaper, the *Glasgow Herald*. Both were class newspapers with substantial circulations in Scotland, especially among the business community. They advocated increased rearmanent less out of a concern for national defence than for the contracts which would come to the Clydeside shipyards; and as the *Scotsman* put it:

Things have improved and with the Government promising naval increases the yards-minded voters may return a Unionist.[119]

Both newspapers deplored the split in the Scottish Liberal Party in October which had led to the expulsion of the followers of Sir John Simon. The *Scotsman* commented bitterly that Samuel and Sir Archibald Sinclair

ought still to be giving their talents to the service of national administration; but they have chosen the political wilderness and they will die in it.[120]

The general strategy of both newspapers was to attack the policy and leaders of the Labour and Liberal Parties, rather than defend the National Government's record in Scotland.

Another independent regional newspaper with a substantial readership was the *Birmingham Post*. An enthusiastic supporter of the National Government since 1931, it was confident that most of the Birmingham seats captured from the Labour Party in 1931 would be retained. Among the points it impressed upon its readers was the obvious prosperity of the city, the failure of the Labour Party to honour Birmingham 'with the attentions of candidates of big calibre', and the weakness of Labour's national leadership: 'Put Major Attlee alongside Mr. Baldwin – the contrast is comic.'[121] None of these points was put with equal conviction by the *Liverpool Daily Post*. In the first place it was clear that Liverpool was not sharing in the increased prosperity of southern England; and, indeed, that some of the government's policies may well have worsened local conditions. With this consideration in mind the *Post* was anxious to see a reduction in the size of the government's majority: 'Ministers cannot fail to benefit from this.'[122] Nevertheless, in the last resort the *Post* trusted Stanley Baldwin,[123] and therefore advised its 46,000 readers to vote for the National Government.

The other great northern newspapers, the *Leeds Mercury* and the *Yorkshire Post*, strongly supported the National Government.[124] Owned by the Yorkshire Conservative Newspaper Company, of which the Hon. Rupert Beckett was chairman, both newspapers maintained close links with Ministers of the National Government, particularly Anthony Eden and Stanley Baldwin.[125] Occasionally Arthur Mann, the editor of the *Post*, would venture a criticism of the government;[126] but he did so in the full knowledge that his readers were committed Conservative businessmen. At the election he had no doubt that the government would win: 'The reason is that the world of industry, trade and business generally – which means the wage earners world – look forward confidently to another four years of sane finance and sound administration.'[127] If Linton Andrews, the editor of the *Leeds Mercury*, felt uneasy about any issue, he was less likely to voice his unease because his readers were thought to be Liberals and Socialists, and in Andrew's words:

> I wanted to convert them to national unity on the questions of the League of Nations, rearmament, and air defence.[128]

The last of the independent newspapers of electoral significance are the three Sunday newspapers: the *News of the World*, the *People* and the *Sunday Referee*. The first of these, the *News of the World*, had been owned by Lord Riddell until his death late in 1934 when it was taken over by a group headed by Sir Emsley Carr, who may have been editor at the time of the 1935 election.[129] It enjoyed a circulation of 3,300,000, principally in Wales and England south of the Trent, and among families with an income less than £250 per year. Overall, about one family in three took the *News of the World*. Its great rival, the *People*, appealed to much the same income groups but was far more popular in Scotland and in England north of the Trent. At the time of the 1935 election, the *People* may have been controlled by J.S. Elias of Odhams Press Ltd.[130] While the *News of the World* came out strongly in favour of the National Government and gave election news some prominence, the *People* barely noticed the election, preferring its traditional fare of 'Jealous Wife Kidnaps Her Rival' and 'How Diamond Jim Spent His Millions', and refusing to advise electors on how they should vote. However it gave more space to the government's election campaign and indicated that it expected the National Government to win the election comfortably.[131] The *News of the World* went further than this. In its last two issues before the election there were leaders advising electors to vote for the National Government, which had 'arrested financial collapse', 'stemmed the tide of unemployment' and which was 'sound' on the foreign affairs issue.[132]

The third of the independent Sunday newspapers was the *Sunday Referee*, a pictorial owned by Isidore Ostrer, the president of Gaumont British Picture Corporation. It was widely read in London but not elsewhere. Ostrer seems to have been sympathetic to Ramsay MacDonald and the National Labour Party, for in several editorials the *Referee* expressed a wish to see the National Government made more 'national'. It even went so far as to state that 'On foreign policy, as Labour is less suspect, the Foreign Secretary should be Labour permanently.'[133] Nevertheless, in the final resort the *Referee* advised electors to vote for the National Government.

At the 1935 general election the newspapers controlled by the Harmsworth Group, headed by Lord Rothermere (Harold Harmsworth), had a combined circulation of over 5,000,000. It published two morning newspapers, the *Daily Mail* and the *Daily Mirror*; two Sunday Newspapers, the *Sunday Pictorial* and the *Sunday Dispatch*; and twelve evening newspapers. The group's readership was confined to England south of the Trent, and was particularly strong in the South-West and London. Readers of Harmsworth newspapers were

mostly to be found among income groups of more than £250 per year,
though the *Daily Mail* was also popular with the income group £125-250
per year, which comprised over 50% of families in Britain. All the
Harmsworth Group newspapers supported the National Government at
the 1935 election, but in the case of some of them did so more out of a
passionate hatred of the Labour Party than a stolidly held belief in the
virtues of national government.

In his recent history of the *Daily Mirror* Maurice Edelman has written
that 'After 1934 it expressed the social revolution of the twentieth
century.'[134] Edelman had in mind the accession of H.G. Bartholomew
(the 'common man') to the editorial directorship, the increasingly
important part being played by Cecil King, and the arrival on the staff
of the *Mirror* in 1935 of two brilliant journalists, Hugh Cudlipp and
William Connor ('Cassandra'). This formidable quartet, he believes, gave
a 'shouting age' 'shouting headlines', lifted sales greatly, particularly
among the working class; and eventually adopted a leftist political stance.
However, little of this 'revolution' was evident at the time of the 1935
general election. In 1931 Lord Rothermere had ended his journalistic
overlordship of the *Mirror* and the *Sunday Pictorial*, though he continued to write occasional articles.[135] Nevertheless, the *Mirror* by and
large continued to reflect his views right up to the 1935 general election, though it did not join him in his flirtation with the blackshirt
movement. In the course of 1935 the *Mirror*'s circulation began to
climb for the first time since the 1920s, but at the time of the election
was still under 1,000,000. The miracle of the *Mirror* had not yet
occurred.

Nevertheless, the *Daily Mirror* and the *Sunday Pictorial* supported
the National Government more strongly than did the Harmsworth newspapers subject to Lord Rothermere's editorial control. Perhaps
conscious of its growing working-class readership, and in the knowledge
that over 60% of its readers were women, the *Mirror* stressed the twin
themes of 'work' and 'security'. Its daily campaign caption was
'Support the National Government. They have done much. They can do
more. They will.'[136] It carried a series of articles on the 'Voice of
Industry', in which formerly unemployed workers talked about their
new jobs; and considerable prominence was also given to the government's announcements about cruiser construction in the Tyne dockyards and the projected roads expansion scheme.[137] The *Mirror* mixed
humour with politics, particularly in the cartoon strip 'Jane's Journal',
but also in an occasional editorial.[138] Overall, electoral politics received
little space and election news shared the headlines with '7 times wed at

78' and 'Fire Kills Ten'. But the message was clear enough: support the National Government at all costs.[139]

Lord Rothermere exercised direct editorial control over the *Daily Mail* and the *Sunday Dispatch*: both stood for 'King and Empire' and both lampooned Labour as a party of 'cranks'. Since 1931 the *Mail* had been one of the National Government's bitterest opponents. Indeed right up to the commencement of the election campaign it deplored the government's failure to introduce massive rearmament as well as its continuing commitment to the League of Nations. The League of Nations, so the *Mail* contended, was a 'League of Mischief', and Britain should 'Arm to the Teeth';[140] and a poll it conducted showed that its readers agreed.[141] But while it was critical of the National Government's foreign policy (and it was not interested in domestic issues), the *Mail* reserved its keenest barbs for Labour, whose foreign policy of disarmament and sanctions against Italy was ridiculed in a cartoon which had a 'Socialist Theme Song':

We're all out to fight
And by jingo! if we do
We've cut the ships
We've cut the men
We've cut the money too![142]

During the election campaign the *Mail*'s only concession to impartiality was to extend invitations to leading politicians of all parties to contribute articles. The final editorials, however, were 'Keep the Socialists Out' and 'Vote for the National Government'.[143]

Unlike Lord Rothermere, Lord Beaverbrook maintained close editorial control over all his newspapers — the *Daily Express*, the *Sunday Express* and the *Evening Standard*.[144] Apart from the evening newspaper, which had a large circulation in London and the neighbouring counties, the Beaverbrook newspapers were widely read in all parts of the country, even Scotland, and by all income groups, though especially those below £500 per annum. A Mass Observation report in the late 1940s estimated that about half the *Express*'s readers were Conservatives and a quarter were Labour sympathisers.[145] The distribution pattern of the *Express* in the 1930s would seem to suggest that these findings would also apply to the 1930s. Beaverbrook was a Conservative himself, but a highly idiosyncratic one. For most of the early 1930s he was in conflict with the leader of the Conservative Party, Stanley Baldwin, and at the election only swung in behind the National Government with the greatest reluctance.[146] As he put it in an editorial, 'the Conservatives at least won't go to war without some weapons', a course that Labour was seemingly bent upon.[147]

For much of the campaign Beaverbrook railed against what he regarded as the government's feeble policy. Baldwin had recently described 'Splendid Isolation' as 'Selfish Isolation', to which Beaverbrook replied that as late as 1934 Baldwin himself had described a collective peace system as 'perfectly impracticable', and that in any case Baldwin had misjudged the protection and agriculture issues in 1929 and might well be wrong about 'isolation' now.[148] While Beaverbrook welcomed the early reports that the government seemed to be holding up well in key areas like the Midlands, the Black Country and Yorkshire, and while he was happy enough to see the 'Tories Sweep Council Polls [and] Rout Socialists in the Cities',[149] he hoped that at the general election there would be a low turnout — not so great a fall in turnout as would bring the government down, but sufficiently large to allow him to claim that the country did not care for either the National Government or the Labour Party.[150] The Beaverbrook newspapers' favourite politician was Winston Churchill, whose speeches received greater coverage than did Baldwin's; and apart from Baldwin their greatest target for abuse was Lloyd George and the Liberal Party.[151] In the last number of the *Sunday Express* before the election, Peter Howard, the feature writer and a former Mosley supporter,[152] noted gleefully in a jumble of metaphors:

> On Thursday we shall hear the swan song of the Liberal Party. We shall witness their goose step to perdition.[153]

Interested in foreign affairs only, unconcerned about the possibility of considerable Labour gains, Beaverbrook was no friend to the National Government. It is little wonder that Baldwin, even as late as 1943, spoke bitterly of him.[154]

At the time of the 1935 general election the only mass circulation newspaper which supported the Liberal Party was the *News Chronicle*, controlled by the Cadbury family since 1930. The executive head of the *News Chronicle* was Sir Walter Layton, whose views more closely approximated Lloyd George's than Sir Herbert Samuel's. Layton had worked closely with Lloyd George in the autumn and winter of 1934 when the latter was preparing his New Deal proposals.[155] He had publicly welcomed Lloyd George's return to national politics in January 1935; and from mid-year he had kept the *Chronicle* steady in

support of Lloyd George's Council of Action for Peace and Reconstruction. Throughout 1934 and 1935 Layton described the *Chronicle*'s
policy as being 'half-way between Maxton and Samuel'.[156] The
Chronicle was read principally in London and the South-East, East
Anglia and the North-West (Westmorland): it scarcely penetrated
Scotland, a fact which might in part account for the strength of the
Liberal National Party in that region. It was read mainly by people on
incomes of less than £250, though within this group the *Daily Herald*
and the *Daily Express* were the more popular newspapers.[157]

Like nearly all the mass circulation newspapers, the *News Chronicle*
believed that the National Government was in no danger of defeat by
Labour. In its election coverage, therefore, it tended to ignore the
Labour Party while focusing attention on the failings of the National
Government and the virtues of the Council of Action's peace and reconstruction programmes.[158] It also gave Samuel a kindly hearing, especially after he stated that in constituencies where there was no Liberal
candidate, Liberal sympathisers should vote for the candidate who had
signed the Council of Action's questionnaire. The *Chronicle* urged its
readers not to accept Baldwin's election slogan of 'You May Safely
Trust Me'; or, as it put it in another editorial entitled 'The Tory Horse',

Trust not the Greeks even with gifts in their hands.[159]

This theme was developed in a series of editorials with headings like:
'Plan to Remove Mr. Eden from his Post as League Minister', 'Diehard
Cabinet if the Tories Win — Place Found for Mr. Churchill' and 'Tories
Plan Big Arms Race'.[160]

The *Chronicle* had no illusions about how the Liberals were going
to fare at the polls. After a week-long tour of the constituencies the
eminent columnist, A.J. Cummings, reported that the Liberals 'will
be lucky to hold what they have'.[161] However, if only for the sake of
appearances, the headline for 13 November read 'Tories will be Badly
Shaken at the Polls'; and on polling day the *Chronicle* exhorted its
readers to 'Vote for the Candidate — whatever his Party — who is
Pledged to end Inaction and Support the Policy of Peace and Reconstruction.'

Apart from the *News Chronicle*, the Westminster Press Group
published the London evening newspaper, the *Star*, and nearly forty
provincial newspapers, of which the most representative were perhaps
the *Birmingham Gazette* and the *Nottingham Journal*, both of which
had circulations in excess of 20,000. All the Westminster Press pro-

vincial newspapers modelled themselves slavishly on the *News Chronicle*, indicating a degree of proprietor editorial control far greater than that exercised over the Berrys' provincial newspapers. Indeed, leading and feature articles, notably J.A. Spender's, were syndicated. In Birmingham the *Gazette* was in the unhappy position of writing about constituencies where there were neither Liberal nor Council of Action candidates; but its editorial advice to electors to remain 'neutral'[162] may have been responsible, at least in part, for the very low turnout in several of the Birmingham constituencies. And in general this was probably the most important effect of the Westminster Press newspapers at the 1935 election.

The only other newspaper sympathetic to the Liberal Party was the *Manchester Guardian*. Owned and edited by the great C.P. Scott it had been since the turn of the century a powerful mouthpiece of organised Liberalism. At the time of the 1931 political crisis, however, C.P. Scott was dying and unable to follow events closely and formulate clear editorial policies.[163] Under the influence of W.P. Crozier, the *Guardian* had welcomed the formation of the National Government in August 1931, but in October, fearful that the proposed election would result in a massive majority for the Conservative Party, the *Guardian* opposed the government. At the election it instructed its readers to vote for free-trade Liberals, especially Lloyd George's few followers, and Labour candidates. This change of policy was due in part to the ability of some of the younger *Guardian* men to secure Scott's support for a tougher line against the National Government. Scott died in January 1932, and his family appointed the elderly and more conservative Crozier as editor. Even Crozier, however, was roused to anger when the government introduced protection (early 1932), and thereafter he was one of its fiercest critics. Crozier flayed the Samuelite Liberals, and even when they crossed the floor into opposition late in 1933 he continued to regard them with suspicion, offering them only guarded support.[164]

At the 1935 election the links between the *Guardian* and Samuel were still rather weak, but readers were encouraged to vote for Liberal candidates; where no Liberal was standing they should vote for Labour. Lloyd George's Council of Action was given considerable publicity throughout the campaign. The *Guardian*'s principal grumble was that Baldwin was too weak to stand up against his party's right-wingers; that the government's manifesto was 'weak and dangerous' — 'weak' for the little it offered the unemployed, 'dangerous' because it sought a 'blank cheque' for rearmament.[165] The *Guardian* recognised that the Liberal Party was a spent electoral force; it recognised also that the National

Government was in no danger of defeat from Labour. The best it reasonably hoped for was a substantial reduction in the size of the government's majority.

Throughout the election campaign Labour's only mass circulation newspaper, the *Daily Herald*, whose editorial policy was controlled by the TUC, was mostly on the defensive.[166] October opened badly with news of the resignations of Cripps and Lord Ponsonby from the National Executive Committee, followed by the resignation of Lansbury as leader of the party.[167] Then, just as the *Herald* was beginning to strike out at the National Government, the municipal elections demonstrated that in key areas like the Midlands the party's prospects were bleak. The *Herald* was also hampered in that Labour's international policy had been taken over by the National Government, and there was little clear ground separating them. Furthermore much space had to be devoted to defending several of the party's domestic policies, particularly bank nationalisation; but Hannan Swaffer, the *Herald*'s feature writer, did write a powerful series of articles under the general title of 'I Indict the Government'. In general the *Herald* found it easier to attack the government's domestic record and did so partly through the use of photographs of derelict towns, lines of unemployed men, slum dwellings and so on. (*The Times* printed photographs of 'Beautiful Britain'.) But at no time could the *Herald* muster enough confidence to predict a Labour victory.[168]

For its apparent lack of confidence, the *Daily Herald* was castigated by its ostensible ally, the *Daily Worker*, which was the organ of the Communist Party of Great Britain. Following a directive from Moscow in August 1935, the Communist Party of Great Britain had sought an electoral alliance with the Labour Party but had been rebuffed.[169] Through the pages of the *Worker* it accused the Labour Party of flaccidity: it urged the party to 'Wake Up and Win' and electors to 'Vote Down National Government – Unity Will Win Today'.[170] In John Strachey the *Worker* had a feature writer without peer as a critic of the National Government, but his fine articles were read by probably less than 250,000 people, published as they were in a journal whose circulation at the time of the election would have been something less than 100,000, and whose readers were already convinced that the National Government should go.[171]

The third and last newspaper to support the Labour Party at the 1935 general election was the Sunday newspaper owned by the Co-operative Society, *Reynolds' News*, which had a circulation of 400,000, principally in London, South Wales and the East Midlands. Like the

Daily Herald the *News* doubted if Labour could win the election, though it did predict that Labour would 'certainly' win 235 seats, 'probably' a further 40 and 'possibly' a further 80.[172] Its particular *bêtes noirs* were the recently imposed tax on Cooperative Savings and the effects on food prices of the government's marketing schemes. It was also concerned that

> Mr. Neville Chamberlain, having already increased national expenditure on private monopoly manufacture and armaments by £10 million a year, hints plainly the social services will be starved and social progress stayed to 'fill the gaps' in our Defence, to create huge armaments.[173]

It was always on the lookout for the 'Latest Tory Lie',[174] and was not at all anxious to make Attlee, the newly elected leader, the centrepiece of its campaign.[175]

Notes

1. Political and Economic Planning (PEP), *Report on the British Press* (1938), p. 230. This report brings together the results of surveys conducted by the Incorporated Society of British Advertisers and by the London Press Exchange in 1934 and 1935.
2. The percentages are deduced from paid admissions figures calculated by S. Rowson, 'A Statistical Survey of the Cinema Industry in Great Britain in 1934', *Journal of the Royal Statistical Society*, vol. 99 (1936), pp. 72 and 115. The higher percentage for the electorate follows from Rowson's conclusion (p. 70) that children under 15 years represent 'a relatively small fraction only of the total cinema patrons'.
3. This and the following paragraph draw heavily on the pioneering work of Nicholas Pronay: 'British Newsreels in the 1930s: (1) Audiences and Producers', *History*, vol. 56, no. 188 (1971), pp. 411-18; also 'British Newsreels in the 1930s: (2) Their Policies and Impact', *History*, vol. 57, no. 189 (1972), pp. 63-72. Passages quoted in the text are from (1) pp. 412 and and 414; (2) p. 67.
4. *Daily Telegraph*, 1 Nov. 1935.
5. *Daily Herald*, 14 Oct. 1935.
6. Baldwin Papers, vol. 48, Conservative Central Office Memorandum on Publicity (undated, but probably mid-1934). The memorandum recommended the production of films, the purchase of cinemas and securing control of a 'News Film' service for National Government propaganda. Any resemblance between this proposal and Dr Goebbels's activities in Germany is probably not accidental.
7. *The Times*, 18 Oct. 1935; *Morning Post*, 5 Nov. 1935.
8. *Daily Herald*, 18 Oct. 1935.
9. *Manchester Guardian*, 18 Oct. 1935.
10. Private information from Mr Andrew Strang, present secretary of the Scottish Conservative and Unionist Association, and party canvasser in the 1930s. Also many entries in the Minute Book of the Western Divisional Council of the

SCUA for 1935. Mr S.A. Cooke, present secretary of the National Union of Conservative and Unionist Associations, confirmed Mr Strang's recollections of the utility of the cinema vans.

11. *Manchester Guardian*, 25 Oct. 1935.

12. Baldwin Papers, vol. 39, J.M. Horwill to Stanley Baldwin, 11 Nov. 1935.

13. The title of Asa Brigg's second volume of *The History of Broadcasting in the United Kingdom* (1965).

14. Report of the Broadcasting Committee, 1949 (Cmd 8116), p. 18.

15. *BBC Annual 1936* (Dec. 1934 to Dec. 1935), p. 88.

16. Briggs, *History of Broadcasting*, vol. 2, p. 141, citing *Daily Express* and *Daily Telegraph* surveys between 31 Oct. and 12 Nov. 1935.

17. *Daily Telegraph*, 7 Nov. 1935. Wireless manufacturers reported brisk sales in the weeks preceding the election, particularly of the inexpensive superheterodyne model.

18. *Daily Telegraph*, 7 Nov. 1935.

19. Briggs, *History of Broadcasting*, vol. 2, p. 140, citing C. Sharp, 'The Recent War on the Air', *Weekend Review*, 31 Oct. 1931. For the applicability of the comment to the 1935 election see *Daily Sketch*, 14 Nov. 1935, quoting the opinion of an official of Conservative Central Office.

20. At one time or another in the course of the campaign nearly all the national and regional newspapers made this comment.

21. For an account of the strife over political broadcasting at the 1931 general election see Briggs, *History of Broadcasting*, vol. 2, pp. 138-9,

22. *BBC Ninth Annual Report*, 1935 (Cmd 5088).

23. For Mosley's decision not to contest the 1935 general election see *The Times*, 28 Oct. 1935.

24. Briggs, *History of Broadcasting*, vol. 2, p. 135: In 1929 'He [Baldwin] had written asking Reith for information about the social classification of the audience, and he wanted to know whether working men listened at home or in clubs and pubs. Reith helped him, as he had helped him before, with his peroration.'

25. *The Listener*, 30 Oct., 6 and 13 Nov. 1935.

26. In a BBC radio portrait of the career of Stanley Baldwin, broadcast in 1970. The transcript of the programme is printed in G. Tayer (ed.), *Personality and Power* (1971).

27. Briggs, *History of Broadcasting*, vol. 2, p. 139.

28. Minutes of the meetings of the NEC, 22 and 23 Oct. 1935. Many DLPs wished to see Lansbury make an address. In his book *My Quest for Peace* (1938), p. 31, Lansbury noted that 'The General Election followed soon after and I found myself snowed under with appeals from Labour candidates to speak or their behalf.'

29. Briggs, *History of Broadcasting*, vol. 2, p. 141: 'The *Daily Express* questioned people as to whether or not they had listened to Morrison and to Baldwin: 29.5 per cent had listened to the former, it was claimed, 40.9 per cent to the latter.'

30. *The Listener*, 8 Jan. and 10 July 1935. The first broadcast was on the India question; the second on the mid-year ministerial changes.

31. See W. Golant, 'The Emergence of C.R. Attlee as Leader of the Parliamentary Labour Party in 1935', *Historical Journal*, vol. 13, no. 2 (1970).

32. *Daily Herald*, 9 Oct.; *Reynolds' News*, 13 Oct. 1935.

33. See Frances Lloyd George, *The Years That Are Past* (1967), p. 243.

34. See Chapter 3.

35. J.C.W. Reith, *Into the Wind* (1949), p. 234: '5:4:3 it was to be, Conservative, Labour, Liberal, with the usual grievance all round. Samuel gave one of the

Liberal dates to Snowden and another to Lloyd George; the Conservative Whip was very angry; told me it was a breach of contract; asked me to stop it. I said it had been agreed that the Liberals should have three dates; it was none of my business to whom they allotted them.'

36. *The Listener*, 6 Nov. 1935: 'There is no likelihood that Labour will have a majority at this election.'

37. *Picture Post*, 25 July 1942: an article by Reith, 'The BBC Shows a Middle Road', cited in R.H. Coase, *British Broadcasting: A Study in Monopoly* (1950).

38. W.A. Robson, 'The B.B.C. as an Institution', *Political Quarterly*) vol. 6, no. 4 (1935), p. 477.

39. Baldwin's friendship with Bridgeman emerges touchingly from T. Jones, *A Diary with Letters 1931-1950* (1954), pp. xxv, 4, 207, 230. See also A.W. Baldwin, *My Father: the true story* (1955): 'Perhaps for him [Baldwin] an even sharper cut [than the death of King George V] had been the death a short while before of one who may be truly called an intimate friend among his earliest Cabinet colleagues, one whom he loved and who well understood him: William Clive Bridgeman.'

40. *The Listener*, 21 Aug. 1935.

41. Robson, 'The B.B.C. as an Institution', p. 477. The two women were Margaret Bondfield, a member of Ramsay MacDonald's ministry, 1929-31, and M.A. Hamilton, Labour MP for Blackburn 1929-31, and author of several books on the Labour Party.

42. Report of the Broadcasting Committee, 1949 (Cmd 8116), p. 56. For a plea for systematic listener research see Hilda Matheson, 'Listener Research in Broadcasting', *Sociological Review*, vol. 27 (1935), pp. 408-22.

43. Hilda Matheson, 'Politics and Broadcasting', *Political Quarterly*, vol. 5, no. 2 (1934), p. 181.

44. Report of the Broadcasting Committee, 1935 (Cmd 5091), para. 89.

45. *The Listener*, 9 Jan. 1935.

46. Ibid., 6 Feb. 1935.

47. Ibid., 24 Apr. 1935.

48. Ibid., 10 June 1935.

49. Ibid., 26 June 1935.

50. Ibid., 10 July 1935.

51. Ibid., 14 Aug., 18 Sept., 16 Oct., 6 Nov. 1935.

52. Ibid., 14 Aug. 1935.

53. The speakers were Samuel Hoare, Clement Attlee, Sir George Schuster, Lord Lloyd, Isaac Foot, Winston Churchill, George Lansbury, Stanley Baldwin, Lady Layton and Sir John Thompson.

54. *The Listener*, 13 Mar. 1935.

55. The speakers were Lord Hugh Cecil, Sir Ernest Benn, Herbert Morrison, J.A. Spender, J.L. Garvin, Wyndham Lewis, Eustace Percy, Sir T.D. Barlow, Sir William Jowitt, J. Moore, G.K. Chesterton and George Bernard Shaw.

56. H.H. Balfour, Conservative MP, Isle of Thanet, Kent, 1929-45.

57. *The Listener*, 2, 9, 16 and 23 Oct. 1935.

58. Ibid., 30 Oct., 6 and 13 Nov. 1935.

59. Ibid., 18 Sept. 1935.

60. For the Bartlett incident see Briggs, *History of Broadcasting*, vol. 2, p. 146.

61. *The Listener*, 20 Mar. 1935.

62. Ibid., 3 and 10 July 1935.

63. Ibid., 17 July, 16 May 1935.

64. Ibid., 29 May 1935.

65. Ibid., 16 May, 2 Oct. 1935.

66. Ibid., 24 July 1935.

67. Ibid., 9, 16, 23 and 30 Oct. 1935.

68. Ibid., 6 Nov. 1935.

69. Ibid., 14 Aug. 1935; H. Macmillan, *The Next Five Years: an essay in political agreement* (1935).

70. Report of the Broadcasting Committee, 1935 (Cmd 5091), paras. 80-2.

71. *BBC Annual 1935* (Nov. 1933 to Dec. 1934) contains an extensive 'Five Year Review of Broadcasting 1930-1934' in which important programmes are listed under subject headings.

72. Ibid., p. 64.

73. Report of the Broadcasting Committee, 1935 (Cmd 5091), para. 89.

74. Mentioned in Briggs, *History of Broadcasting*, vol. 2, p. 168.

75. *The Listener*, 13 Nov. 1935. The Archbishop of Canterbury said: 'Give your vote on Thursday with something of the same spirit as that with which the men whom we remember gave their lives.'

76. Cited in Briggs, *History of Broadcasting*, vol. 2, p. 38.

77. For a brief account of the newspaper circulation war see R. Graves and A. Hodge, *The Long Weekend: a social history of Great Britain 1918-1939* (1940), pp. 290-2.

78. Baldwin Papers, vol. 48, Stonehaven to Baldwin, 10 May 1934.

79. A.J. Cummings, *The Press* (1936), p. 79. Cummings completed the manuscript before November 1935.

80. D. Butler and E. Stokes, *Political Change in Britain* (1969), p. 229.

81. Mass Observation, *The Press and Its Readers* (1949), pp. 101-2.

82. This and the following two paragraphs are based on the PEP *Report on the British Press*, p. 124, Ch. 10 and pp. 254-5. Leaving aside the question of the general usefulness of such work, the measurement of column inches as an index to the intensity of political enthusiasm has not been attempted here, largely because such measurements are only meaningful within a comparative framework, which is missing in this instance; i.e. neither Rowe's thesis on the 1929 general election, nor McCallum and Readman's book on the 1945 general election measured political enthusiasm in this way; and, of course, there is as yet no full-scale study of the 1931 general election. C. Seymour-Ure's *The Press, Politics and the Public* (1968) is more or less a catalogue of the problems confronting the student of the press: his final chapter is a counsel of despair — e.g. 'It is impossible to say what part the Press plays in the formation of a voter's images of the political parties' (p. 283).

83. See J.E. Wrench, *Geoffrey Dawson and Our Times* (1955), pp. 205-7; and more fully in *The History of the Times 1912-1948* (1952), Part 2, Chs. 13-14; *1921-1948* (1952), Ch. 14.

84. Wrench, *Geoffrey Dawson*, pp. 209-10.

85. Ibid., pp. 290-7.

86. See K. Middlemas and J. Barnes, *Baldwin: a biography* (1969), p. 860.

87. *The Times*, 15 Oct. 1935.

88. Ibid., 3 Oct. 1935.

89. Ibid., 7 and 8 Nov. 1935. Cripps was *The Times*'s particular *bête noir* among Labour leaders.

90. Ibid., 1 Nov. 1935; editorial, 'Vote Today'.

91. For details of Garvin's early career see A.M. Goll in the *Observer* and J.L. Garvin *1908-1914 A Study in a Great Editorship* (1960)

92. *Observer*, 10 Nov. 1935.

93. Ibid., 6 Oct. 1935.

94. Ibid., 27 Oct. 1935.

95. Ibid., 10 Nov. 1935. Like *The Times*, the *Observer* covered the election extensively. It reproduced most of the government's posters, as well as some Labour ones; it reported speeches fully; and it carried detailed articles on changes

214   *Electoral Politics and the Mass Media*

in the structure of the electorate.

96. See PEP, *Report on the British Press*, p. 99. Also Kurt von Stutterheim, *The Press in England* (1934), pp. 199-200, 203-6.

97. Indicative of this is the fact that Baldwin's close friend Tom Jones met Camrose for the first time as late as 1936. See Jones, *A Diary 1931-1950*, p. 277.

98. See Lord Burnham, *Peterborough Court: the story of the Daily Telegraph* (1955), p. 179.

99. *Daily Telegraph*, 9 Nov. 1935.

100. Ibid., 14 Nov. 1935.

101. Ibid., 8 Nov. 1935.

102. Ibid., 12 Nov. 1935.

103. Ibid., 9 Nov. 1935. It believed that only apathy among government supporters would prevent the government from retaining all 12 Birmingham seats; and that overall the government should win with a majority of 150-60 seats.

104. For a note on Sidebotham see D. Ayerst, *The Guardian: biography of a newspaper* (1971), p. 494.

105. *Daily Sketch*, 29 Oct. 1935.

106. *Sunday Times*, 27 Oct., 10 Nov. 1935.

107. *Sunday Chronicle*, 27 Oct. 1935: 'For four years the National Government have led Britain to first place in the march back to prosperity. It is because of this that the people now are in no mood to drop the substance to chase the socialist shadow.'

108. *Empire News*, 10 Nov. 1935.

109. *Sunday Chronicle*, 3 Nov. 1935.

110. *Western Mail*, 14 Nov. 1935. It described Baldwin as the 'Man on the Footplate – True, Trusted, and Tried'. The *Sheffield Telegraph* carried articles like 'How the Government's Policy has helped Sheffield' (13 Nov. 1935).

111. *Daily Record*, 1 Nov. 1935. It had a circulation of 230,000 (von Stutterheim, *Press in England*, p. 166).

112. Editorials: *Sheffield Telegraph*, 13 Nov. 1935: 'Under socialism everybody must be reduced to dependence upon the dictatorial will of the Masters who rule the State'; and the *Newcastle Journal*, 12 Nov. 1935: 'Communist-Socialist Election Alliance.'

113. See for example, *Newcastle Journal*, 2 Nov. 1935: 'The BBC gave Mr. Lloyd George more rope last night, and he proceeded further with the process of hanging himself.'

114. W.H. Hindle, *History of the Morning Post* (1937).

115. PEP, *Report on the British Press*, p. 105.

116. *Morning Post*, 21 Oct. 1935.

117. The *Morning Post* considered Morrison more of a threat than Attlee; see in particular the political cartoon, 8 Nov. 1935.

118. *Morning Post*, 29 Oct. 1935.

119. *Scotsman*, 30 Oct. 1935.

120. Ibid., 18 Oct. 1935. The *Scotsman* also resented Lloyd George's reapparance on the political scene: 'Having had his "New Deal" rejected by the Government Mr. Lloyd George has had the cards redealt by the Council of Action which is one of his aliases' (22 Oct. 1935).

121. *Birmingham Post*, 13 and 14 Nov. 1935. The *Post* believed Labour's candidates to be either extreme left-wingers or party hacks. They included the author G.R. Mitchison, whose book *The First Workers Government* (1934) was used by Conservative leaders to indicate to electors the dangers of electing Labour to office. At the annual conference of the Labour Party in 1935, the Birmingham Borough Labour Party unsuccessfully attempted to get the ILP reaffiliated.

122. *Liverpool Daily Post*, 1 Nov. 1935.

123. Ibid., editorial, 5 Nov. 1935.

124. A misplaced card caused the writer to overlook the *Leeds Mercury* until after his return to Australia where no copies are available. The paragraph on these newspapers was written from four sources: the *Yorkshire Post*; PEP, *Report on the British Press*; the Baldwin Papers; and Linton Andrews, *The Autobiography of a Journalist* (1964).

125. Andrews, *Autobiography*, p. 159.

126. See also Baldwin Papers, vol. 47, Mann to Baldwin, 3 Feb. 1935.

127. *Yorkshire Post*, 1 Nov. 1935.

128. Andrews, *Autobiography*, p. 149.

129. As late as 1937, the PEP *Report on the British Press* (p. 106) was uncertain as to ownership of the *News of the World*.

130. PEP, *Report on the British Press*. The owner of *People* was M.L. Publishing Co. Ltd which had issued a licence to publish to Odhams Properties Ltd, which in turn had granted a sub-licence to Odhams Press Ltd.

131. *People*, 10 Nov. 1935. 'All the Election News' occupied three half paragraphs in the 24-page newspaper.

132. *News of the World*, 10 Nov. 1935. The week before, in an editorial headed 'A Question of Swapping Horses', it had commented that 'there cannot after all be something so very rotten in the State of Denmark when those responsible for its government and those who would relieve them of the burden all sing, with only very slight variations, the same tune'.

133. *Sunday Referee*, 27 Oct. 1935. The *Referee* favoured the introduction of old age pensions at 60 years, and nationalisation of the coal industry, both policies of the Labour Party.

134. M. Edelman, *The Mirror: a political history* (1966), pp. 1-2. See also Hugh Cudlipp, *Publish and Be Damned* (1953); Cecil King, *Strictly Personal* (1969).

135. Edelman, *The Mirror*, p. 26. Rothermere continued to own the *Mirror*, but the chairman of both the *Mirror* and the *Sunday Pictorial*, John Cowley, managed both newspapers.

136. *Daily Mirror*, from 1 Nov. 1935.

137. For example, *Daily Mirror*, 4 and 5 Nov. 1935.

138. It suggested (5 Nov.) that for the entertainment if not instruction of listeners, the party leaders should debate the issues on wireless. An accompanying cartoon showed MacDonald, Attlee and others, having a bun fight in the studios of the BBC.

139. The *Sunday Pictorial* carried the same message, though perhaps with slightly less conviction. While it could acclaim Baldwin, MacDonald and Chamberlain as 'Three Builders of Prosperity' (3 Nov.), its feature writer, Collinson Owen, struck the true Rothermere note in his final article: 'Vote, Vote, Vote, Support the National Government – or Fare Worse!' (10 Nov. 1935).

140. *Daily Mail*, 10 and 12 Nov. 1935.

141. Conducted in September the questionnaire asked:

1) Are you in favour of economic sanctions by the League against Italy if she attacks Abyssinia?

2) Are you in favour of military sanctions against Italy?

3) Are you in favour of Great Britain remaining a member of the League of Nations?

4) Are you in favour of Great Britain rearming in air, on sea, and on land?

The *Daily Mail* was highly satisfied with the result of this poll: 70,000 replies were received, and the voting was 3 to 1 against economic sanctions, 5 to 1 against military sanctions, 2 to 1 against Britain remaining in the League of Nations, and 22 to 1 in favour of British rearmament (Ibid., 30 Sept., 7 Oct. 1935).

142. Ibid., 16 Sept. 1935.

143. Ibid., 13 and 14 Nov. 1935.
144. For a report of dissatisfaction among Beaverbrook's staff see Lloyd George Papers, Sylvester to Lloyd George, 19 Nov. 1934.
145. Mass Observation in *The Press and Its Readers*, p. 110.
146. See A.J.P. Taylor, *Beaverbrook* (1972), pp. 356-8.
147. *Daily Express*, 14 Nov. 1935.
148. Ibid., 1 and 5 Nov. 1935.
149. Ibid., 2 Nov. 1935.
150. Hence headlines like 'Election Too Dull For Words' (5 Nov. 1935) and 'Nobody Cares, that's the Summing Up of the Election' (6 Nov. 1935).
151. In a cartoon entitled 'Invisible Rat Week', Lloyd George is portrayed as the Pied Piper; but, alas, as he piped his way out of the 'Old Party Fortress', no rats were following him.
152. For an entertaining account of Howard's career in the early 1930s see N. Nicolson (ed.), *Harold Nicolson: diaries and letters 1930-39* (1966), esp. pp. 50, 84-97.
153. *Sunday Express*, 10 Nov. 1935.
154. Nicolson, *Harold Nicolson*, p. 308.
155. Lloyd George Papers, G/141/26.
156. A.J.P. Taylor (ed.), *Lloyd George: a diary by Frances Stevenson* (1971), pp. 260, 298, 305 and 314.
157. PEP, *Report on the British Press*, p. 231.
158. The *News Chronicle* 22 Oct. 1935 wrote of the council's programme: 'It represents, in our view, a fair summary of the immediate desires of a great mass of "Left-Centre" opinion in this country.'
159. Ibid., 25 and 31 Oct. 1935.
160. Ibid., 1, 2 and 12 Nov. 1935.
161. Ibid., 6 Nov. 1935.
162. *Birmingham Gazette*, 14 Nov. 1935. The *Gazette* approved of Stanley Baldwin but 'the pity of it is that among his chosen advisers there appear to be so few Baldwins' (1 Nov. 1935).
163. Ayerst, *The Guardian*, pp. 468-74.
164. Ibid.
165. *Manchester Guardian*, 28 Oct., 11 Nov. 1935.
166. The *Daily Herald* was the property of J.S. Elias of Odhams Press Ltd who owned 51% of the shares, and the TUC which owned the remaining 49%. Editorial policy was controlled by the TUC in conjunction with the National Council of Labour.
167. *Daily Herald*, 9 Oct. 1935. The *Herald* did not warmly welcome the election of Attlee as Lansbury's successor.
168. The nearest it came to doing so was on 9 Nov. 1935 when it noted that the Conservatives feared 'enormous Government losses'.
169. A. Hutt, *The Post-War History of the British Working Class* (1937), p. 270.
170. *Daily Worker*, 2 and 14 Nov. 1935.
171. The *Daily Worker*'s circulation was about 30,000 in London, and 20,000 in each of Scotland and Wales. It was not distributed through the normal channels.
172. *Reynolds' News*, 10 Nov. 1935.
173. Ibid., 6 Oct.
174. Ibid., 10 Nov. 1935.
175. Ibid., 13 Oct. 1935.

8 THE CANDIDATES

The number of candidates[1] at the 1935 general election was well below the interwar average of 1,473. In 1935 there were only 1,348, and although this represented an increase of 56 candidates over the total for the 1931 election, it was nearly 300 below the total for 1929. For the most part the reduction in numbers at the 1931 and 1935 elections was attributable to the failure of the Liberal Party to secure funds to support anything like the 442 which they had managed to average in the 1920s, and this was due in large measure to Lloyd George's refusal to grant them access to his fund. Hence at the 1935 election there were only 159 Liberal candidates. The Labour Party nominated 552, an increase of 36 over the 1931 figure, but 17 down on the number who stood in 1929. The Conservatives nominated 514, or 76 fewer than in 1929. The decrease was due primarily to the party's decision to meet the demands of the National Labour Group and some members of the Liberal National Party that Conservatives should stand aside from some contests.

The Liberal Nationals put 46 candidates in the field, a slight increase over 1931. The National Labour Group ran 20 as it had done in 1931. The number of candidates of fringe groups fell from 75 in 1931 to 52 in 1935. Had the British Union of Fascists not stayed its hand this number might well have been considerably larger.[2]

In the inter-election period both the National Government and the Labour Party experienced difficulties over candidatures. The problems of the National Government have been examined at some length in Chapter 1 and need only be briefly restated here. From the outset relations between the Conservative and Liberal National Parties had been amicable and from early in 1935 the Liberal Nationals had more or less completed their electoral arrangements. Relations between the Conservative Party and the National Labour Group had been, and still were, less easy. Lord De La Warr, the representative of National Labour, had repeatedly urged Conservative Central Office to agree to an increase in its MPs at the expense of the Conservatives, but without success. Central Office, partly due to a reluctance to accede to what were in effect National Labour demands rather than requests, and partly due to the intransigence of local Conservative Associations, was unable to accommodate him, even in regard to agreements made in the difficult circumstances of 1931. Part of National Labour's opposition to an election in the autumn of 1935 may have rested on a belief that the Conservatives had yet to deal fairly over the question of candidatures. Aside from the problem of Liberal National and, more particularly, National Labour representation, the National Government had few difficulties with candidatures.[3] The Conservative Central Office occasionally expressed concern over the local associations' apparent willingness to test the pocket of a potential candidate rather than his policies and ability, but this was a hardy perennial in Conservative Party circles, and the party learned to live with it.[4]

Unlike the Conservative Party, the Labour Party was beset with problems concerning candidates. In the first place, as was indicated in Chapter 2, the party lacked funds, and few individuals of independent means presented themselves to the DLPs. Lack of finance had weakened the ability of the party to contest by-elections and was also responsible for the very slow growth in the number of endorsed candidates between 1931 and 1935. Only in the course of 1935 did the number of endorsed candidates exceed 400. Hence in November 1935 over 150 Labour candidates had had less than one year's contact with the constituencies they hoped to represent.[5] In safe Labour seats this was of no consequence but in some of the marginal areas like Birmingham and Salford, for instance, it may have hampered Labour's chances of victory.

The financial weakness of Transport House and the DLPs increased the party's vulnerability to incursions from the Cooperative Party which, despite an unwelcome tax on its profits from 1933 onwards, was anxious and able to sponsor more candidates than it had done in the past. There was more to it than this, however, for the Cooperative Party made as a condition of sponsorship that candidates should not have to sign the Standing Orders of the Labour Party, which in 1931 had been made more restrictive. Such a demand led to friction between the two parties which ended only in mid-1935 with an agreement to disagree. This meant in effect that for the time being the Cooperative Party had its way. At the general election the Cooperative Party sponsored 20 candidates, eight more than in 1929.[6] Finally, although the party was even more heavily dependent on financial support from the unions, union representation did not in fact increase. Indeed at the 1935 election the number of union-sponsored candidates (128) was the lowest for the interwar years.[7]

Throughout its short history the Labour Party had been reluctant to interfere with a DLP's right to nominate a candidate of its own choosing. In the 1930s, however, it did so, more or less with impunity. At the Wakefield and Rotherham by-elections, for instance, the DLPs were 'asked' by Transport House to nominate Arthur Greenwood and W. Dobbie respectively, and they did so, if somewhat reluctantly.[8] In the main this sort of pressure was applied to DLPs in order to strengthen the front bench of the sorely weakened PLP. However, with the party's worsening relations with the ILP, leading to the complete break in 1932, Transport House adopted a more positive approach to candidatures. The NEC made available to the Glasgow Labour Party additional funds with which to fight the seats held by members of the ILP, notably James Maxton at Bridgeton, Rev. Campbell Stephen at Camlachie, John McGovern at Shettleston and George Buchanan at Gorbals. It proved difficult to find candidates, however, and most who came forward were of indifferent quality; at the general election they were routed by the entrenched ILPers.[9]

Apart from the Glasgow seats, there was only one other constituency where a determined attempt was made to prevent the endorsement of a sitting member. This was in Llanelly where the aging Dr Williams, who had held the seat since 1922, retained the support of his DLP by a margin of 45 to 44 votes. Although under some pressure to intervene, the NEC did not do so, and at the election Williams enjoyed an unopposed return.[10] He died in 1936.

The problems encountered by the Liberal Party have been considered in Chapter 3, but should be mentioned in passing here. The Liberal problem was twofold. In the first place the party's apparent failure of will and obvious decline in electoral appeal made it unattractive to aspiring parliamentary candidates. Secondly, the party lacked the finance needed to attract candidates: in this context the death of Lord Cowdray in 1932 was a severe blow. At one time Samuel spoke publicly about the likelihood of 400 Liberal candidates at the next election, but realists like his deputy, Archibald Sinclair, doubted whether 100 could be nominated.[11] As late as mid-1935 even this figure had not been reached, and constituency organisations, where they existed, were in disarray.[12] In the summer and autumn of 1935 Lloyd George spent nearly £400,000 on Council of Action business. He also seems to have made it known that candidates who pledged themselves to support the council's programme would be eligible for a grant from his fund. There was certainly a minor rush of Liberal candidatures, often in the most hopeless of seats from the Liberals' point of view. As Gwilym Lloyd George estimated that outgoings from the fund at the 1935 election totalled £100,000, the support given was not inconsiderable.[13]

As usual the number of women candidates was very small. As a percentage of the total number of candidates, women increased from

2.9% in 1924 to 4.8% in 1931, and to 5.0% in 1935.[14] The Labour Party, historically more sympathetic to the claims of women to a place in politics than the Conservatives, nominated 33 women, but mostly for safe Conservative seats. Only Ellen Wilkinson at Jarrow was successful. Among the defeated women candidates were Susan Lawrence, MP for East Ham North 1929-31; Margaret Bondfield, MP for Wallsend 1929-31 (defeated by the youthful Conservative candidate Irene Ward); Lady Noel Buxton, MP for North Norfolk 1930-1; and Barbara Ayrton Gould, who had come within an ace of unseating Lord Colum Crichton-Stuart at Northwich at the 1929 general election, and who early in 1935 had been selected by the party to contest the important by-election at Lambeth Norwood which she had narrowly lost. The Conservative Party, although it nominated fewer women, was kinder to them. No less than six out of 19 Conservative candidates were elected, including the Duchess of Atholl who in mid-1935 had had the party whip withdrawn because of her opposition to the government's India and agricultural policies,[15] but who had re-entered the party fold in time for the election. The Liberals mustered eleven women candidates, only one of whom, Megan Lloyd George, was successful.

Sixty-eight members of the 1931-5 Parliament did not seek re-election; all but eleven of these were Conservatives. Of the 57 retiring Conservative MPs, 27 had been elected for the first time in the exceptional circumstances of 1931, or at by-elections subsequently; and twelve of the constituencies thus represented reverted to Labour at the 1935 election, while at least a further five were held by the Conservatives by very narrow margins. But at least 40 of the retiring Conservative MPs had sat for safe Conservative seats which at the 1935 election remained loyal to the Conservative standard.

There were only two Labour retirements, both from safe Labour seats. Tom Griffiths and T.W. Grundy retired having represented Pontypool and Rother Valley respectively since 1918. The two retiring Liberal members, Dr Llewellyn Jones (Flint) and E.H. Pickering (West Leicester), did so in the knowledge that to stand again would be to invite certain defeat. A similar consideration induced A.J. Flint, the National Labour MP for Ilkeston, to retire, while at South Nottingham another National Labour MP, Holford Knight, withdrew in favour of another nominee of Ramsay MacDonald, S.F. Markham, who held the seat comfortably, having benefited from the intervention of a Liberal candidate. In the case of the Liberal Nationals, C.H. Summersby retired from the contest at Shoreditch knowing full well that without a repetition of the 1931 crisis his seat would fall to Labour. His fears were realised when at the election Labour won the seat with a comfortable majority. F. Norrie-Miller, the only other Liberal National to retire, had won Perth as recently as April 1935 with the backing of the local Conservative Association. The refusal of some members of the association to endorse his candidature at the general election may have prompted him to retire.[16]

The social backgrounds of the elected candidates have been examined by Professor J.F.S. Ross,[17] and further analysis confirms his major conclusions. In the Conservative Party successful candidates were usually members of a profession (notably law and the armed services) or were in business or had independent means. In the Labour Party the successful were trade union officials, with a sprinkling of professional men (mainly lawyers) and full-time party workers or politicians. The Liberals show no clear deviation from the Conservative pattern. Ross so defined 'Conservative' as to include Liberal National and National Labour candidates; and indeed the overall figures for the Conservatives differ only marginally when Liberal Nationals and National Labour candidates are abstracted from the total. About 50% of the successful Liberal National candidates were drawn from the professions, notably law, whereas the percentage for the Conservatives is closer to 35%; but the percentage for businessmen is the same for both of the major components of the National Government. The National Labour pattern differs sharply from the Conservative one, but National Labour numbers were too small to affect the overall pattern. Most of the successful National Labour candidates were full-time politicians and journalist-writers such as Harold Nicolson; only one of the successful eight was a lawyer.

Ross concerned himself with successful candidates only, perhaps on the assumption that the pattern would be duplicated in the case of those defeated. In fact there are some quite substantial differences in the occupations of the successful and the unsuccessful. In the Conservative Party, whereas about one-third of the successful candidates came from the professions, among the unsuccessful over one-half did so. On the other hand proportionately fewer company directors and farmers are found among unsuccessful Conservative candidates. In the Labour Party too there are differences in occupations as between the elected and defeated. No less than 36% of the unsuccessful Labour candidates were drawn from the professions (law and teaching mostly), while only 20% of the successful came from this group. On the other hand, while nearly half of those successful were workers (mainly trade union officials), less than one-third of the unsuccessful could be so classified. There are no striking differences in the occupational pattern for elected and defeated candidates in the Liberal National and National Labour Parties.

In his study Professor Ross produced some general tables of the previous parliamentary service of those elected.[18] But he did not separate the parties, and he did not examine defeated candidates in the same way. Table 8.1 extends Ross's tables to include this information, together with local government backgrounds of all candidates:

Table 8.1: Previous service of Parliamentary Candidates

	Elected				Defeated			
	Local Govt. Exp.	Parl. Cands			Local Govt. Exp.	Parl. Cands		
		1st Con-test	1929 or pre-	1931 or bye		1st Con-test	1929 or pre-	1931 or bye
Conservative	25%	9%	70%	20%	24%	40%	26%	34%
Liberal National	22%	—	95%	5%	3%	17%	66%	17%
National Labour	50%	—	75%	25%	50%	25%	66%	9%
Labour	56%	10%	84%	5%	45%	49%	37%	14%
Liberal	25%	—	80%	20%	27%	46%	47%	7%

From Table 8.1 it is clear that Labour candidates tended to come from party workers with experience in local government, whereas this was not the case with Conservative candidates. Because the table is in percentage form, it disguises some absolute differences between the two major parties. While no less than 211 Labour candidates were contesting a parliamentary election for the first time, only 82 Conservative candidates were in the same position. On the other hand, while no less than 119 Conservative candidates had first contested a parliamentary election in 1931 or at a by-election since, only 62 Labour candidates were in this category. In the third category, namely those candidates with experience of parliamentary elections in 1929 or earlier, the two major parties had roughly the same number (275 Labour, 290 Conservative).

Statistics on the educational backgrounds of the candidates do not cast doubt on the generalisations made from more impressionistic material. The tables in Appendix 3 show that while two-thirds of the successful Labour candidates had only an elementary education, only two out of 367 successful Conservative candidates had not proceeded beyond this. While 10% of the successful Labour candidates had been to a public school, no less than 65% of the elected Conservatives had enjoyed this privilege; and while 59% of the elected Conservatives had been to university, only 22% of the successful Labour candidates had found their way to university. Not one Labour candidate had been educated at naval or military colleges, whereas over one in ten Conservative candidates had been to them. For defeated candidates the pattern seems to differ, though for both parties the information is less complete than for those elected. While the percentage of university-educated Conservatives would seem to have been roughly the same for both elected and defeated candidates, this was not the case with the Labour Party. Foreshadowing developments among successful Labour candidates from 1945 onwards it would seem that defeated Labour candidates were better educated than those successful. While only 22% of the successful Labour candidates had had a university education, 43% of the unsuccessful ones had been so trained. Of major parties the Liberals were the most highly educated; two-thirds of all Liberal candidates had been to a university. But it was the same with the Liberal National and National Labour.

At the 1935 general election the average age of members of the House of Commons rose from 48 years 6 months to 51 years, or slightly higher than in 1929.[19] This was brought about by the return of many Labour men defeated at the 1931 election. As Table 8.2 shows, the median age of elected Labour candidates was 54 years, compared with 49 years for successful Conservative candidates. The Table also shows that the median age for successful candidates of the minor parties was even higher than for Labour. The difference between the Labour and Conservative Parties is even more striking in percentage terms. Whereas 53% of the successful Conservative candidates were under the age of 50 years, this was true of only 29% of the elected Labour candidates. The difference is not so marked for the defeated candidates of both parties; indeed in the case of Labour, the percentage of defeated candidates under 50 years is almost double the percentage for elected candidates.

Overall, the differences between elected and defeated candidates were not especially great for any party except Labour. For Labour the defeated were considerably younger, were better educated, and proportionately fewer of them were trade unionists.

Table 8.2: Ages of the Candidates by Party

Age in 1935	Conservative		Labour		Lib. Nat.		Nat. Lab.		Liberal		Totals
	Elected	Defeated	Elected	Defeated	Elected	Defeated	Elected	Defeated	Elected	Defeated	
20-29	11	10	2	15	—	—	—	1	1	5	45
30-39	86	26	9	46	6	2	2	1	5	10	193
40-49	98	19	34	61	4	2	1	3	4	14	240
50-59	102	23	58	67	10	2	1	1	5	12	281
60-69	56	6	43	24	10	4	3	3	2	18	169
70-79	14	2	8	3	2	—	—	1	2	1	33
Total	367	86	154	216	32	10	8	9	19	60	961
Median	49	44	54	47	55	58	61	49	53	51	
Age under 50 Nos.	195	55	45	122	10	4	3	5	10	29	478
%	53	64	29	56	30	40	38	56	50	48	50%

Notes

1. In 1935 methods of selection of candidates closely approximated those of 1945, which are discussed in detail in R.B. McCallum and A. Readman, *The British General Election of 1945* (1947), Ch. 4. Such descriptive matter is therefore omitted here. For an account of a Conservative Association's acceptance of a National Labour candidate see Harold Nicolson's *Diaries and Letters 1930-39* (1966), pp. 210-13.

2. See Mosley's announcement as reported in *The Times*, 28 Oct. 1935: no Fascist candidates would contest the present election, 'but electoral machinery would be built up in preparation for the next'.

3. By October the Liberal National Party was in fighting trim. See Simon Papers, diary entry, 22 Oct. 1935: 'I have been very busy with the Liberal National organization, which is now greatly strengthened both as regards personnel and funds.' For National Labour's grumbles on the eve of the election see M. Gilbert, *Plough My Own Furrow: the life and letters of Clifford Allen* (1965), p. 311

4. Percy Cohen, 'Disraeli's child: a history of Conservative and Unionist Party Organization', unpublished typescript, Conservative Research Department Library, vol. 2, pp. 376-82.

5. *The Times*, 26 Oct. 1935 estimated that 40% of Labour candidates in Yorkshire, Durham and Northumberland were new to the constituencies.

6. This paragraph is based on the minutes of the joint meetings of the NEC and the Executive Committee of the Cooperative Party, attached to NEC minutes, 1933-5.

7. Many unions were experiencing financial difficulties as a result of long-term

unemployment and the operation of the 'contracting in' clauses of the 1927 Trades Disputes Act, both of which decreased union membership. See G.D.H. Cole, *A History of the Labour Party Since 1914* (1948), p. 195; also Appendix 4, p. 450.

8. NEC Minutes, 23 Mar. 1932. Under considerable pressure from Transport House, the NUR nominee, G.H. Sherwood, who had represented the seat on two occasions and been a candidate since 1923, agreed to stand down in favour of Greenwood. See also *The Times*, 23 Feb. 1932.

9. NCL Minutes, 17 Dec. 1935. Also minutes of Executive Committee of Scottish Labour Party, 11 Mar., 10 May, 13 June and 19 Aug. 1935.

10. NEC Minutes, 19 Sept. 1935.

11. For Samuel's comment see *The Times*, 19 May 1933. For Sinclair's view see Samuel Papers, Sinclair to Samuel, 21 Jan. 1935: as late as Jan. 1935 perhaps only 60 candidates had been adopted.

12. Lothian Papers, Harcourt Johnstone to Lothian, 19 Nov. 1934.

13. *News Chronicle*, 2 Nov. 1935; F. Owen, *Tempestuous Journey* (1954), p. 692. See also Lothian Papers, James Scott to Lothian: 'I knew about the balance of the £1,000 which was allocated for Scotland by L.G.'

14. F.W.S. Craig, *British Parliamentary Election Statistics 1918-1968* (1968), p. 62.

15. Baldwin Papers, vol. 107, contains a series of letters from the Duchess of Atholl concerning her opposition to the government's policies.

16. See *Scotsman*, 28 Oct. 1935. It seems that Miller at first intended to recontest the seat and that initially both the Liberal and Unionist Associations supported him. However some influential Unionists then expressed their surprise that Miller was again coming forward. Miller seems to have taken the hint and retired in favour of the Lord Provost, Thomas Hunter. The Perth Liberal Association thereupon declared its neutrality at the election, but Hunter was returned with a comfortable majority.

17. J.F.S. Ross, *Parliamentary Representation* (1948).

18. Ibid., p. 36.

19. Ibid., p. 32.

9 THE OUTCOME

Over most of the country the weather on polling day was unsettled, and many places recorded heavy falls of rain, particularly in the afternoon and evening. The falls were heaviest in Scotland and the North of England, and as far south as the Midlands and East Anglia. Elsewhere there were occasional falls of rain, though in the South of England the weather was more temperate; indeed the temperature – in the mid-50sF – was unusually high for November. There seems to be a correlation between regional variations in the weather pattern and change in turnout in comparison with 1931. While there was an overall fall in turnout of about 5%, the percentage fall tended to be greater in the Midlands, the North of England and the east coast of Scotland, and less in the South of England. A number of factors contributed to the overall fall in turnout,[1] but it seems clear that the inclement weather was one of the more important.

Polling day passed off quietly and when polling stations closed at 8.0 p.m. (9.0 p.m. in London) the only disturbing feature of the day for party organisers was the low turnout, the effect of which was difficult to gauge. To most observers, there was little evidence of a massive shift in public opinion against the government, and throughout the day the mood of the Stock Exchange (as it had been since the commencement of the campaign) was one of buoyancy. On the morning of 15 November *The Times* reported that this

confident tone was a clear indication of the City's belief that a good majority for the National Government would be secured.

It was anticipated that overnight the results for about 230 constituencies would be announced on the wireless. Broadcasts were to commence at 10.0 p.m. and were to continue intermittently until 4.0 a.m. In the slack periods listeners were to be entertained with light music played by Reginald King and his Orchestra, the Gershom Parkington Quintet and the Victor Olof Sextet. The BBC tried hard to inject some life into the evening but to no avail. It was too much like continuing to read a thriller when you're absolutely confident that you've worked it all out from the opening lines: one or two of the later passages may increase the pulse rate, but only by a little and that not sustained. *The Times* had warned its readers not to be discouraged if the overnight returns appeared to indicate a strong swing to Labour.[2] It had pointed out that the bulk of the evening's results would be for London and the larger English towns and cities, in which Labour was expected to make a substantial recovery but which were not typical of the constituencies overall. The word of caution was unnecessary, for by the end of the evening the National Government held a comfortable lead and indeed in some areas had done far better that had been forecast.

The first result broadcast was for Cheltenham, where in a straight fight with Labour the Conservative candidate was returned with his majority substantially reduced; more importantly, however, his percentage vote was far higher than it had been in 1929, when the constituency had been contested by all three parties. From this early result it could be deduced that where there was no Liberal candidate, the Liberal vote was not going to be transferred *in toto* to Labour. A result of even greater significance was the third announced, namely Stockton-on-Tees, where it had been thought that Harold Macmillan might well lose his seat to one of Labour's ablest campaigners, Susan Lawrence. In the event Macmillan held Stockton with a comfortable, though reduced, majority of 4,000.[3] It was apparent that he had secured a large Liberal vote, for the Liberal candidate fared disastrously, and Miss Lawrence only marginally increased Labour's share of the total vote over the 1929 figure.

When at 4.0 a.m. transmission ceased, the National Government led the opposition by nearly 100 seats. It had lost nearly 40 to Labour, principally in London, Manchester and Sheffield, though in none of these cities had Labour recovered all the ground lost in 1931. The National Government had even made a handful of gains, largely at the expense of the Samuelite wing of the Liberal Party, indeed at the expense of Samuel himself (defeated at Darwen by a Conservative). A further indication of success for the National Government came with the results of the three Salford seats. At the 1929 general election Labour had been successful in all three. In 1935 it was widely believed that if Labour was again successful in Salford, then it would do as well nationwide as it had done in 1929. In the event the National Government held all three, albeit South Salford narrowly.[4] From this point, therefore, it seemed quite clear that Labour would not emulate its 1929 record.

A signal success for the government came late in the evening when it was announced that East Fulham had been recaptured by the youthful

W. Astor, the Conservative candidate. Equally cheering was the government's clean sweep in Birmingham. At the 1929 election Labour had impressively smashed through the Liberal-Tory Chamberlainism of the city and captured six of the twelve seats. On the eve of the 1935 election it was thought that Labour would again be successful in at least Duddeston and Deritend, and possibly Kings Norton as well.[5] At the election, however, not one of the Labour candidates came to within 3,000 votes of his Conservative opponent. It is hardly surprising to find, therefore, that on the morning of 15 November the National Government press was enthusing editorially over the results known thus far. By highlighting Labour's individual gains the *Daily Herald* put on a brave face, but in comparison with *The Times* and the *Daily Telegraph* its editorial was in a low key. For the *Daily Herald*, indeed for most Labour supporters, the galling thing was not that the party was losing the election, but that it was losing by so wide a margin.

As further results were announced during Friday 15 November, government supporters became even more jubilant. The English county constituencies held firm for the government, while in the celtic fringe, particularly in Scotland, Labour had failed to repeat its 1929 successes, and the Samuelite wing of the Liberal Party had been all but eliminated. By the evening the government had a clear majority of over 200. The leaders had refrained from commenting publicly on the results of the first day, but when in the afternoon of 15 November the government achieved an overall majority, Baldwin issued a statement congratulating the electorate on its collective wisdom; at the same time he promised to justify the confidence shown in him. For Labour, Attlee's views apparently went unrecorded, while Herbert Morrison and the London Labour Party issued a self-congratulatory statement on the London results, thereby dissociating themselves from the party's dismal showing nationwide.[6]

Labour made a net gain of 94 seats and, in all, 116 seats changed hands, fewer by one-third than any other interwar election, and 125 fewer than in 1931 (when the Conservatives made a net gain of nearly 190 from Labour). Labour made a gross gain of 72 from the Conservatives, 8 from the Liberal Nationals, 6 from National Labour and 9 from the Samuelite Liberals. The Conservatives suffered only a low net loss of 70 seats, and even succeeded in recapturing three seats (East Fulham, Swindon and Wavertree) lost to Labour at by-elections. In all, 435 National Government candidates were elected; 388 Conservatives, 35 Liberal Nationals, 8 from National Labour and 4 loosely termed as 'National'. The opposition parties won 180 seats: Labour 154, ILP 4,

Samuelite Liberal 19, Communist 1 and Irish Partitionists 2.[7] Thus the Baldwin administration enjoyed a majority of 255.

The election produced gains and losses at the ministerial level. The only National Government Ministers to go down to defeat were the National Labour leaders Ramsay and Malcolm MacDonald, though at Spen Valley Sir John Simon came perilously close to defeat. Twenty-four former Labour Ministers who lost their seats in 1931 were returned, among them six former Cabinet Ministers; but seven former Labour Ministers, including five members of former Labour Cabinets, were unsuccessful. Labour surrendered three of its ten by-election gains, including Swindon where Christopher Addison, a former Cabinet Minister in MacDonald's second ministry, was defeated. For the Samuelite wing of the Liberal Party the election was an unmitigated disaster: with the exception of Sir Archibald Sinclair, the entire front bench was lost, together with over one-third of the already meagre parliamentary representation.

The swing against the National Government was fairly uniform nationwide, though, as will be shown later, it varied according to the nature of the contest. For the 450 constituencies where valid statistical comparison is possible,[8] there was a nationwide swing to Labour of 9.4%. The use of this swing calculation is limited to giving only the broadest possible picture of the electoral movement between 1931 and 1935, largely because it takes into consideration no less than nine different types of contest. While in the statistical Appendix 1.5 regional swing is calculated on this basis, in the paragraphs following, regional variations are traced through the use of swing for particular types of contest.

In the 230 constituencies where there was a straight fight between Conservatives and Labour in both 1931 and 1935 there was a nationwide swing to Labour of 9.9% (see Figure 9.1). Variations by constituency type were not marked: in both English county and borough constituencies the swing was 9.7%; for Scottish boroughs it was 10.2% and for Scottish counties it was 10%. In London, where recent by-elections and municipal elections had shown a marked swing to Labour due to domestic issues like overcrowding and rent control, the swing to Labour was greater at 12%; while in the Welsh county and borough seats it was rather lower at 8.2% and 8.6% respectively.

Almost every region showed a swing to Labour of within 4.0% of the national average. The movement was above average in London and Outer London, in areas which had seen only marginal improvement in trade and employment like Lancashire, the East Midlands, the West

Figure 9.1: Conservative versus Labour, 1931 and 1935 (230 constituencies)

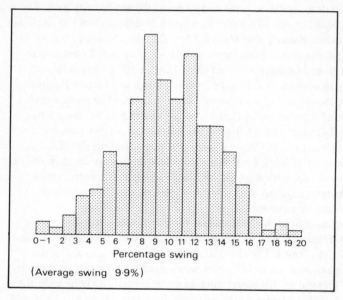

Percentage swing

(Average swing 9·9%)

Riding of Yorkshire, Durham and Northumberland, and southern Scotland. It was below average in south-west England (including Hampshire), parts of the Clyde Valley (which in 1931 had only a low swing to the National Government) and much of north-east England. The areas which deviated most were the prosperous West Midlands, where the swing was barely half the national average, and north-east Scotland, where the swing to Labour was 15.0%. Of the major cities, Edinburgh (4.2%), Birmingham (5.2%), Liverpool (13.2%) and Nottingham (12.7%) deviated most from the national average; also the Hants ports (5%) where the government's rearmament programme held considerable appeal; but Bristol, Hull, Sheffield, Leeds, Manchester and Glasgow were all within 2.0% of the national figure.

Swing in individual constituencies varied greatly. In the Ladywood division of Birmingham the swing to Labour was a negligible 0.1%, in Burton (Staffordshire) 0.2% and in North Portsmouth only 1.8%: in all three cases the decisive factor was Labour's inability to entice the Liberal voters to the polls. At the other extreme were Wavertree (Liverpool) with a swing to Labour of 19.4%, Mitcham (Surrey) 18.8%

and Wallasey 16.5%. In none of these high-swing constituencies was the government defeated. In Wavertree the Labour candidate had to over-come the deficit produced by a strikingly high swing of 24% to the Conservative Party at the 1931 election: in the circumstances he made a better effort of recovery than did many of his colleagues who were placed more advantageously. In Mitcham the Labour candidate achieved a higher swing to Labour than there had been away from Labour at the 1931 election; but the constituency was not marginal, and in 1935 it would have required a swing to Labour of 25.4% for the seat to be captured. Similarly in Wallasey it would have required a massive swing of 34% for the Conservative to be unseated.

The generalisations of the preceding paragraphs are based on swing for constituencies where there was a fight between Conservatives and Labour at both the 1931 and 1935 elections. When swing for constitu-encies where there were straight fights between Labour and Liberal National, and between Labour and National Labour, at both elections is taken into account, a slightly different picture emerges, for Labour did rather better against the non-Conservative components of the National Government than it did against the Conservatives. In straight fights between Labour and Liberal Nationals[9] there was a nationwide swing to Labour of 11%, or 1.3% greater than for straight fights between Labour and Conservatives. Regional variations were marked and did not correspond to the regional pattern for straight fights be-tween Labour and the Conservatives. The greatest movement was in London (16.4%); the least in Wales (5.7%). And in the English counties Labour fared far better in straight fights with the Liberal Nationals (12.4% swing to Labour) than in straight fights with Conservatives (9.7%). In Scotland the swing pattern was roughly similar in both cases: 10.1% versus Conservatives, 9.3% versus Liberal Nationals.

Labour fared best of all in straight fights with National Labour. In the eight constituencies where there were such fights at both elections,[10] the average swing to Labour was 16.8%, or 6.3% greater than for straight fights between Labour and the Conservatives. The swing was most pronounced in London (18.9%), but it was also very high in even the region of lowest swing. Unlike the Liberal Nationals who polled well in Scotland and Wales, National Labour fared disas-trously throughout the country, losing over half its meagre parliamen-tary representation.

The Conservative Party fared exceptionally well in three-cornered contests with Labour and the Samuelite wing of the Liberal Party. In the 32 constituencies where this type of contest took place at both elections,[11] the swing to Labour (calculated in the conventional manner) was only 5.0%; that is, 4.9% below the swing for straight fights between Conservatives and Labour. Even if calculated on a two-party basis the swing to Labour was only 7.6%, still considerably lower than for fights between Conservatives and Labour. Swing in individual constituencies varied greatly, ranging from 4.9% at Basingstoke where an energetic young Liberal, John Foot, staged a remarkable recovery for his party, to 10.4% at Camberwell Dulwich. In no less than eight of the 32 constituencies the Conservative share of the total vote was in excess of the percentage for 1931.

The Conservatives also fared well in straight fights with the Samuelites. In the eleven constituences where comparison is possible, the Liberals failed to make up the ground surrendered to the Conservatives in 1931.[12] Indeed the swing to the Liberals in these constituencies was only 6.3%. In three of the eleven constituencies comparison with the 1929 election is also possible, the Liberal dilemma being seen most clearly in the cases of two, Kincardine and Western Aberdeenshire, and Chertsey. For Chertsey the Conservatives share of the total vote in the three elections was 55.6%, 79.6%; for Kincardine and Western Aberdeenshire, 48.2%, 61.6% and 55.9%.[13] In both cases the Liberals in 1935 failed to regain at least half the ground lost in 1931.

At the 1935 general election the Samuelite and Lloyd George wings of the Liberal Party fielded only 159 candidates – 41 more than in 1931 though 354 fewer than in 1929 when the party last presented a united front to the electorate. The 159 candidates gained only 6.4% of the total vote, 0.8% lower than the percentage (7.2) gained by the 118 candidates in 1931. At first sight, however, it would appear that in comparison with 1929 the Liberal vote was holding up quite well. In 1929 roughly three times as many candidates (513) achieved a percentage of the total vote (23.6) nearly four times greater than that of 1935 – a decline in 1935 but hardly a catastrophic one. This particular comparison, however, disguises the full extent of Liberal electoral decline. In the first place it must be remembered that in 1929 the Liberals were contesting at least 400 seats which they had not even an outside chance of winning, and in many cases were expected to, and did, come third in three-way fights. In fact no less than 259 (or more than half) Liberal candidates finished in third place in 1929, in most cases several thousand votes behind the second place-getter.[14] Secondly, the average Liberal vote per constituency contested was only 8,803 in 1935 whereas it had been 10,348 in 1929, even with so great a number of hopeless seats being contested.[15]

Generalisations about the extent of Liberal decline between 1929 and 1935 can perhaps best be made from a consideration of voting in the 37 constituencies where there were similar contests involving Liberals at all three elections, and where the Liberal vote was particularly strong. In the 34 constituencies where the contest was between the Conservatives, Liberals and Labour,[16] the average Liberal vote at the 1929 election was 12,971, at the 1931 election 10,941; and in 1935 9,654. In terms of the percentage share of the total vote, this represents a fall from 35.8% in 1929 to 29.5% in 1931, and even further to 26.6% in 1935. In the three constituencies where there was a straight fight between the Conservatives and Liberals at all three elections, the average Liberal vote in 1929 was 12,991; in 1931 9,252 and in 1935 11,638. This represents in terms of the Liberal share of the total vote a fall from 47.9% in 1929 to 39.8% in 1935. Both sets of percentages show the extent of the electoral decline of the opposition Liberals, though of the two, the first more accurately portrays their dismal state.

The Liberals also fared disastrously in straight fights with Labour. Comparison is only possible for seven constituencies;[17] in these the swing to Labour in 1935 was 11.2%, higher even than the swing to Labour in constituencies where there was a straight fight between the Conservatives and Labour (9.9%).

The constituencies considered to this point were by and large Liberal strongholds, or at least contained a substantial Liberal vote. To gauge the full extent of Liberal decline, therefore, comparisons must also be made for constituencies where there was a less sizeable Liberal vote. At the 1935 election the Liberals made a comeback in nearly 80 seats which in 1931 they had left uncontested. Of these, 67 can satisfactorily be compared with the 1929 election. In these seats the average percentage Liberal vote fell from 26.4 in 1929 to 13.8 in 1935. Taken overall, 118 seats are comparable for the 1929 and 1935 elections. For these seats the average percentage Liberal vote fell from 30.9 in 1929 to 19.9 in 1935, a loss to the Liberals of approximately one-third of their 1929 voting strength. It has already been shown that in those constituencies where there was a straight fight between the Conservatives and the Liberals at both 1931 and 1935, the Liberals failed to recover fully from the crash in 1931. Furthermore, in 1935 the Liberals failed to contest at least 29 seats in which they had gained over 20% of the total vote in 1929; in no less than 16 of these, Liberal candidates had gained over 30% at the earlier election.

Perhaps the most striking feature of the election was Labour's inability to regain the ground it had surrendered to the National Govern-

234   *The Outcome*

ment in 1931. This failure can best be shown from a comparison between the swing away from Labour in 1931 and the swing to Labour in 1935, for those constituencies where direct comparison is possible. In the first instance this means the 40 constituencies where there was a straight fight between Labour and the Conservatives in all three elections.[18] In these constituencies at the 1931 election there was a swing away from Labour of 15.1%, but for the same constituencies at the 1935 election the swing to Labour was only 9.9%. It would seem therefore that overall in 1935 Labour failed to regain approximtely one-third of the ground lost to the Conservatives in 1931.

In these 40 constituencies between 1929 and 1935 there was an overall swing to the Conservatives of 5.2%. In terms of seats won and lost it represented a gain from the Conservatives of five seats (from 12 seats in 1929 to 17 in 1935). The swing to the Conservatives seems to have been the product of that party's ability to attract newly registered voters, as well as a direct transfer of votes from Labour, rather than a differential turnout of Labour supporters. Table 9.1 suggests that differential turnout was only a factor where the decrease in turnout exceeded 8%. Where this was the case the swing to the Conservatives was more than double the average for the constituencies under consideration. As a result of the differential turnout of Labour supporters at least three of these seats (Birmingham Ladywood, West Birmingham and Liverpool Fairfield) moved from being marginal to being safe for the Conservatives. But the five seats which actually changed hands between 1929 and 1935 did so largely because of a direct transfer of votes from Labour to Conservative.

Table 9.1: Swing and Turnout, 1929 to 1935

		Swing						
	To Labour	To Conservative						
Change in Turnout		Up to 1.9%	2.0–3.9%	4.0–5.9%	6.0–7.9%	Over 8.0%	Average	No. of all seats
Decrease over 8.0%					1	4	13.0%	5
6.0–7.9%	1			1			– 2.9%	2
4.0–5.9%		3		5	2	1	4.7%	11
2.0–3.9%	1				1		3.4%	2
Decrease up to 2.0%		1	1	1	4	1	5.9%	8
Increase		3	4	2	1	2	4.0%	12
All seats	2	7	5	9	9	8	5.2%	40

In the second place, while in three-way fights between Labour, the Liberals and the Conservatives, Labour nearly regained the ground lost in 1931, it strikingly failed to increase its share of the total vote *vis-à-vis* the Liberals. Treating all other factors as equal, it would seem that the greater part of the one-quarter to one-third of the 1929 Liberal vote which went to non-Liberal candidates in 1935 (in constituencies where there was a three-way fight) went to the Conservatives rather than to Labour. This can be seen from Table 9.2, which compares percentage votes for the 32 constituencues where there were three-way contests at all three elections:

Table 9.2: Voting in Three-way Contests

	1929	Diff.	1931	Diff.	1935
Conservatives	38.7%	(+13.5)	52.2%	(−3.6)	48.6%
Labour	25.3%	(− 6.6)	18.7%	(+ 6.2)	24.9%
Liberals	36.0%	(− 6.9)	29.1%	(−2.6)	26.5%

or, more concisely:

	1929	1935	% change
Conservatives	38.7%	48.6%	+9.9
Labour	25.3%	24.9%	−0.4
Liberals	36.0%	26.5%	−9.5

The generalisation made above is valid only if the percentage decrease in turnout in these constituencies is similar to the national average: if it was markedly greater than the national average then it would appear that rather than there being a transfer of Liberal votes to the Conservatives, there was widespread abstention among Liberals at the 1935 election. This does not, however, appear to have been the case. For the 32 constituencies in question, the percentage decrease in turnout between 1929 and 1935 (6.1%) was only marginally greater than the national percentage decrease (5%).

Table 9.3: Turnout in Three-way Contests

	% Turnout			% Change
	1929	1931	1935	1929-35
32 comparable constituencies	81.4	81.2	75.3	6.1
Nationwide	76.0	76.3	71.0	5.0

The figures in Table 9.3 suggest that while there was some abstention among Liberal voters in 1935, in relation to the rate of voluntary abstention among Conservative and even Labour voters it was fairly low: and that the generalisation made in the preceding paragraph, namely that the Liberal vote from 1929, where it did not vote Liberal in 1935, tended to vote, and to vote for the Conservative Party, holds good.

Nevertheless, there is a clear causal relationship in the impact of Liberal candidatures on turnout. Table 9.4 shows the extent to which turnout was affected by the presence or absence of a Liberal.

Table 9.4: Liberal Effect on Turnout

Liberal candidates 1931 and 1935	Change in turnout						All seats	Av. change in turnout
	Increase	Decrease						
		Up to 1.9%	2.0— 3.9%	4.0— 5.9%	6.0— 7.9%	Over 8.0%		
Both elections	4	7	17	20	12	17	77	—5.2
Neither election	25	42	67	99	56	48	337	—4.6
Liberal intervention 1935	4	14	20	14	10	8	70	—4.1
Liberal withdrawal 1935	1	—	2	3	10	10	26	—7.4
All seats (excl. N.I. universities and seats with unopposed candidates 1931, 1935, or both)	34	63	106	136	88	83	510	—4.7

From Table 9.4 it is clear that the decrease in turnout was lowest where there was a Liberal intervention in 1935, and that the largest average fall in turnout occurred in the seats where a Liberal stood in 1931 but not in 1935. The fall was also greater where Liberals stood both times and lost votes, than in fights between the National Government and the rest of the opposition. It cannot be said that in the seats where the Liberal loss of votes was highest the drop in turnout was greatest, because the Liberal loss of votes was greatest in constituencies like West Leicester, East Middlesbrough and East Edinburgh, where in 1931 the Liberal candidate had been the sole standard-bearer for the National

Government, but where in 1935 the Conservatives fielded a candidate
and the fall in turnout was low. Nevertheless, in a number of constituencies where there was a three-way contest or a straight fight between
the Liberals and Labour at both elections, a high percentage loss of
votes by the Liberals was accompanied by a large fall in turnout,
notably in Bethnal Green North East, Manchester Rusholme, East
Nottingham and East Cardiff. However, the fact that the difference in
turnout drop between seats with Liberal intervention (4.1) and those
with no Liberal in either year (4.6) is not great suggests that the overall
rate of abstention among Liberals was not high.

Only 71% of the electorate registered their votes, a fall in turnout of
5% on the 1931 percentage and the lowest turnout since 1923. The fall
in turnout was experienced over most of the country. Some of the fall
was due to a reversion to apathy on the part of electors drawn to the
poll in the extraordinary circumstances of 1931. The fall was due in
part also to apathy on the part of Conservatives who considered that
the National Government was 'home and dry' without any need for
them to cast their votes. Similarly, though for the reverse situation,
Labour abstentions were caused through a belief that Labour had no
chance of winning the election. The age of the register (six months)
may have contributed to the turnout, but only to the same extent as in
1931 and therefore cannot be seen as a factor producing a turnout
lower than 1931. And, as was mentioned at the commencement of this
chapter, the inclement weather was probably an important cause of the
fall in turnout.

The size of the fall was not uniform throughout the country. Turnout change in the English counties — especially in the South — was close
to the national average, though with an above-average fall in turnout
Worcestershire seems to have been affected by the generally large fall
throughout the West Midlands. Indeed, regionally the fall in turnout
was greatest in the West Midlands, and particularly in the cities of
Birmingham and Wolverhampton. No less than nine of the twelve
Birmingham constituencies experienced falls in turnout of over 10% or
twice the national average. There may have been some abstention on
the part of Labour voters, but the fall in turnout seems to have been
caused mainly by the abstention of Liberal voters in the absence of
Liberal candidates. This would be consistent with the claim of the
organ of Birmingham Liberalism, the *Birmingham Gazette* (editorial,
14 November), that, as between the major protagonists in the election,
Liberals would be neutral. In Wolverhampton, Wednesbury and in
some of the neighbouring Staffordshire seats, the fall in turnout was

also well above the national average, due in part to substantial Labour, as well as Liberal, abstentions. For the West Midlands there is a clear causal relationship between the large fall in turnout and the very low swing against the National Government.

Outside the West Midlands the fall in turnout was exceptionally high in the West Riding of Yorkshire, especially in the mill cities of Bradford (three of whose four seats had turnout falls in excess of 10%), Leeds and Huddersfield. For North Bradford and Huddersfield the principal cause of the fall in turnout was voluntary abstention by Liberals; elsewhere in the West Riding the fall in turnout was more obviously multi-causal. For much of Lancashire the fall in turnout was close to the national average but in Liverpool three constituencies had falls in excess of 10%, as did neighbouring Wallasey. Only in the case of Walton was Liberal abstention clearly the cause of the low turnout; elsewhere more general factors, such as the belief that the National Government was heading for a comfortable victory, the wet weather and so on, were probably more important. The fall in turnout was also high along the east coast of Scotland. In three of the Edinburgh seats the fall exceeded 8%, while at Leith it was 9.5%. The fall was greater than 10% in Perth and Central Aberdeenshire, and 9.9% in South Aberdeen. A likely cause of the falls in turnout was the wintry weather, though in the cases of West Edinburgh and Perth voluntary Liberal abstention may also have been important.

The fall in turnout was least in the South of England (excluding several of the Devon seats, where in the absence of Liberal candidates there was a high rate of voluntary abstention), in London, in Durham and in the county seats of Yorkshire, in much of Wales, the west coast of Scotland and the Scottish lowlands. In none of these regions was the Liberal vote a dominant factor affecting turnout, while in several constituencies along the west coast of Scotland the intervention of a Scottish Nationalist Party candidate helped to prevent a marked decrease in turnout. In London political interest had been stirred by several exciting by-elections, as well as by the municipal elections in the previous year.

In a number of constituencies there was an increase in turnout. A few seats were stirred up by recent by-elections. Notable among these were East Fulham where there was a 5.8% increase, West Toxteth, and Rutland and Stamford. There was also an increase in turnout — Isle of Ely, for example — where in 1931, in the absence of a Conservative candidate, electors who usually voted Conservative had refused to accept a Liberal as the standard-bearer of the National Government and abstained, but where in 1935, on the re-emergence of a Conservative candidate, they again came to the polls. This also occurred in several of the constituencies where there was no Liberal candidate in 1931 but where a Liberal again intervened in 1935. Notable among these were Scarborough and Whitby, where there was a 5.2% increase in turnout, Bury and Carlisle. The intervention of candidates of the Scottish Nationalist Party was responsible for the 10% increase in turnout in the Western Isles, and the 4% increase in Greenock, as well as being responsible in part for keeping turnout change to a small decrease in Kilmarnock (where interest stirred up by a recent by-election was also important) and Dunbartonshire. The effect on turnout of Scottish Nationalist Party candidatures at Inverness, West and East Renfrew, was marginal.

There is no evidence to suggest that there was a bonus attached to sitting MPs. Of the 1931-5 Parliament 68 members did not seek re-election. Of these, 2 were for Irish seats, 1 for a University seat. Of the remainder, 56 were Conservatives, 2 Liberal Nationals, 2 National Labour, 1 National, 2 Liberals and 2 Labour. Only 28 of the seats with Conservative retirements lend themselves to valid statistical comparison, and for these the average swing to Labour in 1935 was 9.0%, calculated on a two-party basis. This is actually below the average swing for the nation, where one might have expected it to be higher. And when these constituencies are placed in the regional context, individual swings vary very little from the regional average. This suggests that the electoral impact of the personality factor was not marked.

Finally, the meticulous work of David Butler has demonstrated that the Conservatives and Labour fared more or less evenly at the hands of the electoral system.[19] While geographical chance (that is, boundaries working as if 'gerrymandered' slightly in one side's favour) marginally benefited Labour, the unequal populations in constituencies slightly favoured the Conservatives; that overall, and especially in relation to the 1945 election, the electoral system put neither side at a serious disadvantage in the 1935 general election. The causes of the substantial majority of the National Government must be sought among the factors discussed in this chapter.

Notes

1. See pp. 235-8.
2. *The Times*, 14 Nov. 1935.
3. See H. Macmillan, *Winds of Change 1914-1939* (1966), pp. 425-35.

4. Extensive slum clearance in North and West Salford, and the erection of the new housing estates outside the Salford boundaries, undoubtedly assisted the National Government. South Salford contained many poor districts, and contained a strong Irish Catholic vote; but the Docks area was dominated by a middle-class residential group, which probably voted solidly for the National Government. See *Manchester Guardian*, 16 Oct., 5 Nov. 1935.

5. *Birmingham Gazette*, 14 Nov. 1935.

6. *The Times*, 16 Nov. 1935. A representative Conservative analysis of the election is that of Lord Stonehaven, printed in *Politics in Review*, Oct.-Dec. 1935, pp. 3-9. Stonehaven attributed the government's victory to its 'remarkable' record, its programme of 'industrial and social development', its 'sane and balanced policy . . . on the problems of peace and defence', 'the character and personality of the Prime Minister, Mr. Baldwin', and the 'grotesque' policies and campaign of the Labour Party. The Baldwin Papers contain letters from Conservative candidates which collectively echo Stonehaven's analysis. For the views of two Conservative mavericks see L. Amery, *My Political Life* (1955), vol. 3. pp. 180-1 and Macmillan, *Winds of Change*, pp. 425-35. Labour analyses of the election were less uniform, reflecting the divisions over policy and personnel which had characterised the party since 1931. Cripps and Greenwood might agree that 'we have not yet in our ranks all the industrial workers', but the latter did not agree with the former that this was because the industrial worker wanted Labour to be more clearly Socialist than it was: indeed Greenwood would have agreed with George Dallas that 'the silly propaganda of the Socialist League told against us', and with Morrison that the country was 'not going to vote in a hurry for a first class financial crisis'. Morrison indeed thought that Labour was not winning enough votes from the middle classes, probably because the party's appeal was already 'too narrow and abstract'. Even G.D.H. Cole realised that it had been 'a mistake to place and pressure for too much socialism in party policy'. All the Labour spokesmen referred to the party's leadership problems – from Cripp's 'there is no inspiration in the leadership of the Labour Party today', to Morrison's 'It is the fault of nobody in particular, but since 1931 we have not yet evolved a clear leadership . . . and the British electorate likes to know the kind of people who are going to govern it', and to Cole's the party 'lacks an effective leader more than anything else'. In a sober analysis of the election which bore some resemblance to Stonehaven's, stripped of its rhetoric, Harold Laski also drew attention to the fact that on Labour's side there was no one of equal stature to Baldwin. For the views of Cripps and Dallas see newspaper articles reprinted in *Politics in Review*, Oct.-Dec. 1935; for Morrison's analysis see *Forward*, 23 Nov. 1935; for Greenwood's see *Daily Herald*, 28 Nov. 1935; for Laski's see *Political Quarterly*, Jan.-Mar. 1936, pp. 1-11; for Cole's see *New Statesman and Nation*, 23 Nov. 1935. Writing in the *Contemporary Review*, Jan. 1936, Geoffrey Mander, one of the few successful Liberal candidates, noted that 'Apart from the failure of the distressed areas, trade *was* better, employment *had* improved . . . the sincerity and broadmindedness of the new leaders was liked and trusted by the British people.'

7. These figures differ slightly from those given by F.W.S. Craig in his *British Parliamentary Election Statistics 1918-1968* (1968), pp. 10-11. R.H. Bernays and J.P. Maclay have been included as Liberal Nationals, as being such in all but title. The two MPs listed by Craig as 'Nat.' I have included with the Conservatives. Craig's 'Others' I have retitled 'National' and placed in the National Government total. (Three of the four represented University seats and rarely voted with the opposition; the fourth, A. Hopkinson, although a law unto himself in Mossley, was a close friend of Baldwin – indeed, enjoyed his support at the election – and mostly voted with the National Government.)

8. The Northern Irish (12) and University (12) seats are excluded; also excluded are the constituencies (75) where there was an unopposed candidate at

either or both the 1931 and 1935 elections, together with the 50 or so constituencies where the nature of the contest was such as to preclude meaningful comparison, and two member seats are treated as single units.

9. There are 22 comparable constituencies: Shoreditch, Southwark North, Barnsley, Gateshead, Great Yarmouth, Huddersfield, Newcastle East, Devonport, Luton, South Molton, Consett, Harwich, Holland-with-Boston, Huntingdonshire, Bosworth, Norfolk East, Spen Valley, Swansea West, Dunfermline District of Boroughs, Leith, Montrose District of Burghs, Dumfriesshire.

10. Finsbury, Leeds Central, Tottenham South, Seaham (GPGB 1.3%, 1931), Forest of Dean, Ormskirk, Bassetlaw, Lichfield.

11. Dulwich, Bath, Halifax, Blackley, Rusholme, Nottingham East, Rochdale, Rossendale, Tynemouth, Willesden East, Wolverhampton East, Worcester, Mid-Bedfordshire, Aylesbury, Chester, Penryn and Falmouth, Tavistock, Epping, Thornbury, Basingstoke, Hemel Hempstead, Darwen, Royton, Gainsborough, Yeovil, Chippenham, Westbury, Stourbridge, Holderness, Cardiff East, Carmarthen, Merioneth.

12. East Toxteth, Cumberland North, Barnstaple, Dorset West, Leominster, Chertsey, Devizes, Caernarvon Boroughs, Kincardine and Western, Forfarshire, Kinross and Western.

13. In the third constituency, Leominster, the Conservative vote in 1935 was only marginally greater than in 1929; but it should be noted that in neighbouring Hereford the Conservatives actually improved on their fine performance in 1931.

14. Without the promise of financial backing from the Lloyd George Fund, very few of these candidates could have been persuaded to stand.

15. In 1931 the average vote per contested constituency was 12,768. This high figure covers only a small number of constituencies (118), and is distorted by the fact in nearly one-third of the constituencies the Liberal candidate received votes from electors who in 1929 had supported the Conservative Party, but who now voted for the Liberal as the sole standard bearer of the National Government.

16. The 32 constituencies as listed in Note 11, to which have been added Colne Valley and Camborne which, although not strictly three-way contests, are sufficiently close to being so as to produce little distortion to the calculation.

17. Bethnal Green North-East, Bethnal Green South-West, Lambeth North, Whitechapel and St George's, Bradford South, Cardiganshire, Wrexham. For Bethnal Green South-West, I have combined the Labour and Communist percentage votes for 1931.

18. Kennington, Bow and Bromley, Woolwich East, Ladywood, Birmingham West, Bradford Central, Bristol Central, Edmonton, Leeds South-East, Liverpool Exchange, Fairfield, West Toxteth, Ardwick, Platting, St Helens, Salford South, Sheffield Central, Hallam, Silvertown, Wigan, Jarrow, Spennymoor, Widnes, Newton, Ince, Tamworth, Don Valley, Hemsworth, Normanton, Rother Valley, Aberdeen South, Glasgow Central, Hillhead, Pollok, Kirkaldy District of Burghs, Aberdeenshire Eastern, Bute and Northern, Ayrshire South, Hamilton, Stirlingshire Western.

19. R.B. McCallum and A. Readman, *The British General Election of 1945* (1947), Appendix 3, esp. pp. 284-9.

10 CONCLUSION

The British general election of 1935 was won easily by the National Government. This conclusion canvasses the reasons for the result, briefly compares it with the 1945 general election and, as briefly, discusses the meaning of the result for the last of the years of the peace.

In the inter-election period the National Government had not only kept the country free of financial crises but had also presided over a general increase in the country's prosperity. The most important of the economic factors was the overall decrease in unemployment. In the autumn of 1935 the number of the unemployed fell to below two million for the first time since 1931; and despite a slight upturn again in October 1935, the general expectation was that unemployment would continue to decrease. It was this expectation which explains why many electors in areas of heavy unemployment voted for the National Government rather than for the Labour Party.

In the course of the campaign the government bolstered these expectations by announcing that money was being made available for road construction, and that naval contracts were going to shipyards with heavy unemployment regardless of the size of the tenders. Even the dispirited people of Jarrow were not totally immune from good news, for during the campaign it was announced that Palmer's shipyard would reopen in order to break up the liner *Olympic*. (The surprising feature of the Jarrow election result is not that Ellen Wilkinson won the seat for Labour but that she won it so narrowly from the Conservatives.) The government of course made much of the improvement in unemployment, perhaps most strikingly through the use of an updated version of the famous poster of 1931 which had portrayed an unemployed working man in wretched attire pleading for a job. The revamped version showed the same man well groomed and at work, with the caption: 'They kept their word and gave me a job; help them keep it for me.'

Other economic factors apart from the decrease in unemployment also assisted the government. In 1934 and 1935, particularly in the latter year, there were massive and widespread increases in wages in nearly all industries, coal being the outstanding exception;[1] and early in 1935 the government had restored the last of the salary cuts from 1931. The 1935 budget had seen a measure of tax relief for wage earners. From 1933 the cost of living had gone down, and even a slight increase in October 1935 seems to have produced few shopping-basket anxieties. Finally, in being able to claim that it had built one million homes since 1931, the National Government had a telling, ready-made election slogan.

Of course not all areas and occupational groups enjoyed the benefits equally. It is clear that iron and steel was doing better than wool, that wool was doing better than cotton, that cotton was doing better than coal and that engineering and chemicals were doing better than all of them; and this was reflected in the voting at the 1935 general election. In the inter-election period agriculture had not been free of difficulties; but Labour was never able to break into what was essentially a family squabble between producers and the government — in agriculture there was no electoral mileage for Labour. Labour did assert that very few of the government's one million houses were for letting at low rentals, perhaps with greatest electoral effect in London. But overall, the economic factors overwhelmingly favoured the National Government.

Political factors also favoured the National Goverhment. Riven for much of the inter-election period by the debate over the nature of Conservatism, the Conservative Party presented a united front to the electorate from mid-1935, just at the time when the cracks in the facade of Labour unity became too great to be successfully papered over for electoral purposes. As the Conservative Party swung in behind the new Prime Minister in the summer of 1935, and then the last of the agreements between the Conservatives and their allies were sealed, Labour experienced quakes of seismic proportions with the resignations of Cripps, Ponsonby and Lansbury, and the death of Arthur Henderson; and at the party's annual conference its lack of unity was displayed for all electors to see. In an act of *hari-kiri*, the party elected as its leader a politician unknown to the electorate at large, and then advertised its belief that Attlee was only a stopgap leader. The general election, so impeccably timed by Baldwin, had come too soon for the Labour Party. Unable to resolve its leadership and identity problems before the election, the party used the election as a means of resolving its problems for it; but that the party lacked the will to win the election seems indisputable. And of course, as has been argued in Chapter 7, changes in the nature and influence of the mass media hampered Labour electorally.

If the Labour Party lacked the will to win the election, the Liberals lacked the will to survive. After 1933 Samuel halfheartedly tried to occupy the middle seat in the electoral spectrum, but unfortunately for him he found Stanley Baldwin lounging comfortably in it; and Baldwin was not to be dislodged. His party was driven back to the most isolated parts of Great Britain where the news of the emergence of class politics had not yet filtered through.

For much of the inter-election period Labour's trump electoral card was perceived to be the 'peace and war' or 'rearmament-disarmament' issue. However relatively important this issue was in the inter-election period, it seems that a plea for even limited rearmament was electorally inexpedient. But from March 1935 this was no longer the case. When in mid-1934 the government had announced increases in the size of the Air Force, it received widespread criticism; but its White Paper on Defence, released in March 1935, met with very little hostility outside the House of Commons (though inside, the Labour Party enthusiastically and the Liberals halfheartedly continued to inveigh against increased defence expenditure). As Arthur Woodburn, secretary of the Scottish Labour Party, put it after his party's disastrous showing at by-elections in May 1935, 'the positive passion for Peace which gave us such a powerful plea in earlier elections was not so effective under the shadow of Hitler's threats'. In May the celebrations of the King's Jubilee called to mind the great military and naval achievements of the nation, as well as its present political stability in comparison with developments in Europe; and the Naval Review at Spithead was the best attended for many years. Military fashions appeared again in the autumn of 1935. In May the Liberal Party abandoned its opposition to limited defence increases, thereby dissociating itself from the Labour Party, which clung to its disarmament policy right up to the election. On the eve of the election, the churches proclaimed their support for the National Government, primarily because of its advocacy of limited rearmament. This intervention was probably not without electoral consequences.[2] But apart from questions of security and conscience, defence was a bread-and-butter issue, and in the dockyard towns and towns with armaments factories, with each announcement of further rearmament the government's popularity increased.

A brief comparison of the 1935 and 1945 general elections serves to highlight some of the advantages enjoyed by the National Government in 1935. In 1935 the Labour Party had no clear programme of reform and a divided leadership; in 1945 it had both a plan and a united team of leaders. A related point is that in 1935 Labour's leaders lacked ministerial experience, whereas by 1945 they had had five years of experience, and some of them had been among the outstanding successes of

Coalition Government. In 1935 Stafford Cripps was an *enfant terrible*, used to telling electoral effect by the National Government. In 1945, if not the party's greatest electoral asset, Cripps at least was not a liablity. In 1935 Soviet Russia was generally regarded with suspicion and distaste, and Labour was unable to effectively reply that it was not in alliance with Russia; but in 1945 Soviet Russia was a popular ally of the British and Labour stood to gain from being identified with her. In 1935 Labour was all at sea with the new means of communication with the electors; but in 1945 its leaders handled the media as skilfully as did the Conservative spokesmen; and the weight of press support was more evenly balanced than in 1935. In 1935 Labour faced an opponent which had not clearly failed in any area of activity; but in 1945 it faced a party which had to bear the responsibility for failing to keep the peace and for failing to provide work for over one million men. If in 1945 Attlee had the air of a sound and steady batsman, keeping up his wicket with ease against a demon bowler who was losing both pace and length,[3] in 1935 Baldwin had the air of a sound and steady batsman, keeping up his wicket with ease on a plum batting strip against change bowlers who lacked both pace and length.

The result of the 1935 general election was not without important consequences. Returned with so comfortable a majority the National Government was able to persist with policies which led Britain ultimately into a slide towards war and left one million men unemployed on the eve of war. Had the election produced a more even balance in the House of Commons it is likely that the National Government could have been forced to alter course on a range of policies, much as it came close to doing in the winter of 1934-5, when it feared a severe electoral reverse.

Perhaps most importantly the result of the 1935 general election disguised the growth of class politics. The 1929 general election had shown the unacceptability of the Conservative Party in areas where working-class Toryism had long been a fact of political life. The elections of 1931 and 1935 cut through this development by making it possible for electors to vote for a National Government rather than a Conservative one. In 1945 consciences could not be appeased in this way, and faced with a clear choice between the Conservatives and Labour, the people affected voted Labour, and in such numbers that the backlog in the development of class politics in the 1930s was fully taken up. When the National Government is viewed as a temporary bulwark against the electoral manifestation of the development of class politics, the landslide of 1945 becomes more explicable.

Notes

1. See the useful article by E.C. Ramsbottom, 'The Course of Wage Rates in the United Kingdom 1921-1934', *Journal of the Royal Statistical Society*, vol. 98 (1935), especially Appendix A and Appendix B, pp. 665-70.
2. See *Tablet*, 26 Oct. 1935; *Church Times*, 25 Oct., 8 Nov. 1935; *Methodist Recorder*, 14 Nov. 1935.
3. R.B. McCallum and A. Readman, *The British General Election of 1945* (1947), p. 175.

APPENDIX 1: THE NATIONAL AND REGIONAL RESULTS

1.1 The National Results, 1929-45[1]

	1929	1931	1935	1945
Electorate and Turnout	76.0% 28,854,748	76.3% 29,952,361	71.0% 31,374,449	72.7% 33,240,391
Votes cast	100% 22,648,375	100% 21,656,373	100% 21,997,054	100% 25,095,195
Conservative	38.1% 8,656,225	55.3%[2] 11,978,745	48.1%[2] 10,549,489	36.8%[2] 9,234,278
Liberal National		3.7% 809,302	3.9%[3] 909,797	2.8% 737,732
National Labour		1.5% 341,370	1.5% 339,811	
Liberal	23.6% 5,308,738	7.2%[4] 1,506,630	6.6%[5] 1,399,650	9.0% 2,252,430
Labour	37.1% 8,370,417	29.3% 6,324,737	38.1% 8,325,491	48.0% 11,967,746
Non-endorsed Labour 1931 ILP 1935-45		1.5%[6] 324,893	0.6% 139,577	0.2% 46,769
Others[7]	1.2% 312,995	1.5% 370,696	1.2% 333,239	3.2% 856,240

Notes:
   1. In compiling this table and the one following, I have made use of F.W.S. Craig's invaluable reference book, *British Parliamentary Election Statistics 1918-1968* (1968).
   2. Includes candidates designated by Craig as 'Nat.'
   3. Includes R.H. Bernays (North Bristol) and J.P. Maclay (Paisley), designated by Craig as Liberals. At the 1935 election both men stood as independent supporters of the National Government.
   4. Includes independent Liberal candidates (0.5% of total vote).
   5. Excludes Bernays and Maclay.
   6. Of the 25 non-endorsed Labour candidates, 24 were members of the ILP.
   7. Includes candidates of the Communist Party of Great Britain, the Irish Nationalist Party, Plaid Cymru and the Scottish National Party (1929, 1931, 1935, 1945); the New Party (1931); the Irish Republican Party (1935); the Commonwealth Movement Party (1945); and assorted independents (all elections).

1.2 The House of Commons, 1929-45

	1929	1931	1935	1945
Conservative	260	473^2	388^5	199
Liberal National		35	35^6	11
National Labour		13	8	
Liberal	59	37^3	19^7	12
Labour	287	46	154	393
Non-endorsed Labour (ILP)		6	4	3
Others	9^1	5^4	7^8	22^9

Notes:

1. Includes 3 Irish Nationalist Party members. The remaining 6 are as listed in Craig.
2. Includes 4 MPs designated by Craig as 'Nat.'
3. Includes the Lloyd George family group of 4.
4. Includes 2 Irish Nationalist members.
5. Includes 2 members designated by Craig as 'Nat.'
6. Includes Bernays and Maclay.
7. Excludes Bernays and Maclay.
8. Includes Willie Gallacher, sole parliamentary representative of the Communist Party of Great Britain; also 2 Irish Nationalist MPs.
9. Includes Gallacher and P. Piratin of the Communist Party of Great Britain, and 2 Irish Nationalists; the rest are as listed in Craig.

1.3 Regional Results: Definition of Areas and Sub-areas

A. London (61 constituencies; 62 seats)

1. *South of the Thames*

   Battersea North, Battersea South, Bermondsey Rotherhithe, Bermondsey West, Camberwell Dulwich, Camberwell North, Camberwell North-West, Camberwell Peckham, Deptford, Greenwich, Lambeth Brixton, Lambeth Kennington, Lambeth North, Lambeth Norwood, Lewisham East, Lewisham West, Southwark Central, Southwark North, Southwark South-East, Wandsworth Balham and Tooting, Wandsworth Central, Wandsworth Clapham, Wandsworth Putney, Wandsworth Streatham, Woolwich East, Woolwich West

2. *East End*
   Bethnal Green North-East, Bethnal Green South-West, Finsbury,
   Hackney Central, Hackney North, Hackney South, Poplar Bow and
   Bromley, Poplar South, Shoreditch, Stepney Limehouse, Stepney
   Mile End, Stepney Whitechapel, Stoke Newington

3. *Business and class residential*
   Chelsea, City of London (2), Hampstead, Holborn, Kensington
   North, Kensington South, Paddington North, Paddington South,
   St Marylebone, Westminster Abbey, Westminster St Georges

4. *Remainder*
   Fulham East, Fulham West, Hammersmith North, Hammersmith
   South, Islington East, Islington North, Islington South, Islington
   West, St Pancras North, St Pancras South-East, St Pancras South-
   West

B. **Outer London** (41)

   1. Middlesex county seats:
      Acton, Brentford and Chiswick, Enfield, Finchley, Harrow,
      Hendon, Spelthorne, Twickenham, Uxbridge, Wood Green
      and boroughs:
      Ealing, East Ham North, East Ham South, Edmonton,
      Hornsey, Leyton East, Leyton West, Tottenham North,
      Tottenham South, Walthamstow East, Walthamstow West,
      West Ham Plaistow, West Ham Silvertown, West Ham Stratford,
      West Ham Upton, Willesden East, Willesden West
      and Essex:
      Romford
   2. Kent county seats:
      Chislehurst, Dartford, Gravesend
      Surrey county seats:
      Epsom, Mitcham
      and boroughs:
      Bromley, Croydon North, Croydon South, Kingston-upon-
      Thames, Richmond, Rochester Chatham, Rochester Gilling-
      ham, Wimbledon

C. **South-east England** (22 constituencies; 23 seats)

   1. Kent county seats:
      Ashford, Canterbury, Dover, Faversham, Isle of Thanet,
      Maidstone, Sevenoaks, Tonbridge

2. Surrey county seats:
   Chertsey, Eastern, Farnham, Guildford, Reigate
3. Sussex county seats:
   Eastbourne, East Grinstead, Lewes, Rye, Chichester, Horsham
   and Worthing
   and boroughs:
   Brighton (2), Hastings, Hythe

D. South-central England (15)

1. Oxford county seats:
   Banbury, Henley
2. Berkshire county seats:
   Abingdon, Newbury, Windsor
   and boroughs:
   Oxford, Reading
3. Buckinghamshire county seats:
   Aylesbury, Buckingham, Wycombe
4. Hertfordshire county seats:
   Hemel Hempstead, Hertford, Hitchin, St Albans, Watford

E. The Severn (24)

1. Somerset county seats:
   Bridgwater, Frome, Taunton, Weston-super-Mare, Wells, Yeovil
   Devon county seats:
   Honiton, Tiverton
   and borough:
   Exeter
2. Gloucestershire county seats:
   Cirencester and Tewkesbury, Forest of Dean, Stroud, Thorn-
   bury
   and boroughs:
   Bristol Central, Bristol East, Bristol North, Bristol South,
   Bristol West, Cheltenham, Bath, Gloucester
   Wiltshire:
   Chippenham, Westbury, Swindon

F. Wessex (18 constituencies; 19 seats)

1. Hampshire Ports (boroughs):
   Portsmouth Central, Portsmouth North, Portsmouth South,
   Southampton (2)

2. Rural Wessex:
   Hampshire county seats:
   Aldershot, Basingstoke, Fareham, New Forest and Christ-church, Petersfield, Winchester, Isle of Wight
   Dorsetshire county seats:
   Dorset Eastern, Dorset Northern, Dorset Southern, Dorset Western
   Wiltshire county seats:
   Devizes, Salisbury
   and borough:
   Bournemouth

G. Western Peninsula (13)

1. Cornwall county seats:
   Bodmin, Camborne, Cornwall Northern, Penryn and Falmouth, St Ives
   Devonshire county seats:
   Barnstaple, South Molton, Tavistock, Torquay, Totnes
2. Boroughs:
   Plymouth Devonport, Plymouth Drake, Plymouth Sutton

H. East Anglia (29 constituencies; 30 seats)

1. Norfolk county seats:
   Norfolk Eastern, Norfolk King's Lynn, Norfolk Northern, Norfolk Southern, Norfolk South-Western
   and boroughs:
   Norwich (2), Great Yarmouth
   Suffolk (East and West) county seats:
   Eye, Lowestoft, Woodbridge, Bury St Edmunds, Sudbury
   and borough:
   Ipswich
2. Bedfordshire county seats:
   Bedford, Luton, Mid-Bedfordshire, Cambridgeshire, Huntingdonshire, Isle of Ely
   and borough:
   Cambridge
3. Essex county seats:
   Chelmsford, Colchester, Epping, Harwich, Maldon, Saffron Walden, South-Eastern
   and boroughs:
   Ilford, Southend-on-Sea

I. **Lincolnshire and Rutlandshire** (9)

    Holland with Boston, Grantham, Rutland and Stamford, Brigg,
Gainsborough, Horncastle, Louth
and boroughs:
Grimsby, Lincoln

J. **Eastern Midlands** (30 constituencies; 31 seats)

  1. Derbyshire county seats:
Belper, Chesterfield, Clay Cross, High Peak, Ilkeston, North-
Eastern, Southern, Western
Nottinghamshire county seats:
Bassetlaw, Broxtowe, Mansfield, Newark, Rushcliffe
  2. Leicestershire county seats:
Bosworth, Harborough, Loughborough, Melton
Northamptonshire county seats:
Daventry, Kettering, Peterborough, Wellingborough
  3. Major cities (boroughs):
Derby (2), Leicester East, Leicester South, Leicester West,
Northampton, Nottingham Central, Nottingham East,
Nottingham South, Nottingham West

K. **North-west Midlands** (11)

  1. Cheshire county seats:
Altrincham, Chester, Crewe, Eddisbury, Knutsford, Maccles-
field, Northwich
  2. The Potteries (boroughs):
Newcastle-under-Lyme, Stoke-on-Trent Burslem, Stoke-on-
Trent Hanley, Stoke-on-Trent Stoke

L. **Salop: Shropshire and Staffordshire** (10)

    Shropshire county seats:
Ludlow, Oswestry, Shrewsbury, The Wrekin
Staffordshire county seats:
Burton, Cannock, Leek, Lichfield, Stafford, Stone

M. **South-west Midlands** (33)

  1. Birmingham City (boroughs):
Aston, Deritend, Duddeston, Edgbaston, Erdington, Hands-
worth, King's Norton, Ladywood, Moseley, Sparkbrook, West
Birmingham, Yardley

2. The Black Country:
Staffordshire county seat — Kingswinford
Worcestershire county seat — Stourbridge
Warwickshire county seats — Nuneaton, Tamworth
and boroughs:
Coventry, Dudley, Walsall, Wednesbury, West Bromwich,
Wolverhampton Bilston, Wolverhampton East, Wolverhampton
West
3. Herefordshire county seats:
Hereford, Leominster
Warwickshire county seats:
Rugby, Warwick and Leamington
Worcestershire county seats:
Bewdley, Evesham, Kidderminster
and borough:
Worcester

N. Western Lancastria (30 constituencies; 31 seats)

1. Merseyside:
Cheshire county seat — Wirral
and boroughs:
Birkenhead East, Birkenhead West, Bootle, Liverpool East
Toxteth, Liverpool Edge Hill, Liverpool Everton, Liverpool
Exchange, Liverpool Fairfield, Liverpool Kirkdale, Liverpool
Scotland, Liverpool Walton, Liverpool Wavertree, Liverpool
West Derby, Liverpool West Toxteth, Wallasey
Lancashire county seat — Widnes
2. West Lancashire:
Lancashire county seats:
Chorley, Fylde, Lancaster, Lonsdale, Newotn, Ormskirk,
Waterloo
and boroughs:
Blackpool, Preston (2), St Helens, Southport, Warrington

O. Eastern Lancastria (37 constituencies; 41 seats)

1. Mid-East Lancashire:
Lancashire county seats:
Farnworth, Heywood and Radcliffe, Ince, Middleton and
Prestwick, Westhoughton
and boroughs:
Bolton (2), Bury, Leigh, Rochdale, Wigan

2. Manchester conurbation:
   Cheshire county seat — Stalybridge and Hyde
   Lancashire county seats — Mossley, Stretford
   and boroughs:
   Ashton-under-Lyne, Eccles, Manchester Ardwick, Manchester
   Blackley, Manchester Clayton, Manchester Exchange, Man-
   chester Gorton, Manchester Hulme, Manchester Moss Side,
   Manchester Platting, Manchester Rusholme, Manchester With-
   ington, Oldham (2), Salford North, Salford South, Salford
   West, Stockport (2)
3. North-east Lancashire:
   Lancashire county seats — Clitheroe, Darwen, Royton
   and boroughs:
   Accrington, Blackburn (2), Rossendale, Burnley

P. *West Riding Yorkshire* (42)

1. West Riding conurbation:
   Yorks W.R. county seats:
   Colne Valley, Elland, Keighley, Pudsey and Otley, Shipley,
   Sowerby, Spen Valley
   and boroughs:
   Batley and Morley, Bradford Central, Bradford East, Bradford
   North, Bradford South, Dewsbury, Halifax, Huddersfield,
   Leeds Central, Leeds North, Leeds North-East, Leeds South,
   Leeds South-East, Leeds West, Nelson and Colne, Wakefield
2. Sheffield complex:
   Yorks W.R. county seat — Penistone
   and boroughs:
   Rotherham, Sheffield Attercliffe, Sheffield Brightside,
   Sheffield Central, Sheffield Ecclesall, Sheffield Hallam, Shef-
   field Hillsborough, Sheffield Park
3. Remainder Yorks W.R. (excluding Barkston Ash and Ripon)
   county seats:
   Doncaster, Don Valley, Hemsworth, Normanton, Pontefract,
   Rother Valley, Rothwell, Skipton, Wentworth
   and borough:
   Barnsley

Q. **Remainder of Yorkshire (and Barkston Ash and Ripon) (13)**

East Riding county seats:
   Holderness, Howdenshire

North Riding:
>Richmond, Scarborough and Whitby, Thirsk and Malton

West Riding:
>Barkston Ash, Ripon

and boroughs:
>Kingston-upon-Hull Central, Kingston-upon-Hull East,
>Kingston-upon-Hull North-West, Kingston-upon-Hull South-West

York

R. **Cumbria** (6)

Cumberland county seats:
>Northern, Penrith and Cockermouth, Whitehaven, Workington

Westmorland county seat:
>Westmorland

and borough:
>Carlisle

S. **North-east England** (30 constituencies; 31 seats)

1. Tyneside:

Durham county seats:
>Blaydon, Chester-le-Street, Houghton-le-Spring, Jarrow

and boroughs:
>Gateshead, Newcastle-upon-Tyne Central, Newscastle-upon-Tyne East, Newcastle-upon-Tyne North, Newcastle-upon-Tyne West, South Shields, Sunderland (2), Tynemouth, Wallsend

2. Teeside:

Durham county seats:
>Seaham, Sedgefield

Yorks N.R. county seat — Cleveland

and boroughs:
>Darlington, Hartlepools, Middlesbrough East, Middlesbrough West, Stockton-on-Tees

3. Remainder of Durham and Northumberland:

Durham county seats:
>Barnard Castle, Bishop Auckland, Consett, Durham Spennymoor

Northumberland county seats:
>Berwick-upon-Tweed, Hexham, Wansbeck

and borough:
>Morpeth

T. Wales

1. Industrial and Commercial Wales (23):

Glamorgan county seats:
Aberavon, Caerphilly, Gower, Llandaff and Barry, Neath, Ogmore, Pontypridd
Monmouth county seats:
Abertillery, Bedwellty, Ebbw Vale, Monmouth, Pontypool
Carmarthenshire county seat:
Llanelly
and boroughs:
Cardiff Central, Cardiff East, Cardiff South, Merthyr Tydfil Aberdare, Merthyr Tydfil Merthyr, Newport, Rhondda East, Rhondda West, Swansea East, Swansea West
2. Rural Wales (12):
Caernarvon District of Boroughs
Anglesey (county seat), Breconshire and Radnorshire, Caernarvonshire, Cardiganshire, Carmarthenshire Carmarthen, Denbighshire Denbigh, Denbighshire Wrexham, Flintshire, Merionethshire, Montgomeryshire, Pembrokeshire

U. Scotland (70 constituencies; 71 seats)

1. Highlands:
Argyll, Invernessshire Inverness, Invernessshire Ross and Cromarty, Invernessshire Western Isles, Caithness and Sutherland, Orkney and Shetland, Perthshire Kinross and Western, Perthshire Perth
2. North-east Scotland:
   a. Aberdeenshire Central, Aberdeenshire Eastern, Aberdeenshire Kincardine and Western, Banffshire, Forfarshire, Moray and Nairnshire
   b. Aberdeen North, Aberdeen South, Montrose District of Burghs, Dundee (2)
3. Forth Valley:
   a. Edinburgh Central, Edinburgh East, Edinburgh North, Edinburgh South, Edinburgh West, Leith
   b. Stirling and Clackmannanshire, Clackmannan and Eastern, Stirling and Clackmannanshire Western, Dunfermline District of Burghs, Linlithgowshire, Midlothian and Peeblesshire, Northern, Fife Eastern (county), Fife Western (county), Kirkaldy District of Burghs, Stirling and Falkirk District of Burghs

4. Clyde Valley:
   a. Glasgow Bridgeton, Glasgow Camlachie, Glasgow Cathcart, Glasgow Central, Glasgow Gorbals, Glasgow Govan, Glasgow Hillhead, Glasgow Kelvingrove, Glasgow Maryhill, Glasgow Partick, Glasgow Pollok, Glasgow St Rollox, Glasgow Shettleston, Glasgow Springburn, Glasgow Tradeston
   b. Dunbartonshire, Renfrewshire Eastern, Renfrewshire Western, Greenock (borough), Paisley (borough), Ayrshire and Bute, Kilmarnock, Dumbarton District of Burghs
   c. Lanarkshire Bothwell, Lanarkshire Coatbridge, Lanarkshire Hamilton, Lanarkshire Motherwell, Lanarkshire Northern, Lanarkshire Rutherglen
5. Southern Scotland:
   Ayreshire and Bute, Bute and Northern, Ayrshire and Bute South Ayreshire, Ayr District of Boroughs, Lanarkshire, Lanark, Galloway (county), Dumfriesshire, Roxburghshire and Selkirkshire, Midlothian and Peeblesshire, Peebles and Southern Berwickshire and Haddingtonshire

1.4a Turnout, 1935

		% Voting 1935	Change in % Voting 1931-35
GREAT BRITAIN	(514)*	71.6	– 4.7
England	431	71.2	– 5.0
Wales	22	76.2	– 3.4
Scotland	61	73.2	– 3.8
AREAS OF ENGLAND			
London Area	(97)	63.3	– 4.5
London	57	61.5	– 3.9
Outer London	40	65.9	– 5.4
South and East	(104)	70.5	-- 5.0
South-East	17	66.2	– 4.8
South-Central	10	66.7	– 6.7
Severn	22	74.8	– 5.7
Wessex	17	68.7	– 5.6
Western Peninsula	11	75.8	– 4.9
East Anglia	27	70.0	– 3.6
Midlands	(83)	72.1	– 6.3
Lincolnshire	9	73.8	– 4.7
East Midlands	28	73.9	– 5.5
North-West Midlands	7	76.0	– 4.8
Shropshire & Staffs	9	71.4	– 6.1
South-West Midlands	30	69.2	– 8.1
North of England	(147)	76.4	– 4.4
Western Lancastria	28	73.0	– 5.2
Eastern Lancastria	36	78.0	– 4.1
West Riding	41	74.6	– 5.2
Rest of Yorkshire	9	73.9	– 6.1
Cumbria	4	84.5	– 2.4
North-east England	29	79.8	– 2.7

*Number of comparable constituencies, excluding Northern Ireland and the University seats.

1.4b Turnout and Members Elected, 1935

	Turnout 1935		Members elected 1935 (all seats: 603)								
	% Voting 1935	Change in % voting 1931-35	Con.	Lib.	Nat. Nat.	Nat. Lab.	Govt	Lab.	Lib.	Other	Total

SUB-AREAS OF ENGLAND

London

	% Voting 1935	Change in % voting 1931-35	Con.	Lib.	Nat. Nat.	Nat. Lab.	Govt	Lab.	Lib.	Other	Total
1.	26	63.3	– 3.5	16	1			17	9			26
2.	13	59.3	– 2.7	2				2	10	1		13
3.	7	57.7	– 6.8	12				12				12
4.	11	62.1	– 4.4	8				8	3			11
Total	57	61.5	– 3.9	38	1			39	22	1		62

Outer London

	% Voting 1935	Change in % voting 1931-35	Con.	Lib.	Nat. Nat.	Nat. Lab.	Govt	Lab.	Lib.	Other	Total
1.	27	64.9	– 6.1	16				16	12			28
2.	13	68.0	– 3.8	13				13				13
Total	40	65.9	– 5.4	29				29	12			41

South-East England

	% Voting 1935	Change in % voting 1931-35	Con.	Lib.	Nat. Nat.	Nat. Lab.	Govt	Lab.	Lib.	Other	Total
1.	6	69.6	– 1.9	8				8				8
2.	11	64.4	– 6.3	15				15				15
Total	17	66.2	– 4.8	23				23				23

South-Central England

	% Voting 1935	Change in % voting 1931-35	Con.	Lib.	Nat. Nat.	Nat. Lab.	Govt	Lab.	Lib.	Other	Total
1.	10	66.7	– 6.7	15				15				15

Severn

	% Voting 1935	Change in % voting 1931-35	Con.	Lib.	Nat. Nat.	Nat. Lab.	Govt	Lab.	Lib.	Other	Total
1.	8	93.9	– 6.5	9				9				9
2.	14	75.4	– 5.3	11	1			12	3			15
Total	22	74.8	– 5.7	20	1			21	3			24

Wessex

	% Voting 1935	Change in % voting 1931-35	Con.	Lib.	Nat. Nat.	Nat. Lab.	Govt	Lab.	Lib.	Other	Total
1.	4	67.7	– 7.5	4	1			5				5
2.	13	69.0	– 5.0	14				14				14
Total	17	68.7	– 5.6	18	1			19				19

Western Peninsula

	% Voting 1935	Change in % voting 1931-35	Con.	Lib.	Nat. Nat.	Nat. Lab.	Govt	Lab.	Lib.	Other	Total
1.	8	76.2	– 5.1	6	2			8		2		10
2.	3	74.9	– 4.4	2	1			3				3
Total	11	75.8	– 4.9	8	3			11		2		13

East Anglia

	% Voting 1935	Change in % voting 1931-35	Con.	Lib.	Nat. Nat.	Nat. Lab.	Govt	Lab.	Lib.	Other	Total
1.	11	72.8	– 2.9	10	4			14				14
2.	7	69.4	– 2.9	4	2			6		1		7
3.	9	67.1	– 5.1	8	1			9				9
Total	27	70.0	– 3.6	22	7			29		1		30

Lincolnshire

	% Voting 1935	Change in % voting 1931-35	Con.	Lib.	Nat. Nat.	Nat. Lab.	Govt	Lab.	Lib.	Other	Total
1.	9	73.8	– 4.7	7	1			8	1			9

	Turnout 1935		Members elected 1935 (all seats: 603)							
	% Voting 1935	Change in % voting 1931-35	Con.	Lib. Nat.	Nat. Lab.	Nat. Govt	Lab.	Lib.	Other	Total
East Midlands										
1.	12	74.7	−4.0	6			6	7			13
2.	7	75.8	−5.4	7	1		8				8
3.	9	71.3	−7.6	6		3	9	1			10
Total	28	73.9	−5.5	19	1	3	23	8			31
North-West Midlands										
1.	4	78.8	−5.1	6	1		7				7
2.	3	72.3	−4.7					4			4
Total	7	76.0	−4.8	6	1			4			11
Shropshire and Staffordshire										
1.	9	71.4	−6.1	7		1	8	2			10
South-West Midlands										
1.	12	62.9	−11.0	12			12				12
2.	12	74.2	−6.3	7	1		8	4	1		13
3.	6	71.6	−5.7	8			8				8
Total	30	69.2	−8.1	27	1		28	4	1		33
Western Lancastria										
1.	17	69.2	−6.8	13			13	3	1		17
2.	11	78.8	−2.8	11		1	12	2			14
Total	28	73.0	−5.2	24		1	25	5	1		31
Eastern Lancastria										
1.	9	80.0	−2.8	5			5	6			11
2.	20	74.2	−5.3	16	1		17	5			22
3.	7	86.3	−2.7	7			7	1			8
Total	36	78.0	−4.1	28	1		29	12			41
West Riding										
1.	23	74.0	−6.0	9	2	1	12	10		1	23
2.	8	73.5	−7.2	3			3	6			9
3.	10	76.8	−1.5	1			1	9			10
Total	41	74.6	−5.2	13	2	1	16	25		1	42
Rest of Yorkshire										
1.	9	73.9	−6.1	11			11	2			13
Cumbria										
1.	4	84.5	−2.4	3			3	2	1		6
North-East England										
1.	13	77.7	−3.7	6	3		8	5			13
2.	8	82.9	−3.2	4			4	3	1		8

		Turnout 1935		Members elected 1935 (all seats: 603)							
		% Voting 1935	Change in % voting 1931-35	Con.	Lib. Nat.	Nat. Lab.	Nat. Govt	Lab.	Lib.	Other	Total
3.	8	80.1	– 0.6	2			2	6	1		9
Total	29	79.8	– 2.7	12	3		15	14	2		31
Areas of Wales											
1.	12	75.6	– 3.9	5	1	1	7	16			23
2.	10	76.8	– 2.7	2	2		4	2	6		12
Total	22	76.2	– 3.4	7	3	1	11	18	6		35
Areas of Scotland											
1.	4	60.6	– 4.2	4	2		6	1	1		8
2.	8	70.4	– 5.4	8	1		9	1	1		11
3.	13	74.2	– 3.9	5	2		7	7		1	15
4.	28	75.2	– 3.2	11	2	1	14	10		4	28
5.	8	74.0	– 3.9	7	1		8	1			9
Total	61	73.2	– 3.8	35	7	1	43	20	3	5	71
Northern Ireland				10			10			2	12
Large Cities											
London	57	61.5	– 3.9	38	1		39	22	1		62
Glasgow	15	72.0	– 4.1	6			6	5		4	15
Birmingham	12	62.9	– 11.0	12			12				12
Liverpool	11	67.3	– 6.4	8			8	3			11
Manchester	10	71.5	– 5.9	6			6	4			10
Sheffield	6	72.9	– 7.2	3			3	4			7
Leeds	6	66.8	– 6.1	3		1	4	2			6
Bristol	5	73.9	– 6.7	2	1		3	2			5
Edinburgh	4	67.0	– 9.2	4			4	1			5
Newcastle-upon-Tyne	4	75.6	– 6.2	3	1		4				4
Bradford	4	70.5	– 11.1	2			2	1	1		4
Hull	4	72.2	– 9.1	2			2	2			4
Nottingham	4	69.9	– 7.5	2		1	3	1			4
Leicester	3	69.1	– 8.4	2		1	3				3
Plymouth	3	74.9	– 4.4	2	1		3				3
Portsmouth	3	67.6	– 7.6	3			3				3
Salford	3	75.7	– 3.9	3			3				3
Stoke-on-Trent	3	72.3	– 4.7					3			3
Wolverhampton	3	72.2	– 9.2	2			2		1		3
Cardiff	3	72.5	– 4.3	1		1	3				3

1.5 Regional Results[1] (National Government versus Labour[2])

	Votes (as % of votes cast in constituencies where both sides concerned put up candidates)				Swing (Average of National Government % gain and Labour % loss)
	1931		1935		1931-35
	Nat. Govt.	Lab.	Nat. Govt.	Lab.	
GREAT BRITAIN	450 63.77	32.29	53.85	41.11	– 9.4
England	390 64.52	31.82	54.45	40.59	– 9.4
Wales	13 51.89	39.65	44.02	46.59	– 7.4
Scotland	47 60.87	34.11	51.58	43.91	– 9.5
AREAS OF ENGLAND					
London Area	92 67.05	31.66	54.45	45.34	– 13.1
London	52 66.03	32.44	53.09	45.34	– 12.9
Outer London	40 68.39	30.65	56.21	45.33	– 13.4
South and East	88 70.73	23.28	61.67	31.33	– 8.4
South-East	14 81.57	17.41	71.65	27.34	– 9.9
South-Central	9 72.81	21.97	61.74	31.74	– 10.4
Severn	19 63.64	27.52	54.72	34.94	– 8.2
Wessex	13 72.28	23.22	65.72	28.12	– 5.7
Western Peninsula	8 63.59	22.93	58.46	26.80	– 4.5
East Anglia	25 70.78	25.36	60.26	33.80	– 9.5

	Votes				Swing
	1931		1935		1931-35
	Nat. Govt.	Lab.	Nat. Govt.	Lab.	
Midlands	79 62.74	33.09	55.15	41.20	– 7.9
Lincolnshire	7 65.03	30.99	54.83	39.67	– 9.4
East Midlands	27 62.52	36.25	50.89	45.83	– 10.7
North-west Midlands	7 56.53	34.70	49.97	43.47	– 7.7
Shropshire & Staffordshire	9 64.04	30.36	59.29	40.71	– 7.6
South-west Midlands	29 63.48	31.20	59.17	36.88	– 5.0
North of England	131 59.64	36.65	49.18	46.48	– 10.2
Western Lancastria	23 64.35	33.45	53.43	43.09	– 10.3
Eastern Lancastria	35 58.79	34.06	50.36	43.93	– 9.2
West Riding	38 56.35	40.55	44.20	52.17	– 11.9
Rest of Yorkshire	9 68.33	27.40	55.40	35.44	– 10.5
Cumbria	2 55.30	44.70	48.25	44.95	– 3.7
North-east England	24 58.70	40.13	49.01	48.69	– 9.1

SUB-AREAS OF ENGLAND

London						
1.	25	65.28	32.81	52.75	45.99	– 12.9
2.	9	57.32	40.36	41.83	56.92	– 16.0
3.	7	80.32	19.67	70.30	27.03	– 8.7
4.	11	65.75	33.23	52.13	46.05	– 13.2
Total	52	66.03	32.44	53.09	45.34	– 12.9

		Votes				Swing
		1931		1935		1931-35
		Nat. Govt.	Lab.	Nat. Govt.	Lab.	
Outer London						
1.	27	64.64	34.06	52.29	51.56	– 14.9
2.	13	76.15	23.57	64.33	32.40	– 10.8
Total	40	68.39	30.65	56.21	45.33	– 13.4
South-East England						
1.	5	76.80	23.20	65.34	31.84	– 10.1
2.	9	84.22	14.20	75.16	24.84	– 9.9
Total	14	81.57	17.41	71.65	27.34	– 9.9
South Central England						
1.	9	72.81	21.97	61.74	31.74	– 10.4
Severn						
1.	6	66.75	23.47	56.62	29.22	– 7.9
2.	13	62.20	29.39	53.84	37.58	– 8.3
Total	19	63.64	27.52	54.72	34.94	– 8.2
Wessex						
1.	4	69.93	30.08	65.28	32.20	– 3.4
2.	9	73.33	20.17	65.91	26.31	– 6.8
Total	13	72.28	23.22	65.72	28.12	– 5.7
Western Peninsula						
1.	5	61.36	17.06	56.60	19.82	– 3.8
2.	3	67.30	32.70	61.57	38.43	– 5.7
Total	8	63.59	32.93	58.46	26.80	– 4.5
East Anglia						
1.	10	69.23	30.77	59.60	38.30	– 8.6
2.	6	70.77	22.10	59.80	31.70	– 10.3
3.	9	72.51	21.52	61.31	30.19	– 9.9
Total	25	70.78	25.36	60.26	33.80	– 9.5
Lincolnshire						
1.	7	65.03	30.99	54.83	39.67	– 9.4
East Midlands						
1.	12	57.31	42.55	44.60	52.39	– 11.3
2.	7	66.93	33.07	55.96	41.66	– 9.3
3.	8	66.48	29.24	55.88	39.63	– 10.5
Total	27	62.52	36.15	50.89	45.83	– 10.7
North-West Midlands						
1.	4	61.03	30.60	52.18	36.35	– 7.3
2.	3	50.33	40.17	47.03	52.97	– 8.3
Total	7	56.53	34.70	49.97	43.47	– 7.7

		Votes				Swing
		1931		1935		1931-35
		Nat. Govt.	Lab.	Nat. Govt.	Lab.	
Shropshire and						
Staffordshire						
1.	9	64.04	30.36	59.29	40.71	– 7.6
South-west Midlands						
1.	12	70.56	27.18	65.78	33.86	– 5.7
2.	13	54.26	37.85	51.39	42.11	– 3.6
3.	4	72.20	21.65	64.58	28.93	– 7.5
Total	29	63.48	31.20	59.17	36.88	– 5.0
Western Lancastria						
1.	15	65.29	31.33	54.59	42.03	–10.7
2.	8	62.59	37.41	51.24	45.06	– 9.5
Total	23	64.35	33.45	53.43	43.09	– 10.3
Eastern Lancastria						
1.	9	57.02	40.49	45.70	49.20	– 10.5
2.	19	61.47	32.67	53.19	43.28	– 9.4
3.	7	53.80	29.57	48.69	38.93	– 7.2
Total	35	58.79	34.06	50.36	43.93	– 9.2
West Riding						
1.	20	61.85	33.85	48.63	44.48	– 11.9
2.	8	57.20	38.86	46.25	53.75	– 12.9
3.	10	44.67	55.30	33.70	66.30	– 11.0
Total	38	56.35	40.55	44.20	52.17	– 11.9
Rest of Yorkshire						
1.	9	68.33	27.40	55.40	35.44	– 10.5
Cumbria						
1.	2	55.30	44.70	48.57	44.95	– 3.7
North-East England						
1.	12	59.12	38.64	51.99	46.08	– 7.3
2.	6	60.77	39.02	47.35	48.32	– 11.4
3.	6	55.78	44.22	44.72	54.27	– 10.6
Total	24	58.70	40.13	49.01	48.69	– 9.1
Areas of Wales						
1.	9	54.76	41.96	47.90	49.83	– 7.4
2.	4	45.45	34.45	35.28	39.30	– 7.5
Total	9	51.89	39.65	44.02	46.59	– 7.4
Areas of Scotland						
1.	2	57.75	15.20	65.05	26.90	– 2.2
2.	5	70.90	23.20	57.62	40.16	– 15.1
3.	12	60.93	36.85	50.42	44.03	– 8.8

			Votes			Swing
		1931		1935		1931-35
		Nat. Govt.	Lab.	Nat. Govt.	Lab.	
4.	22	56.54	37.76	47.90	46.74	− 8.8
5.	6	69.32	30.68	57.90	42.10	− 11.4
Total	47	60.87	34.11	51.58	43.91	− 9.5

Large Cities

			Nat. Govt.	Lab.	Nat. Govt.	Lab.	Swing
London	62	52	66.03	32.44	53.09	45.34	− 12.9
Glasgow	15	12	59.37	34.83	49.48	43.42	− 9.2
Birmingham	12	12	70.56	27.18	65.78	33.86	− 5.7
Liverpool	11	10	62.62	32.32	51.85	44.35	− 11.4
Manchester	10	9	62.22	31.82	51.73	42.23	− 10.5
Sheffield	7	6	59.85	37.68	48.50	51.50	− 12.6
Leeds	6	6	63.07	33.97	53.63	44.53	− 10.0
Bristol	5	4	63.23	36.78	52.30	46.53	− 10.3
Edinburgh	5	3	68.50	30.00	62.50	34.03	− 5.0
Newcastle-upon-Tyne	4	4	69.40	30.53	63.73	36.28	− 5.7
Bradford	4	2	66.60	34.40	50.65	43.50	− 13.0
Hull	4	4	62.93	37.08	49.00	46.30	− 11.6
Nottingham	4	4	63.25	28.18	55.25	37.88	− 8.9
Leicester	3	2	72.75	27.25	57.10	38.65	− 13.5
Plymouth	3	3	67.30	32.70	61.57	38.43	− 5.7

		Votes				Swing
		1931		1935		1931-35
		Nat. Govt.	Lab.	Nat. Govt.	Lab.	
Portsmouth	3	3 70.73	29.27	67.27	29.37	– 1.6
Salford	3	2 57.65	31.15	43.65	37.80	– 10.3
Stoke-on-Trent	3	3 50.33	40.17	47.03	52.97	– 8.3
Wolverhampton	3	3 50.90	34.40	47.47	36.37	– 2.6
Cardiff	3	3 55.87	34.27	52.00	41.00	– 5.3

Notes:

1. I calculated constituency percentage votes and swing early in 1968, before Mr Craig gave notice of his intention to publish *British Parliamentary Election Results 1918-1949* (1969). Had I known that he was doing so I would probably have done no more than spot-check his work for accuracy. As it is, I can only assure Mr Craig's readers that his work is very accurate indeed, at least for 1931 and 1935, and, I have no doubt, for the other election years as well.

2. Excluded from this set of calculations (apart from seats uncontested at either or both 1931 and 1935) are University seats; the Northern Irish constituencies; seats where there were straight fights between Conservatives and Liberals and between the Liberals and Labour at both 1931 and 1935 elections, or where a fringe party contested seats with Conservatives and Liberals, or with Labour and the Liberals. Two member constituencies are treated as single units — even Dundee, where the Conservatives refrained from putting up a second candidate at both the 1931 and 1935 elections. Included in this set of calculations are 15 constituencies where in 1931 Labour was represented by the ILP or independent Labour candidates, but where in 1935 official Labour candidates stood.

1.6 Percentage Votes Cast and Swing, according to Type of Context (National Government and Opposition)

	1931 Nat. Govt.	Opp.	1935 Nat. Govt.	Opp.	Percentage swing
Conservative versus Labour 1931 and 1935 (230 constituencies)	66.3	38.7	56.4	43.6	9.9
Nat. Govt. (Conservative and Liberal National) versus Labour 1931 and 1935, and Liberal 1935 (60 constituencies)	69.4	29.2	53.4	34.1	10.5
Nat. Govt. (Conservative) versus Labour 1931 and 1935, and CPGB, ILP, SNP, and independents in either or both 1931 and 1935 (53 constituencies)	59.2	37.0	48.9	46.9	10.2
Liberal National versus Labour 1931 and 1935 (22 constituencies)	69.7	30.3	58.7	41.3	11.0
Liberal National versus Labour 1935, Liberal National (and Conservative) versus Labour non-Liberal fringe parties 1931 (14 constituencies)	57.8	39.6	49.9	47.6	8.0
Conservative versus Liberal 1931 and 1935 (11 constituencies)	61.3	38.7	55.0	45.0	6.3
Conservative versus Liberal and Labour 1931 and 1935 (33 constituencies)	51.5	19.1	47.9	25.5	5.0
National Labour versus Labour 1931 and 1935 (8 constituencies)	63.2	36.8	47.2	52.8	16.0
National Labour versus Labour or ILP and others 1935, and National Labour (or Conservative) versus same in 1931 (7 constituencies)	60.5	39.9	49.3	46.5	8.9

	1931		1935		
	Nat. Govt.	Opp.	Nat. Govt.	Opp.	Percentage swing
Conservative versus Labour 1935, and Labour and Liberal 1931 (15 constituencies)	57.3	26.9	55.4	44.6	9.8

Note: Excludes seats in Northern Ireland, University seats and two member constituencies.

1.7 Regional Occupations, Unemployment and Swing[1]

	Main occupations[2] (over 12%)	Unemployment[3] Moderate (under 20%)	Heavy (over 20%)	% decrease Sept. 1931- Sept. 1935	Swing 1931-35
Great Britain				30	– 9.4
England				34	– 9.4
Wales				+ 1	– 7.4
Scotland				20	– 9.5
Areas of Great Britain					
London & Outer London	Commerce	x		30	– 13.1
South-East	Commerce	x		20	– 9.9
South-Central	Agriculture	x		35	– 10.4
Severn	Agriculture	x		20	– 8.2
Wessex	Agriculture Defence	x		15	– 5.7
Western Peninsula	Agriculture	x		10	– 4.5
East Anglia	Agriculture	x		30	– 9.5
Lincolnshire	Agriculture	x		15	– 9.4
East Midlands	Mining Metals Textiles		x	40	– 10.7
North-west Midlands	Metals		x	40	– 7.7
Shropshire & Staffordshire	Agriculture	x		20	– 7.6
South-west Midlands	Metals		x	65	– 5.0
Western Lancastria	Metals		x	40	– 9.8
Eastern Lancastria	Textiles				
West Riding	Mining Metals		x	36	– 11.6
Rest of Yorkshire	Agriculture Shipping	x			
Cumbria	Agriculture Mining		x	20	– 3.7
North-east England	Mining Metals		x	15	– 9.1
Industrial Wales	Mining		x	1	– 3.9
Rural Wales	Agriculture	x		+ 20	– 2.7
Scottish Highlands	Agriculture	x		+ 30	– 2.2
Forth Valley	Commerce	x		10	– 8.8
Clyde Valley	Mining Metals		x	20	– 8.8
The Large Cities					
London		x		37	– 12.9
Glasgow			x	20	– 9.2
Birmingham			x	66	– 5.7
Liverpool			x	11	– 11.4
Manchester			x	33	– 10.5
Sheffield			x	44	– 12.6
Leeds			x	45	– 10.0

	Main occupations[2] (over 12%)	Unemployment[3]			Swing 1931-35
		Moderate (under 20%)	Heavy (over 20%)	% decrease Sept. 1931- Sept. 1935	
Bristol		x		23	- 10.3
Edinburgh		x		9	- 5.0
Newcastle-upon-Tyne			x	5	- 5.7
Bradford			x	60	- 13.0
Hull			x	12	- 11.6
Nottingham			x	32	- 8.9
Leicester			x	38	- 13.5
Plymouth		x		6	- 5.7
Portsmouth		x		15	- 1.6
Salford			x	30	- 10.3
Stoke-on-Trent			x	41	- 8.3
Wolverhampton			x	52	- 2.6
Cardiff			x	11	- 5.3

Notes:

1. 'Efforts in the direction of electoral geography are likely to be frustrating for their authors and disappointing in their results.' J. Blondel, 'Towards a General Theory of Change in Voting Behaviour' *Political Studies*, vol. 13 (1965), p. 95.

2. Source: *Census of England and Wales, 1931.*

3. Source: *Ministry of Labour Gazette*, Dec. 1931, 1935; also Conservative Central Office, *G.E. Memo 4*, 5 Nov. 1935, for a useful digest of unemployment statistics.

APPENDIX 2: BY-ELECTIONS, 1932-35

2.1a Contested By-elections, 1931-35

Constituency	Date	% Voting	Nat. Govt.[1]	Lab.	Lib.	Others	Swing 1931-Bye	Swing Bye-1935
Croydon, South	1931	68.3	80.3	19.7				
	9/2/32	38.2	67.5	32.5			– 12.8	
	1935	65.2	62.3	29.0	8.7			– 1.7
New Forest and	1931	71.9	83.3	16.7				
Christchurch	9/2/32	48.0	82.0	18.0			– 1.3	
	1935	64.5	74.8	25.2				– 7.2
Henley	1931	68.6	72.2	11.5	16.3			
	25/2/32	48.9	69.9		30.1			
	1935	56.9	70.4		29.6			
Dunbartonshire	1931	82.8	63.3	36.4				
	17/3/32	70.5	43.5	35.6		20.9	– 9.7	
	1935	80.5	50.3	41.9		7.8		+ 0.2
Wakefield *	1931	85.5	57.4	42.6				
	21/4/32	83.0	49.4	50.6			– 8.0	
	1935	84.9	44.0	56.0				– 5.4
St Marylebone	1931	63.5	86.7	13.3				
	28/4/32	30.8	52.3					
	1935	57.9	79.6	20.4				
Dulwich	1931	70.7	71.5	15.6	12.9			
	8/6/32	47.1	61.0	19.3	19.7		– 7.1	
	1935	65.8	60.8	25.7	13.5			– 3.3
Montrose Burghs	1931	74.6	77.0	23.0				
	28/6/32	56.7	46.9	41.4		11.7	– 24.3	
	1935	70.6	69.6	30.4				+ 16.9
Cornwall,	1931	85.7	45.3	5.6	49.1			
Northern	22/7/32	80.8	47.6		52.4			
	1935	79.9	48.7		51.3			
Wednesbury *	1931	89.0	54.5	45.5				
	26/7/32	78.0	45.3	54.7			– 9.2	
	1935	78.1	46.7	53.3				+ 1.4
Twickenham	1931	71.3	74.0	26.0				
	16/9/32	51.9	56.2	43.8			– 17.8	
	22/6/34	55.5	56.1	43.9			– 0.1	
	1935	66.5	62.2	37.8				+ 6.1
Cardiganshire	1931	67.5		24.0	76.0			
	22/9/32	70.4	32.1	19.2	48.7			
	1935	65.1		38.9	61.1			

Constituency	Date	% Voting	Nat. Govt.	Lab.	Lib.	Others	Swing 1931-Bye	Swing Bye-1935
Liverpool, Exchange	1931	69.0	68.8	31.2				
	19/1/33	55.2	55.0	45.0			– 13.8	
	1935	65.7	57.2	42.8				+ 2.2
Fife, Eastern	1931	National Government unopposed						
	2/2/33	65.6	52.2	22.0		25.8		
	1935	71.0	82.3	17.7				+17.2
Rotherham *	1931	82.6	50.8	49.2				
	27/2/33	73.5	30.9	69.1			– 19.9	
	1935	76.7	32.5	67.5				+ 1.6
Ashford	1931	75.6	**					
	17/3/33	70.9	47.7	18.4	33.9			
	1935	73.6	59.2	17.6	23.2			+ 6.2
Rhondda, East	1931	73.7		68.1		31.9		
	28/3/33	74.9		42.6	23.6	33.8		
	1935	80.8		61.8		38.2		
Hitchin	1931	71.1	75.7	24.3				
	8/6/33	51.3	58.4	41.6			– 17.3	
	1935	66.4	63.3	36.7				+ 4.9
Altrincham	1931	National Government unopposed						
	14/6/33	63.4	51.2	16.8	32.0			
	1935	72.0	70.2	29.8				+ 3.0
Clay Cross	1931	74.6	35.4	64.6				
	1/9/33	71.2	19.9	69.3		10.8	– 10.1	
	1935	73.6	25.4	74.5				+ 0.1
Fulham, East *	1931	66.1	68.7	26.1	5.2			
	25/10/33	59.5	42.1	57.9			– 29.2	
***	1935	71.9	51.4	48.6				+ 9.3
Kilmarnock	1931	79.5	59.6			40.4		
	2/11/33	77.3	34.8	27.4		37.8		
	1935	78.8	50.9	33.4		15.7		+ 5.1
Skipton	1931	80.3	68.2	31.8				
	7/11/33	82.7	43.0	33.5	21.8	1.7	– 13.5	
	1935	79.6	56.2	43.8				+ 1.5
Rusholme	1931	80.0	69.3	17.7	13.0			
	21/11/33	60.8	50.8	40.1	9.1		– 20.6	
	1935	69.8	62.6	29.0	8.0			+11.5
Rutland and Stamford	1931	75.3	71.9	28.1				
	21/11/33	77.2	53.3	46.7			– 18.6	
	1935	78.4	59.9	40.1				+ 6.6

Constituency	Date	% Voting	Nat. Govt.	Lab.	Lib.	Others	Swing 1931-Bye	Bye-1935
Harborough	1931	78.1	74.5	25.5				
	28/11/33	72.3	50.9	32.9	16.2		– 15.5	
	1935	72.3	63.2	36.8				+ 4.2
Cambridge	1931	75.6	73.2	26.8				
	8/2/34	67.8	51.2	41.8	7.0		– 18.5	
	1935	73.2	58.5	41.5				+ 3.8
Lowestoft	1931	70.8	67.8	32.2				
	15/2/34	67.9	48.0	42.1	9.9		– 14.9	
	1935	69.0	61.2	38.8				+ 8.3
Portsmouth, North	1931	74.5	68.4	31.6				
	19/2/34	55.7	59.6	40.4			– 8.8	
	1935	64.9	66.6	33.4				+ 7.0

Combined Scottish Universities: by-elections March 1934, June 1935

Constituency	Date	% Voting	Nat. Govt.	Lab.	Lib.	Others	Swing 1931-Bye	Bye-1935
Basingstoke	1931	74.2	69.7	12.2	18.1			
	19/4/34	64.4	53.7	15.5	30.8		– 9.6	
	1935	67.4	57.8	10.0	32.2			+ 4.8
Hammersmith, N. *	1931	69.6	59.2	37.2		3.6		
	24/4/34	56.7	41.9	55.7		2.4	– 17.9	
	1935	65.7	47.2	52.8				+ 3.1
Upton *	1931	70.4	58.5	41.5				
	14/5/34	50.5	40.1	56.4		3.5	– 16.7	
	1935	62.7	46.8	53.2				+ 5.0
Merthyr Tydfil	1931	80.8		69.4		30.6		
Merthyr	1934	81.1		51.8	28.9	19.3		
	1935	68.8		68.0		32.0		
Monmouth	1931	78.0	70.8	29.2				
	14/6/34	69.2	65.0	35.0			– 5.8	
	1935	76.8	63.4	36.6				– 1.6
Twickenham	See by-elections 1932							
Weston-super-Mare	1931	71.8	85.7	14.3				
	26/6/34	57.2	61.5	16.6	21.9		– 13.3	
	1935	66.4	65.6	15.7	18.7			+ 2.5

Fermanagh and Tyrone: by-election 27/6/34

Constituency	Date	% Voting	Nat. Govt.	Lab.	Lib.	Others	Swing 1931-Bye	Bye-1935
Rushcliffe	1931	77.8	72.1	27.9				
	26/7/34	56.5	48.8	38.0	13.1		– 16.7	
	1935	67.9	62.6	37.4				+ 7.2

Constituency	Date	% Voting	Nat. Govt.	Lab.	Lib.	Others	Swing 1931-Bye	Bye-1935
Lambeth, North	1931	64.6		34.9	65.1			
*	23/10/34	52.6	15.0	57.9	25.5	1.6		
	1935	54.2		55.4	44.6			
Swindon	1931	85.5	55.9	44.1				
*	25/10/34	81.8	46.6	53.4			-9.3	
***	1935	84.3	51.2	48.8				+4.6
Putney	1931	66.3	81.6	18.4				
	28/11/34	57.5	54.7	45.3			-26.9	
	1935	68.5	65.1	31.9				+11.9
Wavertree	1931	75.2	77.9	22.1				
*	6/2/35	72.3	31.2	35.4	9.5	23.9	-30.0	
***	1935	73.2	58.5	41.5				+10.6
Norwood	1931	63.9	81.0	19.0				
	14/3/35	53.4	51.1	40.4		8.5	-25.7	
	1935	62.2	66.9	33.1				+11.6
Perth	1931	81.4	50.2		40.1	9.7		
	16/4/35	52.9	68.7	31.3				+5.0
	1935	64.0	73.7	26.3				
Edinburgh, West	1931	79.2	71.2	28.8				
	2/5/35	51.2	53.0	33.9	13.1		-11.7	
	1935	68.1	67.0	33.0				+7.5
Aberdeen, South	1931	75.8	83.7	16.3				
	21/5/35	56.6	66.0	34.0			-17.7	
	1935	65.9	68.1	31.9				+2.1

Combined Scottish Universities: by-election June 1935

Constituency	Date	% Voting	Nat. Govt.	Lab.	Lib.	Others	Swing 1931-Bye	Bye-1935
West Toxteth	1931	76.1	57.9	42.1				
*	16/7/35	53.9	39.1	60.9			-18.8	
	1935	78.6	47.1	52.9				+8.0
Dumfriesshire	1931	77.6	77.7	22.3				
	12/9/35	58.7	60.3	39.7			-17.4	
	1935	73.6	65.4	34.6				+5.1

*Labour gain
**Both candidates stood as supporters of the National Government — one a Conservative, the other a Liberal National
***National Government recovery

Note 1. Either Conservative, Liberal National, or National Labour, except in the case of Dumfriesshire (1935) for 1931 where I have classified T. Hunter as an independent government supporter, which he was in spirit and practice if not at that time in name.

2.1b Uncontested by-elections, 1932-35

1932

Surrey, Richmond	National Government held
Eastbourne	National Government held
Abbey	National Government held

1933

Normanton	Labour
Wentworth	Labour

1934

Hemsworth	Labour

1935

Cambridge University	National Government held
Eastbourne	National Government held
Liverpool West Derby	National Government held
Tamworth	National Government held
City of London	National Government held
Sevenoaks	National Government held

2.2 By-election Issues and Swing, 1931-35[1]

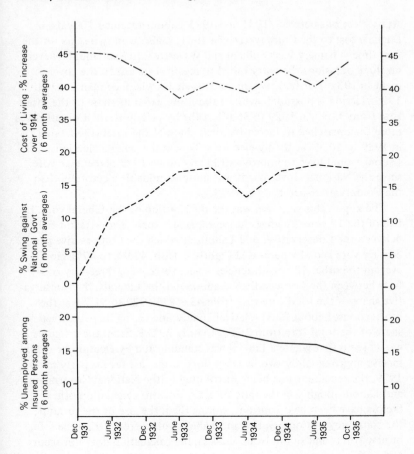

Notes:
1. By-election issues are discussed in my article 'The East Fulham By-Election 25 October 1933, *Historical Journal*, vol. 14, no. 1 (1971), pp. 165-200. See also J.P. Kyba, 'British Attitudes Towards Disarmament and Rearmament 1932-1935, unpublished doctoral thesis, London School of Economics, 1967. The above graph indicates in only the most general way the relationship between swing and nationwide changes in unemployment and the cost of living.
2. Source: *Ministry of Labour Gazette*, Dec. 1935, Feb. 1936.
3. Conventional swing has been calculated for 34 of 50 contested by-elections. The constituencies omitted are: Henley, St Marylebone, North Cornwall, Cardiganshire, East Fife, Ashford, East Rhondda, Altrincham, Kilmarnock, Combined Scottish Universities (twice), Merthyr, Fermanagh and Tyrone, North Lambeth, Wavertree, Perth.

2.3 By-elections and the Distribution of the Liberal Vote

At by-elections between 1931 and 1935 Labour regained 10 seats in England lost to the Conservatives in 1931; it also won two seats for the first time — namely East Fulham and Wavertree. In Scotland, however, on three occasions the party failed to regain seats lost to the government in 1931. Furthermore, in constituencies where comparison with 1929 election is possible[1], while Labour increased its share of the total vote from 33.3% in 1929 to 35.6% at the by-elections, the Conservatives more than matched it, increasing their share of the total vote from 45% in 1929 to 50.3% at the by-elections. To win the general election Labour would have to improve strikingly on its 1929 percentage vote, since the National Government was more formidable electorally than the Conservatives had been in 1929.

The key to this situation was the distribution of the Liberal vote. In five of the 17 constituencies just compared,[2] there were straight fights between the Conservatives and Labour at which the Conservative percentage vote actually decreased slightly — from 47.9% to 47%. However, in the other 12 constituencies where there were three-way contests between the Conservatives, Labour and the Liberals, the Conservative share of the total vote rose from 43.8% in 1929 to 51.7% at the by-elections; Labour fared relatively badly, increasing its percentage share of the total vote from 25.5% to only 29.2%. From these figures it would seem that where a Liberal was standing at a by-election he would receive approximately two in every three votes cast for his party in 1929, the remaining one being distributed to the National Government and Labour roughly in the ratio of 2:1.[3] For this calculation other factors have been held constant, among them the size of the turnout, the constancy of Conservative and Labour voters from 1929, the effect of new voters and so on. None the less, the calculation does not seem out of line with more impressionistic evidence, such as the newspaper reports of the by-elections. Both sources suggest that the Labour Party failed almost completely to garner Liberal votes in Scotland, but was markedly successful in London: elsewhere the National Government did the better. To some extent this was a class matter: Liberals in working-class areas tended to vote Labour; Liberals in middle-class areas tended to vote for the National Government. As Sir Robert Topping put it in a memorandum in April 1935, the National Government was being supported by the sort of Liberals whose names appeared in telephone directories.[4] But in some places — the West Midlands in particular — the distribution of the Liberal vote seems not to have been on pure class lines. Chronology also played a part. Immediately following Samuel's decision to move into opposition, the rate of Liberal abstention at by-elections seems to have increased; but during 1935, particularly at the Scottish by-elections, the National Government seems to have attracted many Liberal votes.

Notes

1. Dulwich, Ashford, Altrincham, Skipton, Rusholme, Harborough, Cambridge, Lowestoft, Basingstoke, Weston-super-Mare, Rushcliffe, West Edinburgh, Liverpool Exchange, Clay Cross, Putney, South Aberdeen, West Toxteth.

2. The last five in the above list.

3. This is close to the ratio arrived at by Butler and Stokes on the basis of their 1963/4 survey of people who remembered their parents as Liberals. Butler and Stokes omit to mention, however, that it was the existence of the National Government which made it possible for former Liberal voters to cast their votes with a relatively easy conscience for Conservative candidates. See D.E. Butler and E. Stokes, *Political Change in Britain* (1969), pp. 251-4.

4. Baldwin Papers, vol. 47, memorandum on the Norwood by-election prepared by Sir Robert Topping, 8 April 1935. Central Office thought that probably one in three voters who supported the Liberal Party in 1929 now supported the National Government.

APPENDIX 3: THE CANDIDATES

3.1 Occupations of Candidates at the 1935 General Election

Occupation	Conservative		Labour		Liberal	
	Elected	Defeated	Elected[1]	Defeated	Elected	Defeated
Professions						
Barristers	58	35	7	34	6	29
Solicitors	7	7	2	12		8
Drs/Dents/Clergy	6	1	6	11		8
Architect/Surveyor	3		1	5		1
Engineer	13	1	4	7		3
Accountant	6	3		8		6
Civil Servant[2]				3		
Armed Services	30	10	1	4		2
Teaching:						
University		2	2	13		3
Adult[3]	4	9	4	23		3
School	3	3	3	20		5
Total	130 (35%)	71 (56%)	30 (20%)	140 (36%)	6 (30%)	68 (51%)
Business						
Co. Director	67	5	4	4	2	5
Businessman	36	15	7	14	4	15
Financier	13	8		3	2	9
Total	116 (31%)	28 (22%)	11 (7%)	21 (5%)	8 (40%)	29 (22%)
Farmer – Total	52 (14%)	9 (7%)	1	6 (2%)	3 (15%)	6 (5%)

Miscellaneous						
'White Collar'[4]	27	3	11		53	9
Private Means	30	5			2	1
Politician/Party Worker[5]		1	17	2	11	3
Journalist/Writer	14	6	8		37	10
Student		1	1		2	
Total	71 (19%)	16 (13%)	37 (24%)	2	105 (27%)	23 (17%)
Workers[6]						
Miners			19		7	
Trade Union Offs.			52		63	
Skilled	2	2	2		29	3
Semi-skilled			1		20	1
Total	2	2	74 (48%)		119 (30%)	4
GRAND TOTAL	369[7]	126	153	19	391	133

Notes:

1. See also W. Guttsman, *The British Political Elite* (1963), p. 238.
2. Includes retired civil servants.
3. Includes social workers.
4. Clerks and secretaries.
5. Includes full-time politicians like Stanley Baldwin and Ramsay MacDonald, as well as officials of Transport House and Conservative Central Office.
6. The distinction made between miners and trade union officials is arbitrary.
7. 25% of the successful National Government candidates held knighthoods; 5% were peers. Only 4 of the Liberal MPs were knights. Labour had only 4 knights.

Sources: *The Times House of Commons 1929, 1931, 1935; Constitutional Year Book; Liberal Year Book; Annual Register; Debrett's House of Commons; Who's Who; Who was Who; Labour's Who's Who* (2nd ed., 1927); *New Statesman's Year Book; Daily Mail Year Book.*

3.2 Parliamentary and Local Government Experience, and the Ages of Candidates at the 1935 General Election

Age in 1935	No.	Local Govt. experience	Elected First contest	Parl. Cands	Pre-1931 & 1931 Bye	No.	Local Govt. experience	Defeated First contest	Parl. Cands	Pre-1931 & 1931 Bye
Conservative Party Candidates										
20-29	11		7	2	2	10		7	1	2
30-39	86	11	11	44	31	26	5	8	14	4
40-49	98	18	10	72	16	19	6		7	12
50-59	102	29	3	80	19	23	7	4	10	9
60-69	56	24	1	49	6	6	2	1	3	2
70-79	14	8		11	3	2	2		1	1
*Unknown						40	8	30	7	3
Total	367	90 25%	32 9%	257 70%	75 20%	126	30 34%	50 40%	43 34%	33 26%
Labour Party Candidates										
20-29	2		1		1	15	1	13		2
30-39	9	5	3	3	3	46	23	25	14	7
40-49	34	16	5	27	2	61	26	16	30	15
50-59	58	32	5	51	2	67	34	15	49	3
60-69	43	28	2	41		24	13	3	18	3
70-79	8	6		8		3	2		2	1
*Unknown						178	77	123	32	23
Total	154	87 56%	16 10%	130 84%	8 5%	394	176 45%	195 49%	145 37%	54 14%

Liberal Party Candidates

Age									
20-29	1		1		5		3	1	1
30-39	5	1	3	2	10	2	4	5	1
40-49	4		4		14	3	1	13	
50-59	5	1	4	1	12	4	2	10	
60-69	2	1	1	1	18	5	5	13	
70-79	2	1	2		1		1		
*Unknown					80	24	49	23	8
Total	19	4	15	4	140	38	64	66	10
						27%	46%	47%	7%

*For the defeated candidates the ages of approximately half are unknown though information about local government and parliamentary experience is fairly complete

3.3 Ages and Education of Candidates at the 1935 General Election

Age in 1935	Elected No.	Elementary	Education Secondary	Public School	RMC RMA Naval	Uni.	Defeated No.	Elementary	Education Secondary	Public School	RMC RMA Naval	Uni.

Conservative Party Candidates

Age in 1935	No.	Elementary	Secondary	Public School	RMC RMA Naval	Uni.	No.	Elementary	Secondary	Public School	RMC RMA Naval	Uni.
20-29	11			9	1	9	10		4	6		9
30-39	86		7	78	10	60	26		5	19	3	18
40-49	98	1	26	71	8	72	19	1	11	5		9
50-59	102	1	45	50	5	44	23		16	6	3	9
60-69	56		20	29	6	27	6		2	2	1	2
70-79	14		4	5		6	2		1	1		
Total	367[1]	2	102	242	30	218	86[1]	1	39	39	7	47

Labour Party Candidates

Age in 1935	No.	Elementary	Secondary	Public School	Labour College[2]	Uni.	No.	Elementary	Secondary	Public School	Labour College	Uni.
20-29	2		1	1		2	15	1	6	4		13
30-39	9	5	1	2	2		46	11	25	10	3	30
40-49	34	19	12	3	3	13	61	20	25	10	7	23
50-59	58	41	11	4	3	11	67	30	28	4	3	18
60-69	43	35	7	4	6	6	24	9	12	2		7
70-79	8	5	2	1		2	3	2	1			1
Total	154	105	34	15	14	34	216[3]	73	97	30	13	92

Liberal Party Candidates

			RMC RMA Naval					RMC RMA Naval	
20-29	1	1	1	1	5		1	2	5
30-39	5	1	4	3	10		2	4	7
40-49	4		3	3	14		5	5	11
50-59	5	2	3	5	12		5	5	6
60-69	2		2	1	18	2	5	6	9
70-79	2	1	1		1			1	1
Total	19	5	14	13	60^4	2	18	23	39

Notes:

1. The ages of 61 candidates could not be traced; and in these cases the educational background too was generally unknown.
2. Excludes Ruskin College (in University list).
3. The ages and educational backgrounds of 182 defeated candidates could not be found.
4. Ages and educational backgrounds of 80 defeated candidates are not known.

APPENDIX 4: ISSUES AT THE 1935 GENERAL ELECTION: CANDIDATES' ADDRESSES

Subjects mentioned in candidates' addresses[1]	Nat. Govt. %	Labour %	Liberal %
Democracy, freedom	11	14	18
'National' Government[2]	35	53	45
1931 crisis[3]	26	12	—
Socialism, anti-Socialism	52	54	40
House of Lords[4]	—	20	—
Labour's leadership[5]	6	—	—
Baldwin	22	12	18
Rearmament (a) 'modernisation' 'state of preparedness'	86	29	38
(b) fear of massive rearmament	—	85	38
Empire[6]	37	7	13
Nearness of war	11	49	15
Disarmament[7]	42	71	48
League of Nations	90	90	93
Italo-Abyssinian war[8]	41	50	38
'Peace Ballot'	2	20	8
Germany	2	7	3
No mention of foreign affairs	—	2	—
Prosperity, cost of living, standard of living, recovery	89	20	18
Tariffs, exports, trade	77	49	93
Taxation	29	36	18
Tax on Cooperative Societies	—	41	—
Employment, unemployment[9]	86	82	83
Means Test, Public Assistance[10]	27	84	63
UAB Regulations	10	56	15
Distressed areas	27	60	38
Public works, 'prosperity loan'	24	32	70
Agriculture (a) general[11]	43	53	65
(b) marketing	26	8	25
(c) land settlement	2	5	13
Council of Action programme			33
Coal industry (a) wages and conditions[12]	8	30	15
(b) unification of royalties; reorganisation	19	—	18
Nationalisation (a) coal	—	65	5
(b) land	—	66	3
(c) Bank of England	—	69	8
Repeal of Trades Disputes and Trade Union Act (1927)	—	41	—
Education (a) general	61	76	33
(b) school-leaving age	47	62	23

292 *Appendix 4*

Subjects mentioned in candidates' addresses		Nat. Govt.	Labour	Liberal
Health (e.g. maternal mortality)		44	60	18
Pensions	(a) general	53	61	33
	(b) at 60 years	2	62	10
Housing	(a) general	72	67	35
	(b) built 'to let'	11	51	28
	(c) Rent Restrictions Act (1933), rents	3	15	3
	(d) slum clearance	51	53	10
Local[13]		35	25	25

Notes:

1. A full set of interwar election addresses is held by the Conservative Research Department.

2. Most of the National Government candidates who referred specifically to the 'national' character of the government had been elected for the first time in 1931, when they received votes which would normally have gone to the Liberal and Labour Parties.

3. The percentages refer only to addresses containing detailed discussions of the crisis.

4. In style and content about half the Labour addresses followed the party's manifesto closely, but less than one quarter followed the manifesto call for the abolition of the House of Lords.

5. On the hustings, National Government spokesmen made much of Labour's divided and weakened leadership; but this was not reflected in the election addresses.

6. Only about 2% of the addresses contain a direct reference to India, the subject of considerable debate in the inter-election period. National Government candidates viewed the Empire as a defence problem, while Labour candidates referred to the need to have all British possessions brought under the mandate of the League of Nations.

7. Labour candidates not referring to disarmament were generally contesting seats in London and the South-East, areas already sensitive to the need for air defence.

8. In many National Government addresses the Abyssinian crisis was referred to as a 'border dispute', whereas in Labour and Liberal addresses it was described as a 'war of aggression'.

9. In approximately 16% of the addresses there was no reference to the unemployment problem. The constituencies concerned either had such heavy unemployment that mention of it in an address would have been superfluous (e.g. East Rhondda), or they were free of unemployment (e.g. Cheltenham).

10. Most Liberals wished to abolish the Means Test; a minority, however, endorsed the government's declared policy of 'humane administration' of the test.

11. In the great cities very few candidates referred to agriculture; but in parts of Wales and Scotland and for south England (excluding London and the sea ports) very few candidates failed to raise the issue.

12. Throughout the campaign there were 'stay-in' pay strikes at pits in Wales, Durham and Nottinghamshire.

13. Included are regional industries like fishing, fruit, tin-mining and so on, as well as the tithe issue in parts of south-east England.

BIBLIOGRAPHY

1 MSS Sources

Alexander Papers, Churchill College, Cambridge
Baldwin Papers, University Library, Cambridge
Bevin Papers, Churchill College, Cambridge
Cecil of Chelwood Papers, British Museum
Neville Chamberlain Papers, Birmingham University Library
Dalton Diary and Papers, British Library of Political and Economic
    Science, London School of Economics
Hannon Papers, Beaverbrook Library, London
Lloyd George Papers, Beaverbrook Library, London (now in House
    of Lords Record Office)
Lothian Papers, Scottish Record Office, Edinburgh
Samuel Papers, House of Lords Record Office
Simon Papers, on temporary loan to the Institute of Historical
    Research, London (Dec. 1970)
Templewood Papers, University Library, Cambridge
The Attlee Papers, University College, Oxford, contain nothing
    earlier than 1940. Lord Stonehaven's papers were destroyed
    during the blitz. Lord De La Warr believes he has mislaid or lost
    his papers on the National Labour Party
Thurso (Archibald Sinclair) Papers, Churchill College, Cambridge

2 Public Records

Minutes and Memoranda of the Cabinet, 1931-5, Public Record
    Office
House of Commons Debates, 5th series, 1931-5
Census of England, Wales and Scotland, 1931
Boundary Commission for England, Wales, and Scotland (Representa-
    tion of the People Bill, 1917; Redistribution of Seats) 1917-18
    (Cmds 8756-9)
Returns of Election Expenses, 1931-2, 1935-6 (PP Nos. 109, 150)
Report of the Broadcasting Committee, 1935 (Cmd 5091)
Report of the Broadcasting Committee, 1949 (Cmd 8116)
BBC Ninth Annual Report, 1935 (Cmd 5088)
Royal Commission on the Press, 1947-9 (Cmd 7700)
Ministry of Labour Gazette/Board of Trade Journal, 1931-5

3 Party Records and Ephemera

Minute Book of the Central Council of the Conservative and Unionist Associations, 1931-5 (Conservative Central Office)
Minute Books of the Eastern and Western Organizing Committees of the Scottish Conservative and Unionist Association (Glasgow Office of the Association)
P. Cohen, 'Disraeli's Child: a history of the Conservative and Unionist Party Organization', unpublished typescript, Conservative Research Department
Conservative Agents' Journal
Gleanings and Memoranda, 1931-4/*Politics in Review*, 1934-5
(Conservative Party) *Notes for Speakers at the 1935 General Election*
Reports of the Annual Conferences of the Conservative and Unionist Party 1931-5
Constitutional Year Book
Minutes of the meetings of the National Executive Committee of the Labour Party; reports of the several subcommittees of the party; and minutes of the meetings of the National Joint Council/National Council of Labour (Transport House)
Reports of the annual conferences of the Labour Party, 1931-5
The People's Year Book
Labour (A Magazine for All the Workers)
Liberal Magazine
Liberal Year Book
Minute Books of the Scottish Liberal Federation (University of Edinburgh Library)
Election ephemera of all parties is held at Transport House, the British Museum, the British Library of Political and Economic Science (series JF2 42), and the Lloyd George Papers (G/141); election addresses are held at the Conservative Research Department and the Library of the National Liberal Club

4 Yearbooks/Handbooks

Annual Register
BBC Yearbook/Handbook
Daily Mail Yearbook
Debrett's House of Commons, 1930
Labour's Who's Who (2nd ed., 1927)
Mitchell's Newspaper Directory
The Statesman's Yearbook

The Times House of Commons, 1929, 1931, 1935
Whitaker's Almanack
Who's Who
Who was Who
Willing's Press Guide

5 Newspapers and Journals

Daily Telegraph
The Times
Morning Post
Daily Sketch
Daily Mirror
Daily Mail
Daily Express
News Chronicle
Daily Herald
Daily Worker
Daily Dispatch
Truth
Manchester Guardian

Sunday Times
Sunday Graphic
Empire News
Sunday Chronicle
Observer
News of the World
Sunday Pictorial
People
Sunday Dispatch
Sunday Express
Sunday Referee
Reynolds' News
Evening Standard

Nottingham Journal
Western Mail
Sheffield Telegraph
Daily Record
Newcastle Journal
Scotsman
Birmingham Post

Liverpool Daily Post
Yorkshire Post
Birmingham Gazette
Glasgow Herald
East Anglian Daily Times
Yorkshire Observer

The Listener
New Statesman and Nation
Spectator
Economist
Church Times
Methodist Recorder
Tablet
Forward

Political Quarterly
Nineteenth Century and After
Quarterly Review
Round Table
Contemporary Review

6 Autobiographies, Memoirs, Biographies*

Amery, L.S. *My Political Life* (1955), vol. 3

Andrews, L. *The Autobiography of a Journalist* (1964)

Angell N. *After All* (1951)

Attlee, C.R. *As It Happened* (1954)

Baker, A. *The House is Sitting* (1958)

Baldwin, A.W. *My Father: the true story* (1955)

Bondfield, M. *A Life's Work* (1949)

Boothby, Lord *My Yesterday, Your Tomorrow* (1962)

Bowle, J. *Viscount Samuel: a biography* (1957)

Brockway, F. *Inside the Left* (1942)

——*Socialism Over Sixty Years: the life of Jowett of Bradford (1864-1944)* (1942)

Bullock, A. *The Life and Times of Ernest Bevin* (1960), vol. 1

Butler, J.R.M. *Lord Lothian* (1960)

Butler, Lord *The Art of the Possible* (1971)

Campbell Johnson, A. *Viscount Halifax: a biography* (1941)

Cecil, Viscount *All The Way* (1949)

Churchill, W. *The Second World War* (1948), vol. 1

Citrine, Lord *Men and Work: the autobiograpy of Lord Citrine* (1964)

Clynes, J.R. *Memoirs 1924-1937* (1937)

Cole, M. (ed.) *Beatrice Webb's Diaries 1924-1932* (1956)

Cooke, C. *The Life of Sir Richard Stafford Cripps* (1957)

Coote, C. *A Companion of Honour: The Story of Walter Elliot* (1965)

Cross, C. *Philip Snowden* (1966)

Cross, J.A. *Sir Samuel Hoare: a political biography* (1977)

Cudlipp, H. *Publish and Be Damned* (1953)

Dalton, H. *The Fateful Years: memoirs 1931-1945* (1957)

Duff Cooper, A. *Old Men Forget* (1953)

Eden, A. *Facing the Dictators* (1962)

Estorick, E. *Stafford Cripps* (1949)

Feiling, K. *The Life of Neville Chamberlain* (1st ed., 1946: reissued with new Preface and Bibliography, 1970)

Foot, M. *Aneurin Bevin* (1962)

Gallacher, W. *Last Memoirs* (1966)

Gilbert, M. *Plough My Own Furrow: life and letters of Clifford Allen* (1965)

——*Winston Churchill 1922-1939* (1976)

Halifax, Lord *Fulness of Days* (1957)

*Place of publication is London, unless otherwise indicated

Hamilton, M.A. *Arthur Henderson: a biography* (1938)
——*Remembering My Good Friends* (1944)
Harrod, R. *Life of John Maynard Keynes* (1951)
Heuston, R.F.V. *Lives of the Lord Chancellors 1885-1940* (Oxford, 1964)
Jenkins, R. *Mr. Attlee* (1948)
Jones, T. *A Diary with Letters 1931-1950* (1954)
——*Lloyd George* (Oxford, 1951)
Kilmuir, Lord *Political Adventure* (1964)
King, C. *Strictly Personal* (1969)
Lansbury, G. *My Guest for Peace* (1938)
Lloyd George, F. *The Years That Are Past* (1967)
McCormick, D. *The Mask of Merlin: a critical study of David Lloyd George* (1963)
McGovern, J. *Neither Fear Nor Favour* (1960)
Macleod, I. *Neville Chamberlain* (1961)
Macmillan, H. *Winds of Change 1914-1939* (1966)
Marquand, D. *Ramsay MacDonald* (1977)
Martin, K. *Editor* (1968)
Marwick, A. *Clifford Allen: the open conspirator* (1964)
Middlemas, K. and Barnes, J. *Baldwin: a biography* (1969)
Minney, R.J. *The Private Papers of Hore-Belisha* (1960)
Minney, R.J. *Viscount Addison* (1958)
Montgomery Hyde, H. *Strong for Service: the life of Lord Nathan of Churt* (1968)
Morgan, K.O. *Lloyd George* (Cardiff, 1963)
Morrison, H. *An Autobiography* (1960)
Mosley, O. *My Life* (1968)
Nicolson, H. *George V: his life and reign* (1952)
Nicolson, N. (ed.) *Harold Nicolson: diaries and letters 1930-1939* (1966)
Owen, F. *Tempestuous Journey. Lloyd George: his life and times* (1954)
Page Croft, Sir H. *My Life of Strife* (1947)
Pelling, H.M. *Winston Churchill* (1974)
Percy, Lord *Some Memories* (1958)
Pethick-Lawrence, F.W. *Fate Has been Kind* (1942)
Ponsonby, C.E. *Ponsonby Remembers* (1964)
Postgate, R. *The Life of George Lansbury* (1951)
Reith, J.C.W. *Into the Wind* (1949)
Rhodes James, R. *Churchill: a study in failure, 1900-1939* (1970)

—— (ed.) *Chips: the diaries of Sir Henry Channon* (1967)
—— (ed.) *Memoirs of a Conservative: J.C.C. Davidson's memoirs and papers 1910-1937* (1969)
Roberts, B. *Stanley Baldwin: man or miracle?* (1936)
—— *Sir John Simon* (1938)
Salter, A. *Personality in Politics* (1947)
Samuel, Viscount *Memoirs* (1945)
Shinwell, E. *Conflict Without Malice* (1955)
Simon, Viscount *Retrospect* (1952)
Snowden, Lord *Autobiography* (1934), vol. 2
Somervell, D.C. *Stanley Baldwin: an examination of some features of Mr. G.M. Young's biography* (1953)
Stocks, M. *Ernest Simon of Manchester* (1963)
Swinton, Earl *I Remember* (1947)
—— *Sixty Years of Power* (1966)
Sylvester, A.J. *The Real Lloyd George* (1947)
Taylor, A.J.P. *Beaverbrook* (1972)
—— *et al. Churchill: four faces and the man* (1969)
—— (ed.) *Lloyd George: a diary by Frances Stevenson* (1971)
—— (ed.) *Lloyd George: twelve essays* (1971)
Templewood, Viscount *Nine Troubled Years: 1931-1939* (1954)
Thomas, J.H. *My Story* (1937)
Thomson, M. *David Lloyd George: the official biography* (1949)
Vansittart, Lord *The Mist Procession* (1958)
Williams, F. *A Pattern of Rulers* (1965)
—— *Ernest Bevin* (1952)
Wilson Harris, H. *J.A. Spender* (1946)
Winterton, Earl *Orders of the Day* (1953)
Woolton, Earl *Memoirs* (1959)
Wrench, E. *Geoffrey Dawson and Our Times* (1955)
Young, G.M. *Stanley Baldwin* (1952)

7 Contemporary Books and Articles*

Allen, Lord *Britain's Political Future* (1934)
Amery, L.S. *Forward View* (1935)
—— 'What is Wrong with the National Government?', *Nineteenth Century and After*, vol. 113 (Apr. 1933)
Attlee, C.R. *The Labour Party in Perspective* (1937)
Baldwin, S. *This Torch of Freedom* (1935)

*Place of publication is London, unless otherwise indicated

Boothby, R. 'Political Parties and the next election', *Political Quarterly*, vol. 5 (Oct. 1934)

Cecil, Viscount *A Great Experiment* (1941)

Cripps, S. *et al. Problems of a Socialist Government* (1935)

Cummings, A.J. *The Press* (1936)

Dalton, H. *Hitler's War: before and after* (1942)

Dean, E.P. 'Trends in British Elections', *Foreign Affairs*, vol. 14, no. 2 (1936)

Graves, R. and Hodge, A. *The Long Weekend: a social history of Great Britain 1918-1939* (1940)

Grigg, E. *The Faith of an Englishman* (1936)

Hannington, W. *The Problem of the Distressed Areas* (1937)

—— *Ten Lean Years* (1940)

Harrisson, T. 'What is Public Opinion?', *Political Quarterly*, vol. 9, no. 4 (1940)

Haxey, S. *Tory MP* (1939)

Headlam, C. 'The General Election – And After', *Quarterly Review*, vol. 264 (1936)

Hogg, Q. 'The Prospects of the Conservative Party', *Nineteenth Century and After*, vol. 115 (Jan. 1934)

Hutt, A. *The Post War History of the British Working Class* (1937)

Laski, H. 'The General Election, 1935', *Political Quarterly*, vol. 2, no. 1 (1936)

Livingstone, Dame A. *The Peace Ballot* (1936)

Lloyd George, D. *Peace and Reconstruction* (1935)

McHenry, Dean E. *The Labour Party in Transition, 1931-1938* (1938)

Macmillan, H. *The Next Five Years: an essay in political agreement* (1935)

Mander, G., Rockley, Lord and Lees-Smith, H.B. 'The General Election and After', *Contemporary Review*, vol. 149 (Jan. 1936)

Matheson, H. 'Politics and Broadcasting', *Political Quarterly*, vol. V, no. 2 (1934)

—— 'Listener Research in Broadcasting', *Sociological Review*, vol. 27 (1935)

Muggeridge, M. *The Thirties* (1940)

Muir, R. 'The Balance of Parties', *Nineteenth Century and After*, vol. 118 (Sept. 1935)

National Liberal Federation *The Liberal Way* (1934)

National Peace Council *Peace and the General Election* (1935)

Percy, Lord *Conservatism and the Future* (1935)

Political and Economic Planning *Report on the British Press* (1938)

Ramsbottam, E.C. 'The Course of Wage Rates in the United Kingdom 1921-1934', *Journal of the Royal Statistical Society*, vol. 98 (1935)

Robson, W.A. 'The B.B.C. as an Institution', *Political Quarterly*, vol. 6, no. 4 (1935)

Round Table, vol. 26 (1935-6): editorial and unsigned article 'Great Britain: The General Election'

Rowse, A.L. 'The Labour Party from Within', *Nineteenth Century and After*, vol. 114 (Dec. 1933)

Rowson, S. 'A Statistical Survey of the Cinema Industry in Great Britain in 1934', *Journal of the Royal Statistical Society*, vol. 99 (1936)

Samuel, H. 'Liberty, Liberalism, and Labour', *Contemporary Review* vol. 146 (Sept. 1934), Samuel's address to the Liberal Summer School in 1934

Strabolgi, Lord, 'The Political Scene', *Nineteenth Century and After*, vol. 118 (Oct. 1935)

von Stutterheim, K. *The Press in England* (1934)

Wickham Steed, H. *The Press* (1938)

Wilkinson, E. *The Town That Was Murdered* (1936)

Wilson, Sir A. 'Walks and Talks', *Nineteenth Century and After*, vol. 118 (Dec. 1935)

Wyatt Tilby, A. 'The Election — and After', *Nineteenth Century and After*, vol. 118 (Dec. 1935)

8   Secondary Books and Articles*

Addision, P. *The Road to 1945: British politics and the Second World War* (1975)

Allen, A.J. *The English Voter* (1964)

Ayerst, D. *The Guardian: biography of a newspaper* (1971)

Bassett, R. 'Telling the Truth to the People: the Myth of the Baldwin "Confession" ', *The Cambridge Journal*, vol. 2 (1948); and later correspondence, especially the letter from Professor Max Beloff

——*Democracy and Foreign Policy: a case history of the Sino-Japanese dispute 1931-1933* (1952)

——*Nineteen Thirty-One: political crisis* (1958)

Beer, S. *Modern British Politics* (1965)

Benney, M. *et al. How People Vote: a study of electoral behaviour in Greenwich* (1956)

Berkeley, H. *The Myth That Will Not Die: the formation of the*

*Place of publication is London, unless otherwise indicated

National Government 1931 (1978)

Blake, R. *The Conservative Party from Peel to Churchill* (1970)

Blewett, N. *The Peers, the Parties, and the People: the general elections of 1910* (1972)

Blondel, J. 'Towards a General Theory of Change in Voting Behaviour', *Political Studies*, vol. 13 (1965)

Blythe, R. *The Age of Illusion: England in the twenties and thirties* (1963)

Booth, A.H. *British Hustings 1924-1950* (1956)

Briggs, A. *The History of Broadcasting in the United Kingdom* (Oxford, 1965), vol. 2.

Buck, P. *Amateurs and Professionals in British Politics, 1918-1959* (University of Chicago Press, 1963)

Budge, I. and Urwin, D. *Scottish Political Behaviour* (1966)

Burnham, Lord *Peterborough Court: The Story of the Daily Telegraph* (1955)

Butler, D.E. *The Electoral System in Britain Since 1918* (Oxford, 1963)
—— *The Study of Political Behaviour* (1958)
—— (ed.) *Coalitions in British Politics* (1978)

Butler, D.E. and Freeman, J. *British Political Facts 1900-1960* (1963)

Butler, D.E. and Pinto-Duschinsky, M. *The British General Election of 1970* (1971)

Butler, D.E. and Stokes, D. *Political Change in Britain: forces shaping electoral choice* (1969)

Butler, Lord (ed.) *The Conservatives: a history from their origins to 1965* (1977)

Carlton, D. *MacDonald versus Henderson: the foreign policy of the second Labour Government* (1970)

Cline, C.A. *Recruits to Labour: the British Labour Party 1914-1931* (Syracuse University Press, 1963)

Coase, R.H. *British Broadcasting: a study in monopoly* (1950)

Cole, G.D.H. *History of the Labour Party from 1914* (1948)

Cook, C. *The Age of Alignment: electoral politics in Britain 1922-1929* (1975)

Cook, C. and Ramsden, J. (eds.) *By-Elections in British Politics* (1973)

Cook, C. and Peele, G. (eds.) *The Politics of Reappraisal 1918-1939* (1975)

Cook, C. and Stevenson, J. *The Slump* (1977)

Cowling, M. *The Impact of Hitler: British Politics and British Policy 1933-1940* (1975)
—— *The Impact of Labour: the beginning of modern British politics*

(Cambridge, 1971)

Craig, F.W.S. *British Parliamentary Election Statistics 1918-1968* (Glasgow, 1968)

—— *British Parliamentary Election Results 1918-1949* (Glasgow, 1969)

Douglas, R. *History of the Liberal Party from 1895 to 1970* (1971)

Downs, A. *An Economic Theory of Democracy* (New York, 1957)

Dowse, R.E. *Left in the Centre: The Independent Labour Party 1893-1940* (1966)

Dunbabin, J.P.D. 'British Rearmament in the 1930s: a chronology and review', *Historical Journal*, vol. 18, no. 3, 1975

—— 'Parliamentary Elections in Great Britain, 1858-1900: a psephological note', *English History Review*, vol. 81 (1966)

Edelman, M. *The Mirror: a political biography* (1966)

Gathorne-Hardy, G.M. *A Short History of International Affairs 1920 to 1939* (Oxford, 1942)

Ghosh, S.C. 'Decision Making and Power in the British Conservative Party: a case study of the Indian Problem 1929-1934', *Political Studies*, vol. 13 (1965)

Golant, W. 'The Emergence of C.R. Attlee as Leader of the Parliamentary Labour Party in 1935', *Historical Journal*, vol. 13, no. 2 (1970)

Guttsman, W.L. *The British Political Elite* (1963)

Gwyn, W.B. *Democracy and the Cost of Politics in Britain* (1962)

Harrison, M. *Trade Unions and the Labour Party Since 1945* (1960)

Heller, R. 'East Fulham Revisited', *Journal of Contemporary History*, vol. 6, no. 3 (1971)

Hyams, E. *The New Statesman: the history of the first fifty years 1913-1963* (1963)

Jackson, J.A. *The Irish in Britain* (1963)

Kinnear, M. *The British Voter: an atlas and survey since 1885* (1968)

Lewis, E.G. *British By-Elections as a Reflection of Public Opinion* (University of California Press, 1943)

Lloyd, T.O. *Empire to Welfare State: Britain 1906-1967* (Oxford, 1970)

Lyman, R.W. 'The British Labour Party: the conflict between socialist ideals and practical politics between the wars', *Journal of British Studies*, vol. 5, no. 1 (1965)

McCallum, R.B. *Public Opinion and the Last Peace* (Oxford, 1944)

McCallum, R.B. and Readman, A. *The British General Election of 1945* (1947; new imp., 1964)

McKenzie, R.T. *British Political Parties* (1955)

Madge, C. *Pilot Guide to the General Election* (1945)

Marsh, D.C. *The Changing Social Structure of England and Wales 1871-1951* (1958)

Martin, R. *Communism and the British Trade Unions 1924-1933* (Oxford, 1969)

Marwick, A. *Britain in the Century of Total War: War, Peace and Social Change 1900-1967* (1968)

—— 'Middle Opinion in the Thirties: Planning, Progress and Political "Agreement" ', *English Historical Review*, vol. 79 (1964)

Marwick, W.H. *A Short History of Labour in Scotland* (1967)

Medlicott, W.N. *British Foreign Policy Since Versailles, 1919-1963* (2nd ed., 1968)

—— 'Britain and Germany: the search for agreement 1930-1937', *The Creighton Lecture in History, 1968* (1969)

—— *Contemporary England 1914-1964* (1967)

Miller, F.C. 'The Unemployment Policy of the National Government, 1931-1936', *Historical Journal*, vol. 19, no. 2, 1976

Morgan, K.O. 'Twilight of Welsh Liberalism: Lloyd George and the "Wee Frees", 1918-35', *The Bulletin of the Board of Celtic Studies*, vol. 22, pt. 4 (May 1968)

Mowat, C.L. *Britain Between the Wars 1918-1940* (1955)

—— 'Baldwin Restored?' *Journal of Modern History*, vol. 27 (June 1955)

Naylor, J.F. *Labour's International Policy: the Labour Party in the 1930s* (1967)

Nicholas, H.G. *The British General Election of 1950* (1951, new imp., 1968)

Northedge, F.S. *The Troubled Giant: Britain among the great powers 1916-1939* (1966)

Page Arnot, R. *The Miners in Crisis and War* (1961)

Pelling, H. *A Short History of the Labour Party* (1965)

Pollard, S. *The Development of the British Economy 1914-1950* (1962)

Pronay, N. 'British Newsreels in the 1930s: (i) Audiences and Producers', *History*, vol. 56, no. 188 (1971)

—— 'British Newsreels in the 1930's: (2) Their Policies and Impact', *History*, vol. 57, no. 189 (1972)

Pulzer, P.G. *Political Representation and Elections in Britain* (1967)

Ramsden, J. *A History of the Conservative Party: the age of Balfour and Baldwin 1902-1940* (1978)

Ranney, A. *Pathways to Parliament: candidate selection in Britain* (1965)

Rasmussen, J. 'The Disutility of the Swing Concept in British Psephology', *Parliamentary Affairs*, vol. 18, no. 4 (1965)

Raymond, J. (ed.) *The Baldwin Age* (1960)

Richardson, H.W. *Economic Recovery in Britain, 1932-1939* (1967)

Robertson, J.C. 'The British General Election of 1935', *Journal of Contemporary History*, vol. 9, no. 1 (Jan. 1974)

Rose, R. (ed.) *Studies in British Politics* (1966)

Ross, J.F.S. *Elections and Electors: studies in democratic representation* (1955)

Ross, J.F.S. *Parliamentary Representation* (rev. ed., 1948)

Routh, G. *Occupations and Pay in Great Britain, 1906-1960* (Cambridge, 1965)

Rowse, A.L. *All Souls and Appeasement: a contribution to contemporary history* (1961)

Russell, A.K. *Liberal Landslide: the general election of 1906* (1973)

Sanderson, G. 'Swing of the Pendulum in British General Elections, 1832-1966', *Political Studies*, vol. 14 (1966)

Saville, J. *Rural Depopulation in England and Wales 1851-1951* (1957)

Self, P. and Storing, H. *The State and the Farmer* (1962)

Seymour-Ure, C. *The Press, Politics and the Public* (1968)

Skidelsky, R. *Politicians and the Slump* (1967)

Somervell, D.C. *Between the Wars* (1948)

Stannage, C.T. 'The East Fulham By-Election, 25 October 1933', *Historical Journal*, vol. 18, no. 1 (1971)

—— 'Introduction', *Conservative Campaign Guide 1935* (Harvester Press, 1973)

Symons, J. *The Thirties: a dream revolved* (1960)

Tayer, G. (ed.) *Personality and Power* (1971)

Taylor, A.J.P. *English History 1914-1945* (Oxford, 1965)

Watt, D.C. 'The Anglo-German Naval Agreement, 1935', *Journal of Modern History*, vol. 27, no. 2 (1956)

—— *Personalities and Policies: studies in the formation of British foreign policy in the twentieth century* (1965)

The History of The Times, vol. 4, pt. 2, 1912-1948 (1952)

Wightman, J. 'The Rearmament Issue in the British General Election, 1935', *The Proceedings of the South Carolina Historical Association* (1963)

Williams, G. (ed.) *Merthyr Politics: The Making of a Working Class Tradition* (Cardiff, 1966)

Williams, J.E. *The Derbyshire Miners* (1962)

Youngson, A.J. *The British Economy 1920-1957* (1960)

9 Theses

Blewett, N. 'The British General Elections of 1910', D. Phil., thesis, University of Oxford, 1966

Jupp, J. 'The Left in Britain 1932-1941', MSc. (Econ.) thesis, London School of Economics, 1956

Kyba, J.P. 'British Attitudes Toward Disarmament and Rearmament 1932-1935', PhD thesis, London School of Economics, 1967

Rowe, E.A. 'The British General Election of 1929', B. Litt. thesis, University of Oxford, 1959

Russell, A.K. 'The General Election of 1906', D. Phil. thesis, University of Oxford, 1962

INDEX

Aberdeen
  South: by-election 77
Aberdeenshire: Central 238; South
  238; Western 232
Abnormal Importations Bill 86
Abyssinian crisis 122-5; as 1935
  election issue 155; BBC coverage
  188; Labour party policy 78;
  Liberal party policy 109;
  National Government policy
  proposal to 120, 123-5;
  partition 123-4; *The Times*
  views 196; 1906 Agreement 124
Acland, Sir Francis: into Opposition
  97; Liberal candidate Cornwall
  North favours move 89, 91
Adams, Vyvyan 99
Addison, Christopher 229
Addision, Christopher Dr: and
  Labour agricultural campaign 70;
  Swindon Labour candidate 105
Agriculture 220; Agricultural
  Marketing Bill: Liberal opposition
  93; as 1929, 1945 election issue
  173; as 1935 election issue 154,
  163-5, 243; BBC series on 188;
  Labour Agricultural Campaign 70;
  Labour conference resolution 71;
  National Government legislation
  114
Alexander: defeat in 1931 election
  62
Alexander, A.V.: gives Labour view
  on Navy 139
Allen of Hurtwood, Lord: critical of
  election timing 134; fears re-
  armament 134
Altringham: by-election 41-2
Amery, L.S. 145, 185
Andrews, Linton 202
Angell, Norman 99
anti-Socialism: anti-socialist groups
  45; Baldwin's speeches 42; in

Conservative propaganda 40; in
  the press 201; in 1935 election
  campaign 170-1; resolution of
  Conservative Central Council 46
Archbishop of Canterbury 186, 189
Argyll 101
Armaments *see* rearmament
arms, private manufacture of:
  Labour policy 102; Liberal
  policy 102
arms race *see* rearmament
Ashford: by-election 69, 93
Astor, J.J. Col.: purchase of *The
  Times* 195-6
Astor, W. 228
Atholl, Duchess of 220
Attlee, Clement 146, 148, 176,
  184-5; as leader in 1945 election
  245; denounces 'scare' election
  136; in 1931 election 62; leadership 149, 169, 171, 180-1, 202,
  210, 243; major 1935 general
  election speech 141-2; on unemployment 133; proposes bank
  nationalisation 140; views on
  BBC 187; views on 1935 defeat
  228; 1935 election campaign 147,
  149, 155, 158, 168, 171, 177
Avenol, J. 186
Ayrton Gould, Barbara 220

Baird, William (chairman Scottish
  Liberal Federation): *rapproch-
  ment* with National Government
  108-9; support for Lloyd George
  106
Baldwin, Mrs Stanley 200
Baldwin, Stanley 11, 14, 18, 19, 24,
  26, 33, 35, 40, 139, 141, 146,
  154, 157, 184; and Ottawa Bill
  31-2; attitude to National
  Government 38, 42-3, 49-51;
  becomes Prime Minister 54, 118,

GLASSBORO STATE COLLEGE